A Life in Norfolk's Archaeology

1950–2016

Archaeology in an Arable Landscape

Peter Wade-Martins

ARCHAEOPRESS PUBLISHING LTD
Gordon House
276 Banbury Road
Oxford OX2 7ED
www.archaeopress.com

ISBN 978 1 78491 657 2
ISBN 978 1 78491 658 9 (e-Pdf)

© Archaeopress and Peter Wade-Martins 2017

Front Cover picture: A montage of two images: excavating an Anglo-Saxon post-hole building (Fig.17.2) and squashed and plough-damaged cremation urns at Spong Hill, North Elmham (Fig.17.4) prior to subsoiling and further ploughing for potato and root crops. Agriculture is the greatest threat to archaeological evidence in the East Anglian landscape. There were relatively generous government grants available in the 1970s and 1980s to rescue a small selection of sites like Spong Hill from cultivation. But it is difficult to envisage how such slow painstaking work, conducted to research standards over ten years, plus the conservation of the finds and the highly complex computer analysis which followed, could be funded now. Today, support for rescue archaeology is largely dependent on developer funding: a system from which the farming industry is largely excluded.
Usually the only record we have of plough-damaged sites like Spong Hill comes from aerial photography and surface finds brought in by metal detectorists and fieldwalkers for identification. But there are so many items coming in now that the county's identification service finds it difficult to identify them all. Nevertheless metal detecting is transforming our understanding of Norfolk's past.

Back cover picture: The author at Burgh Castle after the public access works had been completed in 2012 (Courtesy *Eastern Daily Press*).

All rights reserved. No part of this book may be reproduced, in any form or by any means, electronic, mechanical, photocopying or otherwise, without the prior written permission of the copyright owners.

Printed in England by Holywell Press, Oxford
This book is available direct from Archaeopress or from our website www.archaeopress.com

In memory of two great archaeologists:

John Hurst *(1927-2003),*
Inspector of Ancient Monuments, who did so much to promote the study of medieval settlement archaeology and to encourage the formation of the Norfolk Archaeological Unit

and

Philip Barker *(1920-2001),*
Extra-mural lecturer in archaeology, who developed open-area excavation into a fine technique through his work at Wroxeter Roman city and Hen Domen motte and bailey castle.

They both provided real inspiration for a budding young archaeologist.

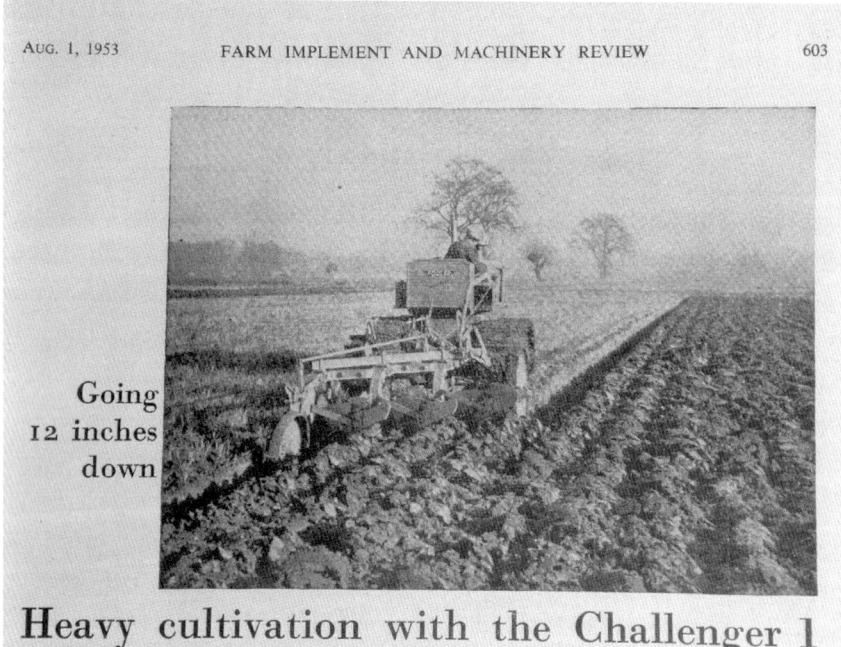

An advertisement published in the Farm Implement and Machinery Review for August 1953 showing the Fowler 'Challenger 1' 50-horse-power Diesel Crawler 'Going 12 inches down' with a three-furrow plough. It was the 1950s which saw the arrival of powerful diesel tractors which started to do so much more damage to archaeology on arable land

Contents

Acknowledgements ix
Abbreviations xi
Norfolk Firsts xiii
Time line of key events most of which feature in the Book xv
Chapter 1: Introduction 1
Chapter 2: The Early Years 3
A farming background 3
Growing up on a chicken farm 4
A first taste of archaeology 5
Bloxham School, 1957-62 6
A volunteer at Norwich Castle Museum 8
Warham Camp excavations, 1959 9
Ashill Roman enclosure and West Acre Saxon cemetery, 1961 10
Thetford Castle excavations, 1962: a near-death experience 10
Report writing 13

Chapter 3: Excavating Deserted Medieval Villages 15
Destruction in the countryside 15
Thuxton deserted village excavations, 1963-64 15
Thetford Anglo-Saxon town excavations, 1964 21
Birmingham University, 1964-67 21
Grenstein deserted village excavations, 1965-66 22
Surveys of other deserted villages 29
Postscript: A nostalgic return to Thuxton 30

Chapter 4: The Launditch Hundred Project, 1967-71 31
Unanswered questions about medieval settlement in the Norfolk countryside ... 31
Fieldwalking: then a new technique 31
Roman and Early Saxon 32
Isolated churches and village greens 33
Rural wealth and decline 33

Chapter 5: North Elmham Park: The Excavation of a High-Status Anglo-Saxon and Early Medieval Settlement, 1967-72 41

The Anglo-Saxon dioceses 41
A strongyloid worm started the excavations 42
Public and press interest 45
Voodoo village 45
How much detail to publish in print? 46
Linking the excavation phasing to the 'cathedral ruins' 47
The pre-Danish Middle Saxon settlement (seventh to ninth centuries: Period I) .47
The timber-lined wells 49
The bishops return (late ninth and tenth centuries: Period II) 52
The Late Saxon timber buildings (eleventh and twelfth centuries: Periods III and IV) ...53
The cathedral cemetery 56
The market place 58
Further areas to be excavated 59
Writing the report 59
Distinguished visitors 61

Chapter 6: Chance Finds 63

A French polychrome jug from Welborne churchyard, 1968 63
A Late Bronze Age metalworkers hoard from North Elmham, 1970 64
An Anglo-Saxon inhumation cemetery at The Paddocks, Swaffham, 1970 66

Chapter 7: Societies 69

Norfolk and Norwich Archaeological Society (NNAS) 69
The Prehistoric Society of East Anglia 70
The Norfolk Research Committee (NRC) 71
Norfolk Industrial Archaeology Society (NIAS) 76
The Norfolk Archaeological Rescue Group (NARG), 1975-1992, and the Norfolk Archaeological and Historical Research Group (NAHRG) 1992 to present 77
The Federation of Norfolk Historical and Archaeological Organisations 80
Norfolk Historic Buildings Group 80

Chapter 8: Amateurs in Action 81
John Owles: the fieldwalker/ farmer 81
John Turner: the lone excavator 82
Brian Cushion who discovered a Roman road and surveyed the majority of the county's earthworks 83
Alan Davison who combined the skills of a highly effective fieldwalker and documentary researcher 84
Silvia Addington who counted hedgerows, fieldwalked and researched the documents 86
The Brampton excavators ('Excavatores Brantunae') 88
TV-sponsored excavations 98

Chapter 9: Metal Detecting: 'The Norfolk System' 101
The 1996 Treasure Act 101
Portable Antiquities Scheme 102
How 'The Norfolk System' all began 104
The 'STOP' campaign 109
The Norfolk way is the only way 110
The Burgh Castle rally 113
Three successful detectorists 114
Geophysics and GPS-recording of coin distribution on Dunston Field 122
The tidal wave continues 123
A well-deserved recognition 125
A happy outcome 125

Chapter 10: Urban Surveys 129
The King's Lynn Survey, 1962-71 129
The Norwich Survey, 1971-2002 129

Chapter 11: The 'RESCUE' Movement, The Scole Committee and Professional County Units 141
'RESCUE' 141
The Norfolk Archaeological Unit: the birth of the first county-based professional field unit in Britain, from 1973 145

Chapter 12: A New County Service for Field Archaeology, 1973-1999 155
The role of a County Service 155
Museum displays 157
The changing legal background 158

Chapter 13: Key Norfolk Archaeological Unit Projects 165
The Sites and Monuments Record 165
Aerial photography 167
Some outstanding aerial photography discoveries 170
The Fenland Survey 180

Chapter 14: The Story of 'East Anglian Archaeology' 189

Chapter 15: County-based Conservation Projects 193
The Barrow Survey, 1973-76 193
A review of barrow protection, 1983 195
The protection of field monuments 196
The Norfolk Monuments Management Project (NMMP), 1990-present 198
The County Earthworks Survey, 1994-2000 203

Chapter 16: National Conservation Initiatives 207
The English Heritage Monuments Protection Programme (MPP), 1986-2001 207
The English Heritage Monuments at Risk Survey (MARS), 1994-1996 209
Natural England's Environmental Stewardship schemes 210
Breckland Archaeological Survey, 1994-96 211
A New Prescription for Preserving Archaeological Sites in Breckland: a significant step forward 212
Protection under the European Common Agricultural Policy from 2005 214

Chapter 17: Some Rescue Excavations, 1972-92 217
Spong Hill Anglo-Saxon cemetery, North Elmham, 1972-81 and 1984 217
Potential disaster averted 220
Anglo-Saxon cemeteries at Bergh Apton and Morningthorpe, 1973-75 224
Sixteenth-century pottery kiln wasters from Fulmodeston, 1974 226
Norwich, Anglia TV site on the former Cattle Market, 1979 228
Norwich, St Martin-at-Palace Plain, 1981 229

Norwich, Fishergate, 1985 231
Thetford, Fison Way, 1980-82 232
Norwich Southern Bypass, 1989-92 236
Barton Bendish parish survey, 1980-90 242

Chapter 18: Clearing the Publication Backlog from the Past, 1977-97 247
The Caistor Roman town excavations of the 1930s 248
Is history now repeating itself? 249

Chapter 19: Re-structuring Field Archaeology in Norfolk, 1991 251
Norfolk Landscape Archaeology (NLA) 251
Archaeological contractors 252
Sites and Monuments Record 252
Archaeology and planning 253
The new Norfolk Archaeological Unit 253
A Five-year Development Plan for archaeology in the Museums Service 254
County standards for field archaeology 255
The County Council's own contracting unit goes into the red 256

Chapter 20: Time to Move On 259
All change 259

Chapter 21: The Norfolk Archaeological Trust: a property-owning conservation trust 261
The early years of the Trust, from 1923 261
Archaeological Trust's first properties 264
The Trust takes a new direction 271

Chapter 22: Caistor St Edmund Roman Town 273
Countryside Stewardship Scheme 274
Site opening 275
Caistor Roman Town Project 278
Dunston Field, 2011 283

Chapter 23: Burgh Castle 'Saxon Shore' Roman Fort 291
Site purchase 291
Site management plan 294

The wildlife 296
The trouble with car parks 297
Site interpretation 299
The need for site wardens 300
Special moments 301

Chapter 24: Two Monasteries 303
Binham Priory 303
St Benet's Abbey, Horning 307

Chapter 25: Other Recent Acquisitions 323
Iron Age fort at Church Field, Tasburgh, 1994 323
Bloodgate Hill Iron Age hillfort, South Creake, 2003 323
Middleton Mount motte and bailey castle, 2006 325
Burnham Norton Carmelite Friary, 2010 327
Fiddler's Hill round barrow, 2012 328
Castle Acre Priory meadows 329

Chapter 26: The Future Role of the Norfolk Archaeological Trust 333
The role of a county conservation trust for archaeology 334
Low membership 335

Chapter 27: A Time to Reflect 337
Where are we now? 337
And now a new, and potentially larger, publication backlog 339
The long-term storage of excavation archives 343
Finding the space 344
Protecting the field evidence in an arable landscape 345

Appendix 1: Alan Davison's publications 351

Appendix 2: Summary of progress set out in the 1996 Five-year Development Plan for Archaeology in the Norfolk Museums Service 353
Recording services 353
Development control 354
Monument conservation and interpretation in the countryside 354
Presenting monuments to the public 355
Identification service 355
Outreach 355

Appendix 3: List of those archaeologists who attended the February 1970 Barford meeting which represented the start of the RESCUE movement 357

Bibliography 359

Index 379

Acknowledgements

This has been a life in archaeology in which so many people have been involved in different ways, and it is difficult to single out just a few to thank in particular. I am indebted to all friends and colleagues mentioned in this book. The period from 1972 to 1991 was one we, as a relatively young and close-knit group of idealistic archaeologists, explored together to discover what was possible and what we could achieve. It was all new ground, and unknown territory lay ahead. There seemed to be no limits on how far we could go, and, luckily, government policy and national guidance on good planning practice just about kept in step, and it was all quite magical. We were riding on the crest of a wave generated by the fathers of the RESCUE movement, of which we were proud to play a part. We also had the kindly support of senior officers and members of the County Council at a time when 'budget cuts' were not yet on the agenda. As I say in the text, these were indeed the 'golden years' to be in field archaeology.

The second part of the book was more of a personal journey. It describes the wonderful opportunities the trustees of the Norfolk Archaeological Trust gave me to demonstrate how a modern county archaeological conservation trust could play a major role in site protection and in opening for public enjoyment a range of properties which would not normally be accessible. I do hope that this is only the beginning and that the momentum can be retained so that we can go further in catching up with the far greater achievements of wildlife conservation movement. In truth there is still a long way to travel.

Unless otherwise acknowledged, the aerial photographs reproduced here were taken by Derek Edwards, and his skills are apparent in his fine pictures. The staff of the current Historic Environment Record at Gressenhall: Heather Hamilton, Alison Yardy and Julia Richards were extremely helpful in retrieving and scanning the many photographs from the Gressenhall archive, and Sue White has performed miracles computer enhancing the pictures.

The author is especially grateful to Steven Ashley, David Gurney, John Davies, Will Bowden, Brian Ayers, Malcolm Atkin, Dave Evans, Catherine Hills, Henry Walker and Peter Griffiths for reading the whole or parts of the book and commenting on the text. But all the views expressed here are my own.

A note on copyright: Unless otherwise indicated, the photo reference numbers at the ends of the captions are those used to identify images in the Historic Environment Service archives at Gressenhall. These include my own early photos which I have placed in the Gressenhall photo archive, and they should all be treated as Norfolk County Council copyright. For just a few black and white pictures no copyright is acknowledged because I have no record of their source and will make the necessary correction at the first opportunity. The later digital colour photography comes from the period I worked for the Norfolk Archaeological Trust, and Trust copyright is gratefully acknowledged. The three photographs provided under the Portable Antiquities Scheme are also Norfolk County Council copyright.

Abbreviations

- CBA Council for British Archaeology
- CEAS Centre of East Anglian Studies at UEA
- *DAFT Dereham and Fakenham Times*
- DCMS Department of Culture, Media and Sport
- Defra Department of the Environment, Farming and Rural Affairs
- DNH Department of National Heritage
- DoE Department of the Environment
- DoT Department of Transport
- EAA East Anglian Archaeology regional monograph series
- *EDP Eastern Daily Press*
- EH English Heritage
- ESA Environmentally Sensitive Area farmland conservation scheme
- FLO Finds Liaison Officer
- GPS Global Positioning System
- HER Historic Environment Record, replacing the SMR
- HES Historic Environment Service
- HLF Heritage Lottery Fund
- HLS Higher Level Stewardship Scheme for farmland conservation
- MAFF Ministry of Agriculture, Fisheries and Food
- MPP Monuments Protection Programme
- NAHRG Norfolk Archaeological and Historical Research Group
- NARG Norfolk Archaeological Rescue Group
- NASAC Norfolk Archaeological Services Advisory Committee
- NAU Norfolk Archaeological Unit
- NCM Norwich Castle Museum
- NFU National Farmers Union
- NHMF National Heritage Memorial Fund
- NIAS Norfolk Industrial Archaeology Society
- NMMP Norfolk Monuments Management Project
- NMS Norfolk Museums Service
- NPS Norfolk Property Services
- NRC Norfolk Research Committee
- PAS Portable Antiquities Scheme
- RCHM Royal Commission on the Historical Monuments (of England)
- SMR Sites and Monuments Record, later to become the Historic Environment Record (HER)
- UEA University of East Anglia (Norwich)
- UPD Updated Project Design
- YOP Youth Opportunities Programme

Norfolk Firsts

- First county archaeology conservation trust, 1923
- First county wildlife trust (The Norfolk Naturalists' Trust), 1926
- First county fledgling Sites and Monuments Record, 1933
- First systematic research-based fieldwalking project (on the Launditch Hundred), 1967
- First government post-excavation grant (for North Elmham Park), 1971
- First county archaeological unit, 1973
- First county air photographs library, 1973
- First full-time county air photography officer, 1973
- First comprehensive county barrow survey (which later became a part of a regional barrow survey), 1973-76
- First county to actively support and encourage legal metal detecting, c. 1975
- First comprehensive county ruined churches survey, 1976-91
- First fully developer-funded urban excavation outside London (from Anglia TV), 1979
- First county to have a 'county from the air' book of aerial photographs, 1987
- Possibly the first county with a strong Structure Plan policy which ensured that the development of sites of archaeological importance (scheduled or not) would only be permitted in exceptional circumstances, 1988
- First comprehensive Monuments Management Project incorporating all earthworks of schedulable quality, 1990
- First comprehensive county-wide survey of known earthworks in grassland, 1994-2000
- First *County Standards for Field Archaeology*, 1998

(with apologies if any of these claims should prove to be inaccurate)

'It is increasingly clear that industrialised agriculture, employing ever larger tractors pulling bigger ploughs, is truncating buried archaeology at accelerating rates. Plough damage remains the single most destructive agent of archaeological evidence in Britain, and continues to occur on an annual basis effectively unnoticed and un-monitored at a national scale ....

If nothing is done to manage the ongoing impact of agricultural damage it is likely that within the next 30 years we will see the majority of the rural archaeology of Britain hopelessly compromised ....

.... if we continue to look the other way as agricultural plant gets larger and the industrial production of root crops, for instance, increases, we will only have ourselves to blame for the devastation of the buried record of the human past that even now barely survives in the ground.

It is essential that we increase public-awareness of the fragility of the buried and invisible archaeological resource if it is to be afforded the same degree of protection that is applied to aspects of the living natural environment.

To face this challenge we have to identify those areas most worthy of preservation, emphasise and make more implicit the link between the human past and the natural world, a world in which the status of archaeology matches that of the living natural world, a world in which humanity is not only contributing to the destruction of the natural environment but is also a key component of the environment. To achieve these aims we will have to adopt novel new approaches and work in new partnerships with farmers, communities and government institutions absorbing rather than rejecting change.'
(Powlesland 2015, 113 and 117)

Time line of key events most of which feature in the Book

1739/75   Publication of F. Blomefield's *Towards a Topog. Hist. of the County of Norfolk.*
1813   The earliest known rescue archaeology on barrow burials at Sporle with Palgrave.
1843   Publication of R. Ladbrooke's *Views of the Churches of Norfolk.*
1844   Publication of Rev. Richard Hart's *The Antiquities of Norfolk: A Lecture.*
1846   Founding of the Norfolk and Norwich Archaeological Society.
1908   Inaugural meeting of the Prehistoric Society of East Anglia.
1923   Norfolk Archaeological Trust formed as a limited company.
1924   Norfolk Archaeological Trust bought its first historic building.
1926   Norfolk Naturalists' Trust also formed as a limited company.
1932   The original Fenland Research Committee was formed.
1933   Norfolk Archaeological Trust bought the earthworks of Binham Priory cloisters.
1933   Rainbird Clarke started the Norfolk card index of archaeological sites and discoveries.
1934   Norfolk Research Committee established.
1935   The Prehistoric Society was formed out of the Prehistoric Society of East Anglia.
1935-48   The first Norfolk barrow survey organised by the Norfolk Research Committee.
1946   The RAF created the first vertical aerial photograph cover of Norfolk.
1948   The Snettisham Treasure discovered after deep ploughing.
1957   Publication of Keith Allison's Norfolk survey of deserted medieval villages.
1959   Norfolk Research Committee excavations at Warham Camp.
1959   Destruction of Grenstein deserted medieval village earthworks.
1960   Publication of Rainbird Clarke's *East Anglia.*
1960-c.1980   John Owles at Witton documented the level of plough damage on farmland.
1962   Norfolk Research Committee Thetford Castle excavations where the trench collapsed.
1962   Destruction of Thuxton deserted medieval village earthworks.
1962-71   King's Lynn Survey excavations.
1963-64   Thuxton deserted village excavations.

1964   Thetford Brandon Road large-scale excavations of Anglo-Saxon town.
1965-66 Grenstein deserted village excavations.
1965-89 Excavations by 'Excavatores Brantunae' of Brampton Roman town.
1967-71 Launditch Hundred thematic fieldwalking project.
1967-72 North Elmham Park excavations.
1970   Foxburrow Farm, North Elmham, Bronze Age hoard excavated.
1970   The Paddocks, Swaffham, salvage excavation of Anglo-Saxon cemetery.
1970   Norfolk Industrial Archaeology Society founded.
1970   Meeting in Barford, Warwickshire, triggered the start of the 'Rescue' movement.
1971   Launch of RESCUE at the large London Senate House public meeting.
1971   Letter in *The Times* started government funding for writing excavation reports.
1971   Launch of the Scole Committee for Archaeology in East Anglia.
1971-78 Norwich Survey excavations
1972-81 and 1984 Spong Hill Anglo-Saxon cemetery excavations.
1973   Start of the Norfolk Archaeological Unit as a county field archaeology service.
1973   Start of the Norfolk aerial photography flying programme.
1973-75 Second Norfolk barrow survey.
1973-75 Bergh Apton and Morningthorpe Anglo-Saxon cemeteries excavated.
1974   Norfolk Archaeological Unit moved into the east wing of the Gressenhall workhouse.
1974   Norfolk Archaeological Unit converted Rainbird Clarke's card index into the SMR.
1975   Norfolk Archaeological Rescue Group founded.
1975   Publication of East Anglian Archaeology No. 1.
1975-76 Tasburgh hedge counting project.
1976   Discovery from the air of the defences of Brampton Roman town.
1976-91 The Fenland Survey followed by the Fenland Evaluation Project.
1977   Destruction of three late twelfth-century houses at 28-34 Queen Street, King's Lynn.
1978   Article by Barbara Green and Tony Gregory on metal detecting in *Museums Journal*.
1978   Norfolk County Council took over the Norfolk Archaeological Unit.
1978   Debate about metal detecting boiled over at a Norfolk Museums Committee meeting.

1978 The Crowther national survey of attitudes towards metal detecting.
1979 Norfolk Archaeological Unit took responsibility for Norwich excavations.
1979 First fully developer-funded excavation on Anglia TV Cattle Market site in Norwich.
1979 The 1979 Ancient Monuments and Archaeological Areas Act passed.
1980 Start of the CBA. STOP campaign against use of detectors on all archaeological sites.
1980-90 Barton Bendish parish survey.
1981 Publication of the regional barrow survey covering four counties.
1981 Norwich St Martin-at-Palace Plain excavation revealed Norman house.
1980-82 Thetford, Fison Way, demonstrated the beneficial use of detectors on excavations.
1983 The National Heritage Act set up English Heritage formed in 1984.
1983 Review of the state of barrow preservation in the county.
1983 Publication of *Digging under the Doorstep* on Norwich excavations.
1984 Norfolk Archaeological Trust received the centre of Caistor Roman town as a bequest.
1984 The first computer arrived at Gressenhall to digitise the SMR.
1985-86 Ground-breaking metal detector survey of scheduled Roman temple site at Caistor.
1986-2001 English Heritage Monuments Protection Programme.
1986 Start of MAFF's Environmentally Sensitive Area (ESA) Scheme.
1987 Publication of first edition of *Norfolk from the Air*.
1987 Formation of the Federation of Norfolk Historical and Archaeological Organisations.
1987-91 Large-scale excavations prior to the Castle Mall development, Norwich.
1988 County Structure Plan provided protection for scheduled and unscheduled sites.
1988 Alan Carter, Director of the Norwich Survey, died.
1988 Norfolk Museums Service bought Spong Hill collection from landowner.
1989-92 Norwich Southern Bypass excavations of Bronze Age and Anglo-Saxon burials.
1990 PPG16 made archaeological assessment and recording a key part of development.
1990 British Museum's excavation of the Iron Age gold and silver torcs at Snettisham.

1990 Publication of a complete fieldwalking survey of Hales, Heckingham and Loddon.
1990 Start of the Norfolk Monuments Management Project.
1991 Organisation of field archaeology in Norfolk re-structured in response to PPG 16.
1991 Start of Countyside Stewardship Scheme managed by Countryside Commission.
1991-95 Fenland Management Project.
1992 Norfolk Archaeological Trust bought the Roman suburbs at Caistor Roman town.
1992 NARG and NRC amalgamated into a new NAHRG.
1993 Publication of the first edition of the *Norfolk Historical Atlas*.
1993 Caistor Roman town formally opened to the public.
1994 PPG 15 applied the principles of archaeological assessment to historic buildings.
1994/95 Annual number of planning consultations referred to Gressenhall reached 1,547.
1994-96 English Heritage Monuments at Risk Survey (MARS).
1994-96 Breckland Archaeological Survey.
1994-2000 County earthworks survey.
1995 Norfolk Archaeological Trust bought Burgh Castle Roman fort.
1995 Some barrows finally scheduled by English Heritage following the 1973-75 survey.
1996 Passing of the 1996 Treasure Act.
1996 New Five-year Development Plan for archaeology in Norfolk Museums Service.
1996 Discovery from the air of the full outline of the Roman fort at Saham Toney.
1997 Start of the Portable Antiquities Scheme by the British Museum.
1998 MAFF introduces archaeology conservation payments into Breckland ESA scheme.
1998 Publication of *County Standards for Field Archaeology in Norfolk*.
1998-99 Millennium Library excavation on site of Norman Borough, Norwich.
1998-99 Time Team filmed excavations at Reedham, Thetford and Bawsey.
1999 Seahenge excavated at Holme-next-the-Sea.
1999 P.W-M retired from Norfolk Museums Service and became Norfolk Archaeological Trust's first Director.
1999 Air photography flying programme brought to a close.

2000 Norfolk Historic Buildings Group formed.
2000 Story broke that the NAU, created in the 1991 restructuring, was deeply in the red.
2002 Publication of East Anglian Archaeology No. 100.
2002-04 Norfolk Archaeological Trust bought St Benet's Abbey.
2002 Norfolk Archaeological Trust bought Binham Priory gatehouse and precinct wall.
2003 Publication of the county earthworks survey.
2003 Norfolk Archaeological Trust bought Bloodgate Hill, South Creake, fort.
2005 Limited protection for old grassland introduced under the EU Common Agricultural Policy regulations.
2006 The Norfolk Archaeological Unit transferred to Norfolk Property Services as 'NPS Archaeology'.
2007-08 Repairs to Binham Priory gatehouse and precinct wall.
2009-10 Improvements to public access at Burgh Castle.
2009-12 Excavations at Caistor for the Roman town research project.
2012 Norfolk Archaeological Trust bought Dunston Field, Caistor Roman town.
2012 Integrated geophysical and metal detector surveys of Dunston Field.
2012-14 Heritage Lottery Fund paid for repairs at St Benet's Abbey.
2013-14 Norfolk Archaeological Trust and Holkham Estate worked to conserve Castle Acre Priory precinct walls.
2014 Andrew Rogerson was honoured with a volume of essays: *Landscapes and Artefacts*.
2015 English Heritage divided into Historic England and English Heritage.
2016 Norfolk County Council cancelled plans to cut the artefact identification service.
2016 Norfolk County Council deleted the post of County Field Archaeologist at end of December 2016.
2016 NPS announced in December that it will close down its archaeology contracting team by March 2017.

Chapter 1:
Introduction

This is very much a personal journey through a life which has been involved with the archaeology of Norfolk from my first visit to the Roman town at Caistor as a small boy, then later working as a young volunteer in the Castle Museum and on Rainbird Clarke's excavations at Warham Camp in 1959 through to my retirement as Director of the Norfolk Archaeological Trust in 2014. The story covers three distinctive periods: my early voluntary work and research up to 1973, as County Field Archaeologist from 1973 to 1999 and then as Director of the Norfolk Archaeological Trust up to 2014. These years covered a period of extraordinary change in British archaeology. In the early years *field* archaeology had not yet become a recognised profession; few people were active, and there were very limited measures to protect the historic landscape. The situation is now so transformed that it seems worth putting on record what one person has witnessed over this period of remarkable change.

My father, who was born in 1887 and lived until he was just over 80, once said that he had seen a complete transition in the countryside from the horse to the tractor in his lifetime and he could not believe that change could go any further. How wrong he has proved to be, and I am sure field archaeology will grow and change again just as much as it has over these 50 or so years. The signs are all very hopeful.

Whatever else happens, it is important that we protect and preserve as much as possible for the future after we have lost so much of our archaeology since the Second World War, both in the countryside and in the towns. We need to take more care of what we have left than we did from the 1950s through to the 1980s. There is no doubt that protection of the cultural heritage is now improving. In the towns and villages planning procedures can now ensure some control over the removal of archaeological deposits. In the countryside new conservation measures under Europe's Common Agricultural Policy do safeguard the archaeology better in arable areas to some extent, but not enough. It is too early to know what difference the vote to leave the European Union will make. Whatever happens, many more sites still need *legal* protection, and sub-soiling of unscheduled sites under cultivation is now the biggest problem. This is where the damage continues unseen, unrecorded and unchallenged. We must watch closely to see what changes there will be following our departure from the European Union.

The growth of evidence from metal detecting since the late 1960s is quite astonishing, and it is giving a whole new group in society an opportunity to be involved in archaeology as never before. Metal detecting in particular is democratising people's involvement in the past, and transforming our understanding of the historic landscape. Better awareness can only help to protect what we have left. The past is very precious, and there is still much to do to ensure some of it survives.

Chapter 2:
The Early Years

A farming background

After my parents married in 1941 they decided not to wait until the war was over before having a child, and I was born on 23rd February 1944 in Norwich Hospital. My mother (1901-1981) was Eileen Frazer-Allen, the daughter of Rev. David Frazer-Allen (1868-1923), the rector of Lyng, where she grew up in Lyng rectory. When my mother talked about her childhood I had a strong impression that being a rector's daughter in a village before the First World War was a fairly lonely existence. Edwardian custom created a strong social divide between those in the wooded grounds of the rectory and 'the parishioners' in the village. Later, she went off to Barts Hospital in London to become a nurse, and her younger brother, Archie, left for the colonies to farm near Mombasa in Kenya. Sadly, he was killed when the tractor he had borrowed from a neighbour caught fire. Their father died suddenly aged 56 in 1923, and his grave is close to the south wall of Lyng church. The organ in the church is dedicated to his memory. My mother returned to Lyng to be with her mother, Agnes, but they had to move out of the rectory because the Church of England provided no housing for widows. They were offered the use of the Mill House in Lenwade by the Sayer family, who ran the animal feed mill there, and she stayed in the Mill House until Agnes died in 1939.

My father was Ernest Martins (1887-1970), but he later changed his name to Wade-Martins, reviving an earlier family name after a bank mix-up when money was paid into the wrong account. He farmed at Clay Hall Farm Great Witchingham until he retired and married my mother in 1941 when they moved to a cottage in Mattishall. He often talked fondly about the flock of breeding sheep he had kept at Clay Hall, and also with great sadness about a fine herd of pigs he had built up until they caught swine fever. They all had to be slaughtered without compensation, and because his men refused to help he had the heart-breaking job of shooting them all himself. He often talked about having to shoot the pigs as his way of coping with the agony of it all. He had fought at Ypres, and he once told me that when he was issued with a uniform there was a bullet hole in the jacket. But, like so many men who had fought in the First World War, he would never talk about his time in the trenches.

Growing up on a chicken farm

My parents started married life at 'The Hollies' on the Welborne Road, Mattishall, and then in the early 1950s they built their dream bungalow further down the road towards Welborne which they called 'The Elms'. At The Hollies my father quickly established a chicken business to produce first-cross laying hens from Rhode Island Red and Light Sussex breeding stock, the purpose being to create prolific layers of brown eggs (*Figures 2.1 and 2.2*). That was before the days of hybrids which later replaced the old-fashioned breeds and their crosses. My parents gave up the chicken business, called Martins & Co. (Norfolk) Ltd, after the incubator house burnt down, but it was probably the right moment to do so anyway with the arrival of the hybrids and industrialised chicken farming with hens in battery cages.

We lived nearer to the neighbouring small village of Welborne than we did to Mattishall, and I was privileged to witness there the last flickering of a way of life much of which went back centuries. A neighbouring farmer, Harry Norton, only used horses. Harvest was cut with tractor-pulled binders (Culpin 1938, 166-177), and later seeing the first combine harvester working in the area was a memorable experience.

Electricity and running water had not yet arrived. In the little shop and post office customers were served by an old lady, actually called Olive Leamon, who had only a paraffin lamp. Water was drawn from wells in the cottage gardens. There was an old wheelwright and carpenter, but the blacksmith had just closed. The pub, called the Horse Shoes, flourished although it was serving a tiny community. The names and trades of the local families, like the farmers called Norton, Curson, Howard, Kerridge and Tooley, the blacksmith called Doy and the wheelwright called Neve, are all there recorded in the pre-war county directories. Sadly, the pub and shop went long ago.

2.1. Father, dressed as usual in thick cord breeches, heavy woollen socks and a flat cap, while feeding his Light Sussex chickens.

2.2. P.W-M helping father to mend a chicken run.

I was taken daily to a small private school in Quebec Hall just to the north of Dereham, and my parents tried hard to avoid the state school system, although I sensed that it cost them more than they could really afford. Judging by the school photo, Quebec Hall had about 40 children (*Figure 2.3*). All I do recall about the school now is standing in rows for assembly listening to the two ladies (in the front row in the picture) playing Chopin to us on the piano. It was nevertheless great fun helping my father with his chickens at the end of the school day.

A first taste of archaeology

At about the age of six I was sent as a boarder to the Town Close Preparatory School between the Ipswich and Newmarket Roads in Norwich. My first taste of archaeology came early when with a school friend, Gerald Townsley, we were taken by his mother to see the Roman town at Caistor St Edmund just to the south of Norwich. We hid from the farmer and walked over the main field, which was still then being ploughed, and picked up pottery which I kept for years afterwards. From that moment there was no turning back; I knew what my career would be, and years later I was able to repay my debt to the site after I took on the

2.3. A school group at Quebec Hall c.1949. P.W-M is fourth from the right in the front row. The two ladies who ran the school are in the centre. This is the only known photograph of the school which closed in the 1960s.

management of the Roman town for the Norfolk Archaeological Trust. After Town Close, education led inevitably into the public school system and to Bloxham just south of Banbury in Oxfordshire.

Bloxham School, 1957-62

My time at Bloxham from 1957 to 1962 was not particularly enjoyable, and when you don't enjoy something you don't remember it well. But I do remember that as a prefect I assiduously avoided dishing out 'points' which could lead to a beating, a system of punishment which seemed degrading and unnecessary. The high moments were starting and running the school Archaeological Society and organising an excavation in 1960 on the Tadmarton Road near to the Quarry Crossroads in a meadow where nothing had previously been recorded, although a Roman cemetery had been found in the ironstone quarry nearby before the war. Below a deep layer of topsoil we came straight onto the foundations of a substantial Roman building. The excavation was published in the school magazine, *The Bloxhamist,* Vol. LXVII, No. 479 (June 1961) and LXVII, No. 480 (November 1961), and in *Cake and Cockhorse: The Magazine of the Banbury Historical Society* (Wade-

Martins 1961) and details are held in Oxfordshire's Historic Environment Record (PRN 4984).

The *Illustrated London News* regularly featured public schools, and it was Bloxham's turn in the 7th May 1960 issue. Amongst the many posed pictures of boys appearing uncharacteristically studious was one of a meeting of the Archaeological Society with us all around a table looking at Roman pottery probably collected from fieldwalking at Swalcliffe Lea a few miles away (*Figure 2.4*).

For my A-level Geography dissertation I found immense pleasure doing a landscape study of Bloxham parish relating it to the pre-enclosure landscape with its ridge and furrow system which had been drawn conveniently as an underlay on

2.4. A very posed photograph published in The Illustrated London News *for 7th May 1960 of a meeting of the Bloxham School Archaeological Society in Oxforshire examining pottery collected from a nearby Roman settlement at Swacliffe Lee.*

the Enclosure map. (There is a reference to the dissertation in the *Victoria County History* volume IX as footnote 1.) The inspiration for this came from reading and re-reading in the school library W.G. Hoskins' *The Making of the English Landscape* (1955). All boys when they left were given a presentation book, and I chose *The Making of the English Landscape* which was signed by every boy in 'Wilson House', and it is still a treasured possession. The other book I devoured was Richard Atkinson's second edition of *Field Archaeology* (1953) which explained brilliantly the techniques of fieldwork at the time. The opening paragraph of the chapter on 'The Publication of the Evidence' resonated always with me after that:

> The importance of publishing proper reports of archaeological research, and especially of excavations, cannot be too strongly emphasised. For, as has already been said, the excavation of a site involves its destruction; once excavated, the evidence cannot be reconstituted except from the records made by the excavator. Failure to publish these records, therefore, is as much a crime against science as the deliberate suppression of a newly discovered historical document.

So, it was quite a shock to realise after he died in 1994 that Atkinson had himself left a major backlog of unpublished excavations, particularly at nationally important monuments like Stonehenge and Silbury Hill.

Academically Bloxham was not that good, and some teaching, particularly for the juniors, was lamentable. No boys from my year went straight on to university. This may explain why I left with only one A-level, in Geography inevitably, and had to go to Norwich Technical College for two years from 1962 to 1964 to take fresh exams, this time in zoology and botany. It was not an easy time when I clearly needed to move on.

A volunteer at Norwich Castle Museum

Meanwhile, in the holidays attending meetings of the Norfolk Research Committee in the late 1950s and early 1960s which were held regularly in the schoolroom at the Castle Museum was wonderful. It was a multi-disciplinary organisation run by the museum's curator, Rainbird Clarke (*Figure 2.5*), and it was a source of pleasure and wonder to attend and listen to the Norfolk personalities of the day, such as Dr Calvin Wells talking about his research on human bones, Charles Green on his excavations on the Roman forts at Caister-on-Sea and Burgh Castle, Charles Lewton-Brain on his flint collecting in West Norfolk, Hallam Ashley on his photography of historic buildings and Tony Baggs on Norwich.

Rainbird Clarke did much to promote archaeology to the public, and I felt very privileged to attend the luncheon in Jarrold's shop in Norwich to launch in 1960 his book *East Anglia* (1960) in the Thames and Hudson 'Ancient Peoples and

Places' series. This quickly became standard reading at the time. He took part in Anglia Television's 1962 'Once a Kingdom' series, and he wrote the Archaeology section of *Norwich and its Region*, published to coincide with the visit of the British Association for the Advancement of Science to Norwich in 1961 (Clarke 1961).

Another real pleasure was travelling to Norwich by bus from Mattishall to work as a volunteer in the museum where large numbers of cremation urns excavated by Guy Knocker from the Illington Anglo-Saxon cemetery in 1949 were to be stuck together. Working behind the scenes in the museum sticking pots in sand trays was a thrilling experience. The smell of that glue will live with me always.

2.5. *Roy Rainbird Clarke, known to everyone as 'Rainbird', curator of Norwich Castle Museum, secretary of the Norfolk Research Committee and originator of the county card index which became the Sites and Monuments Record in the 1970s.*

Warham Camp excavations, 1959

The first excavation I took part in was Rainbird's trenching of the defences at Warham Camp for the Norfolk Research Committee in 1959 to look for dating evidence from under the inner bank (*Figures 2.6 and 2.7*) and from the fill of the outer ditch. My mother, bless her, paid for me to stay in a B&B in Little Walsingham, and it was a great experience taking part in the project. I dug the trench into the inner bank and found hand-made flint-gritted pottery in the old topsoil under the bank, but unfortunately the sherds were not distinctive enough to date the fort with any precision. Perhaps more important was the discovery on top of the bank of a foundation trench to hold upright timbers and post-holes forming a palisade and fighting platform (*Figure 2.8*). I felt very honoured to help Rainbird with the site photography, and several of my pictures were used in the report later written by Tony Gregory and published years later in East Anglian Archaeology (Gregory 1986d).

2.6. An aerial view taken by Mike Page in 2006 of the Iron Age fort, Warham Camp, situated on the eastern slopes of the Stiffkey valley in north Norfolk. This is surely the finest prehistoric monument in the county. None of the three present entrances look original, and there are signs of a causeway across the valley leading to a now-lost western entrance in the valley bottom removed by the straightening of the Stiffkey River.

Ashill Roman enclosure and West Acre Saxon cemetery, 1961

Then followed small-scale excavations at the Ashill Roman enclosure, probably a first-century fort (Gregory 1977), and at the West Acre Early Saxon cremation cemetery in 1961 (unpublished). West Acre was the first time I had the opportunity to see really severe plough damage, with the shattered cremation urns sitting only partly below ploughsoil, a bit like Spong Hill in the 1970s.

Thetford Castle excavations, 1962: a near-death experience

At Thetford is an Iron Age fort remodelled as a Norman motte and bailey castle, and Rainbird excavated the outer defences in 1962 in the hope of finding dating evidence from the original bank and ditch (*Eastern Daily Press (EDP)* 19th September 1962). The trench was cut through the sandy fills of the ditch, 3.3 metres deep,

2.7. P.W-M, wheelbarrow in hand, working in the trench cut into the inner bank on the Norfolk Research Committee's excavations at Warham Camp in 1959.

without any shoring, with potentially fatal consequences. We reached the bottom of the ditch, which proved to be wide and flat-bottomed (Gregory 1992), and it was a real miracle that nobody was injured when the whole trench collapsed just after we had climbed out for a coffee break (*Figures 2.9 and 2.10*). As we sat we watched it just fall in. But for that coffee break, I would certainly have been instantly killed. There was never any explanation from Rainbird as to why he thought shoring at that depth in that sandy

2.8. Post-holes and a slot cut into the top of the inner chalk bank at Warham Camp for a palisade and fighting platform (R20).

2.9. The early stages of the Norfolk Research Committee's deep trench cut through the outer Iron Age ditch at Thetford Castle in 1962 (M4).

2.10. A lesson for all archaeologists who do not shore up the sides of deep tranches: the Thetford Castle trench collapsed just after we had climbed out for a coffee break (M37).

2.11 P.W-M and Susanna Everett on the North Elmham Park excavations in 1969.

soil was unnecessary, but I don't ever remember him going down into the trench himself. Two years earlier, in 1960 he had dug a narrow unshored trench even deeper, to just over 5 metres into chalky loam at the Thornham Iron Age enclosure without any problems (Gregory 1986a), but taking such risks, even by the safety standards of the day, was unacceptable.

Report writing

It wasn't apparent to me then that while Rainbird had the time to excavate in his holidays away from the museum, his museum duties did not seem to permit him time to write up his excavations which lay unfinished at his untimely death at the age of 49 in 1963. The same applied to Charles Green, Guy Knocker and Ernest Greenfield and others when they were excavating at this time for the Ministry of Works. The Ministry's payments covered the excavation but no more, so these early government-funded excavators were all left stranded when they came to writing up quite major projects. Years later in the Norfolk

Archaeological Unit we drew up a programme of report writing funded by the Department of the Environment and then English Heritage to clear up this whole backlog in a series of volumes of East Anglian Archaeology which we completed eventually in 1997 (**p.247-249**).

Chapter 3:
Excavating Deserted Medieval Villages

Destruction in the countryside

The 1950s and 1960s were an awful time to be growing up in the countryside if you were at all aware of the historic environment. Agricultural engineering had reached a stage with the development of the diesel engine which enabled tractors to plough deeper and bulldozers to level uneven ground (*Frontispiece*). The exposure of the Snettisham Treasure of gold and silver torcs in 1948 and 1950 in a field which was being deeply ploughed with a tractor for the first time should have been a warning of what was to happen all over the arable areas of Lowland Britain (Clarke 1956, 21-28). Government grants for improving farmland by removing hedgerows and ploughing up long-established grassland made destruction commonplace. Progress in farming technology was way ahead of the archaeological profession, which did not start to catch up until the 1970s. Old meadowland and heath was being levelled and ploughed everywhere without a murmur of complaint from archaeologists because in practice there were none to take notice outside museums and universities. It wasn't just important monuments which suffered; often it was just small pieces of landscape which disappeared, such as a bank representing an old common edge or a hollow way, each of which had their own story to tell. The examples which follow of the loss of two fine deserted villages at Thuxton and Grenstein were commonplace at the time. The most that Rainbird Clarke could do was fill in record cards of discoveries reported to him and mark up a set of six-inch maps he kept in drawers in the Castle Museum's committee room outside his office and then pass on details to the archaeology section of the Ordnance Survey in Southampton. He started doing this at the suggestion of O.G.S. Crawford, the Ordnance Survey's Archaeology Officer (Daniel 1965; Green 1986), and years later these record cards became the core of the new Norfolk Sites and Monuments Record which we developed in the 1970s (**p.165-166**). Meanwhile, in the 1950s and 1960s anyone who was archaeologically aware must have felt helpless, as I did, while watching post-war redevelopment, without record, of our urban centres.

Thuxton deserted village excavations, 1963-64

Levelling of the village earthworks

My own sense of despair about damage to the countryside was focused on the site of a deserted village at Thuxton not far from home. I found the earthworks of part of the village and moated manor site in pristine condition in 1960 as recorded on vertical RAF air photographs taken in 1946 (*Figure 3.1*). But in 1962 the hedgerows were removed and the earthworks were all levelled and cultivated, leaving soil marks showing where banks and buried medieval clay buildings had been. The village was not scheduled, and the destruction was government-funded and all perfectly legal. While the farming profession was trying to claim that their members were the custodians of the countryside, the need for much stronger conservation measures to control their activities was all too apparent. The memories of what happened at Thuxton certainly motivated me in later years to give conservation a high priority whenever the opportunity arose.

After levelling, the fields where the village earthworks had been were only lightly cultivated, so I could spend the summer of 1963, thanks to the kindly farmer, mainly alone digging on one of the house sites which showed as a clay rectangle on the surface. The buildings of a medieval village on these East Anglian boulder clay

3.1. *The fine RAF vertical aerial photograph taken on 31st January 1946 of the eastern end of Thuxton deserted medieval village showing the main east-to-west street with toft boundary ditches running back from either side and to the east the moated manor site with its outer earthworks all intact up until 1962 (RAF ref: 3 G/ TUD/UK52 5098).*

soils had never previously been excavated, so it was not clear what the evidence might be. I had been on the excavations at Wharram Percy deserted village in Yorkshire run by John Hurst, the Ministry of Works medieval period inspector at the time (1927-2003; obituary *The Guardian* 13th May 2003), and that training was a real help. John was a towering figure in the world of medieval settlement and medieval pottery studies, and he was a great inspiration. Wharram was the training ground for a whole generation of medieval archaeologists, where John had developed the concept of open-area excavation on village sites, derived from Axel Steensberg's work in Denmark, where areas were opened without trenches or box cuttings. This technique was taken to new levels of achievement by the great Phil Barker (1920-2001) with his excavations from 1960 to 1988 at the motte and bailey castle at Hen Domen in Montgomery and with his 1966-90 excavations on the later levels of the Roman town at Wroxeter. So, I applied the same approach at Thuxton with John's enthusiastic encouragement. My philosophy throughout my excavating career was to dig to see what was there and not to be focused on the need to answer academic questions which has a built-in danger of creating a blinkered view of the evidence. I owed much to John for his support in the years which followed.

Air photography from a Tiger Moth

The Thuxton soil marks were so clear on the ground, that it seemed worthwhile recording them from the air. The local flying club were willing to take me up in a two-seater Tiger Moth with open cockpits, and it was really thrilling, with the air rushing past, to see the outline of the village laid out below (*Figure 3.2*). The old RAF verticals and my recent pictures helped enormously in site interpretation and in the planning of the two seasons' of excavation on the village area which followed. These pictures also showed the layout of the outer enclosure of the moated manor after destruction with clay outbuildings ranged around a farmyard (*Figure 3.3*), just as depicted on a late sixteenth-century map of the main manor house at Longham (*Figure 4.5*).

Excavating medieval peasant houses

It gradually became clear in that first year that the medieval houses would be extremely difficult to define and understand because they appeared to be built with clay walls and clay floors similar to the boulder clay sub-soil. Flints were used only sparingly as foundation courses. Otherwise the walls could only be identified as lines of chalk-speckled clay. The edges of flint-cobbled yards *between* the buildings often provided the best evidence for the outlines of the buildings themselves. There was obviously a limit to what one person with a spade, trowel

3.2. Aerial photograph by P.W-M of the levelled and plough-damaged village earthworks at Thuxton in 1963 with the east-to-west street, toft boundary banks and the rectangular clay soil marks of medieval peasant houses and outbuildings. Compare this with the earthworks in Figure 3.1. The straight thin lines show where field drains had just been inserted (TG0408/ABU/slide).

and wheelbarrow could do alone in one summer, with some help from friends who came for a while, but I did expose the plan of one house showing what could be found by gentle open-area excavation.

In the next summer, after the field had been lightly ploughed and sown with barley, I came back after harvest, this time with Ministry of Works funding under the auspices of the Deserted Medieval Village Research Group. The funding was available as part of an initiative organised by the Group to excavate examples of medieval peasant houses threatened with destruction in different parts of the country. The aim was to build up a picture of house types in each region, as explained by John Hurst in a paper he had written on deserted medieval villages in *Recent Archaeological Excavations in Britain,* in which many of the well-known archaeologists of their day had written chapters on their recent research (Hurst 1956, 269-270). This splendid book represented the peak of archaeological activity in the late 1940s and early 1950s.

The Medieval Village Research Group brought in Lawrence Butler (1934-2014) to supervise the excavation. A team of locally-recruited workmen did much of

3.3. Aerial photograph by P.W-M of the moated manor site at Thuxton in 1964 after ploughing of the outer earthworks which revealed the rectangular shapes of clay outbuildings around the outer courtyard. Compare this with the earthworks in Figure 3.1. The layout is similar to that of the moated manor as depicted on a sixteenth-century parish map of Longham in Figure 4.5 (TG0408/D/AEH3).

the digging. Lawrence was a kind and gentle man, and together we developed techniques to expose and record the front part of another toft on the north side of the village street. This revealed the plans of two adjacent houses, again with chalk-speckled clay walls built directly on the medieval ground surface and surrounded by flint-cobbled yards and outbuildings, all dating to the late fourteenth century. Fine air photos of the excavated toft were taken by the wonderful larger-than-life Wing Commander Ken Wallis (1916-2013) from his autogyro which he built himself and flew from his airfield nearby at Reymerston (*Figure 3.4*). This was the machine he later flew in the 1967 James Bond film 'You Only Live Twice'.

Understanding peasant houses

How to visualise the construction of the clay walls was a problem. Was it a form of cob in which the clay was built up between timber shuttering or was it blocks of clay ('clay lump') as widely used in the area in the nineteenth century? Research

3.4. Aerial photograph by Wing Commander Ken Wallis from his autogyro of the excavation of Thuxton Toft 2 from the west in 1964 with the shapes of two medieval peasant houses showing as flat clay rectangles outlined by the surrounding cobbled yards (TG0408/ADK/-).

by John McCann published long after we had finished excavating showed that there is no documentary evidence for the use of clay lump before the late eighteenth century (McCann 1987 and 1997). At the time we looked for traces of breaks in the clay walls which might suggest the divisions between the clay blocks but that was not easy. Malcolm Atkin also considered the excavation evidence for medieval clay buildings in Norwich in 1991 and he favoured the cob option, there being no clear evidence for the post-Roman use of clay lump in the region (Atkin 1991). Adam Longcroft reviewed the evidence in 2004 and concluded that the question of how these clay walls were built should remain open until further peasant houses could be excavated (Longcroft 2004). So there is room for further debate, and there is a need for another excavation of a deserted village not already damaged by cultivation.

The finds included whetstones from Norway and lava querns from the Rhineland, and the few metal finds showed a reasonable level of prosperity on these heavy clay soils. The report was not published in East Anglian Archaeology until 1989; meanwhile Lawrence was excavating at Faxton deserted village in Northamptonshire from 1965 to 1967 and having an active academic career as a lecturer in medieval archaeology at Leeds University (Stamper, Stocker, Rees and Richards 2015). The Faxton report was never published, although it was apparently finished in draft. We did, however, finish the Thuxton report eventually (Butler and Wade-Martins 1989), but lessons still had to be learned about trying to write up important excavations on a shoestring.

Thetford Anglo-Saxon town excavations, 1964

Large-scale excavation of the Saxon town

While waiting for the harvest to be removed from the field at Thuxton in 1964 I joined the excavations just starting at the Anglo-Saxon town at Thetford being run by Brian Davison for the Ministry of Works close to the Brandon Road. Thetford in the tenth and eleventh centuries became a relatively large and prosperous town before it declined during the Middle Ages. This decline left areas of the Anglo-Saxon town undisturbed for several hundred years, but after the war Thetford saw extensive development as part of London's 'overspill' programme. In the 1960s the Borough Council and London County Council announced that this programme was to be accelerated with further housing estates to the south of the river. The only answer was large-scale machine stripping of topsoil to reveal the thousands of Late Saxon pits, ditches and post-holes cut into the sand and filled with darker soil. Over three seasons three acres near the Brandon Road were machine stripped, although excavation was not easy because many of the features were difficult to see and just as difficult to excavate in the dry sandy sub-soils. An important collection of plans of mainly Late Saxon timber buildings was nevertheless recorded, and it was all a remarkable experience and a very useful contrast to digging on the heavy boulder clays at Thuxton.

Susanna Everett

With my little green Austin A35 van I was asked one day to pick up two young ladies from Thetford station who were joining the team. One of them was Susanna Everett. We got to know each other quite well planning the post-holes, and there was one particular line of holes (at the north end of a Building B on Fig 56 of the excavation report!) which Brian Davison made us draw time and again before he was entirely satisfied. We kept in touch after that and married in 1970 (*Figure 2.11*).

Birmingham University, 1964-67

In the autumn of 1964 I went to Birmingham University to read Ancient History and Archaeology and I set out with my head full of the latest thinking about excavation methods and the extra-ordinary benefits of air photography as a method of reading and understanding the historic landscape. But then, I had the biggest culture shock of my life discovering that none of my fellow students had done any excavating or had studied an air photograph. The Department offered no teaching in archaeological method, and the grinding lectures in classical history, Greek sculpture and Greek vase painting nearly finished me. For a country lad to be stuck in the centre of a large industrial city was no fun either. The only saving factor was that the History Department had just appointed Philip Rahtz (1921-2011), described by Mick Aston in his Foreword to Philip's autobiography, *Living Archaeology* (2001), as 'a giant in British archaeology'. Philip had a remarkable excavation record, and he kindly allowed me to attend his lectures and seminars which were always stimulating. He was also fun. To hear at first hand about his excavation of the royal palaces at Cheddar was an experience not to be missed.

Two-week trips to Orkney each June to excavate a Pictist and Norse settlement at Skaill on Deerness with fellow students under Peter Gelling (1925-1983), who lectured on Anglo-Saxon and Viking archaeology, were enjoyable. Peter excavated with Birmingham students for two or three weeks each year at Skaill from 1963 up until 1981, and he died two years later in 1983. Simon Buteux and others have since produced an excellent account of the excavation from the rather incomplete records Peter left behind (Buteux 1997). It appears that the archive was hardly adequate for its day, especially as Skaill was run as a student training excavation. It was the only formal training in fieldwork offered to Birmingham archaeology students during their three-year course.

Grenstein deserted village excavations, 1965-66

Thuxton had taught us quite a lot about the structural evidence for medieval villages in the region, and John Hurst was willing to fund another excavation in the summer of 1965. We chose Grenstein (spelt Greynston in pre-nineteenth-century documents) within Tittleshall parish where the earthworks had been levelled in 1959 (*Figure 3.5*). Again it was on boulder clay, so the Thuxton experience would help with interpretation. A Ministry of Works grant was organised through the Deserted Medieval Villages Research Group, and at the age of 21 I was to be paid to run my first publicly-funded excavation.

Landscape change since the Middle Ages

One of the pleasures of working on Grenstein was that there was a fine series of maps in the Holkham Estate archives, dating from 1596 to the nineteenth century showing how the medieval landscape had gradually been removed. By 1596 the village which stood around Dowes Green, previously called Greyston Green, had been deserted, but the open fields around that were only gradually replaced between the sixteenth and eighteenth centuries by large enclosed fields. In the early nineteenth century Dowes Green was enclosed, and then before the 1880 first edition of the six-inch Ordnance Survey map these enclosures were also swept away by the Holkham Estate to be replaced by the present-day geometric pattern of fields with their dead-straight hedgerows. Locating the details of the medieval landscape by using the old maps, air photographs and surviving archaeology was very rewarding. The village lay on a south-facing slope mainly around a triangular green with a pond for watering livestock at the top (narrow) end (Figures 3.6 and 3.7). The surface pottery suggested that the village had started as a small settlement in the eleventh century around a crossroads to the north of the green and then spread down the hill and around the green in the twelfth and thirteenth centuries. The village was gradually deserted in the fifteenth century. It became clear later that this sequence reflected very similar patterns of village expansion and decline around other village greens in the area, but, unusually for a village of this size, there was no church.

Around the green 26 tofts could be identified. Close by, there were two moated manor sites, Greynston Manor (now obscured in Lounds Wood) and Caley's Manor.

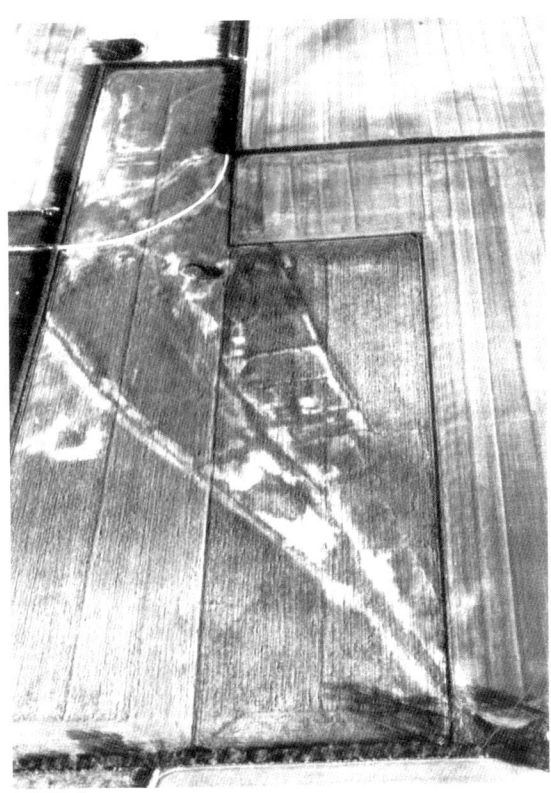

3.5. *Aerial photograph by J.K. St Joseph in 1960 of Grenstein deserted medieval village taken from the north after the bulldozing and ploughing of the village earthworks the previous year. There was a triangular village green with a pond at the narrow end nearest the camera and a row of tofts, some with visible clay buildings along the western side of the street which ran down that side of the green (Cambridge University Collection of Aerial Photography AAQ60: copyright reserved).*

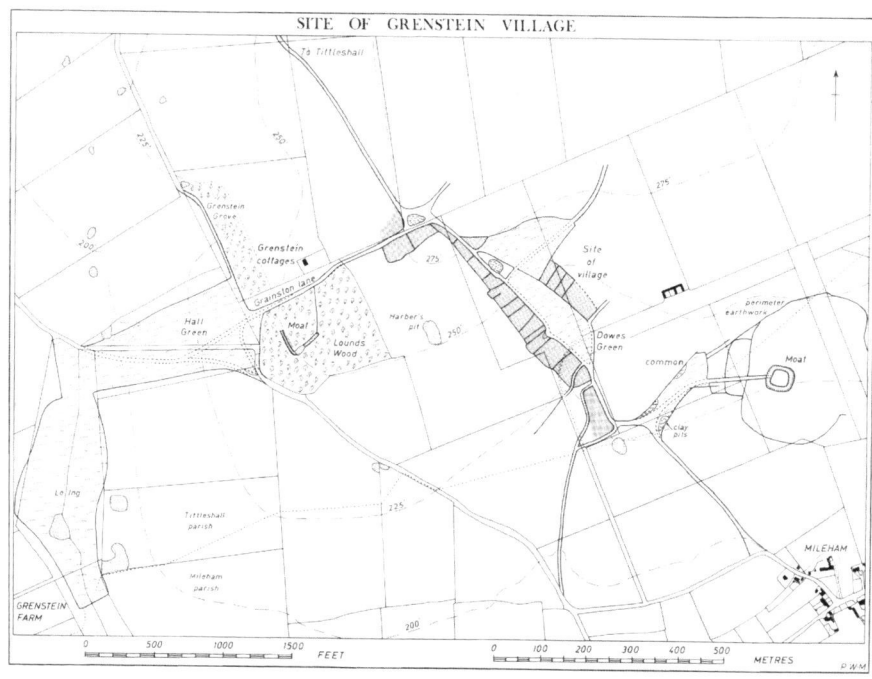

3.6. *An outline plan, based on cropmark, soil mark and earthwork evidence, of Grenstein village and the two moated manors plotted against the background of the modern landscape.*

Stripping a complete toft

In those days student diggers were recruited mainly by advertising in the Council for British Archaeology's *Calendar of Excavations*, and a substantial number of volunteers turned up and had to be housed somewhere. The answer was to borrow a pair of very derelict cottages from the adjacent farmer. We cleaned them out, fastened plastic fertiliser bags over the windows, installed chemical toilets and these cottages became our home for the duration of the excavation. Visits to the Royal Oak pub at Mileham made the evenings more tolerable. A gang of mainly older farm workers was taken on through the Labour Exchange to do the heavier work after the ploughsoil had been removed with a machine. Their foreman was 'Willow' Walpole from Mileham who had been renowned as a batsman in his youth. Janet Escritt, who had been on the Wharram Percy excavations, was the Assistant Director and Susanna was the Finds Assistant. But, shortly before we started, the weather turned incredibly wet, making the machine movement of soil a nightmare. The area around the excavation became such a mess that one

CHAPTER 3: EXCAVATING DESERTED MEDIEVAL VILLAGES   25

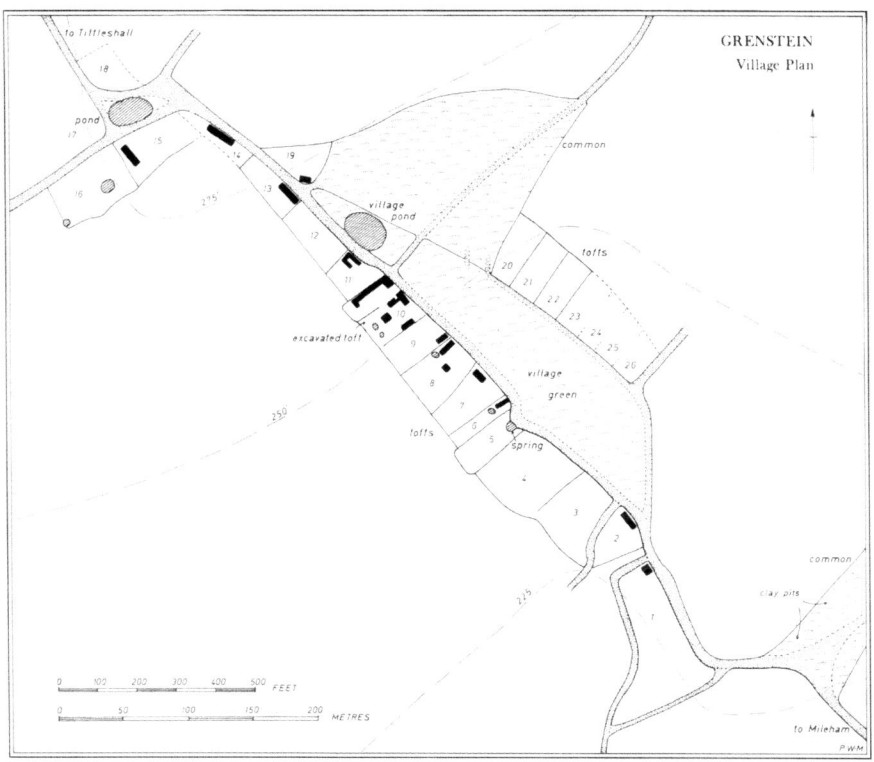

3.7. *A more detailed interpretation plan of the village showing the clay buildings seen mainly on Figure 3.5.*

picture of our topsoil removal was used a few years later in error by Professor Maurice Beresford when he was lecturing on deserted villages as an illustration of site destruction! We put him right on that.

We chose a toft to excavate opposite the centre of the village green (Toft 10) where subsequent documentary research showed some tofts were occupied until the fifteenth century (*Figure 3.8*). After the ploughsoil was removed we found that the plough had largely slid over the flint-cobbled yards without doing too much damage but had cut deep into the higher clay floors. Of the house itself only a depth of 50 mm of the floor remained, and the rest was already a part of the ploughsoil. This explained why the soil marks of the buildings often showed up so well on air photographs. The outlines of the flint-cobbled yards were therefore crucial in locating the buildings, but finding the internal building details was hard. For weeks the

3.8. *A vertical aerial photograph by Wing Commander Wallis of the excavated Grenstein Toft 10 at the end of the 1965 season. We painted a wheeling plank black and white in feet as a scale for this picture (TF9020/F/AED6).*

volunteers trowelled the flint cobbles and scraped the surfaces of the clay floors without complaining. The walls, where they could be seen, showed up as lines of chalk-speckled clay or, occasionally as larger flints forming a foundation course. We developed the use of hoes for the workmen in place of trowels which made scraping the clay surfaces easier and quicker. The men we employed had spent most of their lives on local farm work and so they were very familiar with the use of hoes for thinning out young sugar beet plants, or 'choppen out' as they called it.

None of this would have been possible without the kindness and forbearance of Richard and Rosamund Butler-Stoney of Burwood Hall, Mileham, who let us take over much of their field during those two very wet years and entertained us all every Sunday for supper.

At the end of the first season we had the plan of the whole toft (*Figure 3.9*). There was an entrance bridge over a deep ditch which drained the western side of the green. The bridge led into two cobbled yards with outbuildings on all sides, and towards the back the house was set within its own separate fenced area. In

CHAPTER 3: EXCAVATING DESERTED MEDIEVAL VILLAGES   27

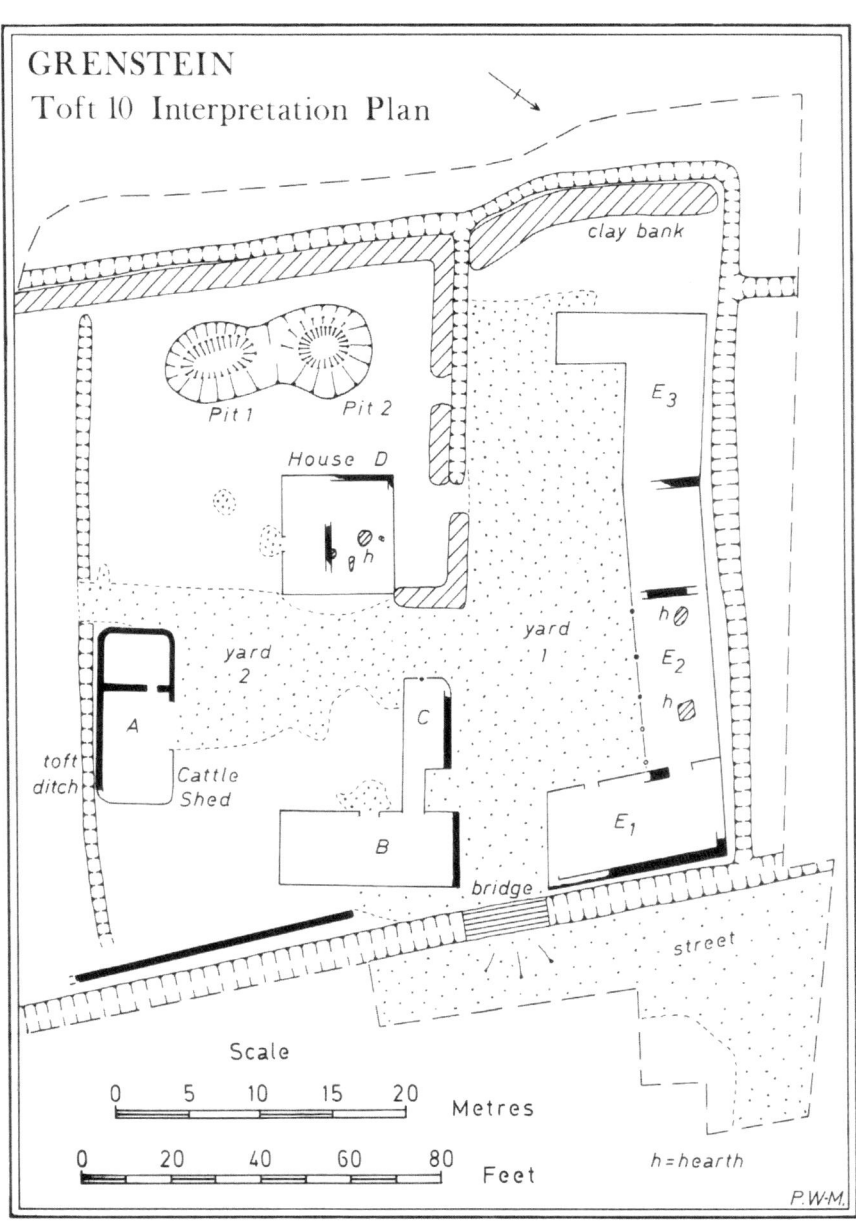

3.9. An interpretative plan of Toft 10 with the house, yards and outbuildings around cobbled yards approached over a bridge from the village street, orientated as in Figure 3.8.

3.10. Building A, the best preserved of the Grenstein clay outbuildings, interpreted as a cowshed because of the wide doorway. The building showed up simply as a clay rectangle defined by the chalk-speckled line of a clay wall to the left and by cobbled yards and a short line of larger flints to the right (BBV9).

this there had presumably been a garden and at the back were two large pits, one apparently kept free of rubbish and probably used for collecting drinking water. At the bottom was the base of a pottery jug to scoop up the water. The best-preserved outbuilding, which we called Building A, had a wide entrance indicated by a cobbled spread in the floor, so it may well have been for cattle (*Figure 3.10*).

The finds

The material from above and under the cobbled yards dated this final phase of the toft probably to the early fifteenth century, a hundred years later than Thuxton. While we had recorded the complete plan of a working farm, the plough damage to the buildings was so severe that it was difficult to identify the details of their plans or how they were used. The metal finds were more plentiful than they had been at Thuxton. There were lots of horse shoes, showing that horses were used more than oxen. Many pieces of lava quernstone from the Rhineland and ragstone whetstones from Norway showed what a large volume of North Sea trade there had been in these commodities. A distribution map of lava quernstone fragments built into Norfolk churches indicates that these were entering the county mainly through the port of Great Yarmouth rather than King's Lynn (Ashley, Penn and Rogerson 2011, Fig 1). The lava quernstones and the animal bones showed that it had been a mixed arable/livestock farm, and sheep bones were the most numerous, along with horse, cattle and pigs (*EDP* 29th December 1965).

Although we returned for a second season in 1966, we did not have the resources to excavate earlier layers in sufficient detail to make that worthwhile. The report recommended that the next excavation of a deserted village should be on a site which had not yet been plough-damaged, and that the resources available should be sufficient to excavate the early layers. The report was published in a volume of East Anglian Archaeology in 1980 along with my subsequent fieldwork on the medieval villages of Launditch Hundred (Wade-Martins 1980). Since then there has been no attempt to excavate any further medieval villages in the region on any scale large enough to understand a medieval toft. It is difficult to see where resources would anyway now come from under the current system where the larger contracts for rescue archaeology are usually won by a process of competitive tendering. Even machine-dug evaluation trenches would tell you relatively little and be very damaging. The very slight and fragile evidence for medieval villages in this area, where there is no suitable building stone, can only be understood by very slow and careful open-area excavation.

Surveys of other deserted villages

My work on deserted villages was not limited just to Thuxton and Grenstein. Following a lecture on both sites I gave to a joint meeting of the Norfolk Research Committee and the Norfolk and Norwich Archaeological Society, Keith Wade and I tried to widen public interest in the subject by writing a guide to the seven best-preserved sites in the county with a 1:500 plan of Pudding Norton, the most complete of all of them. This was published in the Norfolk Research Committee's *Bulletin* in 1967 (Wade-Martins and Wade 1967).

Postscript: A nostalgic return to Thuxton

After we closed the 1964 excavations at Thuxton I didn't return to the field until May 2017: a gap of 53 years. The site was just one continuous barley field with not a weed in sight. A ditch, with banks liberally sown with cowslips, runs through the middle of the field, perhaps as a nod towards modern farm conservation. And elsewhere there are new hedgerows and woodland belts, but while the landscape looks partly restored, the 1960's damage to the archaeology and the historic landscape can never be reversed.

Grenstein, on the other hand, has been down to grass for a while under a Countryside Stewardship scheme, but even here there was too much cultivation in the intervening years for much worthwhile archaeology to remain.

This all makes the few village earthworks we still have left a very special resource.

Chapter 4:
The Launditch Hundred Project, 1967-71

Unanswered questions about medieval settlement in the Norfolk countryside

After Grenstein was finished in 1966 the question was: what next? The opportunity came up to start a major excavation at North Elmham to look for evidence for the Anglo-Saxon village, but there was also a need to develop further our understanding of Anglo-Saxon and medieval settlement patterns in Norfolk. There were a number of key questions which people interested in settlement history in the region had long been asking:

- Can villages ever be traced back with continuity to their Romano-British predecessors?
- Do recent village plans necessarily look at all like their medieval and Anglo-Saxon forms?
- Why is there such a large number of isolated churches in the county? What part have they played in settlement development?
- Does the separation of churches from their villages indicate a movement of the population at some time or were they always isolated?
- Many villages were around greens and commons until these open spaces were enclosed mainly in the nineteenth century. Was this true in the Middle Ages as well and, more especially, at what time did these green villages come into existence?

Fieldwalking: then a new technique

These questions could not be answered without a lot of time-consuming 'fieldwalking', a technique not previously used as a research tool in the region. It involved systematically walking up and down ploughed fields picking up and recording pieces of pottery of different dates and plotting them onto 25-inch scale Ordnance Survey maps and analysing the distribution of these sherds. This was necessary because there was an almost complete absence of relevant recorded archaeology from the chosen study area, the Launditch Hundred in central Norfolk. This contained 29 parishes including Grenstein. Fieldwalking is now a standard technique in British archaeology, but in 1967 it was the first time it had been attempted on a systematic basis in the region, or nationally, as far as I knew. Since then it has been carried out by others in the region with important results, particularly by Alan Davison in Hales, Loddon and Heckingham from 1980 to 1986 (Davison 1990), Andrew Rogerson in Barton Bendish from 1983 to 1990 (Rogerson, Davison, Pritchard and Silvester 1997), extensively for the Fenland Project (**p.180-186**) and more recently by Andrew Rogerson in Fransham (Rogerson 1995), but at the time it was innovative and there was no model to follow. I registered to do a PhD in the Department of Local History at Leicester University, where W.G. Hoskins was still lecturing, although he was about to retire, and I was lucky enough to be awarded a University Research Scholarship which made the whole exercise possible. Later, I transferred to the Archaeology Department under Professor Charles Thomas (1928-2016) who recognised immediately the need to focus on fieldwalking to gather the essential data. Then all was well. Fieldwork was concentrated over the two winters of 1967/68 and 1968/69, and the summers were spent digging at North Elmham. The thesis was submitted and approved in 1971 (Wade-Martins 1971a), and a summary of the main results was published as a chapter in *Recent Work in Rural Archaeology* (Wade-Martins 1975) edited by Peter Fowler who had been my PhD examiner. The full report was published later in East Anglian Archaeology (Wade-Martins 1980) along with the Grenstein excavations.

Of the 29 parishes in the Launditch Hundred, nine contained land owned by the Holkham Estate which had commissioned the mapping of their farms at various times from the sixteenth to the nineteenth centuries. The earliest map was of the parish of West Lexham dated 1575, and maps of this date are quite detailed enough to provide a reliable picture of villages as they were soon after the Middle Ages. With excavation, I always believed it was best to dig to see what was there, but with the fieldwalking with so many villages to cover it was necessary to ask questions of each parish and then select fields to walk to answer those questions. So, fields around isolated churches and village greens in particular were target areas. Alan Davison and Andrew Rogerson years later took much smaller sample areas and gathered evidence as far as possible from whole parishes with much more objective and potentially more reliable results.

Roman and Early Saxon

None of the nine Roman period settlements then known in the Hundred showed signs of Early Saxon occupation, so what happened to the native population from the fifth century onwards remained a closed book. No settlements dating from the fifth, sixth or early seventh centuries could be found except for one close to the great Anglo-Saxon cemetery on Spong Hill, North Elmham, which we later excavated from 1972 onwards (**p.217-223**).

Isolated churches and village greens

For the Middle Saxon period 12 sites produced scatters of hard-fired Ipswich Ware pottery (dating from the early eighth century: Blinkhorn 2012, 8), usually near churches. In some cases the numbers of sherds were very small, and looking back I do wonder if the evidence was strong enough to support some of the settlement models I created. Nevertheless, it was the best I could find to suggest that many of the isolated churches did indeed indicate Middle Saxon village centres. It is time that one of these sites was subject to an extensive research excavation to test the evidence.

Ipswich Ware was followed by Late Saxon Thetford Ware which was manufactured in large quantities across the region from the middle of the ninth century to about the end of the eleventh century. The lack of Thetford Ware around greens was clear enough to show that village greens were not normally centres of occupation until the twelfth century. The twelfth and thirteenth centuries represented the great period of village expansion, often onto these greens. The best and most complete examples of this transition were at Longham, the two Weasenhams (*Figures 4.1, 4.2 and 4.3*) and Grenstein. Mileham had a very fine Middle Saxon centre near the church (*Figure 4.4*), but when expansion took place it was along the main street towards the castle, and no doubt the draw of the castle had some bearing on that. It was at this period that many of the churches, having previously been in village centres, became isolated. It was the twelfth, thirteenth and early fourteenth centuries which saw the full development of village greens as areas of settlement. The permanent pasture provided by the greens was important for the draft animals of the village at a time when more and more of the waste was being taken into cultivation to feed the growing population.

Not a lot of energy went into the study of moated manor sites, but it is worth drawing attention to the depiction of Longham manor on the late sixteenth-century manuscript map of the parish, with its outer enclosure depicting farm outbuildings ranged around a yard with a horse pond (*Figure 4.5*). This 'outer court' arrangement had also been seen at the Thuxton manor site where the clay outbuildings showed up as rectangular soil marks around the perimeter of the outer enclosure after levelling and ploughing (*Figure 3.3*). A similar outer enclosure attached to a moat had been visible as an earthwork at Little Bittering near the church before it was levelled while I was working on the Launditch Hundred project.

Rural wealth and decline

The medieval wealth of the county is best demonstrated by the high density of churches, of which there were just over 900 in Norfolk. A quarter of these have since been abandoned. The population may have halved during the late fourteenth

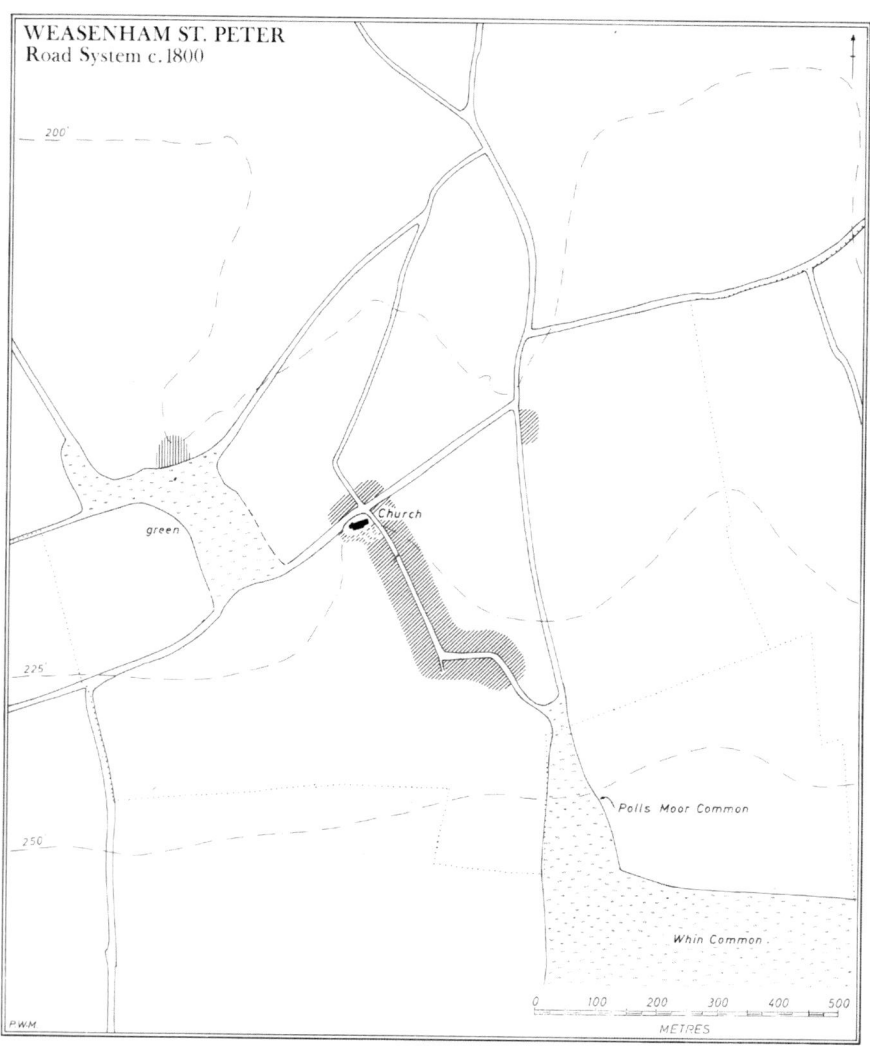

4.1. Weasenham St Peter with shading indicating areas of Late Saxon settlement and the beginnings of the early medieval village on the green, all based on pottery scatters. This distribution is set against the background of the pre-enclosure road system and the areas of pre-enclosure common.

CHAPTER 4: THE LAUNDITCH HUNDRED PROJECT, 1967-71   35

4.2. Weasenham St Peter areas of medieval settlement, based on pottery scatters.

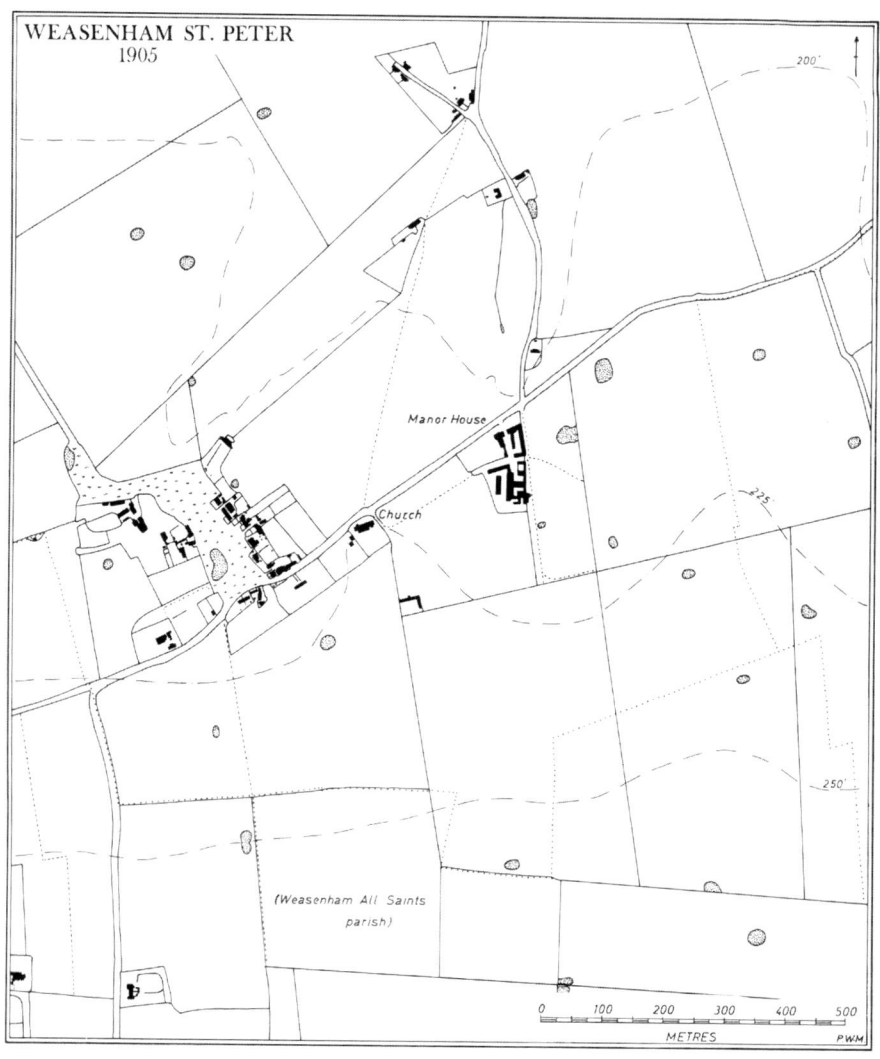

4.3. Weasenham St Peter today with its isolated church standing high on a hill with its quite small village around a green, all surrounded by large rectangular fields laid out in the nineteenth century during the great period of agricultural improvement. The landscape has been almost entirely transformed since the Middle Ages.

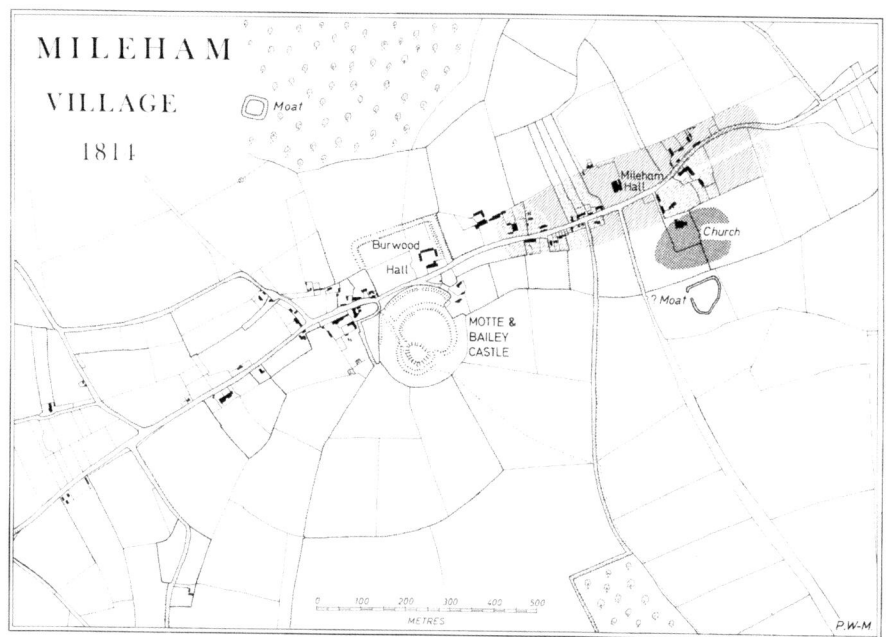

4.4. Mileham village as portrayed on the 1814 enclosure map showing the location of the Middle Saxon settlement around the church and the Late Saxon settlement in a different location along the village street spreading westwards towards the motte and bailey castle.

and fifteenth centuries, but then the decline continued with some villages, like Godwick and West Lexham, only disappearing in the seventeenth century (Davison 2005). In Launditch, 40% of medieval villages have, in fact, disappeared. So, the story of settlement movement and the rise and decline of so many villages was a remarkable one to put together, mainly through the pottery scatters and early estate maps. The lack of any stability of settlement patterns from the Roman period to the enclosure of the greens in the nineteenth century had not been expected, although it has since been recognised as standard in the region.

A recent review of the evidence within the wider East Anglian region by Edward Martin (Martin 2012) has not overturned the Launditch model but inevitably has suggested that it is more complex than I originally proposed. Edward's point that the settlement nuclei around churches are 'unlikely to be the sole source of people

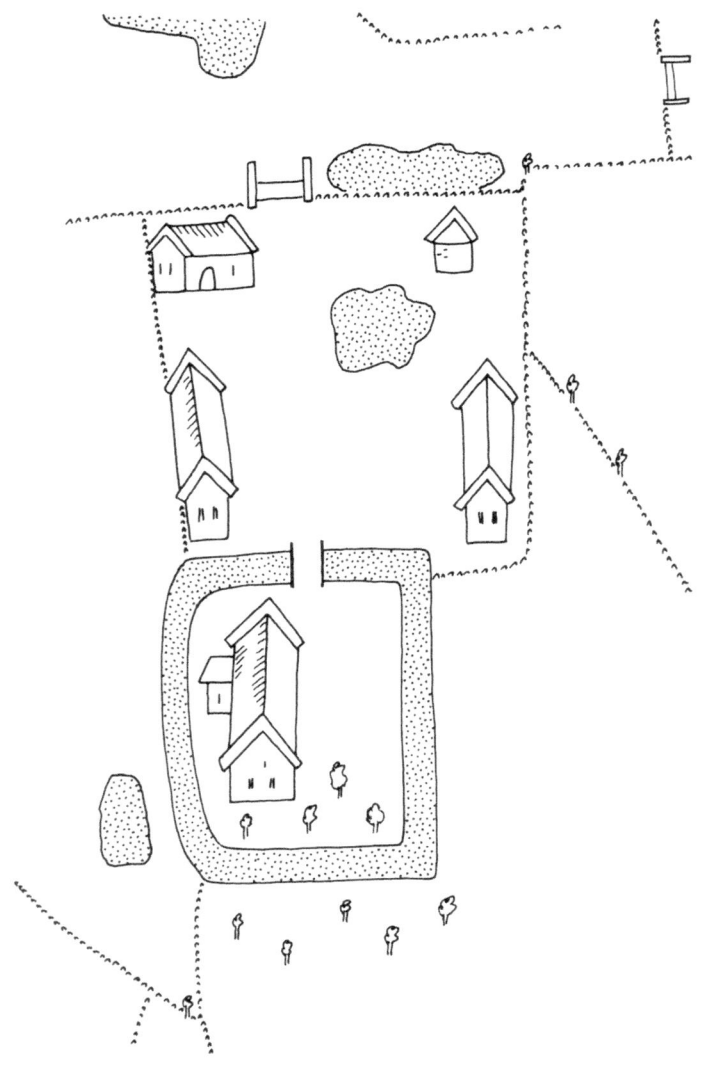

4.5. Maps of parishes once owned by the Holkham estate are a great source of information. This representation of the 'Situs manerii de Longham' of about 1595 shows what must have been a fairly common arrangement of manor house surrounded by its moat and an outer enclosure containing farmyard, outbuildings, stackyard and horse pond as found at Thuxton (Figure 3.3).

for the greenside settlements' is entirely reasonable. And 'the weight of evidence at the moment points to a late eleventh- to thirteenth-century horizon for their establishment' fits the evidence well. Tom Williamson has written generally about common-edge settlement taking place by the time of Domesday with scatters of Thetford Ware on the edges of commons, but he has not given the evidence (Williamson 1993, 169). He has, however, made the point that isolated churches are particularly common simply because many were established by the middle or late eleventh century *before* the villages moved (Williamson 2014, 177).

In a study of the archaeological evidence for the conversion to Christianity in the region Rick Hoggett has recently looked at the Launditch Hundred to see if the apparent date for the earliest settlements around churches would fit his predictions about church foundations (Hoggett 2010a, 147-153; Hoggett 2010b, 207-209). It is gratifying that broadly speaking they were as he had expected from other evidence.

The most comprehensive recently completed fieldwalking and documentary parish survey in the region is Andrew Rogerson's work at Fransham. This is within Launditch, and the full publication of his results is eagerly awaited by all of us with an interest in settlement history (Rogerson 1995). While the full details are yet to be made available, Edward Martin has summarised Andrew's results which show that in Fransham there are 13 sites on or near green edges that can be dated to the eleventh century, 38 to the twelfth century and 53 to the thirteenth century (Martin 2012, 237). So, there is now strong reason to believe that green villages were unusual before the mid eleventh century.

Chapter 5:
North Elmham Park: The Excavation of a High-Status Anglo-Saxon and Early Medieval Settlement, 1967-72

The Anglo-Saxon dioceses

North Elmham has had a special place in the history of the region. The seat of the bishops of East Anglia was established here from soon after 673 until the Viking incursions in the mid ninth century. Then, after a gap of a hundred years or so, the Elmham see was revived about 950 until it was moved to Thetford in *c.*1072 and finally to Norwich in *c.*1095.

The story is complicated by the existence of two Elmhams – North Elmham in Norfolk and South Elmham in Suffolk, and there was much debate in the nineteenth century about which 'Elmham' was the right one (Woodward 1864; Harrod 1864; Howlett 1914). However, the discovery in our Park excavations of substantial evidence for pre-Danish Middle Saxon occupation and a large Late Saxon cemetery removed any lingering doubt that the bishops were at North Elmham. Since the excavations, the ruined church on the cathedral site has been re-interpreted as an eleventh-century Norman chapel and not as the Anglo-Saxon cathedral (Heywood 1982; Heywood 2014, 184-187), but it seems likely that this building, now in English Heritage Guardianship and open to the public, either stands on, or is very close to, the *site* of the Saxon cathedral. This is on the highest part of a spur of land which drops away into the Wensum valley to the east and to Town Beck to the south. It is also in a central position in line with the main street which runs up the hill from the bridge over Town Beck. To the west another street, Walsingham Way, ran up the hill and formed the western side of the excavated area in the Park. To the east of the church was a third street, Rectory Way, and the two formed a triangle at the cathedral site near its centre (*Figure 5.1*).

The story of the early dioceses and the bishops of East Anglia is a complex one, and the details can be found elsewhere (Wade-Martins 1980). Suffice to say that North Elmham had a pivotal role in the region from the seventh to eleventh centuries. Its location close to the main east-to-west Roman road across the county and its proximity to the great Early Saxon cremation cemetery on Spong Hill, just over a mile to the south, were surely factors in the choice of North Elmham for the see. One can easily visualise the positioning of the bishops at North Elmham as a deliberate attempt to create a fresh Christian centre to replace its pagan predecessor. After the Park excavations were concluded we moved on to Spong Hill because that was being damaged by constant cultivation. Here the cemetery was fully excavated over ten seasons from 1972 to 1981 involving the excavation of over 2,000 cremations and 57 inhumations (**p. 217-223**).

5.1. Aerial photograph by J.K. St Joseph of the north end of North Elmham village. The main street heads up the hill directly towards the site of the Norman chapel which probably stands on the site of the wooden Anglo-Saxon cathedral. The earthwork of Walsingham Way to the west lies in the park and the line of Rectory Road to the east completes the triangle (Cambridge University Collection of Aerial Photography ZP71: copyright reserved.)

A strongyloid worm started the excavations

The Park excavations all began after Robin Don, the owner of the Park, called in at the Castle Museum one day at the beginning of December 1966 to say that he had agreed that the eastern part of the Park, which contained interesting-looking earthworks, could be ploughed up for a while to break the life cycle of a parasitic worm in the grass which had caused the deaths of some of the cattle owned by the tenant, Bob Bidewell. That was a civilised gesture at a time when so much of the farming community were ploughing up old grassland with the aid of government grants without much thought to the archaeological

5.2. Tea break with the volunteers on the North Elmham Park excavations in about 1967 with my very faithful little green Austin A35 van which took me to Birmingham University for three years.

consequences. In the discussions that followed Robin and Bob agreed that the area between the earthwork of the old village street, Walsingham Way closed in 1829, and the eastern Park wall would not be ploughed if the Ministry of Public Buildings and Works were to finance rescue excavations. The rest of the parkland with the worm infestation was then levelled and ploughed, and the excavations began in 1967 and ran until 1972 (*Figure 5.3*). When it was all over, Robin, who was a Master of Wine and a real wine enthusiast, decided to plant a vineyard where the excavation had been and this part of the Park remained a vineyard until he gave up the struggle to grow grapes this far north. The area then went back to grass.

It turned out that the most obvious earthworks to the north of the Park driveway actually contained the foundations of post-medieval farm buildings, and below them there was no medieval occupation because the site had been an open market place formed originally from an extension to the Late Saxon

5.3. The top of the church tower provided an ideal photographic platform for set-piece photographs at the end of each season, as here in 1970, showing the multitude of post-holes, pits and ditches cut into the boulder clay subsoil (TX3).

cemetery. So, after some limited hand excavation it was decided that the post-medieval buildings could all be removed by machine in order to reach the evidence for the Middle and Late Saxon settlement beneath, which survived all over the site in the form of pits, post-holes, ditches and burials cut into the boulder clay (*Figure 5.3*). This seemed to be the right decision because where sections through the topsoil over Anglo-Saxon buildings were observed no sign of contemporary floors or occupation levels could be seen. Looking back one has to admit that much of it wasn't in the end a rescue excavation. To the north of the Park driveway the grass could have been ploughed up without cutting into the Anglo-Saxon evidence which could have been left undisturbed. To the south of the Park driveway, where medieval village tofts are still visible and preserved as earthworks, that would have been a different matter. But by the time that was fully apparent the excavation had developed its own momentum, and the evidence was so compelling that it was agreed that we should carry on. Others can judge better if it was the right thing to do. But at least the earthworks of the medieval tofts to the south of the Park driveway along the old street were protected and never ploughed as a result of our negotiations.

Public and press interest

The excavation attracted a lot of public interest, and there were regular features in the local press (eg *EDP* 11th May, 4th June and 6th October 1971); there were guided tours at weekends led by people from the village, and in 1970 we had 2,500 visitors to see the excavations and an exhibition we laid on in the village hall. That was the start of what eventually became an annual event with a festival of flowers in the church (*EDP* 7th May 1971). The Elmham Festival, with Susanna currently the chair of the organising committee, has become the main annual fund-raising event for the parish church.

Voodoo village

There was, however, a downside to the publicity when the burials in the cathedral cemetery were exposed and on show during guided tours (*Figure 5.12*). There was also a skeleton laid out on display on a table in the village hall during the 1970 exhibition. The graves had created a great deal of interest which unfortunately coincided with a number of local road accidents in which five Elmham people were killed early in 1971, all of them pedestrians and two of them children (*EDP* 22nd and 29th January 1971). Such serious road accidents in the village are rare, and suddenly we had these deaths in three totally unrelated incidents over a few months. The press got hold of the notion that the village had becomed cursed in response to the disturbance of the dead, and they labelled us as the Voodoo Village. One shop keeper told the local paper that he had heard it said that 'for every one that was dug up, one of the village would be taken away' (*EDP* 5th February 1971). I had to point out to the press that over the years human bones had often been disturbed in building works and in sewer trenches in this part of the village, and that better traffic regulation was the answer. However, the label 'voodoo' or 'hoodoo' village did stick for a while, and the story also featured in national newspapers. It is, one has to admit, uncanny that there have been no more road deaths in the village before or since.

How much detail to publish in print?

A substantial report filling two volumes containing 661 pages and weighing just over 2.5 kg. was published as East Anglian Archaeology (EAA) No. 9 in 1980 (Wade-Martins 1980b). It contained much more detail than would be permitted today when electronic publication is an easy alternative. It covered not just the excavation but also a strong section by David Yaxley on the documentary evidence, including the topography of the medieval village based on a detailed survey of the bishop's manor of 1454-55 and a description and discussion by Calvin Wells of the human bones from the Late Saxon cemetery. To prevent the report being even longer there was an envelope attached inside the rear cover of Volume 2 containing microfiche with a full gazetteer of the excavated features, an atlas of the excavation plans, a tabulated pottery gazetteer and tables of human bone measurements. But without a good microfiche reader they are of little use, and fiche readers are now hard to find. The good news is that East Anglian Archaeology is having all its back volumes digitised, and that will include the fiche.

Much care was taken in the drawing of the excavation plans to show every detail of the shapes and slopes of the features as they were found cut into the natural, more so than you normally see in recently published computer-generated excavation plans. It was hoped that by making all the details readily available (large-scale plans and sections, pottery and metal finds and human and animal bone etc.) the site could be re-interpreted one day. There has actually been very little comment on the excavation results in the archaeological literature since the report was published, much less so than about the Launditch Hundred fieldwalking results already described **(p. 31-39)**. But the conclusions should be re-assessed in due course in the light of information from other relevant excavations. For me, the most significant outcome was the sequence of timber buildings dating from the Middle Saxon to the Early Medieval periods. This was a large collection of building plans which, with those found at the Thetford Anglo-Saxon town (Dallas 1993) and more recently at Brandon Middle Saxon monastic site (Tester, Anderson, Riddler and Carr 2014), should lay the foundations for the further study of the Middle Saxon and Late Saxon timber building tradition in the region.

If the site was being excavated today there would certainly be more detailed soil analysis and metal detectors would be essential, but they were hardly available at the time. Only two Anglo-Saxon coins were recovered, and one would hope that more will be found if there are further excavations in the area. This should help provide a firmer framework for dating the site sequence. There would also be more use of radiocarbon dating and probably more extensive examination of the environmental evidence. All the data would now be computerised, whereas our working records, all now stored in the Castle Museum, are on index cards and drawing paper. Photographs were mostly taken on 25mm black and white film which needs printing, while they would now all be high quality digital colour images.

Linking the excavation phasing to the 'cathedral ruins'

In one aspect, the excavation report became out of date soon after it was published, because the report attempted to link the phasing of the excavation to the structural sequence of the ruined church then interpreted by scholars as the Anglo-Saxon cathedral (Fisher 1962, 331-336; Rigold 1962-63; Taylor and Taylor 1965, 228-231). However, Stephen Heywood convincingly demonstrated soon afterwards that it was a later Norman chapel for the bishops of Norwich who retained ownership of the North Elmham manor after the see had moved to Norwich (Heywood 1982).

The pre-Danish Middle Saxon settlement (seventh to ninth centuries: Period I)

Period I, the Middle Saxon settlement, was the earliest activity on the site, started in the late seventh century. The significant discoveries for this period were the plans of the first Middle Saxon timber buildings to be excavated in the region, large deposits of Roman tile fragments found in the debris from a burnt-out timber-framed building and two timber-lined wells with the woodwork remarkably well preserved.

Timber buildings

There was good evidence for timber buildings in four locations, all exhibiting a strong tradition for setting the wall posts into continuous foundation trenches (*Figure 5.4*). In the largest building the carpenters managed to span an internal width of just over six metres with the hipped roof sloping down at either end being supported on internal posts. In one the shapes of many of the wall posts could be recognised in the trench fill. These posts were rectangular in section about 30 cm across and spaced about 80 cm between centres, so quite a lot of heavy timber was employed. The gaps between them were no doubt filled with wattle and daub. A central hearth was obvious in one building, but not in the others.

Roman tiles in a Saxon timber-framed building

A few fragments of Roman tiles were found in various places over the site, but not in sufficient quantity to be significant. However, in the upper fills of the two collapsed timber-lined wells were deep layers of charcoal, burnt clay and several thousand Roman tile fragments from a burnt-down timber building.

5.4. The foundation trenches of two superimposed Middle Saxon buildings (Buildings Z and AA). Cutting at right angles to the foundation trenches are a number of emptied Late Saxon graves (TX2).

Many of the pieces of burnt clay daub carried the impressions of the timber frame and wattle infilling with the charcoal wattle sticks still surviving in the clay. The two deposits apparently came from the same building and they had been tipped in from the same north or north-easterly direction. While traces of a white and yellow sandy mortar on the tiles suggested that the primary use of the tiles was in Roman masonry, their secondary use was as broken pieces inserted into clay daub, presumably to fill the smaller gaps in a Saxon timber frame. They were too fragmented to be used on roofs or on floors. There was no trace of Roman occupation in the immediate area, so they had clearly been re-used.

It is not unusual to see Roman tiles as fillers in flint and mortar walls or forming corners or window heads in Late Saxon/Early Medieval churches, but to find evidence for them in the debris of a timber building of this date was new. Was this the debris from the first timber cathedral or another major building burnt down in Viking raids and thrown into these hollows to clear the site when it was re-occupied in the tenth century? The date seemed to fit, and the material had been tipped in from the right direction. But that is as far as speculation can take us.

The timber-lined wells

The discovery of the two timber-lined wells, one sunk deep though the boulder clay into water-bearing sands underneath, came as a great surprise, and the excavation of both wells was technically quite demanding, requiring expensive shoring, electrical lifting equipment and pumps. The two wells did demonstrate the high status of this Middle Saxon settlement, for no ordinary village could have afforded these structures. Original woodwork was found in both and they were constructed by first digging out pits wider than the square timber shafts which were then inserted and held in place by the backfill.

Well I

The digging of this well pit, 4m wide at the top and nearly 12m deep, overcoming the problems of running sand at the bottom was a remarkable achievement. It is still a wonder to me how the pit was ever dug deep enough into the sand below water level to push in the bottom part of the well lining. This bottom section was prefabricated in the form of a straight-sided barrel 90cm wide which was preserved as a strong black organic stain in the sand. The outline of each board was revealed by thin black vertical lines between the lighter-coloured stain of each board (*Figure 5.5*). Above that was another prefabricated cylinder, 1.1m wide, made from woven wattles which showed as slight interlace patterns of clay in the sand. And above that there was a square shaft, 1.5m wide, rising 9m high to the surface, but only the lower part was sufficiently waterlogged to be

5.5. *The bottom of Well I represented as a stain of a wooden barrel pushed into the sand with the outlines of each plank clearly visible (UJ45).*

5.6. The upper square shaft of Well I surviving as a stain rather than as preserved wood (AL34).

partly preserved (*Figure 5.6*). This square lining was constructed in position by using large internal corner posts and horizontal side planks dropped in behind the posts. There were no joints, so one piece of wood was simply lodged behind another, and the whole structure held open by horizontal frames of bracing boards set about every 1.5m apart up the shaft. In neither well was there any trace of saw marks; all the shaping of the wood was done with radial splitting of the timber and the ends were trimmed with an axe or an adze.

5.7. In Well II the timbers in the lower sections were still perfectly preserved (UG26).

Well II

This second well was just over 6m deep and was used to collect surface water. At the bottom of the well the organic preservation was far superior to Well I because the lowest 1.8m of the timbers were completely sealed by the boulder clay and there was no sign of decay (*Figure 5.7*). Above that, the woodwork survived only as dark grey organic stains in the clay.

The well timbers were made from radial planks cut and shaped with axes and adzes (*Figure 5.8*). Well II gave us a rare glimpse of Middle Saxon carpentry, which was unsophisticated but effective. The tree rings were studied by John Fletcher and radiocarbon dates were measured by Roy Switsur, both in Oxford. The outcome was that there was a 67% certainty that the actually felling date for the timber lay between AD 802 and 862. Then, in 1982 John Fletcher revised his conclusions by comparing the ring-width sequences with five other contemporary wooden structures and concluded that the felling date for the North Elmham timbers was AD 795 plus or minus one year (Fletcher 1982).

5.8. The axe and adze marks on the Well II timbers were remarkably clear; saws were not used. The carpentry was quite primitive and the whole structure was designed to remain stable without joints (CB20).

How long the wells were used and regularly cleaned out is unclear, but the absence of rubbish in the fills of both suggested that the site was quite suddenly abandoned and remained empty and unused. The high quality of the organic preservation in Well II showed that branches and twigs from the surrounding trees fell in, as did seeds of stinging nettle, dock, fat hen and elder. From all of this evidence it was very difficult not to conclude that this period of disuse followed a raid by the Danes for whom North Elmham would have been an obvious target. The date of the timbers in Well II and the last evidence for an Elmham bishop in 845 does all fit.

The next event was the tipping in of the debris from the clearance of the burnt-out building followed by rubbish layers containing Late Saxon Thetford Ware pottery which filled the pit up to the surface.

The bishops return (late ninth and tenth centuries: Period II)

There was some rebuilding, mainly in the form of purpose-built latrines, at the north end of the excavated area in Period II when Middle Saxon Ipswich Ware pottery was still in use but after some limited amounts of Thetford Ware had been introduced. So, this revival phase needs to be dated to no later than the end of the ninth century. It is interesting that one of the cess pits in these latrines contained possible Danish loot in the form of the only rich group of metalwork found on the site, including a gilded silver strip, possibly from a shrine, currently on display in the Anglo-Saxon gallery in the Castle Museum.

The first substantial building was a large hall we called Building U dated to the early tenth century by the absence of Thetford Ware in the foundation trenches compared with the amount of material in the later Period II buildings. It had an impressive internal span of 7m, so there must have been tie beams to withstand the outward thrust of the roof.

Then followed the largest building found on the site, Building P. It was an L-shaped structure with the main east-to-west range having an internal span of at least 8.5m which was surely a severe test for the carpenters to span. The foundation trenches were also shallow suggesting that the timber frame was self-supporting and did not derive strength from its setting in the ground. I had to question if a structure of this width could have been roofed successfully, but the clue lay in the greater width and depth of the wall trenches in the angle where the two wings met. This was where the rainwater off the two roofs had poured down the walls rotting the wall timbers causing them to be replaced.

It was frustrating that the north side of the main range of Building P lay just outside the excavation in the shrubbery of the adjacent garden and so was not excavated. Looking back, though, that was actually quite lucky because it means that at some future time the evidence for this wide building, which was interpreted as the bishop's palace, can be re-examined. It was good to leave some of the evidence entirely undisturbed for the future.

The fourth side of the courtyard created by these two large buildings was closed off with a latrine with the floor area filled with cess pits at one end, so it looks as though the bishops had an outside loo across the yard! This period belonged primarily to the use of Thetford Ware pottery, but some Early Medieval Ware was also being introduced into the topsoil during this time, and it then became the predominant pottery type for Period III. The Period II buildings are not illustrated here because of the size of the plans, but they can be seen in the full excavation report in EAA 9.

The Late Saxon timber buildings (eleventh and twelfth centuries: Periods III and IV)

At the end of the tenth century there was a change in the use of the site with the colonisation of the area by village people with their houses and their outbuildings represented by hundreds of post-holes, all of a quite different character to what had gone before. Five house sites were excavated, each containing a sequence of post-hole buildings. Piecing their plans together and devising a sequence based on fairly meagre pottery evidence was fascinating (*Figure 5.9*). No two archaeologists would come up with quite the same results, and some structures were much more convincing than others. A plan of one house and its outbuilding is included here (Buildings K and M in *Figure 5.10*). Comparable post-hole patterns had previously been identified in the Thetford Saxon town excavations between 1964 and 1966 (Dallas 1993).

5.9. The Late Saxon Periods III and IV buildings were represented by a thick scatter of post-holes cut into the boulder clay making building shapes which had to be disentangled (UC3).

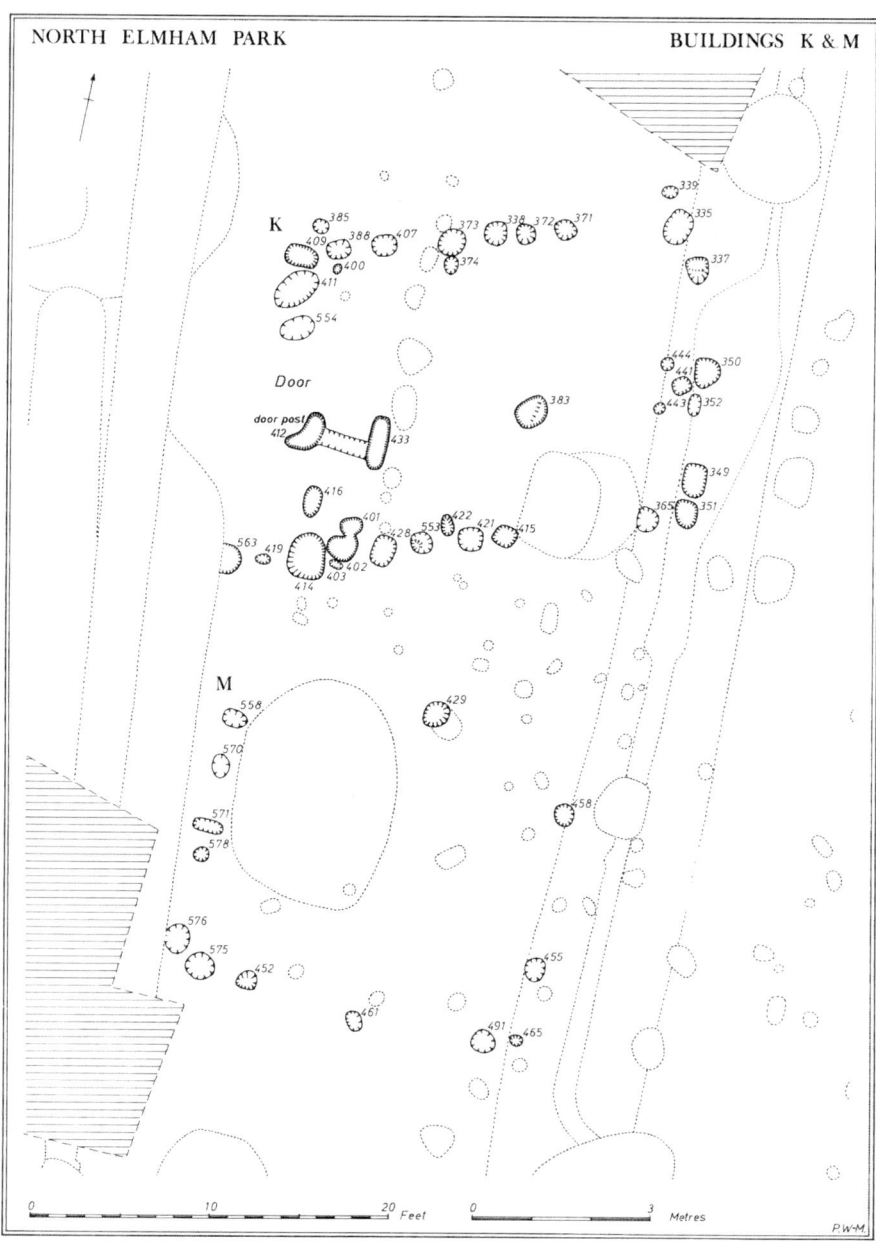

5.10. One of the clearest Period III post-hole buildings was Building K with its outbuilding M.

In the pottery sequence, the proportion of Early Medieval Ware increased in relation to Thetford Ware over Periods III and IV. The first medieval glazed wares came in at the end of the sequence.

During Period IV a new method of erecting the timber-framed houses arrived as exhibited in Building T (*Figure 5.11*) which had seven pairs of larger wall posts each forming a transverse truss, probably linked together at ground level with interrupted ground sills into which wall studs were fitted. With this new construction came a tendency to make the side walls slightly curved or 'bow-sided', which may have had a Scandinavian origin.

The final house in the sequence was a structure 17.5m long and 7.4m wide in the middle and 6.7m wide at the ends (not illustrated). The hearth was in the centre of the floor, and there was a pair of posts on either side forming an aisled truss which served to lift the tie beam out of the reach of the flames. The next bay to the south had a pair of wall posts in the walls acting as door posts, possibly with a cross passage between them. At the doors the interrupted ground sills were set deeper to act as thresholds (*EDP* 4th June 1971). This was the last to be found in the building sequence and the closest we came to finding medieval buildings with continuous ground sills into which the whole timber frame was jointed. A frame like this did

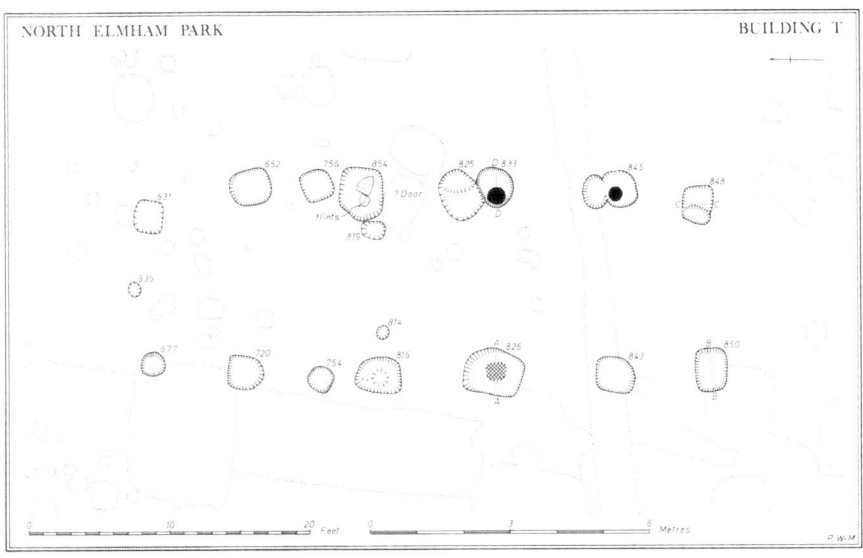

5.11. *Building T, one of the final buildings in the sequence, was constructed with larger wall posts set further apart forming distinctively curved sides, probably indicating Scandinavian influence.*

not, of course, need to be dug into the ground, and, indeed, it would last much longer on a brick or flint sill. As good timber from the woodlands became harder to find, with increased demand through a rising population, this could have been the moment for the switch to building in clay as seen at Thuxton (**p. 15-21**), Grenstein (**p. 22-29**) and Norwich. One can envisage a divergence in building traditions at this point where peasant buildings were built of clay throughout the Middle Ages and only the wealthy in their manor houses continued with ever more elaborate timber-framing.

The unravelling of this sequence of timber building plans covering five centuries was one of the most important results to come out of the Park excavations.

The cathedral cemetery

A total of 194 inhumation graves were uncovered in the north-east corner of the site, without any grave-goods and orientated west-to-east with head to the west (*Figure 5.12*), except for one. Previously, bones had been dug up in the gravel car park across the road in front of the old George and Dragon pub for the installation of the village sewerage system and also to the east of the pub when a bowling green was built. (Subsequently the bowling green was built over without any archaeological recording.) They were all Christian graves and they all appeared to be focused on the site of the cathedral. Around the cemetery was a trench to hold a wooden boundary fence defining a roughly rectangular area which extended 80m to the south and 60 m to the west of the Norman chapel, with an entrance to the south under the present main

5.12. Examples of the Late Saxon burials. None seemed to have marker posts which explains why their locations were quickly lost and inter-cutting was frequent. The widely splayed arms of Grave 99 near the back showed that they didn't all have coffins; indeed no coffins stains were seen (BI3).

road. The pottery from the grave fills strongly suggested a Late Saxon/Early Medieval date, from the late tenth to early eleventh centuries, before the parish church was built by Bishop Losinga. After the church was opened, no doubt the focus of burial switched to the new churchyard.

Calvin Wells, who always had a very colourful way to describe human bones, picked out three burials as being of special interest. He was sure that inhumation 5 was not Anglo-Saxon, nor even European, but a lady of pure black African descent. The skull was characterised by having a very flat nose and a strongly projecting upper jaw.

Inhumation 10 was the only one buried with head to the east and placed outside the area defined by the cemetery fence. He was a powerfully built male with a grossly deformed left leg, with a chronically distorted left knee and thickened femur and tibia, and must have been an unpleasant sight. No doubt for this reason he was buried apart from ordinary folk. Inhumation 171 had met a violent death with sword slashes to head, neck and arm. He was buried actually on the line of the cemetery fence: another example of a social outcast buried away from ordinary people (Hadley 2010, 104-106).

This was the first large group of Late Saxon skeletons from a rural population to be published from East Anglia, and the group provided us with a glimpse into the daily lives of the farming population of Norfolk in the late tenth and eleventh centuries. The bodies were laid out straight with hands to the side or sometimes joined together, and there was no clear evidence for coffins. Indeed, the way the arms were sometimes positioned (*Figure 5.12*) left no room for coffins. It is interesting, however, that in an earlier waterlogged Christian cemetery recently excavated nearby at Great Ryburgh coffins made of dug-out tree trunks were usual (*EDP* 16th November 2016, 6-7). There was no suggestion that the graves were marked with stones or posts, so their positions were soon forgotten, which explains the lack of order or spacing between the graves and why one was frequently cut by another.

A fifth of the population had died by the age of 18. The mean life expectancy of adults was 37 years (35.8 for women and 38.2 for men). Unlike the urban groups Calvin had previously examined, they were well fed and healthy as children. The relatively light deposits of tartar on the teeth argued for a diet of tough meat and coarse bread and an absence of soft porridge and well-cooked stews. Heavy tooth wear was probably caused by grit from the lava quernstones which we know were imported from the Rhineland by Middle Saxon times and found frequently on medieval village sites. The high great frequency of osteoarthritis and osteophytosis pointed to the heavy nature of manual work. Calvin reckoned that 90% of the population had osteophytic changes to the spine caused by excessive manual labour by their mid twenties (*Figure 5.13*). The absence of sinusitis in all except one case suggested that the houses were well ventilated with effective roof openings, even though they had the hearth in the centre of the floor. It is interesting to compare these results with the burials from an urban population of the same date in Norwich under the castle earthworks excavated in 1979 (**p. 228-229**)

The market place

We know that Bishop Despenser converted the Norman chapel, probably on the site of the Saxon cathedral, into a fortified manor house in 1387 by digging the massive earthworks one can see today, with soil actually piled against the walls of the chapel which became the undercroft for his new fortified country retreat. This must have involved the desecration of hundreds, if not thousands, of Anglo-Saxon graves, and the bishop could hardly have been unaware of what he was doing.

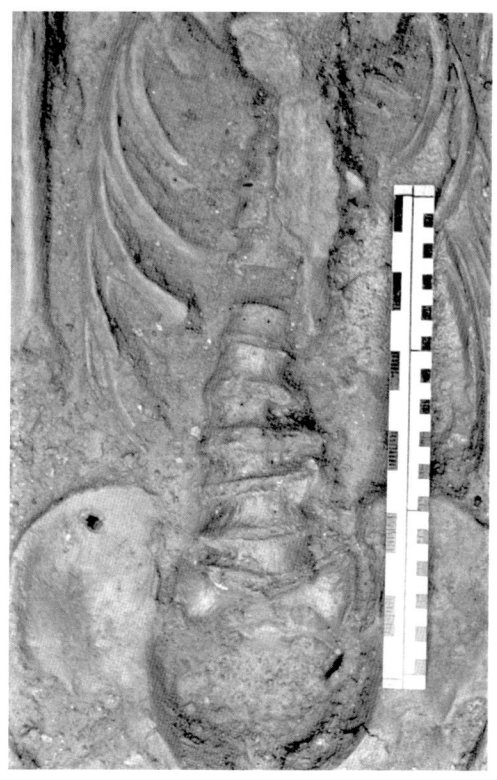

5.13. Inhumation 50 was a good example of severe osteo-phytosis of the spine with distortion of the lower vertebrae suggesting a life of heavy manual labour (AN31).

David Yaxley's documentary research established that there was a market on a green, known as Bell Green in 1572, which was created in the centre of the excavated area. There was a market held here probably by 1326-27, but it had decayed by the beginning of the fifteenth century. The green had been formed partly out of the cathedral cemetery and was extended westwards to cover a wider area, reaching as far as Walsingham Way. This green was thoroughly exploited as a source of clay which was extracted from small circular pits probably for house building. Old clay pits around commons and greens are still a familiar sight, as indeed they are in the nearby village of Brisley.

Further areas to be excavated

The desecration of the cemetery by the Bishop of Norwich and the creation of Bell Green brings the story of the archaeology of the excavated area within the Park to a close, but in the long term there needs to be more excavations in the area. Soon after the excavations were over a part of the hilltop containing an early street frontage was genuinely threatened when the eastern side of the churchyard extension to the south of the church was to receive modern burials. However, despite a number of requests for funding to the Department of the Environment no grant was available. No explanation was forthcoming, but the obvious explanation was that they had already invested heavily in the Park excavations and they were by then also funding the long-term excavations of the very threatened Early Saxon cemetery on Spong Hill to the south (**p. 217-223**). In these circumstances they probably felt that North Elmham was already having more than its share, so the opportunity was lost. Other areas, sooner or later, may well come up for development to the east of the church and to the north of the ruined chapel ruins, so when they do it is important that the opportunity to excavate here is not lost as well.

Writing the report

Having completed the Grenstein and North Elmham excavations, it was time to write, but there was no government funding to pay excavators to work on their reports unless they were prepared to go and work in a miserable little room in a government office in Victoria Street in London. I tried it once or twice, but it was horrible, and the substantial excavation archive you needed to work on had to be taken to London with you.

Early in 1971 the government had announced increased funding for rescue excavations following pressure from RESCUE (**p. 143**), but there was still no pay to help excavators write up their work except through the Victoria Street scheme. So, I wrote a letter to *The Times* which was published on 10th January 1971, a part of which went as follows:

> *If this extra government grant is really to be effective, there needs to be a new system whereby professional field archaeologists can excavate and prepare their results for publication under reasonable conditions. As the number of sites to be excavated grows even larger, so the problem becomes more acute. No figures are officially available, but it is surely no coincidence that under the present system over half the government financed excavations are never adequately published; without vastly improved facilities for archaeologists, over half this new money will also be wasted.*

It seems an obvious point to make now, but at the time it was revolutionary. I must have been working in the Victoria Street building when the *Times* letter was published and John Hurst arranged for me to meet himself and Arnold Taylor, then Chief Inspector of Ancient Monuments. They were clearly upset by the letter and the meeting was heated. However, the outcome was a radical change of national policy. I received the first-ever government-funded post-excavation grant, and this opened the floodgates for post-excavation grants for all those who had run government-funded excavations. We then had no good reason for not producing our excavation reports in good time, and it did make a big difference. The main North Elmham Park report was published in two volumes in East Anglian Archaeology (Wade-Martins 1980b). There were four interim reports in *Norfolk Archaeology* (Wade-Martins 1969a; Wade-Martins 1970b; Wade-Martins 1971b; Wade-Martins 1972) and more popular articles appeared during the excavation in *Current Archaeology* (Wade-Martins 1968; Wade-Martins 1970a; Wade-Martins 1973; Fletcher and Switzur 1973). Various hand-outs were also printed each season for visitors to explain the excavations as they progressed.

5.14. *One visitor who came to work on the excavation from time to time brought her Basset Hound (1013/72).*

Distinguished visitors

The visits of two well-known personalities over the years were particularly memorable. One was Sir Mortimer Wheeler who visited with a lady friend, and I deeply regretted not taking a photograph of him on the excavation. He smoked his pipe constantly, and whenever he threw away a matchstick it was picked up enthusiastically by the star-struck diggers who put all the matches into a polythene bag, labelled the bag, and hung it in the finds hut, and the matches stayed there for the rest of the excavation. Sir Mortimer brought a lady friend who stayed and helped on the excavation for a while with her basset hound sitting next to her (*Figure 5.14*).

The other distinguished visitor was an elderly, and highly respected, Basil Brown, the excavator in 1938-39 of the Sutton Hoo Anglo-Saxon ship burial, and I did take a photo of him on the site, although at his request I took away his walking stick before the picture was taken (*Figure 5.15*).

5.15. A visit from the elderly Basil Brown, the excavator of the Sutton Hoo ship burial in 1939 (BJ19).

Chapter 6:
Chance Finds

In the 1960s there were no full-time archaeologists working outside museums, so there was no publicly-funded arrangement to record important discoveries. People knew that I was interested in archaeology and sometimes brought finds to me. There are three which stand out as being particularly memorable from the period up to 1973 when we started the Norfolk Archaeological Unit.

A French polychrome jug from Welborne churchyard, 1968

There was a knock on the door one day at Mattishall in November 1968, and standing on the doorstep was an old friend, Philip Norton, the churchwarden at Welborne. He was holding the fragments of a very rare but instantly recognisable late thirteenth or early fourteenth-century French hand-painted 'polychrome' jug. A grave digger called Mr M. Johnson had just found all the pieces while digging a grave and because they looked unusual he had collected almost all of them up and passed them to Philip.

The jug had been imported from Saintonge, north of Bordeaux in western France. For Welborne it would have been an expensive item and may have been used for church ritual. The jug was made of fine white clay hand-painted with two birds outlined in dark brown and infilled in green. There were also three shields decorated with horizontal lines and dots. Only the handle was missing (*Figure 6.1*). The jug was drawn and published in *Norfolk Archaeology* (Wade-Martins 1969b), and it was given by the Parochial Church Council to

6.1. A French polychrome jug after repair now on display in Norwich Castle Museum, found by a grave digger close to Welborne church in 1968.

Norwich Castle Museum where it still remains on display in the Fitch Room (NCM 1969.29).

Previous examples had been found only in Great Yarmouth and King's Lynn, both busy medieval ports, and to find one in this remote location was indeed surprising (Wade-Martins 1969b).

A Late Bronze Age metalworkers hoard from North Elmham, 1970

The same thing happened in January 1970. Susanna and I had just returned from our honeymoon in Scotland when there was a knock on the door early the next morning. There stood the burly figure of Fred Nicholson, the farmer of the nearby Foxburrow Farm in North Elmham (and a prominent County Councillor). He was clutching a pair of bronze axeheads picked up the previous day by his ploughman. A further five more and a bronze ingot were on the surface, and their positions were marked with stakes. A 30-foot square was then set out around the finds, and the square was excavated by volunteers in mid February. Nobody had metal

6.2. Volunteers excavating the site of a Bronze Age metalworker's hoard at Foxburrow Farm, North Elmham, in 1970 watched over by Fred Nicholson, the farmer (with a long stick standing beside me), and Harry Apling with a white be ard. Harry had become well known for his research on Norfolk windmills and burial mounds.

detectors then, but a total of 48 bronze objects were recovered, nearly all from the ploughsoil, which was 300 mm deep. When the surface of the gravel sub-soil was scraped using hoes (*Figure 6.2*) the base of the hoard pit appeared as a very shallow feature only 25 mm deep. In the base of the pit were two complete axeheads, parts of another and two ingots.

Of the 48 items catalogued, 33 were whole or fragments of socketed axeheads, two were pieces of socketed spearheads; there was a small fragment of a rapier, parts of two swords, a sword chape and nine bronze ingots (*Figure 6.3*). Axeheads are usually the most numerous items in these metalworkers' hoards, and three decorative vertical ribs on several of them are almost identical to the decoration on those from another hoard previously found at Foulsham only five miles away. Two sword fragments joined to make about two thirds of a comparatively small example of a sword. There was no evidence of a container in the pit, so the items were all probably buried in a sack or leather bag, and their typology suggested a burial date of about 700 BC. Hoards like this are not particularly unusual, but what made this one unique at the time was that it was the first hoard to be excavated archaeologically using modern methods, thanks to Fred Nicholson and the keen band of volunteers put together for the excavation.

The Castle Museum was lucky enough to have Tim McK Clough, a prehistorian, working on the staff at the time and together we wrote up the hoard which was published in *Norfolk Archaeology* later the same year (McK Clough and Wade-

6.3. *A selection of bronze items from the Foxburrow Farm hoard in Norwich Museum, including a lump of slag, parts of a leaf-shaped sword and eight socketed axeheads.*

Martins 1970). Except for an axe and spearhead retained by the family, the hoard was then placed in the Castle Museum on long-term loan by Fred Nicholson. The loan has recently been converted by Mrs Nicholson into a gift (NCM 2015.28).

An Anglo-Saxon inhumation cemetery at The Paddocks, Swaffham, 1970

The third 'knock on the door' happened while we were excavating in North Elmham Park in 1970. We heard that Anglo-Saxon grave-goods and bones had turned up on a building site at The Paddocks housing development in Swaffham, so we responded by diverting the excavation team there at weekends where we were allowed to dig by the developer between the partly-finished buildings, the piles of building materials and the tarmac already laid over the adjoining road. At total of 19 inhumations and a possible cremation were excavated in August and November, but these were obviously only a small proportion of the total. The rest had been destroyed by the house foundations or sealed under the buildings and the road.

Of particular interest were two male graves with their shields and spears laid over them. In one case a tall powerfully built man had been placed face downwards with arms folded under his chest and there was a central shield boss and four decorative discs lying in two pairs to either side on his shoulders. Among the jewellery in the female graves were a fine gilded cruciform brooch and a necklace.

Although organic material had not survived in the sandy soil, impressions on the corrosion surfaces of the metal gravegoods allowed Elisabeth Crowfoot to identify several different fabric weaves on the clothing (Figure 6.4), and some of the objects displayed impressions of bracken laid over the bodies before burial (Figure 6.5). However, the most remarkable discovery was two skulls with gouged-out holes which were interpreted by Calvin Wells as trephinations. These are holes deliberately made in the skull while the patient was alive to relieve pressure on the brain. Calvin had

6.4. *Textile impressions on the corrosion surfaces of an iron buckle from The Paddocks Early Saxon inhumation cemetery in Swaffham (ME34).*

previously found similar well-healed lesions on Anglo-Saxon skulls from Watton, Eriswell and Grimston and concluded that there had been a distinguished Anglo-Saxon surgeon, or more likely surgeons, at work in the area!

Six years later the cemetery was published mainly by Catherine Hills, who was by then excavating at Spong Hill, in East Anglian Archaeology (Hills and Wade-Martins 1976). The finds were given by Swaffham Town Council to the Castle Museum (NCM 1976.314).

6.5. *Braken impressions on the corrosion surface of an iron mount for a wooden shield from The Paddocks cemetery (ME30).*

Chapter 7:
Societies

Possibly the earliest example of archaeological rescue recording in the county took place in 1813 when a local historian, Goddard Johnson Junior, collected and recorded the finds from sixth-century Anglo-Saxon burials removed from three barrows being levelled for agricultural improvement at Sporle with Palgrave (Ashley and Penn 2012). And until 1973 field archaeology in Norfolk, like everywhere else, was almost entirely dominated by amateur enthusiasts who formed themselves into society groupings in various ways. Many carried out excavations on barrows but left little record of their activities.

Norfolk and Norwich Archaeological Society (NNAS)

The 1840s saw the founding of many of the county archaeological societies, many of them inspired by the clergy with their enthusiasm for historic buildings and churches in particular. It was no coincidence that this was the decade when the arrival of the railways made it possible to travel for the day to meetings and excursions. Much of the interest was in church architecture, manorial history and records. The preliminary meeting of the Norfolk and Norwich Archaeological Society was held in Muskett's shop in the Haymarket in Norwich in December 1845. Charles Muskett was a bookseller and printer who published books of antiquarian interest like *The Antiquities of Norfolk* by the Rev. Richard Hart and the immensely important *Ladbrooke's Views of the Churches of Norfolk* in five volumes. The formal inaugural meeting of the Society was held the following January (Wade Martins, S. 2015, 35). Volume 1 of *Norfolk Archaeology,* quaintly subtitled *Miscellaneous Tracts relating to the Antiquities of the County of Norfolk*, was published in 1847. By 1850 the membership had already reached 400. The President was the Bishop of Norwich and of the 18 committee members eight were clergy, with many of the other founding members being from the aristocracy and the gentry.

In the nineteenth century and into the twentieth century there was a particular interest in opening burial mounds; with at least 55 dug into during the nineteenth century and a further 48 by 1950 (Lawson, Martin and Priddy 1981, 37-38). Soil layers were hardly recognised and many of the finds disintegrated in private collections without conservation. A selection of the more robust items was collected in Norwich Castle Museum which was opened in 1894, and a careful catalogue of this material, with accession numbers, was prepared by the great Norfolk historian and antiquarian Walter Rye and published in 1909 (Rye 1909).

The antiquarian clergy were enthusiastic, often over enthusiastic, about restoring their medieval churches, and it is fortunate that Ladbrooke sketched most of them in considerable detail to provide a record of these buildings before Victorian restoration. These sketches were published in five volumes (Ladbrooke 1843). By the end of the nineteenth century antiquarian perceptions of the county's archaeology were still sketchy. While the more obvious field monuments like the Roman town at Caistor St Edmund and the Roman forts at Burgh Castle (then in Suffolk) and Brancaster were recognised, the appreciation of earthworks was in its infancy; the Iron Age fort at Warham was believed to be a 'Danish' (Viking) encampment, while less conspicuous and more subtle earthworks like deserted medieval villages were not recognised until Keith Allison's pioneering work describing and listing most of them was published in *Norfolk Archaeology* in 1957. The wonderful aerial photography by Keith St Joseph at Cambridge University exposed all the detail of these earthworks to close scrutiny for the first time after the war.

A lasting legacy of the Society is the unbroken annual series of *Norfolk Archaeology* in 46 volumes, today filling 2 m of shelf space when bound, full of detail on every conceivable subject. No serious archaeologist in the county can manage without access to a set. Excursions formed an important part of the society's activities, and the annual report for 1900 describes Society visits to seven churches, three great houses, one castle and one other building. At that time churches, monasteries and castles *were* archaeology for many people. The programmes of excursions (*Figure 7.1*) and lectures and the annual arrival of a new volume of *Norfolk Archaeology* still provides members with a rich feast of endless interest right up to the present day.

The Prehistoric Society of East Anglia

The region was an early focus for prehistorians, no doubt encouraged by years of barrow digging and flint collecting on the light Breckland soils. In 1908 a very significant event took place in the rooms of the Norfolk and Norwich Library. It was the inauguration of the Prehistoric Society of East Anglia to be 'an East Anglian society for the study of all matters appertaining to prehistoric man'. The movement to create this new body was led by W.G. Clarke, author of *In Breckland Wilds* (1925) and later expanded by his son Rainbird (1937). It published its own journal: *The Proceedings of the Prehistoric Society of East Anglia,* and its meetings were held alternately in Ipswich and Norwich. In 1935 the society held a ballot of members, and there was overwhelming support for it to become a national society and it burst out of the region to become 'The Prehistoric Society' (Phillips 1987, 51-52). However, probably in anticipation of this event, a year earlier the Norfolk Research Committee was formed primarily to promote locally-based interdisciplinary research (**p. 71-76**).

7.1. Mainly members of the Norfolk and Norwich Archaeological Society on a guided tour of Binham Priory with Michael Begley in 2005.

The Norfolk Research Committee (NRC)

The 1930s seems to have been a period of increased antiquarian interest in the historic landscape. There was a growing feeling that while there was a need for specialist societies, there was also a case for co-ordinating research between disciplines, particularly between those interested in the history of man and his relationship to the natural environment. The Fenland Research Committee was set up in 1932, and on 30th July 1934 a letter was sent out to prospective members of a new Norfolk Research Committee:

> *Dear Sir,*
> *At an informal meeting held at Norwich Castle Museum on June 29th it was unanimously decided to form a Norfolk Research Committee. The meeting, presided over by Mr F. Leney (Curator of the Museum), was attended by delegates representing the Norfolk and Norwich Archaeological Society, the N & N Naturalists' Society, the Prehistoric Society of East Anglia, the county branches of the Geographical and Historical Associations, the N & N Aero Club, the Norwich Science Gossip Club, Norwich Castle Museum and Thetford Corporation Museum.*

The Committee is in no sense a new society. It is rather a co-ordinating organisation to promote researches which, owing to their complex nature, have hitherto lain outside the field of study of the existing local societies. It will endeavour to secure co-operation between experts of local and national standing in an investigation into the archaeology, geology, social and economic history, physical and human geography, plant ecology and climatology of the county. In adopting this wide range of enquiry the committee follows the admirable precedent of the Fenland Research Committee formed in 1932.

The letter went on to invite the recipient to become a member. Invitations were sent to 81 individuals, and 53 then joined the new co-ordinating body.

When the Research Committee was wound up in 1992 and replaced by the Norfolk Archaeological and Historical Research Group I had a chance to read the minute book covering the period 1934-59 before giving the presidential address to the new Research Group. This minute book, assembled by Rainbird Clarke, who was curator of the museum from 1951 to 1963, was partly a scrap book and partly a minute book. It was an account of an active pioneering organisation studying archaeology, geology, natural history and local history in a truly multi-disciplinary manner seldom seen today. But its main focus was on archaeology, and when I started to attend their meetings in the museum in the late 1950s the subjects covered were largely related to archaeology. Nevertheless it played a useful role in stimulating research in a wide range of subjects at the time. The tragedy is that the NRC minute books cannot now be found. The last secretary, Alayne Fenner, says that they were collected from her by someone called 'John' who said he was in the Castle Museum, but they haven't been seen since.

The first barrow survey 1935-1948

On 29th June 1935 the newly-formed Norfolk Research Committee set up a group to carry out a survey of Norfolk barrows; it consisted of well-known names of the period: Harry Apling (prehistorian with an interest in windmills and windmill mounds), Basil Cozens-Hardy (secretary of the Archaeological Society and local correspondent for the Ancient Monuments Board), H. Dixon Hewitt (prehistorian), Leslie Grinsell (national barrows specialist), H.F. Low, Eric Puddy (local historian), Rainbird Clarke (archaeologist), J.E. Sainty (prehistorian and geologist), P. Schwabe, Rev. Tyrell-Green and A.Q. Watson (prehistorian). The purpose of the survey was to check the existence of all known barrows, to measure and describe them, to excavate a number where their identity was in doubt, to list their contents when recorded, and collect folklore about them.

The progress of the survey was reported to a meeting of the NRC in 1948, and manuscript notes by Rainbird Clarke for that meeting were seen by Andrew

Lawson at the Castle Museum when we revived the barrow survey for the Norfolk Archaeological Unit (NAU) in 1973 (Lawson, Martin and Priddy 1981, endnote 4). By 1948 the team had discovered a previously unknown long barrow and had increased the number of recorded round barrows from 131 to 250, although Andrew in his report describes their barrow descriptions as often inadequate. Worse still was their publication record. Andrew calculated that 13 were excavated by members of the group prior to 1935 and a further 13 thereafter, but none, with one notable exception, was published except for a very brief description of the Breckland barrows in Leslie Grinsell's *The Ancient Burial Mounds of England* (Grinsell 1953, 200-203. The notable exception was Norfolk's first known long barrow at West Rudham found by Sainty and Watson in 1935 when they were out visiting the round barrows at Harpley and West Rudham. In 1937 they sectioned the flanking ditches to prove to their satisfaction that the long mound was indeed a long barrow – the first to be recognised in Norfolk (Sainty, Watson and Clarke 1938). They then invited A.H.A. Hogg from Newcastle to complete excavation of the mound in 1938, which was promptly published despite the outbreak of war (Hogg 1938; Hogg 1941). The long barrow proved to be a turf mound covered with upcast from the surrounding ditches, with an area of burnt sand at the south end which he thought indicated the site of a cremation pyre.

NRC Bulletins

From 1949 the Research Committee produced an annual duplicated *Bulletin*, assembled by Rainbird Clarke as Secretary, full of fascinating information about the activities of their members. A set of the Bulletins, recently bound, can be consulted in the Castle Museum library. The first issue listed members' archaeological excavations carried out in 1948, and these are summarised below. (Where these excavations were subsequently published, the references are shown in brackets):

- A 'long mound' at Acle containing medieval pottery sectioned by A.J. Morris and P.E. Rumbelow, possibly connected to a medieval salt-pan (unpublished).
- A rich Bronze Age settlement at Bacton Wood Farm, Edingthorpe found by J. Turner. This excavation continued for several years (unpublished).
- The Anglo-Saxon cremation cemetery on White's Hill, Markshall excavated in 1815-22 and rediscovered by Larwood with some intact cremations in urns (Myers and Green 1973).
- An Iron Age settlement excavated by Dr J.G.D. Clark on Micklemoor Hill, West Harling, largely financed by the Prehistoric Society (Clarke 1953).
- Excavations on four medieval sites within Norwich, mainly directed by E.M. Jope, at Barn Road, St Stephen's Back Lane, Ber Street and Ber Street Gates (Jope 1952).

- A medieval timber-framed well exposed in cliffs and excavated by G. Larwood at Happisburgh (Larwood 1952).
- The western rampart and ditch of Tasburgh Camp sectioned by G.W.T. Barnett (**p. 323**) (unpublished except for schematic re-drawn section in Rogerson and Lawson 1992, 34).
- A large part of a courtyard of the Appleton Roman villa cleared by R.R. Clarke (unpublished).
- The sites of three Iron Age hoards of gold torcs ploughed up in 1948 on Ken Hill, Snettisham, and subsequently excavated by R.R. Clarke (Clarke 1949 and 1952).

That came to 12 different excavations being organised by members of the Research Committee in a single season, and it represented an extra-ordinary level of effort. In addition, Guy Knocker was excavating on the St Mary's housing estate at the Late Saxon town at Thetford for the Inspectorate of Ancient Monuments (Rogerson and Dallas 1984). Guy Knocker then excavated the Illington Anglo-Saxon cemetery the next year (Davison, Green and Milligan 1993) as well as continuing at Thetford. It was these Illington Anglo-Saxon urns which I stuck together as a teenage volunteer ten years later (**p. 9**).

In addition, in 1948 archaeological reports were said to be in preparation on:
- The late Commander Mann's 1932-38 excavations on the Caistor-by-Norwich Anglo-Saxon cemetery by J.N.L. Myres (published 24 years later as Myres & Green 1973).
- Caister-on-Sea Roman settlement by A.J. Morris (unpublished).
- Reffley Bronze Age site excavated by P.L.K. Schwabe and I.J. Thatcher in
- 1937-38 in preparation by Miss F. Patchett (unpublished).
- Illington Anglo-Saxon cemetery by Captain Knocker (published 44 years later as Davison, Green and Milligan 1993).
- A general survey of Roman Norfolk by R.R. Clarke to appear in Norfolk Archaeology for 1949 (Clarke 1952).

For geology there was just one project, the investigation of post-glacial deposits in the Broads with bore holes in the Ant, Bure and Yare valleys by J.N. Jennings.

Two geological reports were in preparation:
- The Cromer Forest Bed by F.O. Whitaker.
- New map of Blakeney Point by J.A. Steers.

There was no let-up in this level of Research Committee activity as recorded in the *Bulletins* for several years. Archaeology was always dominant, although the excavation records were of varied quality and much remained unpublished. There seems to have been no attempt to set standards for recording or publication of work carried out in the name of the Committee.

There was also a healthy level of research into a range of other subjects, particularly post-glacial ecology, mainly in the Broads. In this context the names of J.N. Jennings and J.M. Lambert frequently occur. In the mid 1950s C.T. Smith and J.M. Lambert were writing about their research into the origins of the Broads, which came to fruition in 1960 in the famous Royal Geographical Society Research Series monograph *The Making of the Broads* (Lambert, Jennings, Green and Hutchinson 1960). This completely changed our understanding of the origins of these inland waters. In 1955 Ruth Barnes was describing a new atlas being prepared of British flowering plants. In 1957 E.L. Swann was compiling a new card index of *all* Norfolk plants and B.F.T. Ducker was recording Bryophytes on Scolt Head. At various times Tony Cartwright kept members up to date on the preparation of the Norfolk sheets for the new national Land Utilisation Survey. Meetings were held regularly in the old school room at the Castle Museum and they covered subjects like coastal defences in the two world wars, Roman roads and the Cromer Forest Beds Series.

Study of Iron Age forts

Archaeological initiatives by the Norfolk Research Committee depended heavily on the active leadership of Rainbird Clarke after he was appointed Deputy Curator of Norwich Museums from 1946 and Curator from 1951 until his sudden death in 1963. The City Council would not permit him to run excavations as a part of his work, so his excavating was limited to his holidays and weekends with the help of local volunteers under the auspices of the Research Committee (Green 1986). The Iron Age was his particular interest, and so he embarked upon a programme of investigation of Iron Age defensive sites between 1955 and 1962, all of which were written up years later by Tony Gregory for the Norfolk Archaeological Unit. This proved to be no easy task when Tony frequently had to describe Rainbird's records as being often 'sketchy' and 'incomplete'.

The Iron Age defensive sites, in the order in which they were first excavated, were:
- A first-century AD rectangular ditched enclosure at Thornham in 1955, 1956 and 1960 (Gregory 1986a).
- A first-century AD rectangular ditched enclosure at Wighton in 1957 and 1958 (Gregory 1986e).
- Warham Burrows rectangular ditched enclosure and adjacent Warham Camp in 1959 (Gregory 1986c; Gregory 1986d).
- Thetford Castle, where the castle was constructed in part from the earthworks of an Iron Age fort, in 1962 (Gregory 1992).

The Late Iron Age small 'Thornham-type' rectangular forts, nine in all including the three excavated by Rainbird and the rest found by air photography, were discussed by Tony in the East Anglian Archaeology volume in which the Norfolk Archaeological Unit published these excavations (Gregory 1986f). They were mostly in north-west Norfolk and each had a defensive ditch enclosing an area of about a quarter of a hectare, usually with just one entrance and occupying relatively high ground overlooking river valleys. They formed a coherent group with strong similarities, built in the early first century AD probably during the period of the client kingdom before Boudica's revolt. Evidence for internal structures was sparse. The 1950s was a period when diesel tractors could plough much deeper, and Tony noted how much plough damage there had been to the base of the rampart at Thornham in the short period between the 1956 and 1960 excavations (Gregory 1986f, plates III and IV). Although it is now well established that plough damage was severe and widespread at the time, it is unusual to have such clear well-dated evidence for the damage.

The trenching of the defences at Warham Camp and Thetford Castle confirmed a likely Iron Age date for both, but no more than that. However, strong evidence for timberwork on top of the inner bank at Warham was of particular importance (**p. 9-11**).

Momentum is lost

Gradually after Rainbird's sudden death in 1963 the momentum which had sustained and driven the NRC so effectively and for so long gradually dropped away. By 1969 five of us felt that the NRC had lost its way and we wrote an open letter to the editor of the Newsletter (as the Bulletin had become by then) raising a number of questions about the way it was run and what its future should be. But this made little difference, and so we started the Norfolk Archaeological Rescue Group (NARG) in 1975 to create a fresh momentum in amateur activity.

Norfolk Industrial Archaeology Society (NIAS)

NIAS was founded in early 1970 at a training course to record a fish-curing house due for demolition in Great Yarmouth. It was organised by Susanna soon after we had married and she had moved to Norfolk (Martins, S., 1971), and it followed from her recording of industrial archaeology in Oxfordshire. NIAS quickly developed as a very effective organisation to record industrial sites both on a thematic basis and in advance of demolition or alteration. Monthly meetings were organised in the Bridewell Museum with lectures on various industries or with training sessions to provide tuition in recording techniques. For much of the next 40 years Mary and Derek Manning proved to be great advocates for NIAS and contributed so much to its success (obituary to Mary in NIAS Newsletter September 2015). Survey results were all stored at the Bridewell Museum, where a card index of recorded sites was maintained, with a duplicate set in the Local Studies Library in Norwich until the 1994 Central Library fire. Their full survey records were microfiched with copies retained by English Heritage and at the Sites and Monuments record (SMR) at Gressenhall. Their more important surveys were also published in their *Annual Journal*, although publication of the *Journal* was a heavy cost for the society which had a membership of only about 60. They also worked closely with conservation officers in planning departments and with the SMR at Gressenhall.

NIAS assisted with the Norfolk Windmills Trust at Gunton Park Sawmill to restore the water wheels and the machinery, maintaining the mill in working order and providing stewards and guides on open days. In 1994 they wrote a manual on the operation of the mill. The Society was also the instigator in saving the Fakenham gasworks and setting up the gasworks museum there and again providing stewards on open days. Members were a great help at Gressenhall Rural Life Museum, collecting machinery for the museum and restoring machinery to full working order. The Society was also active in saving New Mills pumping station in Norwich.

Three typical years

In 1993 examples of NIAS activities included recording wartime coastal defences, Norfolk milestones, bridges being repaired in advance of improvements to meet increased weight limits and mineral spas and springs. In 1994 their recording included Smith's Mill at Dickleburgh, Costain's concrete works at Lenwade, Tidmans Ironworks and the Boulton and Paul factory in Norwich. In 1995 they were working again on the Lenwade concrete works, the maltings in Dereham, machinery at Stow Bardolph Hall and the Allen and Page site at Quayside in Norwich. The enthusiasm and achievements of NIAS over these years was impressive and exemplary.

The Norfolk Archaeological Rescue Group (NARG), 1975-1992, and the Norfolk Archaeological and Historical Research Group (NAHRG) 1992 to present

NARG was formed at an inaugural meeting attended by about 80 people at Gressenhall on 22nd February 1975. I invited them all to the meeting when it became clear that the old Norfolk Research Committee was not willing to support the formation of a more active amateur rescue group for the county. It would have been a better option to re-invigorate the NRC, but their committee was not so keen on that. So, at the meeting I outlined a role for NARG which would be to co-ordinate amateur interest in rescue archaeology in the county by:

- providing a local amateur digging force,
- encouraging people to record buildings,
- organising fieldwalking and other forms of fieldwork.

There was much enthusiasm for such a group, and a steering committee was formed to suggest a constitution, and a further meeting was arranged for 10th May (*EDP* 13th February and 24th February 1975).

It seemed better to make NARG entirely self-sufficient rather than have it run by the Norfolk Archaeological Unit, and that worked well from the start under the Chairmanship of George Fenner and the Secretary Norma Virgoe. The Unit and the Group were two parts of a team, and to underline that point we produced a joint leaflet both to promote the Unit and to encourage people to join NARG. The leaflet explained that the Group was:

> .. founded in 1975 specifically to encourage the amateur to participate in fieldwork and rescue archaeology. It publishes a newsletter, which keeps members in touch with surveys and excavation projects. The Group also organises lectures and meetings to hear about the results of recent research and provides members with an opportunity to report on what they have found. Membership is open to <u>all</u>, and it is <u>not</u> limited to those with previous archaeological experience.

Amateur excavations

In the past, excavations had been run largely with volunteers, as at Grenstein and North Elmham Park and as we were doing at Spong Hill with professional supervisors, but that could only work for short summer seasons. It was actually quite difficult for volunteers to participate fully as digging gradually became more professional and full time. Amateurs could still play a major part, as we saw at the Morningthope Anglo-Saxon cemetery which turned up in a gravel pit in October 1974. The joint NAU/NARG leaflet featured a picture of volunteers digging these graves, and there was a similar scene on the cover of the first Morningthorpe East Anglian Archaeology volume, which came out in 1987. This featured John Pope, the farm manager at Brampton Roman town, excavating an amazing large Anglo-Saxon iron-bound wooden tub in a grave (Green, Rogerson and White 1987). Similarly, the sixteenth-century pottery kiln dumps at Fulmodeston were recovered without any paid labour over a few weekends in 1974. Hundreds of these kiln wasters today form by far the largest reference collection of its kind in the county (Wade-Martins 1983 and **p. 226-228**). But, drawing them all for publication proved to be a major piece of work for the Unit's professional illustrator, Sue White. We all recognised that as excavation and recording requirements for publication became more sophisticated and more demanding, so the dilemma of under-resourced volunteer-run excavations grew. Volunteers could continue to participate in various ways, and we later saw them playing a significant role on our excavations on the Norwich Southern Bypass in 1989 and 1990 (Ashwin and Bates 2000) and on the Castle Mall project in Norwich from 1987 to 1990 where they manned the visitor centre and provided guides for school parties and did the pot washing (Shepherd Popescu 2009).

When a small amateur group worked to a carefully structured project design there were some quite notable achievements which concluded with well-presented reports. Shining examples were the Hales/Loddon survey, covering fieldwalking between 1980 and 1986 and documentary research (Davison 1990 and **p. 84-86**). The group was also heavily involved in two studies of deserted villages in Norfolk (Cushion *et. al.* 1982; Davison 1988) which again combined fieldwork and documentary research.

The recording of buildings by NARG members did not take off so well, largely because there was then nobody in the group able to take a lead. However, the NARG survey of chapels and meeting houses was a great success. A group of 37 volunteer recorders led by Norma Virgoe and Janet Ede carried out a comprehensive survey of over 600 chapels between 1988 and 1993, and this was followed by *Halls of Zion* published by the UEA Centre of East Anglian Studies in 1994 (Ede, Virgoe and Williamson 1994). It was a model example of a thematic approach to volunteer survey.

One can add to this the first class work by Silvia Addington to produce a landscape study using hedgerow surveys, fieldwalking and documentary work (Addington 1982 and **p. 86-88**). And also, of course, there were the surveys of moated sites by Bert and Barbara Dollin in north-east Norfolk (Dollin 1986). And then we had Graham Pooley who worked as a photographer in the Gressenhall darkroom every Monday, unpaid, for 16 years!

NARG provided an important meeting ground for amateur field archaeologists in the county aided by its magazine *NARG NEWS*. As an organisation it was also able to discourage most amateur excavations, except for those which were carefully thought-out with limited project designs and achievable outcomes. One of the better examples of this, organised by its successor body NAHRG, was the excavation of the chancel of Oxwick church between 1998 and 2000 where up to five or six NAHRG members and local people worked for three to five weeks each year to examine the evidence for the demolished east end of the church following an informative resistivity survey (Sims 2010).

There will always be a need for an active amateur field group. This role is likely to remain quite separate from that of the long-established county archaeological society, which focuses primarily on the publication of a journal, winter lectures and summer excursions. There is certainly room for both.

The Norfolk Research Committee ran from 1934 to 1990 and NARG from 1975 until 1991 when the two were joined together. The first meeting of the new successor body, NAHRG, was held on 4th July 1990 following a final meeting of the NARG/NRC Joint Steering Committee. The aim of the new NAHRG was to continue the best traditions of the old group and it has produced two regular publications, the *Annual* and the *Quarterly*, and is currently enjoying an upsurge in activity under its very efficient Secretary, Tony Bradstreet.

The tragedy is that the minute books and records of NARG, other than their publications, have disappeared. The secretary of NARG has since died and the whereabouts of the papers is unknown. It is bad enough that the minute books and papers of the Norfolk Research Committee from 1934 to 1990 have been lost and even the archive of Norfolk Archaeological Unit has been shredded **(p. 146)**, but to lose all of the NARG papers as well is distressing. These papers were a record of a very formative stage of research into the county's cultural heritage and they should have been safely stored. Once again, we are reminded about the need to deposit all important documents in the county Record Office.

The Federation of Norfolk Historical and Archaeological Organisations

The Federation was formed in 1987 with the aim of providing a link between the many organisations in Norfolk concerned with history, archaeology, genealogy, heraldry and conservation in the county. It currently has an impressive membership of 31 organisations ranging from village societies like the Garboldisham History Society to the Norfolk and Norwich Archaeological Society, all working in their own areas of interest. The Federation's role to start with was running the Norfolk History Fair, but that ceased some years ago. It does offer small research grants, but its main activity is the production of the Federation's Diary which is a most useful six-monthly list of events and meetings of its constituent members. This is produced in conjunction with Poppyland Publishing, and details of the Federation's constituent bodies can all be found on the Poppyland website at www.poppyland.co.uk/federation.

Norfolk Historic Buildings Group

The Historic Buildings Group was founded in 2000, so it is really outside the timespan of this part of the book. But it has been so successful that it needs to be mentioned, if only to say that it organises thematic surveys of the buildings of places like New Buckenham and Little Walsingham and of building types, such as rural schools. The schools project was organised by Susanna and Adam Longcroft of the University of East Anglia in conjunction with the Norfolk Record Office and the University of East Anglia (Longcroft and Wade Martins, S., 2013). Details are on the group's website www.nhbg.org.uk.

Chapter 8:
Amateurs in Action

Amateur archaeology has contributed so much to our understanding of the past, and this great tradition will surely continue. There will always be a role for the amateur fieldworker however sophisticated professional techniques do become. Having looked at the contribution made by societies, it is now worth focusing on the achievements of a small selection of individuals, and it is such a pity there is only space for a few.

Amateur effort has mainly focused on helping on excavations, with fieldwalking, earthwork surveying, building recording, documentary research, finds' processing and metal detecting. In recent years most, but not all, have wisely avoided running their own excavations because of the resources required to produce an acceptable report. There have been some notable achievements when the two sides have worked closely together, often with professionals assisting with publication. What follows are some stories usually with happy, but in one case with unhappy, outcomes.

John Owles: the fieldwalker/ farmer

John Owles (1914-1996) farmed *c.* 230 hectares of mainly arable land at Park Farm, Witton, in north-east Norfolk covering about a quarter of the parish. John found his first flint blade on the surface after ploughing in 1960, and from that moment he developed a passion for collecting material off his fields. He was not selective, so after nearly 20 years he had accumulated an unbiased picture of the archaeology of the farm from the Mesolithic to post-medieval. When fields were ploughed a little deeper than usual for root crops he would walk the plough furrows collecting pottery and flints. When he thought he had found something of particular interest he marked the spot with a pile of oyster shells, which he kept for feeding his chickens, and went back after harvest to dig the feature his finds had come from. His method was not the structured fieldwalking as we know it today, and he was simply taking opportunities as they arose. He had no training in archaeology, and, as he was entirely self-taught, his digging and recording was not up to modern standards. But nevertheless over the years he collected a lot of material, much of which would otherwise have been destroyed in subsequent cultivations and sub-soiling (*Figure 8.1*). John had kept all the finds safe in his house, and so in 1978 Andrew Lawson, then employed as the prehistorian in the recently-formed Norfolk Archaeological Unit, was able to draw up catalogues and maps showing the locations of all John's discoveries which were published as a volume of East Anglian Archaeology (Lawson 1983). In this report Andrew wrote 'The result of John Owles's collection is a staggering range of artefacts ranging from Mesolithic microliths to post-medieval porcelain' (Lawson 1983, 1). As far as we knew, this was the first time an archaeological survey had been carried out by a farmer. Outside John's farm there were almost no recorded finds, yet his own collection contained 1,695 flint flakes and flint tools and 4,948 sherds of pottery of all periods (*EDP* 11th August 1983).

We hoped that our publication in 1983 would do justice to John Owles's perseverance. I remember so well after the volume was published that I had such a nice letter from John thanking the Norfolk Archaeological Unit profusely for bringing his work to publication, and he concluded by saying 'You have done me proud.' It also demonstrated just how much archaeology was being lost on the surrounding farms at the same time by deeper cultivation which was under way from the 1950s. John has since passed away, but most of the finds remain with his family (obituary *EDP* 15th May 1996).

8.1. John Owles at home in 1983 with his substantial collection of finds which he had collected on his farm (CCA2).

John Turner: the lone excavator

A nearby farmer, John Turner, who was also interested in archaeology, took a different approach and completely excavated an unscheduled round barrow on Witton Heath by himself in his spare time over two years in 1954/5. He produced an interpretative report which he deposited in the Castle Museum in 1955 to explain a complex stratigraphic sequence he had found consisting of a primary burial, subsequent mound enlargements and secondary burials producing seven Bronze Age urns. Nowadays we would have strongly discouraged John from excavating a well-preserved barrow, but at the time everybody was doing it. About 1970 John retired from farming and moved to Cringleford and then enjoyed helping on other people's excavations, especially at our Anglo-Saxon cemetery on Spong Hill (Knowles 1983). Luckily, Andrew Lawson was able to discuss John's Witton Heath manuscript report with him before he died, and Andrew's report on the barrow was then included in the Witton volume. John's report was accessioned into the museum collections (NCM 955.124), but it now cannot be found.

If we hadn't stepped in to create a record for publication of the work of both Johns much of their data would ultimately have been lost. One has to say that there is always a risk of taking a project too far without the skill, time and resources to bring it to a satisfactory conclusion. But, this can apply to both professional and amateurs alike.

Brian Cushion who discovered a Roman road and surveyed the majority of the county's earthworks

While working for the Ordnance Survey in 1973 Brian Cushion spotted on a series of Ordnance Survey vertical air photographs a remarkable alignment of roads, hedgerows and soilmarks running over a distance of eight miles from Billingford, through North Elmham, Brisley, Horningtoft to Toftrees. At Billingford the alignment joined a straight road from the east which was already recognised as Roman (Margary 1967, 272) and at Toftrees it joined another Roman road running north to Holkham (Margary 1967, 273). Brian's new section was not quite straight all the way, but the evidence he had noticed was so convincing that it was beyond argument (*Figure 8.2*). This new Roman road joined the two well-known roads together, and Brian and I worked on his discovery which we published in EAA (Wade-Martins 1977b).

8.2. A part of the line of the Billingford to Toftrees Roman road showing as soil marks through Horningtoft parish (Crown Copyright 2017 OS licence number 100058448).

The one place where the road survived as an upstanding bank (or *agger* as Roman road enthusiasts like to call it) was across Brisley Common. So, in November 1976 members of the newly-formed Norfolk Archaeological Rescue Group dug two trenches across the bank revealing a dense concentration of flints in the topsoil. It became clear, though, that the common had been deep ploughed once, probably during the Second World War, thus destroying much of the road surface. But, while the ploughing had turned the gravel over in the furrows, at the bottom between the plough grooves there were still just enough clean made-up sandy gravel to show there had been a continuous road surface (Wade-Martins 1978).

The gratifying end of the story was that the words 'Roman road' afterwards appeared on the next edition of the Ordnance Survey map (Ordnance Survey Explorer map 238 1:25,000 scale).

After Brian took early retirement from the Ordnance Survey, the Norfolk Archaeological Unit engaged him as a part-time consultant to record all the known earthwork monuments in old grassland in the county over a six-year period from 1994, and he jointly assembled with Alan Davison a fine EAA volume *Earthworks of Norfolk* (Cushion and Davison 2003; **p. 203-206**).

Alan Davison who combined the skills of a highly effective fieldwalker and documentary researcher

Few amateur archaeologists in recent decades have achieved more than Alan Davison (1930-2006) did before he was tragically killed in a car accident in 2006. From the time he retired from teaching geography in 1985 he devoted his considerable energies and ability to the understanding of the Norfolk landscape (Barringer 2006; Rogerson 2007). He was a skilled fieldwalker; he was equally good as a documentary historian, and he wrote so well that his texts seldom needed much editing (*Figure 8.3*). He was not so good at identifying pottery but when he was unsure he turned to Andrew Rogerson at Gressenhall to check his conclusions. They

8.3. *The only known photograph of Alan Davison fieldwalking.*

made a good team. I was able to suggest a number of projects which Alan took up enthusiastically, producing an extra-ordinary flow of articles from 1980 onwards in *Norfolk Archaeology,* East Anglian Archaeology and the Annual Reports of the Deserted Village Research Group (subsequently the Deserted Medieval Settlements Research Group). From 1990 to 2006 he jointly edited *Norfolk Archaeology,* mainly with Trevor Ashwin, and he also co-operated with Trevor in the editing of the acclaimed third edition of *An Historical Atlas of Norfolk* (Ashwin and Davison 2005), with far fewer spelling mistakes than I let through when editing the first two.

One particular fieldwalking project stands out amongst Alan's achievements: the complete survey of Heckingham, Hales and Loddon with the help of a small band of supporters. Documentary research was by Alayne Fenner and it was published in 1990 as East Anglian Archaeology 49 (Davison 1990). The report concluded with a very useful summary of the evidence for all periods with suggestions for further research. This paper has been described by Andrew Rogerson as:

> *A work of great importance, this volume has achieved the status of a text book in East Anglian studies. Its great significance lies in its interpretation of settlement shift in the Early and Middle Saxon periods against the backgrounds of soil and climate (Rogerson 2007).*

Hales still has a large unenclosed green, and it is of particular interest that Alan demonstrated that settlement around the green had started by the first half of the twelfth century at the latest. Research like this, encompassing fieldwalking, documents and where possible the buildings are just the sort of projects that future amateur researchers and groups could well aspire to.

One of Alan's last projects was the joint volume with Brian Cushion published in 2003 on *Earthworks of Norfolk.* Brian heroically surveyed all the 141 significant earthwork sites he could discover by searching old grassland on air photographs, ranging from Roman to post-medieval settlements, manorial complexes, monasteries, fishponds, oyster-fattening beds, water meadows, ridge and furrow and parks and gardens. Barrows were excluded because they had already been covered in a regional survey by Andrew Lawson and others in East Anglian Archaeology 12 in 1981. Brian surveyed the sites just with tapes, ranging poles and a compass, without the satellite positioning equipment which is so easily available now. Alan wrote up the documentary background, and this provided an invaluable contribution to our understanding of each site. All land agents, conservation advisers and project officers in government conservation agencies would be hard pressed now to fulfil their roles properly without access to a copy. It provides key information about *why* earthworks and landscape features are important and *why* they need protection (eg Castle Acre Priory: *Figure 25.9*). Alan also completed by himself a very useful parish survey of West Acre with the archaeological and documentary research presented in two separate reports in *Norfolk Archaeology* in 2003 and 2004.

For the layman, Alan's *Deserted Villages of Norfolk* (1996) in Poppyland's Norfolk Origins series is a superb review of the evidence for the most significant deserted village sites in the county. And overall, his detailed, but always readable, writings on the Norfolk landscape have left a remarkable legacy. A tribute to Alan by Andrew Rogerson can be found in his introduction to Alan's final papers on Godwick and Beeston (Rogerson 2007). A list of most of his publications is included as **Appendix 1**. His exceptionally careful fieldwalking, his meticulous documentary research and his unending flow of published papers represents for me the pinnacle of amateur achievement. Nobody could have made better use of their early retirement.

Silvia Addington who counted hedgerows, fieldwalked and researched the documents

Silvia Addington and her husband David were farmers who lived at the Old Hall at Tasburgh close to the possible Iron Age fort (**p. 323**). He kept pigs and enjoyed his flock of ornamental ducks on the large pond near the farmhouse. She was deeply fascinated by the Norfolk landscape and was concerned that the hedgerows were disappearing all around her on other farms (*Figure 8.4*). She fieldwalked; she was

8.4. Silvia Addington recording hedgerows in Tasburgh in 1983 (Courtesy Eastern Daily Press).

an accomplished potter and she enjoyed photographing woodwork in medieval churches. Sadly, she died of cancer in 1987 when she was still in her prime, and she and David are buried together in Tasburgh churchyard. We were great friends, and I much admired her enthusiasm for the countryside.

Silvia wrote two important papers for *Norfolk Archaeology*. The first was on the 'Hedgerows of Tasburgh' (1978), and the second 'Landscape and Settlements in South Norfolk (1982), which took a broader view of landscape change in the same area. Her hedgerow work was a rescue effort, but she applied scholarship to the results. As she said in the summary to her first paper: 'Since the 1906 25-inch Ordnance Survey map of Tasburgh was made roughly one third of the hedges in the parish have gone, and they are still going.' Thankfully, since her death new planning regulations and the prospect of farms losing some subsidies as a result of landscape damage have brought that destruction to an end.

Following the work of Hoskins and Hooper (Hoskins 1967, 118-130) and Pollard and Hooper (1974), Silvia set about recording the species in all the hedgerows in Tasburgh parish. But she soon realised that the identification of the hedgerow species and the ground-covering plants under them, could tell us much more about landscape change than just a possible date of each hedge. While acknowledging that there was a generalised link between species' numbers and hedgerow date, she was very careful to treat this theory with some caution. Indeed, in a separate statistical paper in *Norfolk Archaeology* for 1982 Wendy Johnson had demonstrated that there were dangers in trying to tie species' numbers to the age of hedgerows too closely (Johnson 1982). This has since been confirmed more recently in a general study of Norfolk hedgerows by Gerry Barnes and Tom Williamson in the book *Hedgerow History* (2006, 83).

In 1975 and 1976 Silvia counted the species of every hedgerow in Tasburgh in units of 30 yards and compared the results with the Enclosure and Tithe maps. In the following spring each hedge was revisited to record the ground-covering plants, such as dog's mercury and primroses as indicators of early woodland. Dog's mercury was almost entirely confined to the heavier soils where fields had been carved out of old woodland. Her maps showed hedgerows (a) with an average of over seven species, which were the oldest, (b) with an average of four to seven species, which were mainly Tudor and (c) those with under four and others known to have been planted since the 1818 Enclosures. Hedgerows with high counts seemed to contain species which were seldom found in other hedgerows, particularly dogwood, hornbeam, holly, spindle and spurge-laurel.

Silvia concluded that species' numbers, the composition of hedgerows and the identity of ground-covering plants were all factors which needed to be considered together when assessing the age of a hedge. The creation of a local chronology based on the three characteristics was necessary for the study of any given area.

In the 1982 paper Silvia took a larger block of South Norfolk parishes to understand the former woodland, the fields and the settlements. It was a major piece of work, too detailed to summarise here. She confirmed that there was evidence for Middle Saxon and Late Saxon settlements near some churches and there was no substantial move onto common edges before the twelfth and thirteenth centuries. High hedge counts were concentrated on clay in the edges of parishes where former woodland, with reservoirs of woodland seeds, were the last to be brought into cultivation. These were more datable by species' types than by species' numbers.

This was the first time in Norfolk that all the techniques of fieldwalking, hedgerow and undergrowth recording, field names and documentary research had been brought together, and it was presented in a masterly piece of work. This is surely the best way to understand any piece of countryside (*EDP* 21st June 1983).

The Brampton excavators ('Excavatores Brantunae')

Twenty-four years of excavation

The Roman small town at Brampton was the largest Roman settlement in Norfolk after Caistor St Edmund, but unlike Caistor, which was called *Venta Icenorum*, we do not know its original name. It had its own defences and a major pottery-producing industry (*Figure 8.5*). From 1965 until 1989 Dr Keith Knowles and his wife Vivienne excavated almost every Sunday with the help of six or seven volunteers calling themselves the 'Excavatores Brantunae' (*Figure 8.6*). They also excavated a Roman cemetery at Bawburgh in 1971 (Gurney 1998). Keith was a busy GP and a doctor for students at the University of East Anglia. During the late 1960s and early 1970s he gave a number of entertaining talks about the group's work at meetings of the Norfolk Research Committee, and typescript annual reports were produced each year. Copies of just four of these for 1968, 1969, 1970 (described as the fourth report) and 1971 are held in the Historic Environment Record at Gressenhall, but that is not the full set. A set of these reports previously held in Norwich Castle Museum cannot now be found (Green 1977, endnote 5). Keith also wrote an interim summary of the group's work covering the years 1965 to 1975 published in *Britannia* (Knowles 1977), but nothing further was published for the years 1976 to 1989, except for very brief notes in *Britannia* for most years from 1970 to 1987). Two small-scale Brampton building plans were published in a paper by Barry Burnham on buildings in Roman small towns (Burnham 1995). There is a useful summary of the site by David Gurney in a volume on Roman small towns (Gurney 1995, 56-57), and the pottery industry was summarised by Vivien Swan in her *The Pottery Kilns of Roman Britain* (1984, 121-122). In the *Britannia* article Keith wrote 'No final report can be published until more large-scale excavations have been carried out', but he did not justify that view.

8.5. Aerial photograph of Brampton Roman town showing cropmarks of the town defences in 1976 (TG2223/ACX/AFF11).

Over their first 11 years the group excavated 2,300 square metres (Edwards 1977, 232), and went on to do a lot more. They sectioned the defensive ditch twice and excavated a timber wharf beside the old course of the River Bure, exposed various timber buildings, a number of timber-lined wells, a bathhouse and 13 out of a total of 141 pottery kilns which Keith and the farm manager, John Pope, located from surface evidence in 1968 (Green 1977, 94). The kilns were making buff wares, including *mortaria* with the potter's stamp AESUMINUS on the rim and a lot of burnished grey wares. The *Britannia* article contained only the briefest summary of all this early work. John Pope also did a lot of metal detecting by himself over

8.6. Members of 'Excavatores Brantunae' standing in an excavated Roman well. Keith Knowles is at the back on the left and John Pope, the farm manager, is at the front on the right. John was an enthusiastic amateur who also helped on many NAU excavations in the 1970s.

many years, but most of the finds were not recorded by an archaeologist. The final years were spent excavating deeply stratified deposits in an area they called 'the cottage garden', a garden of a former cottage within the defences close to the railway line.

Air photography, site scheduling and grant applications

During the latter stages of the excavations the Norfolk Archaeological Unit carried out regular aerial surveys of the site recording the crop-marks from 1974 onwards, and the results were published in East Anglian Archaeology (Edwards 1977, 230-232). These revealed the earthwork defences enclosing a hexagonal area of 6 hectares beside the old course of the River Bure and more extensive crop-marks of industrial suburbs to west and to south (*Figure 8.5*). There are a number of breaks in the defences where Roman roads radiated from the town in different directions. The whole complex covered 30 hectares, and most of it was ploughed. To assess plough damage the Norfolk Archaeological Unit excavated one pottery kiln and an area of timber buildings in the industrial area to the south-west of the town in 1973-74 (Green 1977) to assist the case we made for scheduling, and the whole town was then scheduled in September 1983 (list entry no. 1003698). It was remarkable at the time that the whole place was so easily scheduled based on the crop-mark and excavation evidence while extensive areas of the Roman town at Caistor St Edmund even now have no formal protection. Brampton was put on the English Heritage *Heritage at Risk* Register and remains on that list. This is presumably because it is still under plough.

When it was becoming clear that the Brampton excavators were showing no sign of producing a site archive or publishable reports, the NAU did raise a small grant of £750 from the British Academy to start the study of the Brampton pottery industry. Under Tony Gregory a type series of 272 sherds was extracted to create a range of vessel types ranging from the early contexts to the later kilns covering most, if not all, of the production period of the Brampton pottery industry. A second grant application in 1979 by the NAU to the British Academy for £5,430 to take the work a stage further by assembling a site archive, studying the pottery and re-boxing all the material excavated up to that point was not successful, presumably because there was no clear strategy for concluding the project as excavation continued.

The scheduling of the whole town in 1983 did not stop the excavations, as I had hoped it would, and the group was allowed by the Department of the Environment on the advice of the Historic Buildings and Monuments Commission (later called English Heritage) to continue excavating 'the cottage garden' up until Keith's retirement in 1989. But this was on the condition that he would produce a summary report within six months of the completion of the excavation and a full report by 1994. He did neither and it is believed that the Ancient Monuments inspectors did not inspect the excavation, did not check the site records and did not require compliance with their conditions.

Report to the Scole Committee

The group continued digging without there being any indication that they were thinking about how to produce an excavation archive or a final report for publication. This was causing increasing concern, and on 12th June 1985 the Scole Committee, the regional committee for archaeology in East Anglia **(p. 144-145)**, decided to ask Keith Knowles if he would be willing to consider letting the committee arrange for a professional archaeologist to go through the finds and excavation records to assess the size of their backlog problem. The minutes of the committee held in the Norfolk Record Office (ACC 2008/77 and 2011/16) and files at Gressenhall record what then happened. In March an impressive and detailed report by David Gurney, then a Project Officer with the Norfolk Archaeological Unit, on the feasibility of publishing the excavations was prepared, and this was considered by the committee on 16th April 1986. The thrust of the report was that the excavation could still lead to a worthwhile publication, but finance would have to be raised. Everything depended on Keith's willingness and ability to manage the work and raise the considerable sums needed to buy in specialists' time. The time was quantified and costed in detail in the report. The estimate at 1986 prices was £5,303 for the site report, £17,440 for the excavated finds and £6,450 for the surface finds. This would involve employing a research officer to edit and assemble the report, an illustrator to draw the maps, plans, sections and the many finds, a photographer and eight specialists to write up the finds. This would be a major piece of research and Keith insisted on retaining overall control. A long list of bodies which might be willing to fund the report was also assembled for him so that he could submit grant applications.

In the background was the realisation that the quality of site recording was well below the standards of the time. A lack of section drawings made the stratigraphic sequence difficult to reconstruct, the recording in the site notebooks was superficial (*Figure 8.8*), there was a lack of soil and environmental samples, and the recovery of animal bones had been too selective for them to be of much value. The finds were mostly stored in old boxes, some of which were collapsing in Keith's garden sheds as a result of water penetration, and the finds from different sites were becoming mixed. The iron objects had not been conserved and were suffering from significant decay. Considerable effort had already been put into cataloguing the 2,000+ Roman coins, but the standard reference works had not been used, so the results were totally inadequate.

Since the 1970s the farm manager, John Pope had been metal detecting the town, but that was stopped with the 1983 scheduling. However, in 1988 David Gurney obtained a licence from English Heritage to allow John to resume detecting, provided that a detailed record was made of the survey and a report was submitted to English Heritage. That was done and the report approved by English Heritage in 1990.

Keith was due to retire in 1989, and he would then have the opportunity to work full time managing this complex project supported by a team of professionals. The Committee congratulated David on his excellent report and decided to approach Keith to offer further help and advice. To this end, a small sub-committee consisting of the Chairman (George Fenner – a keen amateur himself), Tony Gregory and David Gurney was appointed. The aim was to advise Keith on how to prepare the academic case to support grant applications which he would need to organise. A letter was sent and a reply was awaited.

Five months later David Gurney reported back to the Scole Committee that he had not heard from Keith about his reaction to the proposal, so the Committee urged the sub-committee to meet Keith and come back at the next meeting. In December 1986 George Fenner reported that they had met Keith and they were optimistic about him raising the funds, and could see no reason why David Gurney's proposals should not be carried out in full. Keith had one more season of excavation in the 'cottage garden' as permitted under the terms of the Scheduled Monument Consent, and although there was a feeling that he should be discouraged from any more digging, the committee was anxious not to upset him, so they took the matter no further. There was to be another meeting with Keith in 12 months time. A year later, in December 1987, that meeting had not yet taken place, so George Fenner promised to organise one.

In April 1988 David reported that some finds from the bathhouse excavation and the 'cottage garden' had just been handed over to the Museums Service and moved to a store, but without any accompanying records; they were being re-boxed by museum staff into 68 new boxes and retained in that store. There had been no progress so far in applying for post-excavation grants. If Keith was to bag and re-box the material in the garden sheds at Bawburgh Lane in boxes to be supplied by the Museum Service, all this material could be moved to a museum store as well.

On 13th July 1988 there was a site meeting in the 'cottage garden' between myself, the Ancient Monuments Inspector, David Gurney and Keith at which Keith was not persuaded to stop digging a year early and to start the preparation of the site archive. On 12th December 1989 David submitted another report saying that the final season of excavation had been completed, and the 'cottage garden' was being backfilled. But Keith would not have time to discuss, or start to prepare a report for publication before May 1990. So, another meeting would be convened with him in May 1990.

By August 1991 David reported that a number of meetings had in the meantime been held with Keith 'with the intention of' sorting out and compiling an archive site by site. With only a little more work an archive on some eight small sites would be ready for post-excavation purposes. The hope was that the process would then continue on all the other sites, and it was envisaged that this archiving would be complete by early 1993. Meanwhile David's priority was to collect and photocopy all the records to which Keith gave him access with funding from the Scole Committee – a wise move in the circumstances. In fact, Keith and his team took archiving no further at all. The Scole Committee gave up after that because their efforts and David's efforts were making little difference. In June 1996 David did write to Keith once more saying that priority should be to the preservation of the finds and asked three questions:

1. How much more is there?
2. When would it be available?
3. How would he feel about depositing the (paper) archive with the Museum Service at the same time?

The answers on a brief card came back as follows:
(1) heaps,
(2) can't answer that one really
(3) to be discussed ....

He said that there seemed 'an awful lot to do and not enough time'. The indications were that he had done nothing.

For many archaeologists who were working in the region at the time and who were aware of the situation it was deeply distressing and frustrating, but little more could be done without funding and without Keith's blessing. So much information was still only in Keith's memory, and his active involvement in completing the archive was essential before the writing of a final report could even begin. It must be said, though, that conversations with him at the time suggested that there was real doubt about how much detailed information he could still recall.

This whole sequence has been described in detail to show that everything which could have been done was done to avoid the catastrophe which then followed. There was an interesting division on the Scole Committee between the professionals who could see what was coming and the non-professionals who still believed blissfully that the 'Excavatores Brantunae' with minimal resources and extremely limited skills, would somehow pull off a miracle.

The final outcome

What then happened should be seen as a lesson to all those who might think of embarking on an excavation without the time, inclination, skills or resources to see the project through to a full and final research report. The archive, consisting of the paper records, the photographs and the finds remained stored at the Knowles' Bawburgh Lane home on the outskirts of Norwich, except for a few choice items on loan for displays at Norwich Castle Museum and Lowestoft and Cromer museums. The records were kept in the house, but most of the finds were stacked in hundreds of collapsing cardboard boxes in the loft and in garden sheds which were by then leaking badly and actually falling over. Vivienne died in December 2002 after Keith nursed her for several years, and then after her death he showed no further interest in Brampton and was moved into a care home himself before he died in February 2010.

Before Keith died the family decided to clear the house to realise its capital value to pay for the cost of his care. One of their sons, Peter, recalls that Keith and Vivienne had often said to them with bitterness that the Castle Museum would not take the excavation archive because it was too big and the museum had no room; they said repeatedly that 'no-one was interested'. The documents quoted above show that was not the case, although today there are no members of staff in the museum who were there when those conversations might have taken place, presumably in the 1980s. But it is much more likely that the museum archaeologists were pressing for an archive to be prepared and the finds properly boxed and labelled and integrated with the archive before accepting the whole collection. That was normal practice by then.

Keith made no arrangements for the excavation archive in his will, although we believe it was his hope that the paper record and finds would go to the museum one day. The family tell me that because they remembered that their parents had said that the museum would not take the material, everything was sold to Paul Murawski, a Norwich antiquities dealer and author of *Benet's Artefacts of England and the United Kingdom: Current Values* (2003). Certainly, those members of staff currently in the museum are sure they knew nothing of the sale and were not consulted. Paul Murawski was given the opportunity the search the entire property, including the attic, and he took away all he could find. Mr Murawski then offered the Brampton finds (*Figure 8.7*) and paper archive to the Castle Museum for £10,000. A price of £8,000 was agreed and the museum then raised the money through grants for the purchase (accession number 2007.417), and the collection is now re-boxed. In August 2007 a number of Roman coins were brought into the Castle Museum having been found in a skip at a landfill site just outside Norwich. From other material in the skip the coins were subsequently traced back to Keith Knowles and to the Brampton excavations. They were also acquired and added to the site archive.

The original paper record as it survives contains brief reports of the 1980 to 1982 excavations, photos of various kiln and well excavations, typed notes of various trenches, three notepads with very rough sketches which seem to be the closest the excavators ever came to making measured plans and sections (*Figure 8.8*), a report of a resistivity survey of a part of the defended area, and a typed coin catalogue of 1016 coins, but without their excavation contexts. There are no detailed records of contexts or layers, so it would have been impossible to relate finds to their contexts anyway. It is doubtful now that an adequate site archive or a site report of any value could ever have been written from these records. The pottery, metal finds and coins all lack meaningful recorded contexts, and most of the coins arrived in a single cloth pouch! So the numbering in the coin catalogue does not now relate to the coins. It is known that much of the pottery from the

8.7. The surviving finds from the Brampton excavations in 2015 soon after they reached museum stores, representing what must be a relatively small part of the original site archive.

sheds actually finished up scattered over the Bawburgh Lane garden. And it is certain that the finds now in the museum represent only a small fraction of the original collection. The rest have been lost, and so much of the work carried out by well-meaning enthusiastic weekend diggers over 24 years has been largely wasted. The Museums Service should be commended on recently saving what they could of the finds and the records, but it seems wrong that the Service should have had to pay anything to save this archive.

What can be done now?

Although Keith's excavations and John Pope's metal detecting have long since ceased at Brampton, there are many loose ends which still need to be tied up. Some of the original paper archive is in the Castle Museum, and a small number of other finds are on loan to possibly three other museums. There are David Gurney's photocopies of some of Keith's original records, there may be other photocopies

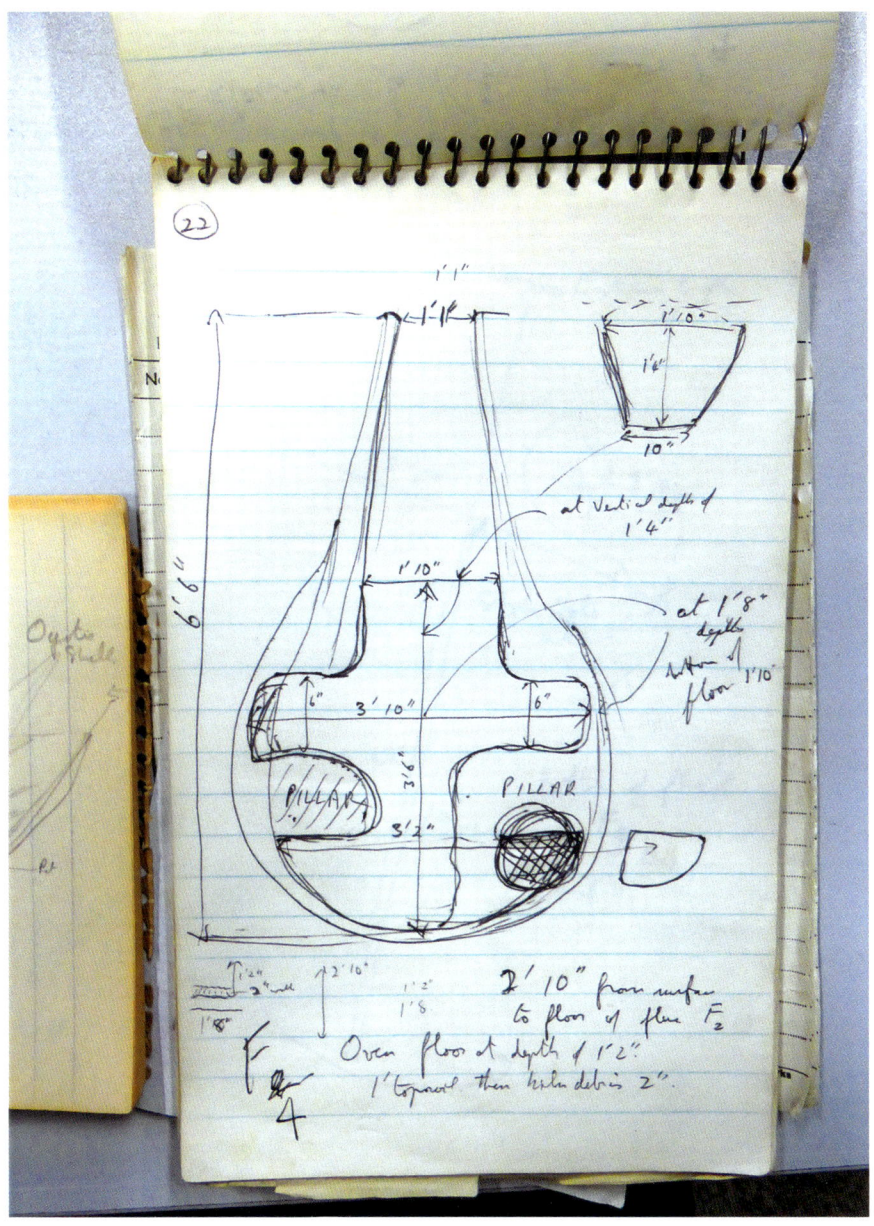

8.8. *A typical record plan by the 'Excavatores Brantunae' of one of the many excavated Roman pottery kilns at Brampton.*

of Keith's paper records and some photographs in private hands. The finds from John Pope's metal detecting are still at Brampton in the landowner's possession. With all this there is surely scope for someone to pull the information together for a post-graduate dissertation, but probably not for a PhD. The museum currently has an experienced volunteer re-organising the archive.

Could this happen again?

It could so easily happen again, particularly with excavations by enthusiastic amateur groups and community projects where there is no one person, or a clearly defined organisation, responsible for the quality of the excavation archive or for the final report. When the number of people who are having fun on a dig is used as the main measure of success, the quality of the archaeological record can be the casualty. It is very tempting to start an excavation, but responsibilities go with it. When grants are relatively easy to obtain from the Heritage Lottery Fund for community archaeology projects, where success seems to be largely measured by the level of public participation, there is a very real danger that without rigorous monitoring of the archives and their deposition and the proper publication of reports there will be more disasters similar to Brampton in the future. There has been little archaeological monitoring by the Heritage Lottery Fund of the projects they have funded so far.[1]

TV-sponsored excavations

The great achievement of Time Team was that it promoted archaeology to a wide public audience.

> *Love it or loathe, it is difficult to deny that television archaeology, and particularly Time Team, led to a general raising of public consciousness of archaeology; 20 years ago, it is doubtful that many people outside the archaeological community would have been even aware of the existence of geophysical survey; now, there are millions of people who know that before you dig, you have to do the 'geofizz' (Blinkhorn 2015, 268).*

The 2003 series had an average of 3.4 million viewers per programme (Blinkhorn 2015, 262). This was impressive, although surely very few viewers believed that you could run and fully record an excavation in just three days. In 1998/9 there were three excavations by the Team in Norfolk: a Dominican Friary in Thetford, the

---

[1] The writer is particularly grateful to David Gurney for providing access to the reports, notes and photocopies which he made while working with the Scole Committee and with Keith Knowles in an attempt to obtain a satisfactory outcome to a deteriorating situation.

crash site of a Second World War *Flying Fortress* at Reedham and a live transmission over the August Bank Holiday weekend of a multi-period settlement around the ruined church at Bawsey near King's Lynn. The post-Roman archaeology at Bawsey is particularly important, and was certainly due for some careful investigation. As usual, the excavation was carried out at great speed with some trenches being opened and finished in a single day, and the TV series as a whole gave the impression that this was an acceptable way to run an excavation.

The series producer did, however, conclude his description of this particular programme in *Time Team 99: The Site Reports* by saying:

> *It all added up to a lot of further work compiling records, updating maps, maintaining archives and studying the finds. Mick said that archaeologists have an unwritten rule: one day in the field equals ten days back in the office and laboratory. The scale of this weekend's operation meant that a lot of people would be kept busy for a long time to come (Taylor 1999).*

So, while Tim Taylor recognised in a subsequent publication that his excavation had created a lot more work, it was not clear to viewers exactly who would be taking this forward. Surely, it would have been better if there had been on site a reputable archaeological contracting team, highly visible, working alongside the TV personalities with full responsibility for recording and with a contract to produce a site archive and final report within an agreed period? There may have been one, but that was not obvious on screen. The impression that you could just swan in, dig for three days and disappear was at best misleading.

Thankfully, reports have after many years been produced on Thetford and Bawsey (Bellamy and Trevarthen 2011 and Pestell 2014) and it is the best possible news that the results of the 2012 excavations at the Brancaster Roman fort on the north coast (*Figure 13.7*) have already been submitted to *Norfolk Archaeology*. There, the Team used Ground Penetrating Radar as well as a magnetometer survey with astonishing results which Tim Taylor has thankfully already published in *British Archaeology* (Taylor 2013) and online (https://www.youtube.com/watch?v=hsGJv-NXmd8).

Chapter 9:
Metal Detecting: 'The Norfolk System'

The difference between excavating and metal detecting is that excavation is usually destructive, but detecting is mostly confined to the ploughsoil where objects are under threat from ploughing and chemical erosion. To rescue them from the plough is for the good, provided they are properly recorded.

Metal detecting is not like any other form of amateur archaeology. It involves people from the whole social spectrum who are all gripped with the same strong enthusiasm for finding things. They are usually very committed to their hobby; they have read avidly about their finds and have an understanding about their subject that is often impressive and surprising for professional archaeologists who meet the hobby for the first time. Most detectorists prefer to work on their own. The hobby is guided by a code of conduct issued by the Department of Culture, Media and Sport (DCMS) which has oversight of the implementation of the 1996 Treasure Act, and full details are on the DCMS website.

The 1996 Treasure Act

Before the 1996 Treasure Act the rules were simple: Treasure Trove just covered gold and silver. When it was hidden in the ground with the intention of recovery, and the owner was unknown, it was declared Treasure Trove at an inquest and belonged to the Crown. But when it was buried with no intention of recovery, as in a grave for instance, it remained with the owner of the land. The classic example of this was the Sutton Hoo Anglo-Saxon ship burial where the grave-goods were declared not to be Treasure Trove and remained the property of the owner, Mrs Pretty, who generously gave them all to the British Museum (Evans 1986, 96).

Under the 1996 Act the following finds are now Treasure:
1. Any metallic object, other than a coin, provided that at least 10% by weight of metal is precious metal (gold or silver) and that it is at least 300 years old when found. If the object is of prehistoric date it will be Treasure provided any part of it is precious metal.
2. Any group of two or more metallic objects of any composition of prehistoric date that come from the same find.
3. Two or more coins from the same find provided they are at least 300 years old when found and contain 10 per cent gold or silver. If the coins contain less than 10% of gold or silver there must be at least ten of them.
4. Any object, whatever it is made of, that is found in the same place as, or had previously been together with, another object that is Treasure.

5. Any object that would previously have been Treasure Trove but does not fall within the precific categories given above.
(Extract from Lewis, M. (ed), 2013. *The Portable Antiquities Scheme Annual Report 2013*)

The discovery of Treasure has to be reported to the District Coroner or a Finds Liaison Officer within 14 days.

Detectorists and landowners are advised always to come to an understanding about the ownership of finds *before* detecting begins. Many detectorists sell their finds, quite legally, once they have been recorded unless the coroner decides they are Treasure. Other detectorists believe that it is better to give them to a museum if that will add significantly to the museum's collections. Some will sell them without reporting their finds and then important information is lost. In the worst cases, 'nighthawks' go on farmland at night without the landowner's permission, which is committing the offence of going equipped to steal. Detecting on a Scheduled Monument without an English Heritage licence is a separate offence. Archaeologists who liaise with detectorists may have all shades of honesty to deal with, and they have to form their own judgements about the reliability of the information they are given.

Portable Antiquities Scheme

The Portable Antiquities Scheme (PAS) was introduced by the DCMS with the participation of the British Museum in September 1997 when the new Treasure Act came into force. The aim was to encourage the voluntary reporting of both Treasure and non-Treasure finds so that they could all be properly recorded. The initial funding from the DCMS provided for a pilot project covering Norfolk, Kent, North Lincolnshire, North-West England and Yorkshire. The prime purpose of the new 'Finds Liaison Officers' (FLOs) was to seek out those who were making the discoveries, principally detectorists, and encourage them to record where their finds were made and make them available for study. The FLOs would identify the finds and put them onto the new online database (www.finds.org.uk). From 1999, with additional funding from the Heritage Lottery Fund, the Scheme was extended to cover half of England. By then it had the active support of all the key national organisations, including the Council for British Archaeology which had in the 1980s been opposed to the 'indiscriminate' use of detectors on archaeological sites. Additional Heritage Lottery Funds from 2003 allowed the Scheme to be extended further to cover the whole of England and Wales, and from 2006 the Scheme was entirely funded by the DCMS, and the various local partners, and managed by the British Museum. In Norfolk's case the local partner was Norfolk County Council.

The national online database provides a description of the find, the name of the finder, the circumstances of discovery and its location, but it is a complex database which is slow to compile, and there have been software problems with transferring the information to the County Sites and Monuments Records (SMRs). The SMRs, now called Historic Environment Records (HERs), have to be the primary record of all archaeological data, so it is important that the data is transferred digitally into the HER.

In Norfolk from the time the Scheme started in 1997 up to 2007 we had 607 Treasure cases out of a total of 3,969 for England (15%). The nearest to that was 324 (8%) for Suffolk and 279 (7%) for Kent. Most other counties were significantly under 100 cases over the same period. In 2013 Norfolk had a staggering 107 Treasure cases (10.7%) out of a national total of 993, compared with 62 for Lincolnshire and 61 for Suffolk. This creates a heavy workload for the staff who form the Norfolk Identification and Recording Service, headed by Andrew Rogerson (*Figure 9.1*). Andrew and his colleague Steven Ashley are funded by Norfolk County Council, along with half the salary of Adrian Marsden, the coins specialist based in the Castle Museum. Then, there is a FLO who handles the administration and legal aspects as well as identifying finds. Half of Adrian's post is PAS-funded. In addition to that, Tim Pestell, an Anglo-Saxon specialist in the Castle Museum, attends detector clubs regularly and museum staff have given a lot of time to finds' identification over the years. Even so, there are never enough of them to keep up with it all.

In 2013 the Portable Antiquities Scheme recorded 80,861 finds for England, of which Norfolk had 14,474 (18%). The good news is that 91% of these nationally were removed from cultivated land where objects are susceptible to damage from ploughing or chemical erosion by fertilisers. Most of this is very much a rescue process. (Further details are in the Annual Reports of the Portable Antiquities Scheme.)

Since the Scheme began the FLOs have recorded a million finds nationally. This was described by Neil MacGregor, the previous Director of the British Museum, which administers

9.1. Andrew Rogerson, a man of many talents, who currently leads the team identifying metal detector finds in the county (CLG 10).

the Scheme, as '.... a testament to the success of the PAS in breaking down barriers between archaeologists and metal-detectorists.'

More background information on the events which led up to the 1996 Treasure Act and the introduction of the Portable Antiquities Scheme (the PAS) can be found in Addyman 2008 and Bland 2008.

There is no doubt that metal detecting since the 1970s has transformed our understanding of the county's archaeology. Norfolk's Identification and Recording Service is fully stretched often identifying up to 16,000 metal, pottery and flints finds each year. This is an astonishing figure, and it is a reflection of: (a) the wealth of the area in prehistoric and later times, (b) the fact that much of the land is under arable and therefore accessible to detectorists, and (c) the trust which has been built up between local detectorists and archaeologists in Norfolk over the years. The way this trust was built up at the beginning is quite a story.

How 'The Norfolk System' all began

9.2. Tony Gregory who showed us the way to develop close ties with the metal-detecting community (CLG 5).

Metal detecting has had an important part to play in the history of Norfolk's archaeology since the first machines appeared in the late 1960s. The first Norfolk archaeologist who really woke up to the need to work with the detecting fraternity, rather than oppose it, was Tony Gregory (*Figure 9.2*) who was appointed in 1974 as Assistant Keeper of Archaeology at the Castle Museum under the Keeper, Barbara Green (*Figure 12.2*). He soon received an increasing number of metal finds for identification as detectors became more affordable and sophisticated. At the same time stories started to circulate from various parts of the country about thefts from archaeological sites. But Tony realised that trying to conceal information about sites would only encourage detectorists not to report their own discoveries and that the two sides needed to be open with each other and to work together. Barbara and Tony decided it was time to come out into the open and express the views of all of us working in Norfolk at the time, and they wrote a paper entitled 'An initiative in the use of metal detectors in Norfolk' in the *Museums Journal* (Green and Gregory 1977-8). This caused a furore. Barbara and Tony were both employed in the Norfolk Museums Service, and the chairman of the Norfolk Museums Committee, Hon. Robin Walpole, took a stand against their views in public.

Reading their article today, it seems to be totally reasonable, but at the time it went against the prevailing mood in museums and amongst the majority of archaeologists nation-wide. Tony and Barbara made the point that despite the establishment of a joint working party of the Museums Association and the Council for British Archaeology in 1975/6 no national policy had emerged. So, in Norfolk, in the absence of a national policy, we were taking the initiative in seeking co-operation and a better personal understanding between detectorists and archaeologists. The first step had been to produce a leaflet *Archaeological finds: some suggestions about the use of metal-detectors* sponsored by the Norfolk Archaeological Rescue Group and the Norfolk Research Committee and distributed through local detector dealers.

In response, a Norfolk and Suffolk Metal Detecting Society had been formed to promote better understanding, and the Society had adopted the leaflet as their Code of Conduct. Tony had been co-opted onto their committee as their archaeological adviser and he was advising them on which sites they could detect and which ones they should avoid, particularly Scheduled Ancient Monuments. The Society, encouraged by Tony, organised a detector survey in advance of the Caister-on-Sea bypass, described by Barrie Sharrock in the website of what is now the East Norfolk Metal Detecting Society:

> Members were instructed in laying out search grids and labelling find's bags and the club organised much of the searching, first of the actual roadway and later the adjoining fields along the route. Liaising with contractors and farmers occupied a lot of time for the officers of the club, so did marking out the fields into grids so that accurate findspots could be recorded.

This method of co-operation was becoming known within the detecting fraternity as 'The Norfolk Example'. Tony and Barbara made it clear that since local Sites and Monuments Records were public documents compiled at public expense, they should as far as possible be freely available to the public. Open access to SMRs would indicate which sites were scheduled, and would provide details of the boundaries of scheduled areas to ensure that mistakes could be avoided. They argued that staff running SMRs could no more deny SMR access to a detectorist than they could to someone writing their local history. The local scheme was going well, and the next step was to re-publish the leaflet as a *regional* Code of Conduct.

Robin Walpole insisted that the matter be brought to the next meeting of his Museums Committee which was held on 24th November 1977. He explained that as he was also Chairman of the Area Museums Service he was opposed to the use of metal detectors on *all* archaeological sites and that the conciliatory approach in the leaflet should not be endorsed by the Museums Committee. This put him on a collision course with the Director of Museums, Francis Cheetham. Francis supported his staff totally but pointed out that while archaeologists in the Service had approved the wording, the Service itself had not been the publisher of the leaflet. He said that the current print run was exhausted and it was due to be re-issued as a regional leaflet. He reminded members that there was no legislation governing the use of detectors, nor was there likely to be. So, it was more useful to encourage detectorists to act responsibly and report their finds to museums.

The Committee asked the Director of Museums to review the wording of the leaflet and report back. Francis then convened an informal meeting of the working party involved with publishing the revised leaflet, and this met in his office on 22nd December 1977. It was a useful discussion anyway since we were due to revise the text as a regional leaflet to be issued by the Scole Committee for Archaeology in East Anglia. The outcome was an expanded version urging detectorists not to dig out finds they might locate below ploughsoil and to report such discoveries to an archaeologist. The leaflet listed seven key points to 'REMEMBER', which were a little clearer than those in the first version. They went as follows:

> REMEMBER *that the permission of the landowner and farmer, or whoever is responsible for the land, must be obtained before searching.*
> REMEMBER *that it is illegal to disturb a site that is scheduled as an Ancient Monument. Information about such sites can be obtained from your local Museum or Archaeological Unit.*
> REMEMBER *that anything other than gold or silver belongs to the land-owner, not the finder, so make arrangements with him first.*
> REMEMBER *that objects of gold or silver are subject to a Treasure Trove Inquest so must be reported. It is illegal to fail to do so, and your Museum will advise you on this.*
> REMEMBER *to record where each find was discovered.*
> REMEMBER *that pieces of pottery and other finds can be as important as metal objects, and should be collected and brought into the Museum for recording.*
> REMEMBER *that digging below the plough-soil will damage archaeological remains, and should not be attempted without the guidance of a professional archaeologist.*

There was an additional section which listed the museums and archaeological units in the region willing to identify and record finds.

The Museums Committee met again on 2nd February 1978. The revised draft was on the Agenda with a bland covering report from the Director of Museums urging members just to 'note' the re-wording and await national developments on the matter. That was all agreed (*EDP* 20th February 1978).

But, the Director of the Area Museums Service for South-Eastern England remained unrelenting in her opposition to the leaflet and threatened to re-consider grants which her organisation was making to the Service unless the Museum Committee did not dissociate itself 'by public statement' from the revised leaflet. The next meeting of the Museums Committee was held on 23rd November 1978 in the Chrome Gallery at the Castle Museum. Because the gallery housed precious paintings of the Norwich School the light levels were kept low to protect the paintings, and this enhanced the drama of the moment. The County Council's Chief Executive, Barry Capon, was there to express his concern about the improper use of the grant-making powers of the Area Museums Service. He had, in fact, objected formally to the standing Commission on Museums and Galleries about the threats from the Area Museums Service, and he was awaiting a reply. The minutes of the meeting are now in the Norfolk Record Office and make interesting reading (ACC 2012/235: Box 47).

The Chairman was quite clearly determined that the committee should make a public statement deploring the use of detectors on *all* known archaeological sites even though that was contrary to the views of archaeologists in his service and indeed most in the region. He threatened to resign over the matter, but in the end after a long debate the Chairman had his way, and a resolution was passed as follows:

> *The Committee disassociates itself from any document which fails to discourage treasure hunting on known archaeological sites.*

So, the Chairman did not have to resign, the Area Museums Service continued to make their grants to the Norfolk Museums Service, and the revised leaflet went ahead anyway, published by the Scole Committee, without further opposition. It was so obviously the right way forward that we heard no more criticism of the 'Norfolk System', which has been our strategy ever since (*EDP* 20th February 1978).

In the spring of 1978 the results of a research project provided a very interesting window on opinions then current amongst archaeologists and detectorists (although it is puzzling to see that no archaeologist or detectorist in Norfolk responded). Questionnaires were distributed to every provincial museum in Great Britain and a selection of archaeological units and every metal detecting club then known to exist. This was organised by David Crowther for a BA dissertation he was writing at the Institute of Archaeology in London (Crowther 1983).

The replies from archaeologists nationwide were analysed as follows:
- Only 14% of museums and 15% of archaeological units had built up any form of regular contact with local detector users.
- 43% of museums and 39% of units had no liaison with detectorists whatsoever.
- Of the units that replied 65% had never heard of a detector being used for 'archaeological purposes', and 42% would not consider using one under any circumstances.
- And for detectorists:
- 85% of the sympathetic clubs agreed that recording was necessary.
- 70% would be willing to engage in an elaborate scheme for finds plotting and recording.

The contrast between the two sides on their willingness and enthusiasm to collaborate with each other was very strong. Archaeologists clearly had a long way to go to catch up with the detecting world. Indeed, the author of the report made his own views about detector users very clear in his concluding remarks:

> *Theirs is a heritage which can be encapsulated within a boxful of metal objects. Ruthless profiteers apart, such hobbyists seek to bring the past to life; an archaeologist would say they trivialise it. Whatever their aims, the net effort tends to remain the same: namely an arbitrary, if generally naive, vandalism of the archaeological record (Crowther 1983).*

Tony Gregory transferred to the Norfolk Archaeological Unit in 1978 to become a Field Officer with us with special responsibility for Roman period archaeology, and the move to the NAU gave him the opportunity to be more involved with fieldwork. He picked up the news after Easter 1980 that a great treasure had been found at Gallows Hill in Thetford the previous year. This was a spectacular hoard of Late Roman gold and silver jewellery and spoons which only came to light thanks to Tony's detective work (Johns and Potter 1983, 13-19; Watts 1988; Marsden 2014, 49-50). 'Here his ability to win confidence was of paramount importance in extracting the truth under very difficult circumstances' (Rogerson 1991). By the time the Treasure Trove Inquest was held the finder had died and his estate only received a fraction of the full value of the find because it had been concealed in a bank vault until Tony brought it to light.

After Tony left the museum Bill Milligan and Sue Margeson continued to record and report on finds brought in for identification. From 1980 to 1982 Tony ran a major excavation on a late Iron Age triple-ditched enclosure next to the treasure find spot and made full use of local detectorists both in searching the ploughsoil before it was removed by machine and in recording the underlying archaeology (**p. 232-235**). This was the first time detectors had been used on an archaeological excavation in the county, and the results more than justified the effort. His policy was to involve the local detectorists in the excavation since they could handle their own machines much more effectively than archaeologists could.

The 'STOP' campaign

However, on 12th March 1980 the Council for British Archaeology (CBA), supported by a number of other leading national bodies, launched a campaign at a London press conference using the strapline 'Stop Taking Our Past' (or STOP). The Council of the CBA had the previous January passed a strongly worded resolution denouncing treasure hunting as inimical to the archaeological heritage of Britain. The other national bodies lending support to the campaign were the Museums Association, RESCUE, the Society of Museum Archaeologists, the Association of County Archaeological Officers, the Standing Conference of (Archaeological) Unit Managers and the United Kingdom Institute of Conservation. They were followed within a few months by the Associations of County and District Councils and the Historic Houses Association.

The STOP campaign in 'defence of our heritage', asked for the support of major landowning institutions to ban the use of detectors and asked CBA members to 'combat the menace that is destroying what the bulldozers have left us of our past' (Cleere 1980a). At the launch the campaign committee made it clear that their aim was to educate public opinion so that 'the indiscriminate use of detectors on archaeological sites becomes as socially unacceptable as bird nesting or the rooting up of rare plants' (Cleere 1980b). That was for all sites – not just scheduled ones.

To promote the campaign the CBA produced lapel badges, car stickers and posters under the slogan 'Campaign against Treasure Hunting'. While the intention was to make the irresponsible aspect of treasure hunting socially unacceptable, it had a wider and much more negative underlying message. Some archaeologists went further, advocating that the locations of sites and finds should be kept secret and that the profession should not co-operate with the hobby. They were recommending that all detectorists should be licensed and that unlicensed detecting should be illegal.

Although the National Trust did ban detectors on their properties, the campaign otherwise achieved little, as we knew it would. The Home Office did not introduce any new legislation as the CBA wanted, or any licensing, and gradually the momentum to ban their use on sites faded away. But this had all made the task of bringing the two sides together in Norfolk much harder.

The Norfolk way is the only way

In 1983 Tony wrote an article for the *Treasure Hunting* magazine on 'Archaeology and Treasure hunting: a view from the other side' (Gregory 1983a). This was a passionate and heartfelt plea to the detecting community to work with archaeologists, to limit their detecting to the ploughsoil and to avoid undisturbed pasture:

> *If found below the ploughsoil, or below the turf on a field which has never been ploughed, then an object is stratified, and if it is removed from its layer without skilled archaeological excavation then the evidence which that object could give is lost. It could have dated the layer in which it was found and also the layers above and below, but once removed that dating is impossible. Clearly then, digging up objects from below the ploughsoil or below the turf of unploughed pasture cannot be part of responsible metal detecting.*

He then went on to explain how on his Thetford excavation the detailed recording of objects from the ploughsoil before the soil was removed by machine had added enormously to his understanding of the site. He argued that this was a good example of how the two communities could and should co-operate:

> *.. the vast majority of detector users in Norfolk are after interest and enjoyment and want to contribute to our study of the past; they are desperately anxious not to break the law or damage the archaeological sites, so at club meetings we can sit down and discuss the sites and finds and avoid problems. We are steadily getting over the archaeologists' fears that sites will be ruined by detecting and the detector users' fears that as soon as the site is reported to archaeologists they will be banned from it.*

Tony's great strength was that although he had a formidable intellect he also had the ability to mix on equal terms with people who had no academic pretensions. He had the rare gift of being able to give a paper at a high-powered conference or talk equally well to detectorists in a pub about their Roman coins. His aim was to build up trust and eliminate barriers between the two communities. He was entirely committed to making archaeology interesting for the readers of *The Sun*; he did not want it to be an activity just for the academic elite (Gregory 1983b). He saw these machines as a wonderful way of engaging with people not in mainstream archaeology, while other archaeologists saw them as 'a problem' (eg Crowther 1983, 9).

Relations nationally went through a bad patch in the 1980s after the site of a second-century Romano-Celtic temple at Wanborough in Surrey was seriously damaged after its location was inadvertently announced at a Treasure Trove Inquest in 1984. Thousands of Iron Age and Roman coins and other votive objects were then looted at night. While the British Museum was able to acquire over a thousand of these coins after they had been seized, most of the material disappeared unrecorded into the antiquities trade. But it did provide a stimulus for both archaeologists and detectorists to start building bridges nationally and to work together more effectively (Hobbs 2003, 142-144).

In 1984 Tony followed his article for the detecting community in *Treasure Hunting* by writing another with Andrew Rogerson on 'Metal Detecting in Archaeological Excavation' in *Antiquity*, a periodical at the other end of the academic spectrum. They were making the same point that detectors used by local enthusiasts had become an essential tool for archaeological excavations (Gregory and Rogerson 1984). In describing the way local detectorists were used on the Thetford excavation Tony wrote:

> *The results were startling, on several levels; the enthusiasm and application of the detector-users was at least as great as any seen from professional or amateur archaeologists. They all displayed a tremendous and infectious excitement at their discoveries and gladly accepted normal archaeological discipline, including the retention of all finds in the excavation collection on behalf of the land-owner. This was all in very marked contrast to the black picture commonly painted by some archaeologists of the motives of detector-users.*

Andrew then went on to describe the excavation in November 1980 of a hoard of mid eighth-century silver pennies of the East Anglian king Beonna found in the ploughsoil:

> *There is little doubt that few, if any, of the ploughsoil objects would have been recovered without the use of a detector.. Future excavations of comparable Norfolk sites with or without a coin hoard will involve the use of controlled metal-detection as a normal tool of archaeological research.*

Nowadays it is almost unthinkable for archaeologists to be running an excavation without a detector to hand, but then it was still a novel and slightly subversive concept.

The local press loved stories about illegal detecting, and there was a particular spate of them in 1985 with headlines like 'Police declare war on plunder gangs' (*EDP* 14th March 1985), 'Night plundering of ancient sites uncovered' (*EDP* 20th March 1985), 'Bid to control metal detector plundering' (*EDP* 12th April 1985) and 'Treasure hunt fines winning Norfolk battle' (*EDP* 24th April 1985). But when Tony was interviewed by Bruce Robinson for the *EDP* in 1986, he said that 'The use of detectors has increased our knowledge of Bronze Age hoards by 200 per cent. Of all new sites, I suppose a third emanate from the use of detectors'. That percentage has surely increased since. He estimated that there were then about 600 detector users, and only about 20 'take a sinister interest'. While he recognised that there was illegal detecting, he believed that was exceptional (*EDP* 28th October 1986).

Over the winter of 1985-86 Tony followed all this by organising a detector survey of the scheduled Roman temple complex at Caistor St Edmund, close to the Roman town, with the full approval of the then Historic Buildings and Monuments Commission (later re-named English Heritage). The site had become notorious for night-time raids, and clearly something was attracting the nighthawks. There seemed little doubt that important material was being stolen from the ploughsoil; but what? The purpose of the project was to demonstrate that a responsibly organised survey to remove objects from the ploughsoil before they could be stolen made good sense. To record their locations properly would add to our understanding of the site. He enlisted the help of four local detectorists, Don Bennett, Paul Butterfant, Steve Dunthorne and Barrie Sharrock, to survey the temple and surrounding fields. This was before the days of the Global Positioning System (GPS), so the land was all pegged out in 20-metre squares and each square was systematically detected by a single individual to ensure an even level of recording. The resultant plan of coin finds was impressive, and a series of graphs was produced showing coin distribution by period. The discovery of eight Iron Age Icenian silver coins from the temple field was the biggest surprise, explaining the principal motive for the nocturnal raids. It is interesting that there were very few votive bronzes which one would normally expect to find on a temple site (Gregory 1991b).

Since then the temple area has been put down to grass by the farm tenant under a Higher Level Stewardship scheme to give it some protection, and the 1985-86 survey provided a thoroughly useful record of the surface archaeology before it was grassed over. The project demonstrated that detecting on scheduled sites, when properly managed, could yield really worthwhile results.

Tony had made his point well, and it was a great loss to archaeology and to his colleagues and friends when Tony died of cancer aged only 42 in June 1991 shortly after moving to Yorkshire (Press interview just before he left: *EDP* 22nd September 1988; obituaries in *The Times* 1st July, *Independent* 29th June, *Guardian* 1st July, *Telegraph* 9th July, *DAFT*, 5th July, 1991 and an appreciation of Tony in the *EDP* 23rd July 1991). None of the rest of us in the old Unit will have so many obituaries! While he was with us in Norfolk he had done more than the rest of us to bring a sense of trust and mutual respect to the relationship between archaeologists and the detecting community. Gradually the 'Norfolk System' of doing things was accepted nationally, and we now have the national network of Finds Liaison Officers described earlier which grew out of this concept.

It should be said that there are, and always will be, nighthawks, and let us hope that they will remain a minority. On 9th September 1993 we arranged for the High Sheriff of Norfolk, Robert Buscall, to launch a 'Campaign Against Illegal Metal Detecting' with the aim of working more closely with the police. This included having an Inspector in each Division as a regular contact and with the police being given (for their eyes only) a register of sites we considered to be particularly at risk. A new leaflet for landowners and farmers was also produced giving advice on illegal detecting. How much long-term difference it made I doubt, but it did underline to landowners that we were on their side. Over the years the damage nighthawks have caused did feature in the press from time to time (*EDP* 6th and 12th March 1993; 10th September 1993; 9th and 12th March 1994; 10th October 1994; 1st March 1996), but the overall benefits of responsible detecting by the many outweigh the damage caused by the few. But the pressure the sheer quantity of metal detector finds submitted for identification was putting on museum staff was highlighted in a short article in the *EDP* on 13th October 1994 under the heading 'Pressure is on History team'.

The Burgh Castle rally

A superb example of close cooperation between the Museums Service, the Norfolk Archaeological Trust and the metal detecting community took place at Burgh Castle in 1995. John Green, the owner of the fort, had been holding metal detector rallies on the fields around the fort and charging £20 a head for some time. This was permitted because most of the land outside the fort walls was then still not scheduled. He had run these rallies with no involvement from archaeologists, but this would stop after I had agreed a deal with him in 1995 to buy the whole place for the Norfolk Archaeological Trust (**p. 291-294**). But John, who never missed an opportunity to earn a few bob, imposed a condition on the sale that he should be able to hold one last rally, even though all the fields were by then scheduled. English Heritage, quite rightly in this case, relented in order not to hold up the sale. On 23rd April the rally took place attended by John Davies from the Castle Museum to identify the Roman objects and by Andrew Rogerson from Gressenhall for the Anglo-Saxon and medieval finds. While the archaeologists at the event must all have found it unsettling to take part in the event knowing that the land was scheduled, the results were quite spectacular. The detectorists were queuing with their finds outside the identification tent. The end result was over 700 Roman coins, an Iron Age coin, three Anglo-Saxon sceattas, one ninth-century half penny, 22 medieval and post-medieval coins and tokens, a Roman bronze bust of Venus, several Roman brooches a Roman phallic mount, three Anglo-Saxon brooches and a fifteenth-century gold finger ring. The detailed identification of these finds, particularly the Roman and Anglo-Saxon coins, has helped us considerably to understand the settlement history of the area around the fort. Quite separately, members of NAHRG organised a detailed and very useful fieldwalking exercise of the same fields so that the pottery could supplement the metal detector evidence. After the purchase by the Norfolk Archaeological Trust, the fields were all put down to grass and then effectively sealed from further disturbance (**p. 295-296**).

Further details of the early years of metal detecting in Norfolk can also be found in Rogerson 2017.

Three successful detectorists

The following profiles of three successful currently active detectorists provide an insight into the hobby as it is today. These three alone are making an enormous contribution to our understanding of the county's archaeology.

Dave Fox

Dave has retired having spent a lifetime working with industrial paints and shot blasting on metal surfaces (*Figure 9.3*). He worked particularly on North Sea gas installations and Air Force bases where metal buildings and pipe-work needed frequent re-coating. Because the work had both busy and some slack periods he found himself regularly with time on his hands and so took up detecting as a hobby. The early machines came in kit form, and he bought his first in the late 1960s as a made-up kit from a jeweller's shop. At that time you needed a 'Pipe finder/metal detector' licence issued under the Wireless Telegraphy Act 1949, costing £1.40 'for the purpose of determining the position of buried or concealed pipes, cables or other metal objects' which lasted five years. They are no longer issued, but he still has one issued to him in 1980.

Better detectors made by C-scope came in during the early 1970s, although they were still very basic machines which could not discriminate between metals. In some fields he found himself picking up whole barrow loads of rusty iron. Discriminating detectors became available in the late 1970s, and they had two tones – a high-pitched noise for non-ferrous and a low groan for ferrous. It was still difficult then to obtain permission from farmers to detect on their land because they thought that if you had a detector 'you were a bit of an anorak', and he therefore started on beaches and commons outside private control. The first ploughed land he had permission to go on was at Stiffkey where in 1985 he stumbled across an undisturbed hoard of Late Bronze Age socketed axes and one small fragment of a sword (unpublished).

The first farmer who gave Dave permission to search on any quantity of land lived at Hindringham. When asked, he said to Dave that he and his father had farmed their land all their lives and had 'never found nothing', but he was welcome to have a try with his 'Geiger Counter' if he wished. That gave him access to several thousand acres of arable land, and the turning point for Dave was when he found a gold *solidus* of the emperor Honorius. He then realised for the first time that what he was doing was actually important and worthwhile and he wasn't just collecting junk. It was a hobby to be taken seriously. He became a keen member of the Norfolk and Norwich Archaeological Society and has followed over the years the reports of his finds which have featured in the pages of *Norfolk Archaeology*.

9.3. Dave Fox, one of the first metal detectorists to be active in the county, with a selection of his favourite discoveries, 2015.

With the new permission, Dave started on a field not far from the River Stiffkey in Great Walsingham which actually turned out to have a rich collection of Roman votive offerings, presumably from a temple. Amongst them were two statuettes of the god Mercury which he found in 1984, and another four years later, and he eventually sold them to the Norwich Castle Museum (*Figure 9.4*). By then archaeologists were recognising that this 'temple field', as it became known, was part of a larger Roman settlement best classified as a small Roman town possibly covering up to three hectares, although the whole complex may cover up to 84 hectares (Gregory 1986b; Gurney 1995, 57-59; Davies 2008, 181-182). Dave found many Roman coins and brooches on the temple field, but it was the votive offerings to the gods which were of particular importance. Many were on show recently in a temporary Roman exhibition at the Castle Museum. This is one of the few detector collections from the county which has been subject to detailed published academic scrutiny (Bagnall Smith 1999; Marsden 2014, 47-48). There

9.4. *A statuette of the god Mercury found by Dave Fox in the 'temple field' at Great Walsingham (15.7 cm high). (Portable Antiquities Scheme)*

are seven concentrations of building material, and at least five of these represent the remains of substantial buildings, including a bathhouse and a temple. In addition, there are possibly dispersed Iron Age Icenian silver hoards. Of the greatest interest is a ploughed-down oval earthwork enclosure in neighbouring Wighton which may be of Late Roman or sub-Roman date, where the Norfolk Archaeological Unit carried out some sample excavations in 1974 (Lawson 1976b). It is distressing that this whole complex with strong and extensive evidence for structural remains was not scheduled by English Heritage years ago.

With Tony Gregory's support, Dave obtained permission in 1985 to detect the rest of the town owned by neighbouring estates. But, while the Hindringham farmer showed no interest in the objects, the two estates which owned the additional land agreed to settle for a 50/50 split of the finds. Dave honoured that agreement by passing on half the material after it had all been fully recorded. He is determined that most of the items he has been allowed to retain under his understandings with the landowners will all finish up in the Norwich Museum collections. It is nevertheless Dave's philosophy that it is the *information* which is of primary importance and what happens to the objects in the end is a secondary consideration. Early on, Tony Gregory provided Dave with large-scale maps on which he marked the location of every non-coin find with a find number. So, all his detecting over the years was well recorded both by him and by archaeologists in the Castle Museum or the Norfolk Archaeological Unit at Gressenhall.

However, there are two less satisfactory aspects to the story which do need to be mentioned. One is that as the temple field became better known within the detecting community it was regularly hit by nighthawks, mainly from outside the county. The details of some of them are known because three times they were caught by police at night leaving the site *with* their metal detectors and *with* their stolen finds. In September 1991 six men from Wisbech, Thetford and Essex were arrested late at night as they were leaving the site with metal detectors, shovels, a fork, a torch and Roman coins. The case came to Crown Court in September 1992, and the defendants were charged with theft and going equipped to steal. The confiscated detectors and the finds were all exhibited as evidence at the trial. The arguments put forward by the defence were that they were engaged in an innocent hobby, not harming anyone and not removing objects of any great worth. That appeared to convince the jury and the six left the court without convictions.

The problem is that rewards of successful nighthawking can be considerable when gold or silver coins or figurines, potentially worth hundreds of pounds are found. The only solution is for Historic England, as it is now, to ensure that sites like this are properly scheduled. The legal significance of the site is then clear in court and a charge is much more likely to lead to a conviction.

The other part of the story is that Dave has now been told not to go on the temple field because it is being regularly used for commercial detector rallies. There are a number of businesses who run rallies like this, and the finds from them seldom reach an archaeologist for recording, so the information is usually lost. Because the Walsingham rallies attract so many people Dave thinks that it is quite possible that they have found just as much as he has in the past, and there could be little left in the ploughsoil now. Archaeologists are seldom given the opportunity to attend rallies and are reluctant to do so anyway because of the high level of dishonesty involved with people bringing items to the rally to win the prize of best find of the day. Also, once a find has a reported provenance at a rally, it can be sold on with that provenance wherever it was actually found; it is a method of laundering objects removed illegally from sites elsewhere. It is sometimes said, but never proven, that some organisers actually salt a field before an event with a few attractive coins to encourage more customers. However, there is no evidence that any of this happens at the Walsingham rallies.

The County Council's Historic Environment Service has not yet put the Walsingham land forward for protection as a Scheduled Ancient Monument because English Heritage is very reluctant to schedule more sites in ploughed fields, although their reasons for not doing so are usually inconsistent and unconvincing. We would have put Walsingham forward for scheduling years ago, but having failed completely to get English Heritage to even consider the Treasure Field and its environs at Snettisham where the Iron Age torcs were found there seemed little point. Remember, when we completed the barrow survey we wanted to move on to do a survey of major Roman settlements until English Heritage made it clear that they would not be acting on the scheduling recommendations arising from the survey (**p. 198**).

Dave has also made two other significant hoard discoveries. One is part of a Late Bronze Age hoard of socketed axes and sword blade fragments at South Creake on the same spot where nine socketed axes had been found in 1959 and 1968 (Gurney 1997, 540). The other is a massive hoard of Late Bronze Age weapons at Waterden, again where some had been found earlier. In 1959 five sword fragments and two spearheads were 'Found in a round container which disintegrated on removal, probably of pottery, but at the time of reporting (1964) the finder could not be certain'. In 1992 Dave located the hoard with a few pieces actually visible lying on the surface some distance from where the spot had been incorrectly reported in 1992. In September 1994 Andrew Rogerson from the Gressenhall Field Archaeology office and John Davies from the Castle Museum hired a digger and with Dave doing the detecting they removed the ploughsoil in thin layers until the bottom of the topsoil had been reached. By the end they had recovered over 80 sword fragments, representing a minimum of 13 swords, 12 complete or near complete spearheads, plus a further 60 more spearhead fragments. There were several joins between the 1952 and 1994 pieces suggesting it was all one deposit. No trace of the hoard pit remained below ploughsoil, so it must have been disturbed and spread by cultivation since the first ones were found in 1959. The Waterden hoard is now close to publication, along with another hoard from Fincham, in East Anglian Archaeology.

Dave is still reporting finds regularly to the Finds Liaison Officers at Gressenhall and Norwich over 50 years after he bought his first kit-built machine, which is an impressive record. When asked which is his favourite find you have the impression he has several, but he is certainly proud of the Lombardic gilded silver radiate-head brooch made probably in Italy in the early seventh century (Figure 9.5). How it finished up in Walsingham is a mystery (Ager, Ashley and Rogerson 1993).

9.5. An early seventh-century Lombardic gilded silver radiate-head brooch also found by Dave Fox at Great Walsingham (7.3 cm long).

Steve Brown

Steve has spent much of his life involved in engineering in various ways, as a fitter installing machinery in King's Lynn factories and in fabricating welding. He was also the skipper on a pilot boat in King's Lynn docks for 15 years. Currently he runs grass cutting machinery on a farming estate at Wormegay, near Kings Lynn. His wife is a full-time nurse in King's Lynn Hospital, and when he is not looking after their two small children he is out detecting several days a week. He holds the record for reporting more Treasure finds to the Portable Antiquities Scheme than any other detectorist in England (eg *EDP* 26th January 2016). The transcripts of all the inquests for his Treasure finds make quite a pile (*Figure 9.6*). On average he has had five or six Treasure discoveries a year. He alone has more finds than Finds Liaison Officers in Norfolk can really cope with. He is sitting on a lot of items waiting to go into the Gressenhall office for identification at the moment. Steve believes that over the years he has had more than a million metal finds to his credit, all of which, of course, need identification. In two weeks he collected a very large number of Roman coins from one Roman site, and they are in the Castle Museum awaiting identification. A recent discovery is a curious gilded silver object he first thought was the silver crest off the top of an Anglo-Saxon helmet, but it is now believed to be an Early Saxon buckle tongue. It featured in a Treasure inquest reported in the *EDP* on 26th January 2016 (Ref NMS-816603), and it has been acquired by the Castle Museum.

9.6. Steve Brown, who holds the record for reporting more Treasure finds to the Portable Antiquities Scheme than any other detectorist in England, 2015. The pile of papers on his desk are the transcripts of the many Treasure inquests at which his finds have been considered by the Coroner.

Steve is full of praise for Andrew Rogerson and his team in the Identification and Recording Service, and he is the first to recognise that they are over-stretched even with Andrew working into most evenings and some weekends.

Steve has permission to go on several large estates in north-west Norfolk, and he has no trouble obtaining permission because he is so well known to the farm managers in the area and he has been active on their patches for so long. With every estate he has a written access agreement, and there is always a 50/50 split. Usually the estate decides to keep all the items after they have been identified and recorded, and the estate pays him half of the value which they agree between them. On one estate he actually arranges the finds in purpose-made showcases in the farm office. As a result, he doesn't have a collection of his own; the pleasure for him comes from the discovery.

Steve keeps away from known sites where finds are already recorded and he does not have much enthusiasm for Roman period archaeology – 'the finds are all too similar', he says! He prefers more of a challenge and likes Anglo-Saxon and medieval sites, and as a consequence he has located several previously unknown Anglo-Saxon cemeteries. He prefers to follow his hunches and to go where nobody has thought of going before, and he doesn't feel the need to check the online data in the Historic Environment Record first. He records most finds by taking a GPS reading of the centre of a field, although with Treasure items he takes an 8-figure

9.7. A small Early Saxon gold and glass oval pendant found by Steve Brown in Gayton (2.8 cm long). (Portable Antiquities Scheme)

grid reference reading of the find spot by GPS which he believes is accurate to within one metre. When the information is put into the HER the online data is limited to a four figure reference, so the *exact* spot is not made public, although it is available to specialists.

He recognises that all his finds, after they are recorded into the Portable Antiquities system, will be entered into both their online database and the HER and they are both public documents. So when he is working a field and is finding important material he usually withholds the information until he is satisfied he has finished because he knows that nighthawks will follow behind him as soon as the data is online.

Steve's favourite finds are a seventh-century gold and glass pendant from Gayton (Rogerson and Ashley 2009, 564-565), now on display in King's Lynn Museum (*Figure 9.7*), and a gold pendant in the shape of a cross, possibly eleventh-century, from a field near Holt. This can be viewed on the Portable Antiquities Scheme website reference number NMS 8D82BB. He thinks it may be earlier than that, while the specialists believe it is a bit later. Who can say who is right when he has handled so many comparable examples himself? Anyway, the field is full of Middle Saxon Ipswich Ware, which gives the pendant an early context which he believes is correct. Steve doesn't just pick up metal. He records pottery and flints as well, so that wherever he works there is a more than an adequate record of the surface archaeology.

Mark Turner

Mark, who lives close to Caistor St Edmund Roman town, runs a wholesale autoparts business in Norwich and he distributes goods to customers over south Norfolk. He devotes most of his spare time to detecting, and, probably because he is an engineer by trade, he is exceptionally committed to accurate recording. He has a policy of never selling his finds, and all his important discoveries are given to the Norfolk Museums Service. He started detecting in 1996 with a friend in his garden at Caistor and found 'a few bits and pieces'. His first significant find was a Roman *denarius* of the Emperor Augustus, and then he became increasingly involved in the hobby. He bought his first GPS position-recording device in 1998 and then started to build up distribution maps of his finds and was fascinated to see what his maps revealed. At that time the GPS system was not entirely accurate because the Americans who controlled the satellites introduced different 'errors' each day of up to 200 metres for security reasons. However, he worked out how to overcome this at the start of each day by checking the GPS location of a mapped landmark and then adjusting accordingly.

Once GPS was made widely available for car navigation the system became accurate to within less than a metre. Since 1998 Mark has recorded about 4,500 finds and catalogued each one using software he devised himself. He has a separate catalogue for each farm he works on so landowners can have access to all the data for the finds from their land. The items are catalogued with a code number, the date found, item description, GPS location, a photo when appropriate, notes on the object and its period, Norfolk Museums Service identification number, and the county Historic Environment Record reference number when allocated. Each find is kept in a separate labelled paper envelope (*Figure 9.8*). The find which has given him most pleasure is a large and very rare seventh-century Spanish Visigothic buckle plate found just to the west of the river at Caistor (Rogerson and Ashley 2011, 254-256). This is on display in the museum (*Fig 9.9*).

9.8. Mark Turner who records his finds in great detail on computer and puts each item in a separate labelled envelope, 2015.

While Mark doesn't resent detectorists who sell their finds, he believes passionately that archaeology is our common inheritance and that finds are everybody's heritage. So he passes on to the Castle Museum the items which they need for study purposes, and some of his best finds are on display. Mark chairs the Norwich Anglian Metal Detector Club, which has about 16 or 17 members, and he encourages his members to record their finds as accurately as they can, although he is the first to admit that only about four use GPS-recording. The rest just report their finds as having come from a particular field. This is a normal ratio for most clubs.

When talking to Mark, he is quick to praise the work of the Norfolk archaeologists who are employed under the umbrella of the national Portable Antiquities Scheme. He is keen to say that the trust which has been built up between the two sides since the 1970s is 'the best in the country'.

Geophysics and GPS-recording of coin distribution on Dunston Field

In 2012 the Norfolk Archaeological Trust bought the 22-hectare Dunston Field at Caistor Roman town to save it from further plough damage and nighthawking. The field, like the Caistor temple field, had become well known by less respectable

9.9. A substantial Hispano-Visigothic seventh-century buckle plate found by Mark to the west of the River Tas at Caistor St Edmund Roman town (10.5 cm long). (Portable Antiquities Scheme)

detectorists as a place to find both Roman and Anglo-Saxon coins. After purchase, the Trust put it down to grass as a protective measure, but before the grass grew up it arranged for a geophysical survey by Dave Bescoby of the University of East Anglia and for Mark Turner to make a very detailed detector survey of the same area. Because Mark's finds were GPS-recorded and the geophysical survey was also recorded by satellite navigation, it was possible to plot the distribution of Roman and Anglo-Saxon coins against the background of the buried features found by geophysics. We believed that this was the first time the two methods had been attempted together using GPS technology, and the resulting plans have told us much about Late Roman and Anglo-Saxon settlement west of the river without ever putting a spade in the ground (*Figures 22.12 and 22.13*). The Roman coins were clustered west of the point where the Roman bridge crossed the River Tas and also alongside the Roman road approaching Caistor from the south, probably representing an area of Late Roman industrial activity. Mark's coin finds, along with others from the Caistor Roman Town Research Project's detector survey of the field, are all at the moment being identified at the British Museum. When the results are available it should be possible to see exactly how and when the town expanded to the west of the river.

The tidal wave continues

From this small sample of three very enthusiastic detectorists some interesting trends emerge. With their engineering backgrounds, they all take pleasure in using their machines systematically, and the satisfaction comes from discovery. I saw no strong enthusiasm for holding on to most of the items they find; they are not primarily collectors and do not have a collector's mentality, quite different from people who buy detector finds on eBay. Some sell their material, but I saw no suggestion that they were motivated by profit. The motivation comes from the pleasure of finding lovely and interesting things.

These are just three out of about two or three hundred detectorists who are now working in the county reporting their finds regularly to the Finds Liaison Officers. There are far more active detectorists than there are other active amateur archaeologists. The quality and richness of the collections they are bringing in for identification is far greater than the profession has ever had to handle before. We are seeing so much important information now that it will transform our understanding of the county's archaeology, yet the sheer quantity of the items is far outstripping the resources which the profession has at its disposal to record it all. In 2014-15 the Norfolk Historic Environment Service recorded 15,207 archaeological finds, mainly from metal detecting. These included 119 cases of Treasure. Of all the finds recorded on the Portable Antiquities database for England and Wales 20% come from Norfolk which is an extra-ordinarily high figure (Norfolk Historic Environment Service Annual Review 2014-15).

An assessment of the development of the national database as a tool for research can be found in Pett 2010. A paper by Jean Bagnall Smith published in *Britannia* in 1999 on the Roman votive objects from the Walsingham temple field is a rare example of a detailed synthesis of detector finds from a single location. There are also six notable studies based largely on metal detector discoveries: *Early Anglo-Saxon Communities in the Landscape of Norfolk* by Mary Chester-Kadwell is a very perceptive study of Anglo-Saxon settlements and cemeteries in the county primarily from detector material (Chester-Kadwell 2009). Then, there is Kathrin Felder's dissertation on *Girdle-hangers in fifth- and sixth-century England: A key to Early Anglo-Saxon Identities* (Felder 2014), Jane Kershaw's *Viking Identities: Scandinavian Jewellery in England* (2013), Steven Ashley's *Medieval Armorial Horse Furniture in Norfolk* (Ashley 2002) and his review of early medieval elite metal fittings (Ashley 2015). There is also the substantial corpus being assembled gallantly by Andrew Rogerson and Steven Ashley of every medieval seal matrix recorded in Norfolk, published in *Norfolk Archaeology* each year since 1999 (eg Rogerson and Ashley 2009). But the lack of resources to study and publish the important group of Early Roman military metalwork from the Roman fort at Swanton Morley is an example of how the current recording system has been overloaded (*Figure 13.5*). Usually, little more than a quick identification, and sometimes a drawing, put into the annual list of outstanding finds published in *Norfolk Archaeology* and on the online Portable Antiquities Scheme database and in the HER is the maximum that the present system permits. But without that system the loss to knowledge would be unimaginable.

The good news is that there is now a multitude of research students nation-wide working on the results of the Portable Antiquities Scheme; in December 2015 there were 98 research students working on the data, 20 at PhD level. While the Scheme cannot fund the research, they are able to facilitate much of it with advice and guidance. It is just a pity that Tony Gregory is not with us now to see what he achieved.

Elsewhere the tension between the archaeological and detecting communities often remains strong (Wilson 2015), and it has been said that:

> .... the perennial problem of metal-detecting .... lies at the heart of one of the most pernicious and profound conflicts within British archaeology (Cumberpatch 2015, 277).

But, while detectorists are contributing so much to our understanding of the county's past, it is best to keep the few nighthawks we know are active in perspective.

A well-deserved recognition

As a recognition of Andrew Rogerson's contribution to archaeology his friends and colleagues wrote a volume of essays in his honour (Ashley and Marsden 2014) with the very apt title of *Landscapes and Artefacts* reflecting his contribution to landscape studies and to finds recording. This was presented to him while we were all enjoying his hospitality on the lawn at his house in Fransham in July 2014.

A happy outcome

In the autumn of 2015 it was announced that *all* the County-funded members of the team identifying metal detector finds at Gressenhall and in the Castle Museum and the Historic Buildings Adviser in the Historic Environment Service at Gressenhall were to be made redundant in budget cuts from April 2016. This was unbelievably shocking, and it represented the biggest potential setback to the recording and conservation of the county's archaeological heritage for decades. The public response to the proposal was immediate, strong and unprecedented. The following email from Clive Cheesman, an expert in heraldry, was just one of more than a thousand representations made to Norfolk County Council in emails, letters, press articles (*EDP* 13th October 2015, 20th January and 29th[h] January 2016) and in an online petition over the following weeks:

> To whom it may concern:
> I write to express my personal view of the proposed cuts to the budget for identification and recording of archaeological small finds in Norfolk, and specifically the loss of the 2.5 posts funded by the County Council.

> Norfolk's identification and recording service has long been a by-word nationally for an extremely high standard in assessing archaeological small finds and publishing the data. The Norfolk approach to its local small finds was a large part of what inspired both the overall ethos and the detail of the national Portable Antiquities Scheme (PAS), and in the following respects it has continued to embody the spirit of that national initiative:
> - it employs persons of real, relevant archaeological expertise and local knowledge;
> - it lays the foundation for an extremely successful partnership between professional archaeologists, amateur detectorists and other finders;
> - it disseminates information about the county's past quickly, accurately and in a way that is accessible to a very wide public – locally and nationally.
>
> The 2.5 posts under threat are at the core of the service currently offered by the Council, being held by highly respected experts whose reputations extend far beyond the county. Their loss would radically diminish the service's fitness for purpose. The statutory obligations of the Council in regard to treasure would remain, while there would be a serious negative impact on the provision of the identification and advice service under the PAS which do so much to foster good relations between professionals and amateurs, detectorists and landowners, experts and the public..

The All Party Parliamentary Archaeology Group of MPs and Peers wrote to the Council on 17th November 2015 to express their real concern. That was followed by a letter from Professor Lord Renfrew, Chairman of the Treasure Valuation Committee, on 4th December 2015, making the point that:

> Between them, the Norwich Castle Museum and Lynn Museum have acquired 63 cases from Norfolk reported under the Treasure Act in the last two years alone. This represents by far the greatest number of Treasure cases acquired in a single county in England and Wales, a testament to the outstanding work of the Portable Antiquities Scheme (PAS) in Norfolk.

The Norfolk Coroner also wrote to say that she needed the expertise of the team from the Historic Environment Service to give evidence at her Treasure inquests (*EDP* 29th January 2016). The point was made that if she had to obtain that evidence from elsewhere it would certainly cost more.

Some County Councillors were surprised that so many people had said that they would prefer increases in Council Tax than see the HES cut back. Terry Jermy, ward member for Thetford West, said:

I was genuinely surprised when I saw just how many people are in favour of council tax increases. They say turkeys do not vote for Christmas but clearly in Norfolk we do (EDP 30th January 2016).

Then, on January 30th the good news came through that the members of the Environment, Development and Transport Committee had taken note of the comments received and would recommend cancellation of all the proposed cuts to both the Historic Environment and the Record Office budgets and would support an increase in Council Tax instead (*EDP* 30th January and 3rd February 2016). The post of the Historic Buildings Adviser in HES was also to be protected. This was approved by the County's Policy and Resources Committee on 8th February, when councillors were clamouring to be the ones who proposed that this cut be deleted from the 2106/17 budget! Then the decision was confirmed by full Council on 22nd February when the cuts totalling £172,000 to the Historic Environment Service were removed, followed by press headlines 'Archaeology will not be hit by budget cuts' (*EDP* 30th January 2016). The Service had been saved from devastation, and this episode genuinely did show how much Norfolk people do care about their past.

It is often said that the work we did in the early years in co-operating with detectorists later laid the foundations of what became the national Portable Antiquities Scheme (eg Thomas 2008, 2), and I think that is probably a fair and accurate assessment. But, there was actually no other way, and the rewards in terms of our increased understanding of the county's archaeology all speak for themselves.

Chapter 10:
Urban Surveys

The King's Lynn Survey, 1962-71

The King's Lynn Survey was a remarkable project with excavations spanning most of the 1960s, leading to the publication of three fine and important volumes. This was one of the first urban surveys and it was founded following a visit to the town by the Society for Medieval Archaeology in 1962 in response to the obvious need for archaeological recording in advance of the (some would say hideous) redevelopment of much of the town centre. The survey was launched the next year, but work was already under way with Vanessa Parker recording the historic buildings for the King's Lynn Preservation Trust and the Society for the Protection of Ancient Buildings. Her volume, *The Making of King's Lynn: Secular Buildings from the 11th to the 17th Century* appeared in 1971, and it was one of the first comprehensive surveys of the historic buildings of a provincial town. Forty-five years later it is still a very useful study.

The first archaeologist appointed to carry out excavations for the Survey was Helen Parker (now Dr Helen Clarke), followed by Eric Talbot and then by Alan Carter. Between 1963 and 1970 they carried out five major excavations and many smaller ones focusing particularly on the medieval waterfronts. Helen's most memorable discovery was the thirteenth-century timber wharf excavated within the courtyard of Thoresby College in 1964. The volume on these excavations by Helen and Alan came out in 1977 as a Society for Medieval Archaeology Monograph *Excavations in King's Lynn 1963-1970* with an important concluding chapter on the development of the town. This monograph helped to bring the archaeology of King's Lynn to a wider audience, and it became a standard well-used reference work for many archaeologists. Finally, Dorothy Owen's work on the documents was published in 1984 as *The Making of King's Lynn: A Documentary Survey*.

As one of England's four most important ports during the Middle Ages, King's Lynn, with its strong Hanseatic presence and exceptionally good organic preservation, is a place with great archaeological potential. It was a pity that the Survey came to an end when Alan moved to Norwich to run the Norwich Survey in 1971.

The Norwich Survey, 1971-2002

The story of the Norwich Survey is one of triumph and tragedy. The concept of setting up this entirely new organisation to study the archaeology and history of the city was born out of a lecture given by Martin Biddle to the Regional History

Dining Group at the UEA on 5th December 1969. When the after-dinner coffee was cleared away Martin gave a brilliant lecture on his Winchester excavations, as he always did, and those present were fired up to go away and start a similar project for Norwich. Leading the initiative was Dr Alfred Hassell Smith (known to everyone simply as 'Hassell'), an historian and the first Director of the Centre of East Anglian Studies (CEAS), which he had set up within the university in 1967 (obituary *The Guardian* 5th September 2013).

Survey structure

The CEAS was designed to be an interdisciplinary bridge within UEA and a link between the UEA and the wider community. It was not attached to any one School of the university, and membership by people outside the university was encouraged. So, it was logical that the Norwich Survey should be based in the CEAS where it was established in 1971. The Survey's role was to study the evidence for the origins and development of the city by researching the archaeology, the architecture and the documents. There was a new 'Norwich Survey Committee' with a chairman appointed by the main Centre committee, and it had 19 members representing the various interested parties as follows:

4 academics representing the Centre,
4 from the City Council,
3 from the Department of the Environment,
2 from Norfolk County Council,
1 one from the Norfolk and Norwich Archaeological Society,
1 from the Cathedral Dean and Chapter,
1 from the Norfolk Association of Architects,
1 from the Norfolk Research Committee,
1 from the Norwich Society.

There was also an executive subcommittee, chaired mostly by Dr Roger Virgoe (1932-96; obituary *EDP* 26th October 1996).), an academic who taught fourteenth- and fifteenth-century history in the School of English and American Studies. A publications sub-committee was later formed and chaired by Don Macreth, who was also running excavations at the time for the Nene Valley Research Committee. The executive sub-committee reported twice a year to the main committee, and the minutes of both committees are preserved in the Norfolk Record Office (ACC 2005/388: Boxes 3,5 and 26). These minutes are both elaborate and very formal, and over the years the Survey staff, except for the Director, had no direct access to either committee. There appears to have been no opportunity for a debate between the two committees and their staff, and when reading the minutes one has the impression that this top-heavy structure created a situation where the committee members were hardly involved in the issues the staff had to face. The lack of anyone with real management expertise on the main committee or its executive sub-committee is now obvious. There appears to have been a lack of control over the running of the Survey, with everything essentially in the hands of one hard-pressed iconic figure, Alan Carter, who was appointed Director in 1971. Alan was a brilliant and highly-respected archaeologist who had a real vision for developing an integrated multi-disciplinary approach to the research. This enabled him to build up a team of archaeologists, historic building specialists and documentary historians to do really worthwhile research. But it was not easy for an academic to run a complex project and be responsible for the finances with funding coming from many different sources, each with their own expectations. The Norfolk Museums Service contributed one post, initially filled by Jan Roberts and then by Malcolm Atkin, to supervise the excavations. They were expected to work in the Castle Museum and not with the rest of the team at the university, which in itself created a divided structure with poor communication between the two locations. In the 1970s and 1980s good managers were not as valued as they are today, and research ability counted for more. It appears that by 1980 communication between the committees and their staff in the various locations had all but broken down.

Excavation programme

Funding came from the Department of the Environment, Norwich City Council, the County Council, the Royal Commission on Historical Monuments and the UEA itself. It covered an eight-year programme of excavations run between 1971 and 1978. A Gazetteer of the 30 excavations and the 15 observations of building sites can be found in the *Norwich Households* volume which mainly describes the small finds (Margeson 1993, 241-242). The excavations ranged from extended watching briefs to large-scale sites covering multiple medieval tenements. Preference was given to those sites which would shed light on the origins and early growth of the city and on the development of late medieval housing.

Dave Evans, who was brought in as a member of the team to assist with publication work from January 1982, has written to say that he has:

> .... *very fond memories of my time at the Norwich Survey; it was a very productive period, working in a wonderfully creative atmosphere, with a very interesting and eclectic mix of people.*

Malcolm Atkin has also written to say:

> *I look back at this time with a strange mixture of pride, sadness and regret. The Norwich Survey did achieve so much. It could have achieved so much more. It was*

> the product of an exciting and wide-ranging partnership – but this led to problems of coordination and control. Alan was the architect of its vision and success, and it is so sad that his illness meant he could not bring it properly to conclusion. I think also that there was a fundamental problem with stand-alone, fixed-term projects which hampered the post-excavation planning.

The site-by-site funding structure required by English Heritage (EH) certainly did not make it easy to manage a closely integrated urban research project, but one can understand that EH did need to have some control over how its money was spent.

Excellent interim reports on all the excavations were published regularly each year in the 1970s in *Norwich Archaeology* (Carter 1972; Carter and Roberts 1973; Carter, Roberts and Sutermeister 1974; Roberts, Donaldson, Cleary and Dunmore 1975; Atkin and Carter with Baxter, Donaldson and Roberts 1976; Atkin and Carter 1977; Atkin and Sutermeister 1978).

The vision

A booklet entitled *The Norwich Survey 1971-1980* (Carter 1980), written after the excavations had been concluded, described in rather expansive tones what had been achieved by 1980 and what was to happen next:

> The 37 excavations that we have carried out have, for instance, allowed us to produce a reconstruction of the pattern of growth of the 10th- and 11th-century town, the defences of which have been firmly dated to c. 900; while for the later periods we can now produce a convincing and coherent explanation of the pattern of late medieval housing (something which has not yet been attempted in any other English town). On the documentary side we have produced a property-by-property survey of ownership in the period between 1284 and 1346; and for the period between 1580 and 1730 compiled a detailed analysis of all 1500 buildings recorded in probate inventories. The buildings' team has now investigated half of the city's area: producing not just individual descriptions of buildings (including a newly-discovered 12th-century hall and some 53 medieval vaulted undercrofts) but also the beginnings of a synthesised account of their development.

The booklet went on to say that Malcolm Atkin and Alan Carter, with the assistance of Philip Judge as illustrator, were responsible for the publication of 37 excavations, so this must have included both the formal excavations and some of the 15 watching briefs. For the historic buildings, a team consisting of Robert Smith, Frank Woodman and Peter Eden had been working on a house-to-house survey, recording their results on record cards illustrated with small-scale plans and photographs. They were more than half way through that survey by 1980, and once that was finished a selection of 50 to 100 buildings would be chosen for more detailed recording.

Documentary research

On the documents front, the main focus was on the analysis of the city's medieval enrolled deeds dating between 1285 and 1340. When properties were transferred the details of neighbouring holdings were also recorded in the deeds, and so it is possible to build up the tenement pattern of the whole city. The end result was to be an atlas of the medieval properties of Norwich. The initial drive for this came from Helen Sutermeister who was employed to develop the documentary research, but there were many others, some acting as volunteers, who did impressive work – Margot Tillyard, Alayne Fenner, Ursula Priestley, Serena Kelly and Elizabeth Rutledge. This fitted perfectly with the ethos of the CEAS, linking the wider community with academics in the university.

Although no atlas of the properties was published, there is a most useful card index for each transaction recorded by the Court Rolls and an impressive series of 137 hand-coloured reconstruction plans showing the layout of all the properties within each block of streets, and these are available for study in the Norfolk Record Office (NRO MC146/52). This was pioneering work inspired by H.E. Salter who in his *Survey of Oxford* (1966 and 1969) built up similar reconstruction plans of Oxford relating all property deeds to each tenement. The reconstruction plans for Norwich 1285-1340, a much larger city, should be considered a substantial achievement and deserve to be better known. It was possible to relate directly the property boundaries located in several of the excavations to those identified in the enrolled deeds. The fruits of this work first showed themselves in Helen Sutermeister's contribution to the interim report on the Oak Street excavation (Atkin and Sutermeister 1978, 35-44). The key articles on this documentary research are 'The Acquisition by the Norwich Blackfriars of the Site for their Church *c*. 1310-1325' by Margot Tillyard, 'The Economic Topography and Structure of Norwich *c*. 1300' by Serena Kelly and 'Property Transfer and Enrolment in Norwich 1285-1311' by Elizabeth Rutledge all in *Men of Property* published by the Norwich Survey (Kelly, Rutledge and Tillyard 1983).

Building surveys

There was to be a report on the secular buildings of the city for a volume by Robert Smith, a volume on the many Norwich churches by Frank Woodman, and a volume on clay pipes by Suzanne Atkin. There was also a suggestion in the committee minutes that there was to be a concluding volume on the work of the Survey, but none of these materialised, and they were all abandoned by October 1985. The card index of the buildings is in the Norfolk Record Office (ACC 2005/388 and copies of some building reports are held in the Historic Environment Record at Gressenhall). Robert Smith used the data for his M.Phil UEA thesis, and Robert and Alan wrote an important article on Norwich buildings before 1700 for *Vernacular Architecture* Vol. 14 (Smith and Carter 1983). Incomplete copies of drafts of Frank Woodman's church survey reports and plans are held by various people, with some at Gressenhall, but it seems that the most developed version of his text was on a computer disc which became corrupted.

Excavation reports

Part 1 of the excavation reports appeared in East Anglian Archaeology in 1982 (Carter ed. 1982). Part 2 covered excavations with themes such as anti-social industries, the evidence of Strangers in Norwich and the development of investment properties, and this came out in EAA in 1985 (Atkin, Carter and Evans 1985). With Part 2 there were microfiche with detailed site matrices, pottery histograms, detailed listing of all the small finds, clay pipes, ceramic building materials, environmental evidence and additional archive sections.

By 1985 English Heritage funding had dried up, and the Survey committee decided to make the whole team redundant, although many reports still remained unfinished. Reading through the executive subcommittee minutes now, one has the feeling that the committee members were not sufficiently in touch with the staff and were too remote from the problems their decisions were creating. After the team had all moved on to other jobs it was somehow expected that they would continue unpaid to complete the remaining two excavation volumes on a voluntary basis. That was left primarily to Dave Evans who went in February to a job in Aberdeen, Malcolm Atkin who left in June for a post in Gloucester and Sarah Jennings, the pottery researcher, who moved in the autumn to work in Lincoln. With so much work still to be done, both with writing the reports and particularly with preparing the site archives for deposition, the decision to disperse the team looks now thoroughly unwise and unrealistic.

Alan had ceased to have much involvement with the Survey by 1986, having been increasingly off work with a serious mental illness leading to a breakdown in 1984. No doubt this gave the impression to funders, particularly English Heritage, that further grants would not yield results. Non-publication was a problem not peculiar to the Norwich Survey, for many urban units were developing extensive backlogs and making little progress with clearing them. For English Heritage there had to be a cap on funding when expensive urban excavations in particular over-ran their timetables. The Norwich Survey committees needed to act decisively to turn things around and rectify an obviously deteriorating situation. But they probably did not have the understanding or the capability to do that, for the CEAS was not part of a university School and therefore did not have the resources of a larger university body to fall back upon. The Centre was very much on its own. I did attend some meetings of the executive sub-committee during the handover of excavation responsibilities between the Survey and Norfolk Archaeological Unit, and it is interesting that I can remember absolutely nothing about these meetings. There is a sad description by Don Macreth dated 11th May 1987 interleaved with the committee minutes describing how Alan had turned up at the end of a publications subcommittee meeting but 'was clearly not in any state to undertake any work for the Survey'. I am told that Don, as the chair of the publications sub-committee, was a pillar of strength for Dave and Malcolm over these several difficult years.

There are increasingly desperate memos surviving from Sue Margeson at the museum who seems to have been lumbered with closing down the project and archiving the records and finds as best she could without any financial support while having a full-time job in the museum. On 28th May 1987 she wrote to English Heritage:

> **Archiving** *Neither the financial implications, nor the staffing and timetabling implications, of the archiving of the Norwich Survey material have ever been taken into account in applications for funding (despite persistent reminders by EBG at Sub-committee meetings).*
> *The archiving is an enormous problem, as the Norwich Survey is a major project (comparable to Winchester).. The Castle Museum can in no way assist in the preparation of the archive (other than general advice), as the Director is anxious for me to be back full time in the museum as soon as possible and there is no-one else available.*
> (EBG = Barbara Green, Keeper of Archaeology at the Castle Museum)

On 15th June English Heritage wrote to Sue saying:

> *We appreciate the problem that the Norwich Survey project has experienced but I am afraid that we cannot offer a further grant, particularly in view of the final additional funding provided last year. We consider that responsibility for the completion of the project rests with the City Council.*

English Heritage inspectors clearly took the decision that they had already put in enough. Many urban excavations at the time were over-running their budgets and not producing reports, and English Heritage clearly had to bring their funding to a close. The Survey's employment of the last member of staff, the loyal illustrator

Phillip Judge, was concluded at the end of June 1987, and he was moved to another department. Then there was no-one. The Director of the Museums Service would have been quite entitled to say to the Survey committee and to the Centre of East Anglian Studies that he would not accept the archive until it had been assembled to museum standards so that the record could be studied in the future. All excavation projects need to include adequate arrangements in their budgets for assembling and depositing the archives as well the preparation of final reports, and museums cannot afford to be dumping grounds for inadequately prepared archives.

The Survey committees appear to have run out of steam entirely by now, and they were in a state of some paralysis. The last meeting of the main committee was held on 4th November 1987, and Barbara Miller, the chairman, sent a memo around to all members of the main committee and the executive subcommittee dated 18th January 1988 formally winding up the Survey. Thereafter, responsibility passed back to CEAS.

After a long illness Alan took his own life on 13th August 1988 (Obituaries to Alan in *The Times* 24th and 30th August 1988; inquest verdict *EDP* 26th August 1988), and with the team's dispersal, progress became increasingly difficult. It was an act of sheer persistence by Malcolm Atkin and Dave Evans that Part 3 was finished at all. This volume, looking at land use in different parts of the city, was submitted to English Heritage for approval in 1990, but EH then insisted that two animal bone reports be re-written, although there would be no-one available to do that for five years. Dave offered to drop the offending bone reports altogether, but EH would not permit that, and the volume appeared in 2002 (Atkin and Evans 2002). A very useful Discussion section by Dave and Malcolm in that volume brings together the main outcomes of the Survey's archaeological work. The volume was launched at a special reception in the keep at the Castle Museum on 31st October to celebrate both Malcolm and Dave's achievement in getting out what proved to be their final volume and to celebrate the publication of the hundredth volume of East Anglian Archaeology, including 60 on Norfolk and Norwich. We had two guest speakers, Adrian Olivier, Head of Archaeological Policy at English Heritage, who spoke on the achievements of EAA, and Hassell Smith who gave a warm appreciation of Alan Carter and his leadership of the Norwich Survey. The event was a very happy occasion, and it was a real pleasure that Alan's wife, Frances, and their two sons, Tim and Finbar, were able to join us. After the reception 18 members of Alan's team had supper together at the King of Hearts in the city (Smith 2003).

Part 3 brought the number of sites published to 20, with a further ten remaining. Of these only three really merited publication, namely:

70-78 Oak Street (site 351N)
Carrow Abbey (site 296N)
Bacon's House, 31 Colegate (site 172N).

A decision was taken to archive and not to publish nine of the ten and to focus just on the 1977 Oak Street site (interim report in Atkin and Sutermeister 1978) in one further volume.

The 70-78 Oak Street site was a large-scale open-area excavation of a whole block of properties and associated tenements supported with good documentation, and it could have led potentially to a showpiece report (*Figure 10.1*). Dave Evans remembers that Malcolm did write a draft text and a paper copy was deposited with the site archive in the Castle Museum, but four years later it could not be found. Malcolm's computer had died and a digital copy could not be retrieved.

The excavation archives were transferred to the Castle Museum in the late 1980s where Sue Margeson and Bill Milligan in the Archaeology Department did what they could with the material. An archaeologist who has recently attempted to work in the museum on the archive of one of the unpublished excavations has described the state of the archive to me in less than glowing terms. There is certainly no catalogue of the whole Survey archive, and compiling one is surely a high priority for the Norfolk Museums Service, having accepted the collection.

10.1. *An excavation by the Norwich Survey in Oak Street, Norwich with sixteenth/seventeenth-century levels showing the multi-tenement nature of the site with wells and cess pits (Norfolk Museums and Archaeology Service).*

Nevertheless, three fine volumes of excavation reports were published, and it is important to view this achievement in a national context. Given that funding was limited when compared with the income available to the larger urban units in York, Lincoln, Winchester and London it actually completed much good work and left a strong legacy of publications with a substantial academic content. Elsewhere outcomes were mixed. The model for Norwich was Martin Biddle's work in Winchester for which ten interim reports were published in *The Antiquaries Journal*. Had Martin followed these with final reports, the results could have been epoch-making for urban archaeology at the time, but 40 to 50 years later little has appeared other than the report on the Romano-British cemetery at Lankhills, an exemplary study of the Winchester Domesday and a massive finds volume. But there is some encouraging news that the report on the Old Minster, a site of international significance, is due to be published in 2017. The York Archaeological Trust, set up in 1972 and still excavating, has produced a stream of fascicules on various aspects of sites and finds, but only for the Roman sewer has there been a comprehensive report on an excavation. The rest of the information is in archive. For Lincoln few sites excavated between the early 1970s and the 1990s have been fully published; as at York, they have opted to publish selective aspects just as fascicules. The Suffolk Archaeological Unit dug 34 sites in Ipswich from 1974 to 1990 yet little appeared in print. The good news is that the records of the Ipswich work are now on line and there are proposals for at least a summary volume to appear in East Anglian Archaeology. So, in the wider context of urban archaeology in the 1970s and 1980s there is so much the surviving Norwich Survey team can justifiably feel very proud of.

Two further important volumes were published which have become standard works of reference; one describes a fine collection of largely un-stratified pottery from the city (Jennings 1981) and the other is a superb volume by Sue Margeson on the small finds from the excavations entitled *Norwich Households* (Margeson 1993). She very thoughtfully presented these finds in functional categories such as dress accessories, textile-working equipment, horse gear etc, rather than in the traditional material categories, such as 'Copper Alloy' and 'Iron' etc. This was a refreshing change from what we had done before. A 1507 cellar group from Pottergate was deemed to be so significant that it featured in the 1985 British Museum exhibition 'Archaeology in Britain since 1945', and that collection is often cited in overviews of English urban archaeology. A beautifully illustrated booklet, *Life on a Medieval Street*, is an example of how to write a popular account of a complex urban excavation, and it has been widely used as a teaching aid for schools (Atkin and Margeson 1985). Then, *Shops and Shopkeepers in Norwich 1660-1730* is a very readable account of shopping in Norwich in the seventeenth and eighteenth centuries based on shopkeepers' probate inventories (Priestley and Fenner 1985).

Alan wrote an article on the Survey's research on the origins of Norwich (Carter 1978a) and on his sampling strategy for the city (Carter 1978b), although the former has been inevitably superseded by a more recent paper on the early development of the city by Brian Ayers (2011) who ran the excavations in Norwich for the Norfolk Archaeological Unit from 1979. There were also popular books by Malcolm Atkin (1993) and by Brian Ayers (1994a) on the archaeology and history of the city. Brian has since written important articles on the development of the city's urban landscape based partly on the Survey's work (Ayers 1993, 2004 and 2015).

In the background of any discussion about the achievements of the Survey there will always be considerable sadness caused by the pre-mature death from cancer at the age of only 36 in 1979 of Helen Sutermeister, who was leading the documentary research. Then there was Alan's death at the age of 44 in 1988, followed by the deaths after they had left the project of no less than three other key contributors: Jan Roberts, who supervised excavations up until 1975, at the age of 46 in 1992; then Sue Margeson in the Castle Museum, who wrote the 'Norwich Households' volume, at the age of only 48 in 1997 (Obituaries in *The Times* 22nd March 1997; *The Guardian* 25th March 1997; *EDP* 3rd April 1997) and Sarah Jennings, the pottery specialist, at the age of 62 in 2009. Roger Virgoe, the executive sub-committee's chairman, was taken ill with motor neurone disease some time before he was due to retire and died at the age of 64 in 1996. Don Macreth has also recently died. A jinx indeed.

The Survey had many successes, and in addition to the Survey's formal publications, there were significant spin-off publications and articles as well:

Norwich Survey articles in addition to the formal Survey publications:

Atkin, M.W., 1983a. 'The chalk tunnels of Norwich' *Norfolk Archaeology* 38, 313-20.

Atkin, M.W., 1983. 'The Anglo-Saxon urban landscape in East Anglia' *Landscape History* 7, 27-40.

Atkin, M.W., 1988. 'A lost building tradition in Norwich' *British Archaeology* 10, 8-10.

Atkin, M.W., 1991. 'Medieval clay-walled buildings in Norwich' *Norfolk Archaeology* 41, 171-85.

Atkin, M., 1993. *Norwich History and Guide*. Alan Sutton Publishing.

Atkin, M. 1993. 'The Norwich Survey 1971-1985 – a retrospective view' in J. Gardner (ed), *Flatlands and Wetlands*, East Anglian Archaeology 50, 127-143.

Atkin, M., Ayers, B. and Jennings, S., 1983. *Thetford-type ware production in Norwich*, East Anglian Archaeology 17, 61-97.

Atkin, M. W. and Evans, D.H., 1984. 'Population, profit and plague: the archaeological interpretation of buildings and landuse in Norwich', *Scottish Archaeological Review* 3, 92-98.

Atkin, M.W. and Smith, R., 1979. 'Norwich', *Current Archaeology* 68, 280-84.

Atkin, S. 1985. 'The clay pipe making industry in Norfolk', *Norfolk Archaeology* 39, 118-49.

Carter, A., 1978a. 'The Anglo-Saxon origins of Norwich: the problems and approaches', *Anglo-Saxon England* 7, 173-204.

Carter, A., 1978b. 'Sampling in a medieval town: the study of Norwich', *Sampling in contemporary British archaeology*, British Archaeological Reports (British. Series.) 50, 263-77.

Jennings, S. and Atkin, M.W., 1984. 'A 17th-century well group from St Stephen's Street, Norwich (site 301N)', *Norfolk Archaeology* 39, 13-37.

Karshner, M., 1979. 'The tobacco clay pipe making industry in Norwich', in P.J. Davey (ed.) *The Archaeology of the Clay Tobacco Pipe I. Britain: the Midlands and Eastern England,* 295-352. British Archaeological Report (British Series) 63, 295-352.

Luckhurst, D., 1983. *Norwich: An architectural Map.* Centre of East Anglian Studies, University of East Anglia.

Priestley, U.M. and Corfield, P.J., 1982. 'Rooms and room use in Norwich housing, 1580-1730', *Post-medieval Archaeology* 16, 93-123.

Smith, R. and Carter, A., 1983. 'Function and Site: aspects of Norwich buildings before 1700', *Vernacular Architecture* 14, 5-18.

Note: The author is especially grateful to Dave Evans, Malcolm Atkin, Elizabeth Rutledge and Brian Ayers for their many helpful comments and suggestions during the preparation of this chapter.

Chapter 11:
The 'RESCUE' Movement, The Scole Committee and the Birth of Professional County Units

'RESCUE'

The 1960s was the time when British archaeologists gradually woke up to the greatly increased rate of destruction to our archaeology. It could be said that the publication which triggered the debate was a book cleverly called *A Matter of Time*, published by the Royal Commission on Historical Monuments in 1960, demonstrating the great wealth of crop-mark archaeology on the English river gravels. It featured impressive aerial photographs, mainly by J.K. St Joseph, of enclosures, circles, cursuses and pit alignments, many vulnerable from impending gravel quarrying. The report, written by H.C. Bowen and R.M. Butler in a rather archaic, but no less effective, style underlined the urgency for action. It drew attention to parishes like Maxey in Northamptonshire with its extra-ordinarily rich concentration of crop-marks under immediate threat from gravel workings. The report's Summary and Recommendations concluded:

> ..time is short, for, as the demand for gravel increases and more efficient machinery is introduced, the process of destruction becomes faster and more thorough. Survey and excavation achieved now will disclose information about the settlement of ancient Britain and its peoples which must otherwise be irretrievably lost (RCHM 1960, 46).

But the profession's response was slow, partly because at that time there were still not many of us, and those who could be concerned were mostly too ensconced in museums, universities and university extra-mural departments to appreciate the scale of the damage. But what happened next is well documented in a chapter by Phil Barker on 'The Origins and Development of RESCUE' in *Rescue Archaeology*, a Penguin book edited by Philip Rahtz (Barker 1974).

A conference of university archaeology extra-mural tutors meeting in Bristol in May 1969 heard a talk by an un-named delegate who castigated members of the profession for being 'diffuse in its aims, woolly in its thinking, disunited, unaggressive and complaining' from their ivory towers. That moment was like pulling a trigger, and it was followed by a meeting of some 30 archaeologists at Westham House at Barford in Warwickshire over three days in February 1970 to discuss what should be done. A copy of the minutes of that event, marked 'NOT FOR

PRESS', is preserved in Norfolk Research Committee box files in the Castle Museum which suggests that the minutes may well have been distributed fairly widely at the time. The list of the 30 attendees at the event now reads like a checklist of the most forward-thinking British archaeologists prominent in their day (**Appendix 3)**. It is interesting to read their perception of the current state of archaeology in Britain after they had all had witnessed rampant destruction over the previous 20 years. Their assessment was:

(i) The rate, extent and completeness of the destruction of archaeological sites of all periods is increasing nationally so rapidly that few intact sites will remain by the end of the 20th century unless positive action is taken now.

(ii) Many more sites exist than all previous estimates have indicated and therefore the scale of current and predictable destruction, with all that this implies in terms of lost knowledge and amenity, is and will be absolutely greater.

(iii) Present archaeological resources and organisation are inadequate to cope with either the minimum necessary recording and excavation in advance of and during destruction or with the conservation of our field antiquities if we want even a representative sample of our formerly rich archaeological heritage to survive into the next century.

Their consensus was:

The present organisation of British archaeological resources is largely fragmented .... it is in any case inefficient, and quite inadequate to cope with the present and foreseeable problem of archaeological destruction.

They discussed a range of options, but it appears that there was most support for a 'completely new National Archaeological Service, independent or state-run, primarily to tackle rescue work'. The Minister was also to be pressed to make a decision on the recommendations in the 1969 Walsh Committee report on the management of field monuments (Wade Martins, S. 2015, 146-147) and to revise the 1931 Ancient Monuments Act.

The original six convenors of the Barford meeting (John Alexander, Philip Barker, Martin Biddle, Barry Cunliffe, Peter Fowler and Charles Thomas) were appointed as a working party to take further action. The Barford event was followed by a repeat at Newcastle in November, attended by 50 archaeologists, many from the north of England, Scotland and Northern Ireland. The Newcastle gathering proposed that there should be a public meeting to be held in London in January 1971. This took place in a large lecture theatre in the Senate House on 23rd January attended by over 700 people with an average age of about 30. The atmosphere at the meeting was electric. Like many at that meeting, I thought that things could never be quite the same again.

There were two key proposals put to the Senate House meeting. One was a long-term aim to set up a state antiquities service which would, through 20 regional centres, provide an effective service capable of responding to emergency situations well in advance of development. The service would also store the data from surveys so that threats to sites could be dealt with properly in advance of destruction. Presumably that meant that each area would organise surveys of their local archaeology and then feed the data into local Sites and Monuments Records. The meeting also agreed to set up a new organisation to be called RESCUE which would obtain funds through individual subscriptions, donations and appeals. RESCUE would raise public awareness, work towards revised antiquities legislation, promote the need for better data collection through surveys and publication, improve training and record and preserve the remains of Britain's past. A RESCUE deputation went to see the Minister of Housing and Construction, Julian Amery. A set of 30 colour slides were made available and a panel of 70 speakers were urged to take the case for change to the wider public. An immediate government response was to almost double the money available to rescue archaeology in 1972 which was doubled again in 1973. The RESCUE logo of a large bulldozer scooping up a part of Stonehenge was deeply effective.

In 1973 RESCUE published a formidable document by Martin Biddle and others *The Future of London's Past* with large maps and overlays of London showing the city period by period with two impressive overlays on which were marked in bright red areas to be developed in the near future (permission outstanding) and areas of proposed redevelopment at September 1972. The text was Biddle at his best:

> *By the end of the 1980s the archaeology of the City will survive only in a few isolated pockets: below some open spaces, below a few churches, beneath some buildings in the conservation areas. The surviving areas of archaeological deposits will be entirely insufficient to preserve an adequate picture of the City's origin and development. (Biddle, Hudson and Heighway 1973, 51)*

The City Corporation's response was immediate. A Department of Urban Archaeology was set up in the Guildhall Museum before the end of that year, later becoming a part of the new Museum of London in June 1975 (Sheldon, Dennis and Densem 2015, xxii).

The idea of a National Archaeological Service operating through regional offices was repeated in a joint statement by RESCUE and the Council for British Archaeology (CBA) in 1974. But that was not to be, probably because more local alternatives were already emerging (Sheldon, Dennis and Densem 2015, xix).

The Scole Committee

By 1970 there was a real feeling amongst those of us working in archaeology in our region that something needed to be done locally to reflect the RESCUE initiative; a new start was necessary. The first local response to 'Barford' was that the Norfolk Research Committee and the local Group of the Council for British Archaeology wrote co-ordinated letters to Norfolk County Council in December 1970 urging the Council to appoint a County Archaeology Officer, but their requests were declined. So, Alan Carter, by then Director of the Norwich Survey, Stanley West, who had taken on the part-time role of setting up a Suffolk Sites and Monuments Record with some support from Suffolk County Council (West 2015), and I decided to call our own Barford meeting. This was held on 26th November 1971 at the Old Scole Inn on the Norfolk/Suffolk border. The village of Scole was actually built on a Roman settlement at the river crossing of the main Roman road from Colchester up to the Roman town at Caistor St Edmund. The centre of the Roman town was threatened with extensive housing development, so it seemed a very appropriate place to meet. Scole was also a central place for the Norfolk and Suffolk area.

The reasons we gave for the meeting were three:
1. There was an urgent need to co-ordinate effort amongst field archaeologists in Norfolk and Suffolk
2. There was an equally urgent need for detailed discussions on priorities in East Anglian archaeology
3. We felt that 'an organisation' of some sort should be formed to prepare and implement practical policies to deal with the situation in East Anglia and to promote the aims of RESCUE.

The Scole Committee was all part of the national awakening and the realisation that a new profession of 'field' archaeologists, as opposed to 'museum' archaeologists, was the only way to face up to the many challenges we were facing in the towns and in the countryside. We had to teach ourselves to be assertive, and we were determined locally not to be outshone by national RESCUE. The minutes of the Scole Committee are, thank goodness, preserved in the Norfolk Archives Centre (ACC 2008/77 and 146, 2009/712011/16), although one has to say that the early minutes are not particularly informative, and several of the agenda papers are missing. David Penrose was elected chair, Stanley West was made secretary and John Wymer was a willing treasurer. The committee agreed that:
1. In principle it should act as the regional group for RESCUE
2. A report on the present state of archaeology in East Anglia should be prepared with details of the numbers of destroyed and threatened sites
3. That a system of priorities be established for rescue excavations in East Anglia.

On 11th February 1972 the Committee discussed possible dates for public meetings. The idea of having travelling exhibitions would also be explored, although neither, as it turned out, were necessary.

At the third meeting on 16th June, Graham Arnold, RESCUE's publicity officer, attended and explained how they were promoting the cause through public meetings, posters, brochures and travelling exhibitions. His advice was to focus public attention on one particular issue for the region, and the committee agreed that the issue for us should be the threat to archaeology in Ipswich from development proposals.

A *brief spell in Winchester*

In March 1972 I took up the newly-created post as City Rescue Archaeologist in Winchester, but while it was an honour to be asked, it soon became clear that I had made a big mistake. Martin Biddle's major programme of excavations had just come to an end, and funding was, quite rightly, all going into his publication programme. There was no new money for further excavations, and I quickly realised that it was not possible to run a worthwhile urban excavation programme just with volunteers. Those days had gone. Within a few months I had, regretfully, handed in my notice and was returning home rather wiser.

The Norfolk Archaeological Unit: the birth of the first county-based professional field unit in Britain, from 1973

Proposals for a Norfolk Archaeological Unit

Meanwhile, during early 1972 I had been in touch with John Hurst, the Ancient Monuments Inspector who had been so supportive with funds for my own excavations at Grenstein and at North Elmham. He offered us a block grant to set up a Norfolk Archaeological Unit as from April 1973, so I was able to present proposals for a Unit at the June 1972 meeting of the Scole Committee. The committee warmly supported the idea, agreed to take responsibility for the Unit and for the funds on offer. The estimates for the Unit's excavations would need to be agreed by the Scole Committee in order to maintain and develop a co-ordinated regional programme. They would also, of course, need approval from Ancient Monuments inspectors. But, we now had a structure in place, a method of employing staff and a procedure for having key projects approved well in advance, all within seven months.

At the fourth meeting of the committee on 14th October 1972 a formal constitution for the Unit was agreed, particularly to satisfy the wishes of the staff who wanted it to be run as democratically as possible. That tradition of democratic decision making, where members of the staff were closely involved with every significant management decision, lasted until the original NAU was split up in April 1991. Indeed, I don't believe that there was ever any sign of a worker/management dispute. It was not in our thinking. We did later have a union representative on the staff, Sue White, but she was usually as involved as I was in the key decisions. To make the Unit as democratic as possible we held staff meetings on the first Tuesday of each month when we all reported, and key issues were thoroughly discussed.

These meetings were minuted, and it was my intention that they would form a key part of the Unit archive in due course. However, the whole collection was put through the shredder a few years after I left the office by a new secretary who said she had been told that these papers were no longer needed. Who gave that instruction I could never discover. The lesson to be learned from this dismal story is never to rely on offices taking care of their own out-of-date documents and to give them as soon as possible to a county Record Office. That applies equally to museum records. I gather that none of the office files for the rescue excavation projects described in later sections of this book are likely to survive either, which is a great pity because background information about an excavation is often an important part of the story. There is surely no good reason why these office files should not be deposited as a part of the excavation archive after the project is published.

Because of the destruction of the Unit archive, some details which follow are not always quite as precise as they should be. The main sources have been the minutes and papers of the Scole Committee and the County Council's Norfolk Archaeological Services Advisory Committee, or NASAC as it was usually called, set up when the Unit was transferred to Norfolk County Council. These are full of useful detail.

Some of the proposed Norfolk Unit staff, namely Keith Wade, Andrew Rogerson, Bob Carr and Derek Edwards, had been excavating at North Elmham Park. But this left us short of expertise for prehistory and for the Roman period, so the two posts were advertised. Andrew Lawson, who later went on to run Wessex Archaeology, was appointed as Field Officer for pre-history and Chris Green (or Christopher Sparey Green, as he later wished to be called) was appointed as Field Officer for the Roman period in October 1972. Edwin Rose was appointed in 1974 as Records Officer to develop and run the Sites and Monuments Record.

At the fifth Scole Committee meeting on 25th November 1972 it was agreed that a whole-day seminar for the committee on 'The State of Archaeology in East Anglia' should take place on 18th December at Stanley West's house at Walsham-le-Willows. This was to write a report on the situation in the region. Also, the constitution of the NAU was revised in the light of comments

Chapter 11: The 'Rescue' Movement, The Scole Committee and Professional County Units

from the Department of the Environment which insisted that the Unit had to be run by a Director. I was then appointed Director as from 1st April 1973.

At the sixth meeting on 6th February 1973 the final draft of *The Problems and Future of East Anglian Archaeology* was agreed (*Figure 11.1*). It had been no easy task writing a report by committee but it had been achieved with remarkable speed. At the seventh meeting on 18th April it was announced that the report would be printed by May, and that £50 grants had been offered to cover printing costs from The Suffolk Institute of Archaeology, The Centre for East Anglian Studies at UEA, The Norfolk and Norwich Archaeological Society and the Norfolk Research Committee. After

11.1. The report published by the Scole Committee in 1973 on the state of archaeology in East Anglia which was used to argue the case for County Council funding for rescue archaeology in Norfolk and Suffolk.

the report was published it strangely disappeared from view, in that I can't recall it being launched with any publicity or being referred to or used much to make the case for funding. We hardly looked at it again, probably because we were already pushing at open doors with regards to Department of the Environment (DoE) and County Council funding in Norfolk and Suffolk.

The Norfolk Archaeological Unit, as the first county-based field archaeological unit in Britain, came into existence in April 1973. This was followed by Oxfordshire that October (although that was primarily a rescue excavation unit separate from local government) and by the Suffolk Archaeological Unit in April 1974 (Wade-Martins 1974b).

The regional units that never were

However, there was a real problem looming. In the meantime, the Ancient Monuments Inspectorate in the Department of the Environment had decided that although they were now funding the Norfolk Unit, they really wanted to establish a network of *regional* units instead to create a structure which would resemble the state antiquities service that RESCUE had asked for. But these units would have to be funded primarily by county councils. The story was covered in *The Times* on 15th June 1973, when it was explained that the Department of the Environment wanted to see 13 regional centres plus one for Wales and one for Scotland, each with a staff of 50 to run rescue excavations. The Department would fund the initial establishment costs of each centre plus the salary of the regional directors. Otherwise running costs would be covered by local authorities. We all thought the idea was unrealistic because if county councils were to be the main funders, then the organisations they would be supporting would have to be county-based and accountable to those councils. That was the only time I fell out with John Hurst, although I was pretty sure the idea did not originate from him. So, a meeting was held in London on 16th May 1973 (only a few hours after I had been with Susanna when she gave birth to our first child, Richard, in King's Lynn Hospital), with John, myself, Francis Cheetham, who was Director of the Norfolk Museums Service, and Stanley West as Secretary of the Scole Committee. The meeting broke up with a complete impasse. The Department of the Environment started to set up their network of Area Archaeological Advisory Committees by the summer of 1974 in the context of a government policy document produced by the Department of the Environment called *Rescue Archaeology: the Next Phase*. This set out proposals for Area Archaeological Advisory Committees to support the multi-county archaeological units. At the same time, the DoE Ancient Monuments inspectors were actually saying to Norfolk County Council that this regional arrangement would not be allowed to conflict with the new Norfolk Unit. There could still be county units if the counties were willing to pay for them. That did rather sound like a contradiction, and I think the inspectors knew it.

In 1973, as a sign of County Council support for what we were trying to do, the Council offered the Unit temporary accommodation in a redundant workhouse at Pulham Market close to the Ipswich road, just north of Scole. It was a large building, too big for our needs, but it gave us a foothold. Then, in 1974 we were given permanent use of the east wing of the redundant Gressenhall workhouse near East Dereham (*EDP* 20th November & 12th and 14th December 1973 and 16th January 1974; *DAFT* 14th December 1973). The rest of the building was later to become the new county Rural Life Museum. Our telephones were installed on 23th October 1974, and the building has remained the main field archaeology offices

CHAPTER 11: THE 'RESCUE' MOVEMENT, THE SCOLE COMMITTEE AND PROFESSIONAL COUNTY UNITS   149

for Norfolk ever since. The aim was to provide a comprehensive field archaeology service for the county, with a new and more sophisticated Sites and Monuments Record, a remarkably successful programme of air photography which led to so many important discoveries, an advisory service to county and district planning officers and a mechanism which allowed us to set up and run rescue excavations as required. It was later very gratifying when the Unit was described by David Dymond in the Preface to his book *The Norfolk Landscape* as 'that remarkable 'power' house at Gressenhall' (Dymond 1985, 9).

The first season of survey and excavation, 1973

The *EDP* on 20th November 1973 carried a well-informed summary of what we had achieved in our first seven months. It explained that the Scole Committee was advising the county councils and the Department of the Environment on an archaeology policy for the region and that the plan was to set up a Suffolk unit the next year. The Norfolk unit was developing as an effective county archaeology service and would be carrying out field surveys and rescue excavations on a 'large scale'. Just after the unit had started it had been able to organise a rescue excavation on a previously unknown Anglo-Saxon cemetery in a gravel pit at Bergh Apton (**p. 224-226**) (Green and Rogerson 1978). After that, the planned excavation of the Anglo-Saxon cremation cemetery at Spong Hill in North Elmham continued where a further 250 burial urns had been lifted from the field believed to contain several thousand urns which were being slowly eroded by ploughing (Hills 1977). At Scole, on the main Caistor to Colchester Roman road, limited funds had allowed some excavation on the Roman town centre where three carefully turned waterlogged wooden table or stool legs had been found in a well (Rogerson 1977). At the Roman town at Brampton there had been trial excavations of a pottery kiln site (Green 1977). At Harpley a ploughed-down Bronze Age round barrow was being excavated (Lawson 1976a), and at Witton work had just finished on an Early Anglo-Saxon village found by John Owles, the farmer (Wade 1983). At Brancaster our air photography had located an extensive Roman settlement outside the Roman Saxon Shore fort (Edwards 1976). Finally, at Yarmouth a medieval brick-built house due for demolition had been recorded (Dunmore 1978). The supporting photograph with the article showed the restoration of a plough-damaged Spong Hill urn.

1974 Season

Press reports of the Unit's work in 1974 appeared in the *EDP* on 7th October 1974 and in *The Times* on 4th January 1975. That year we excavated the ploughed-down defences of a strange earthwork fort close to the Roman town at Great Walsingham

(p. 115-117). It has never been securely dated, but it remains a possibility that it is a late or sub-Roman fort and is of the greatest importance (Lawson 1976b). At Brancaster we were faced with a planning decision already taken to allow development over all of the extra-mural settlement to the west of the Roman fort. The DoE's advice to the planning authority was that there should just be a watching brief, as if that could ever be enough! Even in those days, the Department of the Environment should have urged a delay of the planning decision until there had been some evaluation excavation to assess the impact of the housing estate on this major Roman monument. The area we could afford to excavate was minimal and much of the site was later built over unexcavated, although the DoE's own Central Excavation Unit did their own excavation in 1977 (Hinchliffe and Green 1985). At Brampton we completed our excavation of a Roman kiln and post-hole Roman buildings threatened by cultivation. At Spong Hill work continued on the Anglo-Saxon cremation cemetery, and on the site of the old Lacons Brewery in Great Yarmouth we excavated deep into the Late Saxon levels of the town prior to a supermarket development. This was a fascinating site with layers of wind-blown sand ten feet deep built up over several centuries. The occupation levels, interspersed by the sand layers, were full of fish bones, highly indicative that Yarmouth flourished on the fishing industry in the early medieval period (Rogerson 1976). It was believed that this excavation yielded the largest quantity of fish bones and fish hooks ever recorded in Britain! At Fulmodeston we chanced upon a remarkable pottery dump from a sixteenth-century kiln **(p. 226-228)** (Wade-Martins 1983), and at King Street, King's Lynn, we worked with the Royal Commission on Historical Monuments on the recording of a Norman waterfront house encased by later walls (Richmond and Taylor 1976). Following the subsequent loss of another early building in Queen Street **(p. 161-163)**, this is now the oldest known house in King's Lynn.

Steady growth

Meanwhile, the Department of the Environment's funding for the Unit remained strong (*EDP* 10th January 1975), and by July 1975 they had agreed to the appointment of a conservator to work in Norwich Castle Museum to conserve the finds from both the Norfolk and Suffolk excavations. By October 1976 they had also agreed to fund a regional environmentalist to work in the School of Environmental Sciences at the University of East Anglia in Norwich on the environmental samples from both counties. This post was ably filled by Peter Murphy who made a major contribution in the region for many years. The DoE also agreed to provide additional money to start clearing the backlog of unpublished excavations that both the DoE and its predecessors had funded in the past, particularly Group Captain Knocker's and Brian Davison's excavations in the Anglo-Saxon town at Thetford and Charles Green's excavations on the Roman fort at Caister-on-Sea **(p. 247-248)**.

By September 1977 the DoE had set up a new Fenland Research Committee to put greater emphasis on the study and conservation of the archaeology of this important, and deteriorating, wetland (**p. 180-188**). Stanley West and I were invited to join the committee. As the years went by the local press continued to give us good detailed coverage (*Lynn News and Advertiser* 2nd March 1979 and *EDP* 15th April 1983; *DAFT* 22nd April 1983).

While all this was going on we still had to rely entirely on Department of the Environment funding to cover staff salaries and excavation costs until the County Council could be persuaded to take over running expenses. The crucial watershed moment came at a meeting of Norfolk's Policy and Resources Committee chaired by the Leader of the County Council, Ian Coutts, on 8th September 1977. A record of the meeting is preserved in the minutes of the committee held in the Norfolk Record Office (2012/235 Box 35 A284D).

The County Council decides

The Committee received an excellent seven-page report by John Brighton in the County Solicitor's Department which explained that the Department of the Environment was funding Norfolk as a pilot project, and there were not enough funds to go around other counties as well. The average county was receiving £10,000 a year for rescue archaeology, while Norfolk had been given £40,000 plus a further £15,000 for the Spong Hill Anglo-Saxon cemetery excavation. That level of funding could not be sustained for much longer. Some cutbacks would be necessary if no County Council funds were forthcoming. A working party had been formed, chaired by the Hon. Robin Walpole, the chairman of the Norfolk Museums Committee, 'to consider how the position desired by the Department might be achieved.' The report made mention that there had been much debate within the Working Party over which department of the County Council would be most appropriate for the Unit to join. Although the report skates over the details, the truth was that I had argued that the Planning Department was the right place to be to ensure that the Unit could link fully into planning procedures. Francis Cheetham, however, argued with equal determination that we should go into his new Norfolk Museums Service. He had been Director of Norwich Museums since 1963 and during the local government re-organisation of 1974 he had been very successful in creating a county-wide service by persuading all the Districts with museums in the county to form a new Norfolk Museums Service which he then ran (obituary in the *EDP* 11th November 2005). Francis was awarded an OBE in 1979 for his services to museums and he retired in March 1990 (*EDP* 15th March 1990).

Francis won the battle but it was acknowledged that special procedures were needed to ensure that the Unit was still integrated into the planning process and not regarded as an external agency. The outcome was a proposal to set up a 'Norfolk

Archaeological Services Advisory Committee' with representatives of the Museums Committee, the Planning Committee, the District Planning Committees, the University, the Scole Committee and the Department of the Environment to bring this about and ensure that the Unit was able to give independent archaeological expert advice on planning matters. It was a clever formula devised by John Brighton, as the Working Party's legal adviser, which ensured that the academic integrity of the advice would be guaranteed in a local authority environment. The papers of the Advisory Committee, known ever since as 'NASAC', are maintained in the Norfolk Record Office (ACC 2012/235, box 49), and since the shredding of the Archaeological Unit's archive (**p. 146**), they are a key source of information.

It was a memorable moment when the Policy and Resources Committee had to decide if the Council should take over the core salaries and administration costs of the Unit step by step over a five-year period from 1978/79 to 1982/83. If that was successful then the Department of the Environment's funding could by the end of the five-year period just be used for excavations. The proposal had the full support of the local press (*EDP* leading article 7th September 1977). The motion was proposed by the Hon. Robin Walpole, chair of the Norfolk Museums Committee, and seconded by a good friend and senior councillor, Fred Nicholson, the owner of Foxburrow Farm in North Elmham, where I had excavated the Bronze Age hoard in 1970 (**p. 64-66**) and where we had started the excavations on the Spong Hill Anglo-Saxon cemetery in 1972. The motion was passed unanimously, subject to consultations with the Museums Committee and the District Councils. Following those consultations, the resolution was fully endorsed by Policy and Resources on 13th February 1978. After six years of struggling since the formation of the Scole Committee in 1971 we had made it! The future of professional field archaeology in Norfolk seemed assured. Almost inevitably, Suffolk County Council followed suit the following year. Field archaeology then had a sound basis on which to develop further in East Anglia. The DoE's own Area Archaeological Advisory Committees did not last long; there was never a regional unit and the Scole Committee continued as the regional co-ordinating committee. The role of the Scole Committee had been crucial in maintaining regional cohesion, and it served its purpose well until it was eventually wound up at a formal celebratory luncheon at the Scole Inn on 10th February 2009. It was good to have a formal closure in this way rather than let the committee just fizzle out.

The Norwich excavations

The County Council's Working Party on the future of the Unit had been told that the Norwich Survey would continue digging in the city until 1980. But after a rather sudden and unexpected decision by the Survey to cease excavating in the City in April 1978 we had to move quickly. The City Council generously agreed to fund the appointment of a Norwich Field Officer for two years and the County Council agreed to fund a third year. This then allowed us to go ahead with plans to excavate the Anglia TV site in 1979 before the TV company erected their new office building within the north east bailey of the castle (**p. 228-229**) and before the new magistrates' courts were built on the Late Saxon and early medieval waterfront in 1981 at St Martin-at-Palace Plain (**p. 229-231**).

The DoE were by now urging us to ask developers to carry their share of excavation costs, and it was a great breakthrough when Anglia TV agreed to find the £21,000 to meet the full cost of their excavation. This decision did ensure that the development was not held up while we tried to raise the money elsewhere, and it was made after I gave their Chief Executive a private re-assurance that there was no possibility of an over-run of the excavation timetable. Anglia TV also had the benefit of being able to make a documentary film, directed by Paul Jordon, of the whole project as the excavation progressed. We now had the funding from Anglia TV, and we appointed Brian Ayers from Hull as our new Norwich Field Officer for both projects.

Over the years that followed, Brian did much to promote the archaeology of the city and produced three popular booklets on his projects which sold well: *Digging under the Doorstep* (Ayers with Lawson 1983), *Digging Deeper* (Ayers 1985) and *Digging Ditches* (Ayers, Bown and Reeve 1992). The Anglia TV excavation was the first in a fine series run by Brian in the city (**p. 228-231**). But by far the largest was the removal of the whole castle bailey in advance of a new underground Castle Mall shopping precinct in 1989/91 (Shepherd Popescu 2009). However, some of the later excavations in that series, particularly the church of St Margaret *in combusto* in Magdalen Street in 1987 and the Late Saxon town defences in Calvert Street in 1989/90, still unfortunately await publication (**p. 340**).

The 'golden years'

People who worked at the Gressenhall office in the 1970s and 1980s tell me that the 20 years or so following the birth of the Norfolk Archaeological Unit in 1973 now seems like a golden period when we were constantly pushing boundaries and innovating in ways we had never dreamed would be possible (*Figures 11.2 and 12.1*). It was liberating. We were integrating ourselves steadily into the planning system well before PPG 16 (**p. 159-161**), and our work with metal detectorists in particular was immensely gratifying. But with the full commercialisation of contract archaeology from 1990 onwards the formal separation of curating and contracting had to come, although the magic and informality of those early years would not then be possible. But once we were in the era of developer funding there was a requirement, quite rightly, to be totally professional, with our two functions quite separate.

11.2. P.W-M as County Archaeologist in the Gressenhall office in 1983.

Chapter 12:
A New County Service for Field Archaeology, 1973-1999

The role of a County Service

From 1973 until 1978 the Norfolk Archaeological Unit was responsible to the Scole Committee, and then from 1978 it was fully integrated into the County Council as a part of the Norfolk Museums Service. The intention was that the Unit would not be just a rescue digging organisation, but a team which could provide a comprehensive field archaeology service for the county, covering the following areas:

- **Sites and Monuments Record** Building up a detailed database of the county's archaeology, which was computerised from 1984.
- **Air photography** Initiating an air photography programme to record not just archaeological sites, but a wide range of historic landscape features.
- **Planning advice** Giving advice to County and District planning departments on both conservation policies and on planning applications.
- **Surveys** Organising thematic surveys of archaeological sites and buildings.
- **Advice to farmers** Providing advice to farmers and the Ministry of Agriculture, as it was then, on the conservation of archaeology on farmland.
- **Protecting significant sites** Recommending to the Department of the Environment additional sites and buildings to be added to the registers of Scheduled Ancient Monuments and Listed Buildings.
- **Rescue recording** Organising a limited number of rescue excavations and building recording projects.
- **Identifying and recording finds** Identifying metal detector finds pottery and flints from amateur fieldwalking and other accidental discoveries in close association with the Archaeology Department in the Castle Museum. This all formed an increasing part of our work.
- **Clearing the publication backlog** Writing up the numerous excavation reports left unfinished by our predecessors.
- **Community engagement and outreach** Keeping the people of Norfolk aware of all we were doing was essential. Tony Gregory took part in a series of television programmes called *Now, Then*, which brought archaeology into the homes of thousands who had never seen an excavation. The local newspapers were always willing to carry stories of our discoveries, and metal detecting finds never failed to attract press attention. The publications *Norfolk from the Air* and the *Historical Atlas of Norfolk* sold well in several editions. Brian Ayers' books on excavations in Norwich, *Digging*

Under the Doorstep (Ayers with Lawson 1983), *Digging Deeper* (Ayers 1987) and *Digging Ditches* (Ayers, Bown and Reeve (1992) and his English Heritage *Book of Norwich* (1994a) were particularly successful in keeping the people of Norwich aware of what we were doing in their city. There was a public viewing area for most of the time the large Norwich Castle Mall excavations were in progress from 1987 to 1991. Members of staff also contributed to the 'Norfolk Origins' series with titles like 1: *Hunters to First Farmers* (Robinson 1981), 2: *Roads and Tracks* (Robinson and Rose 1983), *3 Celtic Fire and Roman Rule* (Robinson and Gregory 1987) and *4: The North Folk; Angles, Saxon and Danes* (Bond, Penn and Rogerson 1990).

12.1. *The NAU Gressenhall team in about 1987 (left to right):*
P.W-M., Carolyn Dallas (Post-excavation projects), Bob Silvester (Fenland Survey Project), Julie Gardiner (East Anglian Archaeology Assistant Editor), Hoste Spalding (Illustrator), David Gurney (Project Officer), Joy Lodey (Secretary/office librarian), Kenneth Penn (Spong Hill Project), Frances Healy (Post-excavation projects), Sue White (Senior illustrator), Tony Gregory (Roman Period Field Officer), Jane Everett (Secretary/administration), Derek Edwards (Aerial Photography Officer), Margaret Matthews (Illustrator), Edwin Rose (Sites and Monuments Records Officer), Steven Ashley (Illustrator), Joan Daniels (Secretary/EAA page layout), Brian Ayers (Norwich Field Officer), Andrew Rogerson (Medieval Period Field Officer), Robert Rickett (Spong Hill Project), Dave Wicks (Photographer).

General descriptions of our work were also published from time to time in the local press (eg *Lynn News and Advertiser* 2nd March 1979; *EDP* 15th April 1983; *DAFT* 22nd April 1983) as well as reports of specific discoveries.

Museum displays

But we completely failed to utilise opportunities to present the results of our activities in museum displays. One of the main justifications for putting us in the Norfolk Museums Service, rather than in the County Planning Department, was so that we would be able to use museum facilities to show the results of our fieldwork to museum visitors. But the Museums Service always had other priorities. Several times I had money put into the capital programme for display cases for us to use, but each time other needs asserted themselves. At my last attempt our display cases were replaced with toilets for the disabled at the Castle Museum. That, in itself, was perfectly commendable, but it did emphasise the great divide between museums who really were only interested in displaying their collections and field archaeologists who wanted to display the *totality* of the evidence for the past, including air photographs, excavation plans, site photographs and reconstructions. I personally found it enormously depressing every time I walked into the archaeology gallery, as it was then, in the Castle Museum to see row upon row of Spong Hill Anglo-Saxon burial urns we had excavated without so much as a photograph showing how we had found them, an air photograph of the site showing how the cemetery had been located largely within a Roman enclosure or even a plan of the excavation. What the public saw in the museum was a completely inadequate representation of a major research project. The cultural divide between museums and field archaeology was, and still is, considerable. There is still little sign of the gap closing significantly.

There is a strong case to be made for encouraging museums to design

12.2. Barbara Green, who was Keeper of Archaeology at the Castle Museum until she retired in 1992, with whom we all had the warmest possible working relationship over many years.

displays which are not so object-based but rather ones which represent, as far as possible, total immersion in all aspects of the cultures they are presenting (the houses people lived in, their farming, their technologies, their rituals and the languages they spoke). This wider evidence is often available. More regular and more fruitful debates between museums, field archaeologists and anthropologists before displays are designed could only be beneficial. If museums are not to provide a *rounded* view of past cultures where else will it come from?

The changing legal background

There were a number of significant local and national developments which gradually strengthened our hand over site access and funding in the coming years. These were as follows:

The 1979 Ancient Monuments and Archaeological Areas Act

This Act was crucial in giving better protection to Ancient Monuments along the lines already available to Listed Buildings. The proposal to create 'Archaeological Areas' in towns was seldom implemented, but there could now be no damage to a monument without Scheduled Monument Consent. Before then, a landowner was only required to give four months' notice of his intention to disturb or destroy a scheduled site, and there was little that could be done to stop the destruction. The landowner could even refuse access for a rescue excavation before the destruction took place. The only option was for the Ancient Monuments Board to recommend to the Minister that a Preservation Order be issued, but compensation had to be paid equal to the full market value of the land (Thurley 2013, 78). This option was rarely used in Norfolk, except to stop ploughing in three instances, within the Roman fort at Burgh Castle, within the Roman town at Caistor St Edmund and for a group of round barrows at Little Cressingham.

The 1979 Act is still not ideal because disturbance to a monument is by itself not an offence. We saw the consequences of that at Horsford Castle, a fine motte and bailey castle where the bailey was ploughed in 1986 but the tenant was not prosecuted because English Heritage believed it would be difficult to *prove* damage to the earthen monument (*Figure 15.2*). This was the case even though the clarity of the earthworks within the bailey had clearly been reduced (Scott 1989). The Act was nevertheless much better than before.

The Act by itself still gave no protection to the many *unscheduled* sites of schedulable quality. We saw this in 1986 over a large housing development at Caister-on-Sea to the west of the Roman fort where we knew there would be an extensive Roman period extra-mural settlement. We were permitted only very limited access, and the whole development went ahead with only minimal recording, yet the developers had the temerity to call their site 'Tessera Park' after Roman tessellated pavements! Had the planning application been submitted after the new County Structure Plan had been approved in 1988, the situation could have been very different.

In 1983 the National Heritage Act led to the creation of English Heritage which took on the roles previously performed mainly by the Department of the Environment to secure the preservation of Ancient Monuments and historic buildings, to promote the preservation and character of conservation areas and to encourage the public's appreciation of the historic environment. It practice that made little real difference.

The 1988 County Structure Plan

The new Norfolk Structure Plan came into force in March 1988 with two key archaeology policies, E.17 (1) and E.17 (2), which did not just apply to scheduled sites but to *all* important sites threatened with development. Many were still not scheduled, so these policies were a great step forward.

> *Policy E.17 (1)* Development which would affect sites of archaeological importance will only be permitted in exceptional circumstances.
>
> *Policy E.17 (2)* On other sites of archaeological importance and where there is no overriding case for preservation, development will not normally be permitted unless agreement has been reached to provide for the recording and, where desirable, the excavation of such sites.

Policy E.17 (1) did provide for the first time strong grounds for recommending the refusal of planning permission on unscheduled sites we believed to be of archaeological importance. And E.17 (2) provided an opportunity to require developer-funded excavation as a condition of planning consent.

The 1990 Planning Policy Guidance No. 16 (PPG 16)

This key policy document for England and Wales was to have the most profound impact on the whole structure of rescue archaeology. The driving force behind this initiative was Geoff Wainwright (1937-2017; obituary *The Guardian* 17th March 2017), the Chief Archaeologist in English Heritage from 1989 to 1999. Geoff's conviction that the 'polluter pays' was the over-riding logic behind this new government initiative.

PPG16, *Planning and Archaeology,* published by the Department of the Environment in November 1990, fully integrated archaeology into the planning process. It was not legislation, but it was good clear guidance on best practice to planning authorities in England and Wales on how to take proper account of archaeology before determining a planning decision, and it set out advice for both developers and for planning officers. The developer was advised to consult the relevant Sites and Monuments Record before purchasing a site to see if their proposals might have archaeological implications. The developer might then need to commission an archaeological evaluation if one was thought to be necessary by the County Archaeological Officer. This usually involved evaluation trenching by an archaeological contractor. Planning consent could be withheld until the results of the evaluation were presented to the planning officer, and the results could form a relevant part of the formal planning application (*EDP* 23rd July 1991). A reluctance to carry out an evaluation could by itself be grounds for a planning refusal.

If planning permission was to be granted, there would need to be a condition, or a legally binding agreement, requiring a developer to make arrangements for recording (usually by excavation) to a Specification which would have to be agreed between the developer and the planning authority. That would usually require the developer to:

(1) employ a consultant to devise a Specification or Method Statement for the excavation in response to a Brief issued by the County Archaeological Officer,
(2) provide for the full costs of the excavation to be run according to the agreed Specification and the post-excavation analysis and subsequent publication.

There were two ambiguities arising from this procedure which have not, even now, been fully addressed; there was no clear guidance on the deposition of the excavation archive, consisting of the paper record and the finds. The finds still belonged to the landowner. The landowner could retain the finds and could not be required to make them available for further study. Worst still, some museums did not have the capacity to store these archives anyway, a situation which had deteriorated in Norfolk until recently (**p. 343-344**). There was also scope for the archaeological contractor to delay or not produce a final report and instead to carry out further excavations to generate yet more income from other developers. It was quite easy for the archaeological contractor not to produce a report at all. By this stage it could all become rather messy. More of this later (**p. 339-342**).

PPG 16 did ensure that archaeology was recognised as an important planning constraint and it did inject a considerable amount of new money from developers into British archaeology. Similar measures were introduced in Scotland. However, compromises were at times necessary in order to avoid 'archaeological blight' over some urban areas where profits from development were marginal and where there was considerable political pressure for development to proceed. These compromises were over the size of excavations, rather than over whether they should take place, and the thinking was that potential archaeological costs would be reflected in lower property values.

This was all a far cry from the early days of the Norfolk Archaeological Unit when we were sometimes refused all access, even to watch the digging of foundation trenches. By the Nineties one could feel that the RESCUE movement of the Seventies had largely succeeded, to the great credit of all those who had been originally involved in the Barford meeting (**p. 357**).

The 1994 Planning Policy Guidance No. 15 (PPG 15)

After PPG 16 had come out I well remember having arguments with my historic buildings colleagues in the County Council Planning Department over the need to subject standing structures to the same evaluation and archaeological recording procedures as we were applying to below-ground archaeology. They just couldn't see the need for it and believed that they had the situation fully under control. But in 1994, PPG 15 *Planning and the Historic Environment* provided the opportunity to change all that, although it is fair to say that conservation officers were generally very slow to require developer-funded evaluation and archaeological recording as a condition of Listed Building Consent. It was not a part of their mind-set.

The need for building evaluations was really highlighted for me over the loss in January 1977 of one of the oldest and most important buildings in King's Lynn. It was a late twelfth or early thirteenth-century house built on the line of the original twelfth-century waterfront at 28-34 Queen Street (Richmond, Taylor and Wade-Martins 1982). The building was not listed but it was in a Conservation Area. The early stonework was concealed behind modern rendering, but 1913 photographs and an 1860 sketch in King's Lynn Museum as well as a watercolour in King's Lynn library showed remarkably early stonework in the front wall before some of the rendering had been applied. There was a public enquiry, but at that stage nobody with any knowledge of historic buildings had examined the structure or looked at the publicly accessible records in King's Lynn. So, the developer argued that because the building: (a) had not been listed, (b) was in a poor state of repair and (c) possessed no architectural merit, it should be demolished. It was only as demolition progressed, and the modern rendering was removed, that it became clear that the masonry front wall of the house dated from *c.* 1200 (*Figures 12.3a, 12.3b & 12.3c*). But anyone with any skill in historic building investigation who had been asked to evaluate the building and produce a report for the public enquiry would have quickly recognised its great historical significance. After demolition had started the Department of the Environment decided to issue an Interim Preservation Notice, but the developers returned during the night and demolished the front wall of No. 32 (*Figure 12.3c*). The Department then decided not to issue the Notice because there was by then not enough of the building left to justify preservation. It was strange that the District Planning Officer had his office in the window directly across the street, but we saw no sign of him. We never knew

12.3. Photographs by Colin Shewring (1914-1994), then the district council's Conservation Officer, who did all he could to save 28-34 Queen Street, King's Lynn from demolition in 1977: (a) The front doorway dating to c.1200 revealed after we had rapidly removed the rendering, (b) Then, as we were exposing an upper window police stopped the work as pieces of the rendering were falling into the road, (c) The front wall of No.32 after it was demolished during the night. This was probably pulled down first because it appeared to be the most interesting part of the structure.

who tipped off the developers that an Interim Preservation Notice was on its way, although we had our suspicions because so few people knew. To see a house of that antiquity needlessly pulled down was a devastating gut-wrenching experience. I wrote an illustrated report on the whole dreadful saga which led to a question being asked in the House of Commons (Wade-Martins 1977a), and I like to think that this may in some way have contributed to the thinking behind PPG 15.

The two PPGs were later amalgamated into one Planning Policy Statement 5, so the new planning requirements to take due regard of the historic environment were clearly here to stay.

Chapter 13:
Key Norfolk Archaeological Unit Projects

The work of the Norfolk Archaeological Unit between 1973 and 1999 has been described and summarised in various articles (Wade-Martins 1974b; Wade-Martins 1992; Wade-Martins 1999) and in numerous project reports in East Anglian Archaeology and *Norfolk Archaeology* and sometimes in the *EDP*. So in this section we can take just a few projects and assess their contribution to our understanding of the county's past.

The Sites and Monuments Record

The earliest SMR in Britain

The original Norfolk Sites and Monuments Record consisted of a card index and a set of six-inch maps held in Norwich Castle Museum. It was started in 1933 by Rainbird Clarke as one of the local correspondents appointed to assist O.G.S. Crawford, the Ordnance Survey's Archaeology Officer, with the revision of antiquities on Ordnance Survey maps (Green 1986). The cards were hand-written either by Rainbird or by his successor in the Archaeology Department, Barbara Green, and were kept in metal drawers by period and then by parish. When we took it over in 1974 the index had already reached about 8,000 cards, mainly of chance finds reported to the museum. It was quite a major task photocopying all these cards onto our own larger-format versions and then adding new County Primary Record Numbers. Photocopiers in those days were as big as large cabinets, and the cards endlessly jammed in the machine. Edwin Rose, our Records Officer, later copied the records from King's Lynn Museum on sites and finds in the West Norfolk area as well (*EDP* 12th October 1974).

Data retrieval system

Our aim was to build up the Record as a fully comprehensive index of all historic landscape features including chance finds, crop-marks, earthworks, ancient hedgerows, parks and historic buildings. It was modelled on the SMR created by Don Benson in the Oxfordshire City and County Museum in Woodstock where Susanna had worked with Don as Assistant Field Officer before we were married (Benson 1972; Benson 2013). For each item there was to be a *Primary Record Card* held sequentially by Primary Record Number. We had a set of six-inch *Record Maps* printed onto plastic film so that copies could easily be run off for the District planning departments so they could check planning applications as they came in against our Record Maps. These copies in the planning departments were replaced with updated versions from time to time. The retrieval system used 'optical co-incidence' *Feature Cards* with each card representing a feature or characteristic. These were rigid plastic sheets about a foot square covered with a printed matrix of small squares with each small square representing a Primary Record Number. There was one Feature Card for each characteristic, so the Feature Card representing churches would have all the squares for the County Numbers for churches drilled out. Another would be for a particular period and another might be for a parish name.

So, if you wanted to find the County Numbers for all the crop-marks of Bronze Age ring-ditches in a particular parish, you overlaid sheets representing 'Bronze Age', 'ring-ditches' and the parish name on a light box, and where the light showed right through the drilled-out holes, those were the Primary Record Numbers (the County Numbers) you were looking for. If you drilled the wrong hole by mistake you had a problem, and whenever Edwin Rose was at work on the index there was the constant sound of drilling. By 1977 the cards had grown to 10,000 and by 1984 they had reached 20,000 which was the limit of this data retrieval system.

In addition to that, there were the *Secondary Files* in rows of filing cabinets with additional information in numbered hanging files. The SMR was kept in the largest room in the building which soon filled up with rows of these cabinets. All air photographs were kept in a separate room, and here we filed the prints in cabinets not by Primary Record Numbers but by National Grid kilometre squares, following the practice of the National Monuments Record Air Photography Unit. So we were making full use of the space available in the large rooms we had at our disposal in the east wing of the Gressenhall workhouse.

Our first computer

In March 1984 we received a grant from the Department of the Environment to buy our first office computer for the SMR, which arrived just in time to supplement the optical co-incidence Feature Cards. A grant followed so we could employ an assistant to computerise the data and eventually we were able to abandon the Feature Cards. By 1992 the index had reached 28,000 entries, and it continued to grow mainly from fieldwalking, chance finds, metal detecting and excavations. The term 'Sites and Monuments Record' was traditional at the time, although now these records are usually called 'Historic Environment Records', or less attractively, 'HERs'. This reflects the fact that they are a record of *the whole of* the historic landscape and not just individual archaeological sites and monuments.

Historical Atlas

In 1993 it was time to produce an historical atlas along the lines of one already published for Suffolk in 1988. Using a base map of parishes as they were in 1923, or modern parishes in some cases, 61 contributors prepared maps of 93 different topics. For subjects like moats or non-conformist chapels the distribution could be accepted as largely complete and accurate, but for others, like Roman settlements where the distribution depended on chance finds recorded in the SMR, it was more of a progress report. Contributors were confined to 900 words per topic, but a 'Further Reading' list was also included for each subject. The book was assembled in conjunction with the Federation of Norfolk Historical and Archaeological Organisations (**p. 80**) which sponsored the preparation of the distribution maps. It was printed as a paperback and sold extremely well following a launch by the Lord Lieutenant, Timothy Colman, in the Castle Museum on 8th March 1993 (*EDP* 9th March 1993). A second edition came out the next year (Wade-Martins 1993a and 1994).

There was then a gap of ten years until an entirely new hardback edition, very competently edited by Trevor Ashwin and Alan Davison, was published in 2005 with superb computer-designed graphics by Trevor which were not available for the first two editions (Ashwin and Davison 2005). The whole concept of an atlas like this was an immensely good way of making the information in the SMR available to the widest possible audience. The first two editions had been published by the Norfolk Museums Service, and the third was ably published by Phillimore after the Museums Service seemed to withdraw from publishing. Ten years on again, perhaps it is time for a new edition?

Aerial photography

Aerial photographs library

When we allocated jobs in 1973 to staff within the new organisation I saw that there could be a special role for Derek Edwards because of his technical skills, and when I suggested he should be our aerial photography officer he jumped at the chance (*Figure 13.1*). There seemed to be enormous potential in starting our own aerial photography programme rather than relying on others taking the occasional photo for us.

In other counties they usually stuck air photo prints, when they had them, into the appropriate file in the SMR, but since many of our pictures could not be allocated to one particular SMR entry it seemed best to have an entirely separate index based on the Ordnance Survey National Grid. So, all the photos we took were catalogued by one-kilometre grid square followed by an alphabetical sequence within each square (Edwards 1976, 254-258). We also made a point of keeping the negatives in a separate building to the prints for fire security reasons because the old workhouse we were in was a potential tinderbox. Luckily, though, that did not prove to be necessary. The whole project created a great deal of interest both locally and nationally (*EDP* 10th July 1984; *The Independent* 4th July 1983).

13.1. Derek Edwards who took 41,000 photographs while Aerial Photography Officer at Gressenhall from 1973 to 1999 (FJS1).

By the end of March 2000 Derek had spent 676 hours in the air on 397 flights and had taken 41,000 photographs. The Royal Commission on the Historical Monuments of England and later the Department of the Environment were very supportive and made two black and white prints of each picture so that we had one and they had the other after the pictures had been catalogued. In addition, they generously made annual grants for the hire of aircraft.

We were lucky enough also to acquire pictures taken by others. Early on we were given by the Norfolk Research Committee a collection of 1,792 vertical air photographs taken by the RAF in 1946 as a part of the Royal Air Force National Air Survey of England and Wales. That coverage was spectacularly important because it recorded the countryside as it was just after the war at a scale of six inches to one mile before there was so much damage with hedgerow removal and earthwork levelling in the 1950s through to the 1970s. I had already had first-hand experience of the importance of these pictures when it turned out that they represented the only good record of the Thuxton deserted village earthworks before they were levelled in the early 1960s **(p. 15-16)**. It was an enormous pleasure then to receive in 1992 from the County Council's Planning Department a much larger collection of 9,000 prints from the same survey.

The addition of the Norfolk County Council-funded 'Geonex' colour vertical survey of 1988 at a scale of two and a half inches to one mile further augmented the collections, as did the purchase with a grant from the Science Museum of some

7,000 glass plates and negatives dating between 1907 and 1974. These, plus other donations, created a vast archive of comparative material.

By the early 1990s the air photos library had grown to some 50,000 prints. In addition, we acquired all the 1:2,500 scale (25 inch to 1 mile) Ordnance Survey prints taken from 1960 to 1976. The library had now become a remarkable resource for researching the historic landscape.

Ring-ditches: a measure of achievement

One way to measure the success of the air photography programme was to count the numbers of indicator sites, particularly the crop-marks of ring-ditches, which we had recorded. These are the circular crop-marks, usually representing quarry ditches surrounding Bronze Age burial mounds which had once stood before they were levelled and cultivated. In 1975 we knew of 196; in 1977 that number had risen to 549; in 1982 to 899 and in 1987 to 1,100. By May 2015 the number stood at 1,741! There can surely be no more cost-effective way of recording the historic landscape than by aerial photography.

Norfolk from the Air

There was so much public interest in our aerial photography work that it seemed a good idea for the Norfolk Museums Service to produce a book of air photos, which we called *Norfolk from the Air*. It was the first such county volume to be published, and after that a number of other counties followed suit. The first paperback edition with photographs principally by Derek came out in 1987 with a picture of Cromer pier on the cover (Wade-Martins 1987). This showed the full range of historic features such as crop-marks, earthworks, monasteries, churches, market towns, boatyards in the Broads, airfields and the suburbs of Norwich. Each black and white photo was captioned by a specialist. A few colour pictures were included, but they actually added little.

Some 450 hardback and 11,000 paperback copies were sold. To promote the book we organised an exhibition of photos which opened on 25th July 1987 as a part of the King's Lynn Festival. It then moved to the Castle Museum for August (*EDP* 20th July 1987; *DAFT* 24th July 1987) and on to the foyer of County Hall in September. The book was reviewed by Charles Roberts of the *EDP* who described it as '.. a totally compulsive book which will fascinate and engross all those with an interest in the county ..' (*EDP* 10th August 1987). The exhibition then went to the main Norwich press office in the January. The first edition had to be reprinted within a few weeks of being released. A second edition was published in 1997 as Volume 1 (Wade-Martins 1997), followed by a new Volume 2 two years later which benefitted greatly from a fine new layout designed by Dick Malt who took advantage of more advanced printing techniques which allowed black and white and colour to be intermixed (*EDP Magazine* 24th July 1999; Wade-Martins 1999). It was interesting that, despite the numbers sold, one seldom saw the books for sale second-hand, suggesting that their owners liked to hold on to their copies, and still do.

Some outstanding aerial photography discoveries

The following examples of 10 aerial photographs represent my personal choice of pictures which embody the success of our aerial photography project. They show different periods and types of site, from crop-marks, to earthworks to standing buildings, including industrial archaeology, which all featured in the two volumes of *Norfolk from the Air* (Figures 3.2 to 13.11).

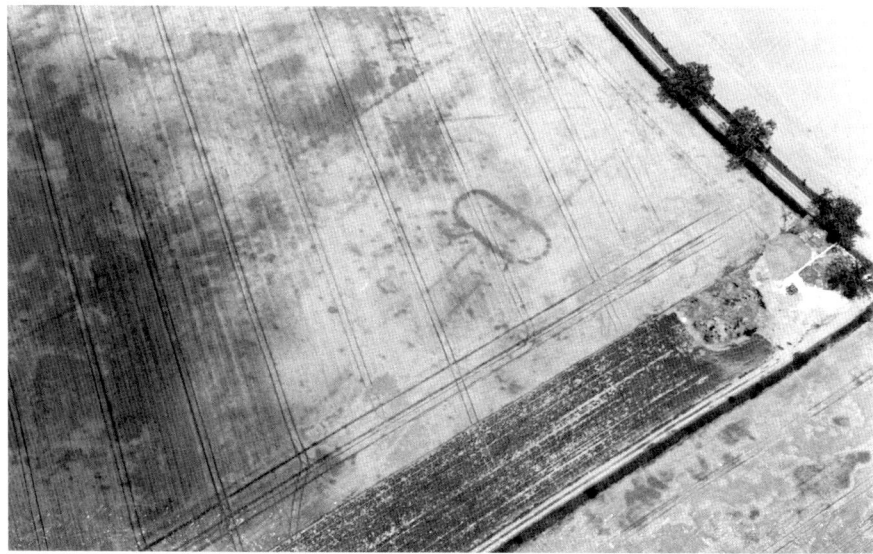

13.2. A possible Neolithic long barrow at Tuttington found in 1996. The soil from the ditches of this oval enclosure was used to create a long mound in the middle which has since been ploughed away. The features at the bottom (east) end of the enclosure may have held heavy timber uprights to form a monumental facade as part of the same cultural tradition seen in megalithic monuments in Wiltshire and the Severn valley (TG2326/P/HJV7).

CHAPTER 13: KEY NORFOLK ARCHAEOLOGICAL UNIT PROJECTS   171

13.3. *An interrupted ditched enclosure and a long barrow at Roughton, both possibly Neolithic. This roughly circular enclosure with the ditch divided into 11 sections separated by causeways would previously have been described as a 'causewayed enclosure'. They are thought to represent tribal gathering points for ceremonial purposes, but actually we are only guessing at their true purpose. Beyond the long barrow is a circle of large holes which looks like a previously un-recognised woodhenge (TG2235/F/AKP24).*

13.4. A group of Bronze Age ring-ditches at Broome. Having several times referred to ring-ditches, it is time to illustrate some. This picture has a group of four showing in a crop of cereals. There are two small ones, a much larger one, with an in-turned entrance on the right-hand side, and another double or triple-ditched circle intersecting with it. There may also be another just beyond, partly lost in the darker crop (TM3493/AP/AXH16).

13.5. A first-century Roman fort at Swanton Morley. These remarkable crop-marks in a field of cereals show the outline of a Roman fort with rounded corners overlooking the River Wensum. A modern hedgerow neatly bisects the fort, and the triple ditches and an entrance are very clear to the left. Over the years the site has produced a collection of surface finds, including coins of the emperor Claudius to pay the army, a wide range of military metalwork as well as native metal items, possibly recycled from a battlefield. Studying this collection could be a worthwhile PhD project for a budding archaeologist (TG0119/ADA/DJB11).

13.6. A second-century Roman fort at Saham Toney. The discovery of these crop-marks in sugar beet can best be described as a miracle. Although there had been metal detector finds in the area, the site was not seen to be a fort until 1987 when one rounded corner provided the first clue. In the following years Derek Edwards regularly checked these fields and in 1996 this photograph finally revealed the full outline of this triple-ditched enclosure. The two inner ditches probably held timber palisades with a large open ditch in front. There are two clues which show that this is Roman; one is the rounded corners (as at Swanton Morley), usual for Roman forts like this, and the other is the white line of the Peddars Way Roman road running in through an entrance on the left-hand side (TF8800/AU/HVN4).

CHAPTER 13: KEY NORFOLK ARCHAEOLOGICAL UNIT PROJECTS   175

13.7. Roman 'Saxon Shore' fort at Brancaster with the civilian settlement beyond. The rectangular outline of this fort, where the walls were pulled down in 1747, had been known for a long time, but beyond that is a pattern or crop-marks indicating the outlines of a civilian settlement found in 1974. There were internal square turrets in each corner of the fort and an entrance in the centre of each side. Running out of the far side was a street which met other streets at a crossroads, and the settlement spread out from there. In 2012 our understanding of this site was greatly enhanced by Time Team's geophysical surveys inside and outside the fort (TF7844/G/AAE12).

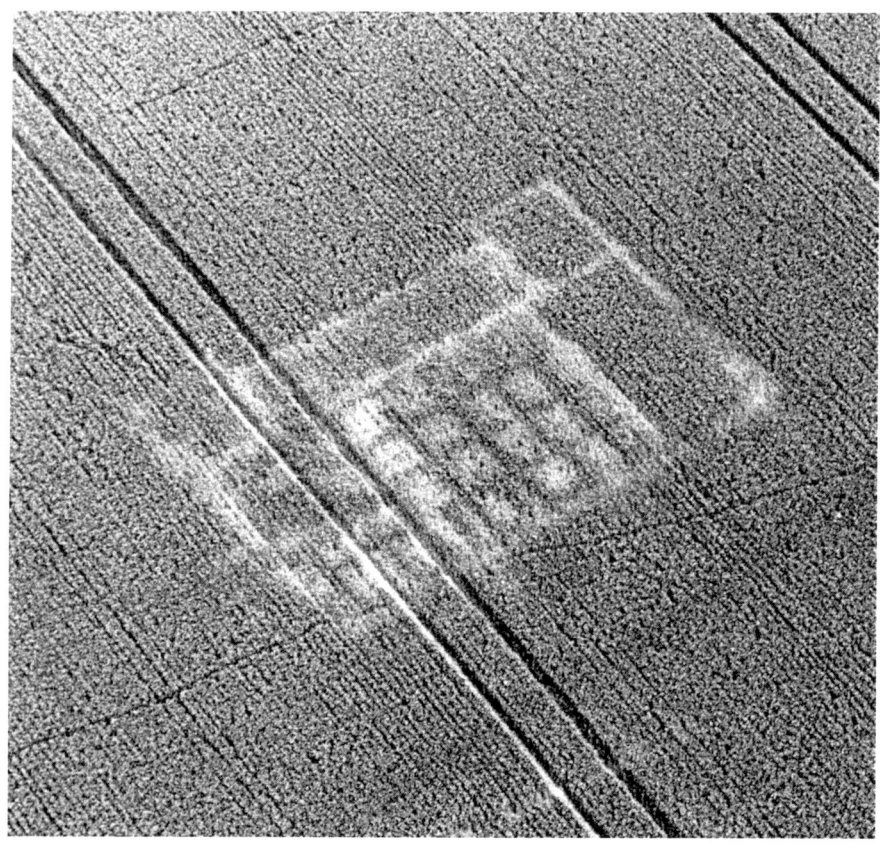

13.8. A Roman villa near Swaffham. It is possible to see the complete plan of this villa showing as parchmarks in a field of cereals when found in June 1996. The most obvious feature is the hypocaust for the under-floor heating system in the main room, and a corridor along the front flanked by projecting wings providing access to the ground-floor rooms. Ploughing must have caused severe damage to the archaeology for the crop-marks to be so clear (TF8605/ABH/(HKB8).

13.9. Crop-marks of a long-lost church at Itteringham discovered in 1986, about which we know little. To the left is a small Norman church or chapel consisting of a nave and apse. The door and the arch between nave and apse are not visible because there are no breaks for these openings in the foundations. There are also rectangular buildings to the south. This group may be the site of Nowers Manor and the chapel of St Nicholas mentioned in documents of 1310 and 1430 (TG1530/A/DBM8).

13.10. Earthworks of Rougham deserted village probably deserted by the early sixteenth century. Extensive earthworks survive, including the fine street running up the photograph and another coming in from the left. Alongside the streets are rectangular enclosures for house sites. Hidden in the woodland to the left are the well-preserved remains of eighteenth- and nineteenth- century estate brickworks (TF8220/L/AUG25).

CHAPTER 13: KEY NORFOLK ARCHAEOLOGICAL UNIT PROJECTS 179

13.11. Thorpe station, Norwich. Part of the appeal of the Norfolk from the Air volumes was the coverage we gave to more recent landscapes. At Thorpe station many of these landmarks have been changed this photograph was taken in 1985. The original station building has been demolished and replaced with a car park, and most of the sidings and the Boulton and Paul works beyond have all been removed and a new road now cuts through the area to the Carrow Road football stadium beyond (TG2308/AU/AYQ22).

Flying programme is closed down

Only months after Volume 2 of *Norfolk from the Air* was published and I had left the Museums Service, Derek was made redundant in a re-structuring exercise in the autumn of 1999. The flying programme was then brought to a close. While a very substantial backlog of un-catalogued pictures had built up, described by the Head of the Museums Service as 'massive' (*EDP* 20th November 1999), this move was strongly criticised in a series of letters to the local press from distinguished scholars. There were headlines like 'Big mistake to drop the pilot' (*EDP* 27th October) and 'Wrong to axe air lensman' (*EDP* 24th November 1999) and 'Aerial pictures are invaluable' (*EDP* 4th December 1999). Although there was a rebuttal from the Head of the Museums Service in 'Aerial photo work goes on' (*EDP* 14th December 1999), she seemed unwilling to recognise that the flying programme had actually been closed down. The re-organisation and cost-cutting was much criticised (*EDP* 6th January 2000). It was the end of a bold and innovative idea which had lasted 26 years and had produced extraordinary discoveries and a multitude of new sites for the Sites and Monuments Record. Some 1,500 or more of Derek's pictures appeared in over 500 books and publications, including a volume with Tom Williamson on *Norfolk Country Houses from the Air* published in 2001 soon after Derek had left. No other county had invested so heavily in a full-time air photography post, and it was always a prime target at a time of cost-cutting and re-structuring. Since then my successors have focused, quite rightly, on clearing the backlog and plotting the discoveries as part of the National Mapping Programme sponsored first by English Heritage and then by Historic England.

The Fenland Survey

The Fens are the largest area of uninterrupted wetland in England covering close on 400,000 hectares. They started as a dry basin with rivers flowing through, and over the following 6,000 years sea levels fluctuated so that sometimes salt waters flooded in leaving blankets of silt and then these silts allowed freshwater lakes and bogs to form behind the silts to create extensive areas of peat fen. The end result was silt fen in the north bordering the Wash and the east and peat fen in the south. Much of the peat fen was originally above sea level, but drainage since the seventeenth century has caused the peat to shrink losing up to 5 to 6 metres of its original height in some places. As the peats dry out so they suffer spectacular windblows lowering their levels still further. Today, rivers through the peat are heavily banked carrying water well above the surrounding land which is intensively cultivated. Buried in this complex landscape, the once well-preserved waterlogged archaeology covering thousands of years of human activity is disappearing under the pressures of drainage and cultivation. A precious archaeological resource is rapidly disappearing, and for the wildlife the last 300 years has been an ecological disaster. As Ian Rotherham says in *The Lost Fens* (2013, 22):

> The consequences of the changes wrought over three centuries probably constitute the greatest single loss of wildlife habitat in Britain and maybe in Europe. This was an ecological catastrophe almost beyond comprehension.

From the mid 1970s the Department of the Environment and then English Heritage commissioned archaeological surveys of the main low-lying wetland areas of England (the Somerset Levels, the Fens, North-West England and the Humberside Levels). This was, for them, a heavy investment:

> The primary purpose of this protracted campaign of field survey and associated research was to identify the archaeological component of England's major wetlands and to use this information as a firm basis for the future management of this important resource .... The outstanding results of all the wetland surveys, published in 45 monographs, provide a solid foundation for English Heritage to turn its attention to the development of a forward strategy for conservation, protection and management of the archaeology of England's wetlands (English Heritage Strategy for Wetlands 2004).

The Fenland Survey, covering the Fens of Cambridgeshire, large parts of Norfolk and Suffolk and some parts of the Lincolnshire Fens, was a bold Department of the Environment/English Heritage initiative to examine and record the archaeology of this vast area of wetland to see what still survived. The cost was over £650,000 and was the largest fieldwork project ever grant-aided by English Heritage (Silvester 1993, 24). The initiative followed the ground-breaking work of the old Cambridge-based Fenland Research Committee of the 1930s when their research first showed the remarkable archaeological potential of the sometimes still deeply stratified waterlogged deposits of the area (Phillips 1951 and 1970; Godwin 1978; Clark, Godwin and Clifford 1935).

In 1976 David Hall was appointed the first Fenland Field Officer as an experiment to carry out a preliminary fieldwalking survey of the Cambridgeshire Fens to see what could be found, and over the years which followed David made an enormous contribution to Fenland studies (Lane and Coles 2002). Amongst his initial discoveries were a Mesolithic settlement covering over a hectare at Crooked Bank near Littleport, a Neolithic site at Swaffham Prior which produced 35 polished stone axes and thousands of flints and 25, or more, burial mounds emerging from the shrinking peat in Borough Fen. For the Iron Age he found 10 ha of occupation debris at Honey Hill, Chatteris and in 1978 a Roman building at Stonea Grange showing as a mound of roof tiles and building rubble 1m high!

Following these discoveries the Department of the Environment asked Professor John Coles at Cambridge to chair a new Fenland Project Committee with representatives of the Royal Commission on Historical Monuments, the British Museum and the various county organisations charged with initiating and co-ordinating archaeological surveys in their areas. This fieldwalking project ran from 1981 to 1988. Further Fenland Field Officers were appointed for Lincolnshire and Norfolk, and ongoing survey work in the Suffolk Fenland was also incorporated into the project. The aim was to expand the original Cambridgeshire survey, including environmental research, and to feed the information into the County Sites and Monuments Records. The results were also to be presented in a series of county volumes (Coles and Hall 1983). Bob Silvester was appointed for Norfolk (*Figure 13.12*) (*EDP* 7th May 1989) and Tom Lane and Peter Hayes for Lincolnshire. An environmental archaeologist, Anne Alderton, to be followed by Martyn Waller, was also appointed. The end result was an impressive eight volumes of primary parish-based surveys (Hall 1987, 1992a and 1996; Hayes and Lane 1992; Lane 1993; Silvester 1988 and 1991), an environmental report (Waller 1994) and several auxiliary volumes on related subjects (Healy 1996, Pryor, French, Crowther, Gurney, Simpson and Taylor 1985; Simpson, Gurney, Neve and Pryor 1993). Finally, there was a summary volume published by English Heritage (Hall and Coles 1994). Annual reports called *Fenland Research* were also published each year as the fieldwalking progressed.

John Coles and David Hall produced at the end a popular booklet *Changing Landscapes: The Ancient Fenland* (Coles and Hall 1998). The whole project was a monumental success. It was well organised, completed on time to a high standard, and fully published, except for the Suffolk volume which never did materialise. Bob Silvester also summarised his own impressions of the main outcomes of the survey as a paper in a celebratory volume of East Anglian Archaeology, with a golden cover, to mark the publication of the fiftieth volume in the series (Silvester 1993).

13.12. Bob Silvester, the very successful Norfolk field officer for the Fenland Project (CLG 3).

I went out with Bob Silvester once when he was in the field, and after walking with him all that day at quite a pace I went home very impressed and totally exhausted! The field surveys of Cambridgeshire, Lincolnshire and Norfolk were completed by 1988, covering 249,000 ha out of a total Fenland area of 420,000 ha. Not all of the Norfolk Fens could be covered in the time available, and for Lincolnshire only a selection of the area could be surveyed because the Lincolnshire Fenland is so vast and it was simply not possible to cover it all. In the course of the survey over 2,000 sites were discovered and recorded, in addition to a further 400 already known. Perhaps inevitably, the most productive period was the Roman with about 820 sites.

The ideal conditions for fieldwalking were over-cast but bright days with the ground ploughed and weathered so that there was a clear view of the soils and the artefacts washed clean by the rain. About six months each winter were considered suitable for this intensive work. To assist with assessing the results a parish map was published alongside the survey information showing field by field the conditions at the time of survey ranging from very good to poor and unvisited. Fields were all walked in transects 30m apart. When a site was located it was then walked more closely to record its extent and to gather artefacts to help identify its date and cultural status. Deep drainage ditches around fields were also checked to record buried deposits.

The results were varied and complex and are not easy to summarise simply. The earliest evidence for man is scatters of Mesolithic flints, dating from the time that the area was dry land, some still deeply sealed while some are eroding as they emerge from the peat. In the Neolithic and Bronze Age settlement was concentrated around the Fen edge. Some of these sites were submerged within the Fen deposits as the wetland expanded and are primary candidates for long-term preservation. Salt making became an important industry during the Iron Age and Roman periods. In the Roman period the Fens became highly regulated and exploited as grazing land with well-organised systems of roads and canals linking extensive areas of settlement. After a post-Roman decline, Saxon settlement became widespread, and radiocarbon dates demonstrated beyond doubt that the well-known Sea Bank around Marshland, despite being known widely as a Roman Bank, is of Late Saxon date and was part of an early land reclamation scheme for the Fens. The silt lands were extensively exploited by the early Middle Ages.

The Fenland Project created a substantial database of field evidence showing how man has lived and worked in the Fens from the Mesolithic period to the present day. The project officers were only able to walk some 60% of the total area, and there are still major gaps in Lincolnshire where 70% of their Fenland remains to be studied, particularly in the Witham valley.

With current cuts to Historic England's budget, it is difficult to imagine a situation in which further surveys on this scale could be contemplated, despite the large sums of agricultural subsidies going into supporting Fenland farming, which is, of course, doing the damage.

Excavations at Stonea Grange

Meanwhile, the British Museum ran their own excavations between 1980 and 1985 on the spectacular Roman site at Stonea Grange discovered in 1978 by David Hall during the trial period before the Fenland Project was fully established (Jackson and Potter 1996; Malim 2005, 97-132). This large stone building, quite alien in the Fenland landscape, was erected apparently as the centre of an imperial estate and for the marketing of its produce, which was mainly salted meat for the army. In front of this prestigious building there was a market place and nearby there was a temple to Minerva. The place continued throughout the Roman period as a market centre even after the main building was demolished and there was then a short period of occupation during the Early Saxon period which had ceased by the mid seventh century. Nothing else quite like it was found in the Fens.

Hay Green, Terrington St Clement

A discovery which I personally found most interesting was a large Middle Saxon settlement strung out along a roddon – the silt ridge left from an old watercourse – at Hay Green, Terrington St Clement in Marshland. The spread of nearly 1,000 sherds of Ipswich Ware pottery stretched along the roddon for at least 1.5 km covering about 7 ha. (Rogerson and Silvester 1986; Silvester 1988, 37). No other settlement in Norfolk of this date has produced so much pottery and that raises interesting questions about what it could be.

Fenland Evaluation Project

After the fieldwalking project was concluded a year was spent evaluating the 2,400 sites identified in the Survey and from previous discoveries. From them, 148 were selected for further investigation. This shortlist contained sites from the Mesolithic to medieval and included settlements, field systems, canals, industrial sites, burial mounds and ritual centres. Some were still probably waterlogged with organic material and some were chosen as representative samples of much larger groups of monuments. All were believed to be of national importance where damage would seriously diminish the record of human activity in the Fens. These sites were visited to collect more surface finds, to sample the deposits by coring or digging test pits or to carry out geophysical surveys. The aerial photographs were examined in detail, and then dossiers were assembled for each site and presented to English Heritage which had essentially only two options:

- take steps to arrest site decay, or
- to record by excavation where physical preservation was unrealistic.

Fenland Management Project

The site dossiers from the Fenland Evaluation Project were the starting point for English Heritage to take site management options a stage further. But Stanley West and I were not invited to be on that committee, and it was already clear that the project did not have the resources or commitment to buy expensive Fen farmland to take whole areas out of cultivation and to organise any sort of re-wetting exercise to prevent further loss of archaeological evidence. In the end, the 'Management Project' just became a well-structured excavation project, summarised in *Fenland Management Project Excavations 1991-1995* (Crowson, Lane and Reeve 2000). Over the years 1991-95, an impressive 41 surface artefact scatters under arable were sampled by small-scale trial trenching or by more extensive area excavation, all published to a high standard – a remarkable achievement. Sites excavated included a burnt mound (Crowson 2004), seven prehistoric sites (Lane and Trimble 2010), the Deeping St Nicholas barrow complex (French 1994), many prehistoric and Roman salt production sites (Lane and Morris 2001), two Roman canals, the Fen Causeway (Wallis 2002) and ten Anglo-Saxon settlements (Crowson, Lane, Penn and Trimble 2005).

Two trenches were dug across the Hay Green Middle Saxon settlement at Terrington St Clement which had produced so much Ipswich Ware, but the finds were of 'low-status' suggesting that the large quantity of pottery on the surface did not reflect its wealth – a rather puzzling outcome which needs further investigation (Crowson, Lane, Penn and Trimble 2005, 147-171).

While these excavations provided a very useful window into the below-surface archaeology, they did not lead directly to the long-term conservation of any sites on arable land. However, 24 earthworks under pasture (a rare sight in the Fens), 8 earthworks under arable and 18 other sites under arable were recommended for scheduling under the Monuments Protection Programme (Hall 1992b), although the outcomes of those recommendations were never announced.

In the final chapter of the Management Project's summary volume, entitled *Fenland Management Project Excavations 1991-1995*, David Hall and John Coles concluded that there was room for both despair and some optimism:

From aspiration to reality

> Contrary to common thought, the early prehistoric sites, believed to be more deeply buried than later sites, were in very poor condition. Their sealing peats had dried out and wasted away, and deterioration of structural features was almost total. In contrast, sites sealed beneath silts were better preserved, although their original

> organic elements had not long survived their submergence. Another interesting conclusion was that Lincolnshire sites were appreciably in better condition than those of Cambridgeshire, possibly because of the differences between the overlying, sealing and protecting sediments – mostly silt in Lincolnshire and peat in Cambridgeshire .... (Crowson, Lane and Reeve 2000, 241).

But, they explained how the high hopes for site conservation had gradually been replaced by realism:

Management?

> Although the Fenland work in the four years 1991 to 1995 was officially termed the Fenland Management Project, it will have become apparent that the name is a misnomer. What has been achieved is beyond an Evaluation, but well short of Management. Essentially what has been accomplished is a preparation for management, an assessment of the potential for management, and an important trial run at the sites to see what is possible .... We have to remember, however, and accept that the Fenland has many interests focused upon it. Archaeological remains are but one interest and not necessarily at the top of all priority lists (Crowson, Lane and Reeve, 234).

The wildlife lobby would not have made such a defeatist statement about the possibilities for protecting and restoring habitats, but Philip Walker, writing as the English Heritage Ancient Monuments inspector in the same volume, did suggest a possible way forward:

> Archaeologists acting alone will not necessarily have the resources and expertise to secure long-term preservation. Water Level Management Plans on a wider catchment basis will be important .... In conclusion, the preservation and management of wetland archaeological sites in the Fenland is complex and is likely to depend on partnership efforts. Funding and expertise would need to be harnessed to shared objectives. The 'Wet Fens for the Future' project offers the best current hope for practical and sustainable results, allied to positive management of Sites of Special Scientific Interest and Water Level Management Plans, and carefully focused field evaluation (Crowson, Lane and Reeve 2000, 9-10).

Wet Fens for the Future

It is not clear why archaeology conservation measures were actually not considered as the historic environment's contribution to 'Wet Fens for the Future' project. There is nobody now in English Heritage who can remember the reasons why sites or archaeological areas were not being put forward for long-term protection as a part of this project, which has since been re-branded 'Fens for the Future'. In June 2012 a very detailed final report entitled *A Strategic Plan for Fenland: A Proposal for an Enhanced Ecological Network* was published and is available on the project's website. This report reminds us that only eight wetland areas, occupying 4,792 ha (1.4% of the original) now remain. The report identifies the key priorities for biodiversity action, and, although there is a section in the report on the archaeology written by the Cambridgeshire County Archaeologist, it lacks specific proposals for archaeology protection.

The project's Vision is 'to see sustainable wetlands restored, re-created and reconnected across the Fens for the benefit of people, our natural and historic heritage and the rural economy'. The Aims in their Mission Statement involves starting with 'Core Areas' which are the remnants of original Fen, such as Wicken Fen in Cambridgeshire, and entirely new creations like the RSPB's Lakenheath Fen in Suffolk and building out from these to create habitats large enough to be sustainable. At Lakenheath between 1996 and 2002 the RSPB converted over 200 ha of arable farmland into reed beds and damp meadows and planted a third of a million reeds (Rothcram 2013, 198). These areas were to be connected by a network of wildlife corridors formed by enhancing rivers, waterways and riverside areas to join together habitats across the Fens 'to help species disperse and increase resilience'.

The Wet Fens report was produced by a partnership, just as Philip Walker had suggested in 2000, but English Heritage/Historic England was not one of the 18 partners, although it included the Environment Agency, the National Trust, Natural England, the RSPB, the Wildfowl Trust and the Wetlands Trust. So, one should rightly ask 'Where was English Heritage?' After all, their involvement in 'A Strategic Plan for Fenland' would have been in line with their own 2004 *Strategy for Wetlands*:

> *Waterlogged sites can only be preserved in situ if their associated hydrology can be controlled. The protection of whole wetlands rather than 'monument islands' must therefore be the basis for future action. This must be done in co-operation with all other agencies involved in wetland management (especially English Nature and the Environment Agency) .... English Heritage will develop site-specific conservation management strategies for the most important wetland monuments at risk and co-operate in the development of wetland landscape conservation management strategies with other relevant agencies.*

In the Fens their own impressive strategy was not followed through by English Heritage or its successor Historic England. With hindsight, it seems a pity that

English Heritage ever wound up its Fenland Management Committee, for it is surely needed now more than ever to take a lead on archaeology conservation policies for the Fens. The failure of English Heritage to engage fully in more recent wetland conservation management in the Fens has been difficult to comprehend.

The reason for the difference between the cultural heritage and the natural heritage when it comes to conservation is probably a simple lack of passion for conservation generally amongst archaeologists, who feel more at home following the academic pursuits of researching and digging rather than just protecting. That needs to change if we are ever to catch up with our wildlife colleagues for whom the survival of biodiversity is an imperative.

Flag Fen, Peterborough

No discussion about the conservation of Fenland archaeology would be complete without a mention of the heroic endeavours of Francis Pryor and the Fenland Archaeological Trust to re-wet, preserve and study a prehistoric waterlogged landscape of timber structures dating from 1350 to 950 BC at Flag Fen near Peterborough. The Bronze Age waterlogged timbers were discovered when a drainage dyke through the area was deepened in 1982, and to save the timbers from drying out an artificial lake was constructed over most of the area by digging a trench around it and inserting a vertical plastic skirt. As Francis said in an article in *Antiquity* in 1992:

> It is sobering to reflect that the large mere was constructed with less than 12 months to spare – after the timbers had spent more than 3000 years below ground. It is very doubtful whether it could have been made today (Pryor 1992, 443).

They caught the drying-out process just in time. The Trust also constructed a visitor centre with a museum partially floating on the new mere. So, while some of the site has been excavated and published in an impressive English Heritage volume (Pryor 2001a), the larger part will be safe for a long time to come. The evidence here shows that if it is not possible to preserve waterlogged archaeology as part of a wider landscape conservation scheme, then some relatively small and isolated Fenland sites could still be given protection in this way. But that could not be achieved easily without the very active participation of Historic England which is now the national lead body for designation and conservation. More on this later (**p. 344-349**).

Chapter 14:
The Story of 'East Anglian Archaeology'

Going back to the Scole Committee's meeting on 1st March 1974, we realised that plans would have to be drawn up for a fresh approach to archaeological publication in the region. There was a long tradition that the annual county journals, in our case *Norfolk Archaeology* published by the Norfolk and Norwich Archaeological Society, were the appropriate outlets. But, that would soon prove to be unworkable with the extra reports coming from the active excavation programmes in our respective counties. A new regional series seemed to be the answer. At a meeting held on 10th April the Scole Committee was told that the Department of the Environment still preferred all reports to go into county or national journals. So, we decided to write to the editors of both the Norfolk and Suffolk journals for their views fully expecting them to say they could not take on more reports in addition to those they were already handling.

The answers came back just as we had expected, and on 14th January 1975 the Scole Committee agreed to a proposal that we establish a numbered monograph series to be called *East Anglian Archaeological Reports*, in association with the Scole Committee with the originating unit being the publisher and funder of each volume, The name of the series was later modified to the less wordy *East Anglian Archaeology*. The reports were to have a uniform format and house style, and the three Unit Directors for Norwich, Norfolk and Suffolk (Alan, myself and Stanley) were appointed as the editorial sub-committee. Alan Carter was to be the first chairman. In the years that followed Alan played a very significant role as chair, where his reading of texts submitted for publication was extraordinarily perceptive.

There was a slight hiccup when Suffolk produced East Anglian Archaeology Report No. 1 without any discussion about a house style or format, but it was already printed so there was nothing we could do. This does explain why the first volume looks very different from the rest. After that, we had the design of the series under some control. The concept of 'East Anglia' was later stretched to include Essex, and the County Archaeologist, John Hedges, joined the editorial sub-committee in 1982. The Cambridgeshire County Archaeologist, Adrian Tindall, joined us in 2004, followed by the Hertfordshire County Archaeologist, Stewart Bryant, in 2007. That was big enough, although we did include Lincolnshire for a volume of salt-making sites and for various Fenland Survey volumes. Essex's first volume was EAA No 25 which came out in 1985, by which time Norfolk had produced seventeen volumes, Suffolk three, Norwich three, and all four counties contributed to the regional barrow survey volume in 1981.

As the series has progressed, numbers generated by each county have partly evened out, and East Anglian Archaeology has been one of the outstanding successes of the whole story of how field archaeology became established as a profession in the region. An EAA promotion leaflet we distributed with Report No 2 announced that the series 'will be the main vehicle for publishing final reports on archaeological excavations and surveys in the region'. Up to October 2016 there have since been 159 volumes filling over two metres of shelving. Up to EAA 102 the volumes were published in conjunction with the Scole Committee, but by then the Committee had become less relevant, so the local branch of the Association of Local Government Archaeologists (ALGAO EAST), which had become the main co-ordinating body for local government archaeology in the region, took over.

14.1. *Jenny Glazebrook, the Managing Editor of East Anglian Archaeology, celebrating the publication of her 100th volume in the EAA series (No 155 Before Sutton Hoo) at a meeting of the Editorial Committee on 21st January 2016: a remarkable achievement.*

As a source of information on the archaeology of the region the series is unrivalled. Its success has depended particularly on the skill and commitment of the Managing Editors, employed through Norfolk County Council and funded by the contributing archaeological units: Julie Gardiner from 1985 to 1989, Susie West from 1989 to 1992 then Jenny Glazebrook from 1992 to present. Jenny has just edited her 100th volume (*Figure 14.1*).

The design of the cover of any journal is important for the journal's image, and the early ones were a disaster. The colour on the cover was meant to have a prestigious tan, but the printers could never quite give us the tan we wanted, and instead it was an unpleasant brown! Then Sue White, the NAU's senior illustrator, produced a fine colourful layout for the cover of No 18, which gave the series a big lift. Later, Steven Ashley and Mark Hoyle provided a new design to give it a fresh look to mark No 100 in 2002 (*Figure 14.2*).

14.2. The changing cover styles of East Anglian Archaeology from No. 2 (1976) onwards as printing and design for the series developed.

Alan Carter was the chairman of the EAA editorial Sub-ommittee from its inception until his sudden death in 1988, and then I took over after No. 44. The next few years were a very rewarding and satisfying experience. But all things must end, and after my retirement from the post as County Archaeologist in 1999 I quickly felt out of touch with the projects the series was publishing, and by 2010 it was time to go. I can be very emotional at difficult moments, and when I told the committee that they needed to find someone new, tears came, no doubt to the embarrassment of all in the room. I was subsequently given a copy of the hardback EAA 132 with a sticker inside which read:

Presented to Peter Wade-Martins, a founder member of East Anglian Archaeology, by the editorial board with thanks for his loyal support over thirty-five years, for chairing eighty-six editorial meetings and for steering one hundred and fifty-five volumes into print – no small contribution to the success of the series.

Long may the series continue, and perhaps we may see other regions follow suit one day by setting up their own series. It was the early collaboration of archaeologists in the region through the Scole Committee which made the whole concept possible.

Chapter 15:
County-based Conservation Projects

The Barrow Survey, 1973-76

When the Unit started in 1973 the countryside had been subject to 25 years of deeper ploughing and sub-soiling following the introduction of more powerful diesel tractors. John Owles, the farmer at Witton, had been collecting and recording the finds in the ploughsoil on his own farm and had saved much fragile prehistoric pottery from rapid disintegration under plough conditions (**p.81-82**). But how had other sites fared under cultivation? It seemed that the best county-wide thematic survey we could start with was a barrow survey, especially as there was already some data available from the Norfolk Research Committee's own barrow survey of the 1930s **(p. 72-73)**. The starting point was a set of hand-written notes for a progress report given by Rainbird Clarke to a meeting of the Norfolk Research Committee on 31st January 1948. With it was a card index with measurements recorded in paces hand-written by Leslie Grinsell. These were all seen by Andy Lawson, our prehistorian, in the Castle Museum in 1973, although they cannot now be found. Rainbird's notes showed that the early searchers had been very successful in increasing the numbers of known round barrows from 131 to 250, but what condition were they in now?

Andy Lawson started our own survey with real enthusiasm and it gave him a chance to get to know the county where he had not worked before. Most of the survey was conducted from 1974 to 1976, and the aim was to record every barrow we could find, to assess its condition and history and make appropriate recommendations for its future protection. Just after we started, Suffolk joined in and then Essex followed. Towards the end Cambridgeshire came in too, so the final report came out as *The barrows of East Anglia* in East Anglian Archaeology 12 (Lawson, Martin, Priddy and Taylor 1981).

Andy created his own gazetteer to include for each barrow its County Number, an eight-figure grid reference, the Ancient Monument number (where scheduled), date of record, condition, measurements and further details. It included all barrows and possible barrows reported up to 30th October 1974. And, it included all ring-ditches recorded up to 31st March 1977. The end result was 625 recorded examples, of which 228 survived as recognisable mounds.

Barrow survival

The condition of the surviving mounds was as follows:
   72 were under grass or bracken,
   104 were under trees and bushes,
   <u>52</u> were under plough.
   228

It was possible to show that at least 220 barrows had been on heaths in the 1930s, but that figure had in the meantime been drastically reduced to 54, so the destruction was mainly due to the ploughing of old heathland during and after the war. And, of course, it is on sandy heathland soils where mounds under plough are subject to additional erosion from windblow. From an available sample of 39 barrows, where measurements of the heights of barrows under plough were recorded in the 1930s, a striking fact emerged: it was possible to calculate that *the average rate of destruction was two centimetres a year, or one metre in fifty years.* So, mounds under plough were disappearing within 30 years, although there was some evidence that once the mound was reduced to a low profile the rate of erosion did accelerate. That was remarkably important data.

Scheduled barrows

Scheduling had offered minimal protection, since 33 of the 162 examples scheduled since the 1930s had been lost and a further seven were currently subject to regular ploughing (Lawson, Martin, Priddy and Taylor 1981, 34). The one ray of hope was that a scheduled group of four at Little Cressingham were taken out of the plough and surrounded with marker posts when the Department of the Environment issued a Preservation Order in 1976.

In March 1982 the Unit prepared an annotated list for the Department of the Environment of all scheduled barrows indicating which ones urgently needed attention, but there was absolutely no response. When Andy Lawson left the Unit for a more senior post at the end of March 1983, John Wymer, a well-known prehistorian, was appointed in his place. (A record of John's first few days in the Unit is reproduced from his field notebook in Powell 2009; a volume of papers in John's honour edited by Ashton, Healy and Pettitt was published in 1998; obituary to John in Rogerson 2006).

Responsibility for the protection of Ancient Monuments was being passed from the Department of the Environment to a new body to be known as the Historic Buildings and Monuments Commission (English Heritage) in April 1984. So, John's first step was to recommend urgent conservation measures for barrows to the new English Heritage.

A review of barrow protection, 1983

Except for a very small number of other monuments, barrows are the only prehistoric features which survive above ground in Norfolk, and with numbers so reduced every surviving barrow was worth protecting. John re-visited a selection of the 228 surviving sites between August and December 1983, ten years after our previous survey had began. He drew up a detailed list of *all* barrows he could find in need of protection with a scale of priorities of 'High', 'Middle' and 'Low'. The list included scheduled barrows and those unscheduled barrows still half a meter high or more. A few had rather sad entries in his list like '1 m (high) at time of Barrow Survey, now levelled'. By 1984 five of the marker posts around the barrows at Little Cressingham which had been taken out of cultivation in 1976 had already been knocked over. We suggested that concrete blocks would last longer, although they were, understandably, considered to be unsightly.

The summary of his recommendations for High Priority included:
- taking two scheduled barrows out of plough immediately and surrounding them with concrete blocks,
- surrounding three scheduled barrows being encroached upon by the plough with concrete blocks,
- having trees removed from one scheduled barrow,
- having eight unscheduled barrows over 0.5m high scheduled immediately, ploughing stopped and surrounding them with concrete blocks.

This was all incorporated into a very detailed, and, we hoped, helpful, report with the names of the farmers concerned and detailed recommendations for action required in each case. This confidential report was endorsed by the Norfolk Archaeological Services Advisory Committee (NASAC) and various district councils in the county. It was then sent on 4th May 1984 to English Heritage by the County Council's Chief Executive. There was, I sensed, some irritation at English Heritage that we had raised the matter again, and a formal reply dated 6th August 1984 from the English Heritage inspector offered little short-term hope of any action at all (*EDP* 14th September 1984):

> The report makes a number of telling points about the rate of erosion of burial mounds caused by ploughing (it is significant that the rate of destruction, about 2cm per year, appears to accelerate once a mound is reduced to a low profile). A number of recommendations for new scheduling are made. I should say that we shall wish to view these and the recommendations for action in lower priority cases mentioned in the report in the context of a proposed re-scheduling exercise (akin to the re-listing of Historic Buildings programme) which the Inspectorate

> hopes will be undertaken by the Commission. Such an exercise, which is still being discussed internally, would involve the injection of much-needed new staff and resources into this branch of our work, the careful checking of all existing scheduling data, with a view to preparing the ground for a large new scheduling (and perhaps de-scheduling) programme. Norfolk's barrows would be viewed in a regional and national context. It seems sensible to await such a re-scheduling exercise, unless an urgent and over-riding case can be made for immediate new scheduling action.
> You will appreciate that a low level of Inspectorate staffing and the resultant very heavy commitments over a wide area are problems which we have had now for some years. This should not excuse us, however, from taking action on the higher priority cases mentioned in the barrow report, and I shall do all I can, within the constraints of a heavy workload in a large number of counties, to ensure that further damage to important monuments is prevented. We shall keep the Committee informed of progress.

So, there was the prospect of a new English Heritage exercise to catch up with scheduling along lines similar to those used previously by Michael Heseltine, the Minister, to update the listing of historic buildings. We were greatly encouraged by the prospect of their 'proposed re-scheduling exercise', later labelled the 'Monument Protection Programme', or the MPP as it became known. In February 1985 English Heritage did agree to the idea of surrounding some scheduled barrows with concrete blocks, and a group of barrows on the Houghton Hall estate on Harpley Common was chosen for the experiment, although they were later removed when the whole field was put down to grass and such markers were no longer necessary. English Heritage also responded positively to some of John's detailed comments about negotiating management agreements to take some scheduled barrows out of cultivation. So there were some limited benefits while we waited for the MPP. But we had to wait a while.

The protection of field monuments

In the 1970s it had been relatively easy to arrange for sites to be scheduled, but after that it had become virtually impossible. First we were told that the scheduling criteria were being re-examined and we would have to wait; then it was difficult because of the extra workload created by the 1979 Ancient Monuments and Archaeological Areas Act; then scheduling was being held up while preparations were in hand for the MPP. In 1988 we were urging English Heritage to start the MPP, but there still seemed no prospect of that. They were then saying that nothing could be done until our Sites and Monuments Record was fully computerised, but with such a large database that was at least two years away. We didn't believe that a fully computerised database would anyway make much difference. For barrows we had already conducted two comprehensive county-wide surveys and knew *exactly* which sites needed immediate protection. There was also a legal loophole which allowed farmers to continue ploughing scheduled monuments if they had been ploughed between 1976 and 1981. This was called a 'Class Consent', and we were urging the Minister to review these Consent Orders. The Minister, Lord Caithness, wrote to Norfolk MPs on 15th January 1988 in response to letters we had asked them all to send to him saying 'We recognise a need to review the present Class Consent Order, particularly in relation to Class 1 works (agricultural horticultural and forestry) and we are discussing this matter with English Heritage', but we heard nothing further on the matter. (In 1994 the second Class Consent regulation was introduced so that routine cultivation of scheduled monuments could continue, but the right to cultivate would lapse if it was not exercised for six years or more.)

We also suggested that English Heritage should consider developing a partnership with the County Council for organising locally negotiated Management Agreements with farmers and then re-charge those costs to English Heritage. The response to that was much better, and in November 1988 a letter arrived from English Heritage with a positive outcome to our suggestion for a partnership whereby if the County Council were to fund a member of staff to negotiate Management Agreements with farmers under Section 17 of the 1979 Act, they would refund the actual cost of the Agreements for items like new fencing, scrub clearance and rabbit control. That was an improvement, and it led to the start of the Norfolk Monuments Management Project (NMMP) in 1990 (**p.198-203**). But, we were still in a situation where the ploughing of old meadows containing unscheduled earthworks, the removal of ancient hedgerows and the continuous ploughing of scheduled sites could continue unabated. There was much for the new NMMP project to do, and there was widespread support in the local press for Norfolk's conservation initiative with headlines like 'Protection urged for old sites' (*EDP* 12th April 1988) and 'Delays pose threat to valuable ancient sites: English Heritage accused' (*EDP* 1st March 1989).

Records kindly made available to the writer by the new Historic England's Designation Team in July 2015 showed that following John Wymer's 1984 report there have been 24 further barrows scheduled as follows:

1995: 12
1997: 1
2000: 1
2001: 1
2004: 9

But we had to wait 14 years between Andy Lawson's Barrow Survey report being published and these fresh barrow schedulings. There has been some progress since, although without detailed site visits it is difficult to know if the barrows John was concerned about in 1984 have all been saved from further cultivation.

After barrows, we had intended to move on to a survey of Roman towns and other large Roman settlements, mainly on arable land, to identify their locations, their extent and their condition with a view to enhancing our records and then preparing scheduling proposals. However, in informal conversations with English Heritage inspectors it became very clear that there was no prospect at all of them acting on our recommendations, so we took the idea no further. They had, though, rather randomly scheduled Brampton Roman town in 1983 (**p. 90-91**).

In 1987 English Heritage produced what could have been an important report on *Ancient Monuments in the Countryside: an archaeological management review* with a section on the management of archaeological sites in arable land, but it contained little new (Darvill 1987, 130-132). There was, however, a tantalising mention that 'a programme to sift out sites which ought not now be on the Schedule, and to add those which have been omitted, began in 1987 and is expected to continue for some ten years, depending upon the availability of resources.' (Darvill 1987, 168). This later developed into their Monument Protection Programme (**p. 207-209**).

The Norfolk Monuments Management Project (NMMP), 1990-present

The damage to the countryside over the post-war years was described so well by Graham Harvey in 1997 in his *The Killing of the Countryside* (1997, 10-12) where he placed the blame for what had been happening squarely on farmland subsidies:

> ..the sole purpose of the countryside is to turn out more and more food, whether or not it is needed, whether or not it has to be 'dumped' on world markets at the expense of ther British taxpayer and poor farmers in the Third World .... Intensive cereal crops and a monoculture of perennial ryegrass have largely replaced the old, flower-rich meadows .... Unbelievably, 97 per cent of Britain's meadowland has perished in the Government-inspired dash for production .... Drive across the Cheshire Plain in summer and you are unlikely to see a primrose. Get out of the car and you probably won't hear a skylark either, just the sound of a tractor and fertiliser spreader applying more nitrogen to the thick lifeless ryegrass sward.

His concern was focused on the wildlife, rather than on the archaeology, but the damage to the historic landscape was just as bad. It is interesting that his book was at the tail end of a whole series of books with the same theme, including Marion Shoard's *The Theft of the Countryside* (1980), J.K. Bowers and P. Cheshire's *Agriculture, the Countryside and Land Use: An Economic Critique* (1983), W.M. Adams's

Nature's Place: Conservation Sites and Countryside Change (1986), Richard Body's *Red or Green for Farmers (and the rest of us)* (1987) and Howard Newby's *The Countryside in Question* (1988), few of which identified the loss of archaeology as a concern. They were mostly focused on the loss of wildlife and the disappearance of landscape character. This showed what a poor job our profession was doing in publicising the equally serious loss to archaeology. The exception was Marion Shoard's *The Theft of the Countryside* published in 1980 which devoted a chapter and more to the loss of archaeology, quoting from significant studies like Peter Drewett's survey of plough damage in Sussex (Drewett 1976) and Alan Saville's survey of similar damage in the Cotswolds (Saville 1977). But her attention to archaeology was unusual at the time. There was so much more we, as a profession, could have done, and should still be doing, to present a better balance so that archaeology and ecology are matters of equal concern.

There were years of frustration over the Department of the Environment's inaction over (a) scheduling sites, (b) advising on conservation when asked by landowners and (c) not prosecuting when real damage was done. This can best be illustrated by quoting three cases concerning deserted medieval villages described in a confidential report on 'The Preservation of Ancient Monuments in Norfolk' I wrote for the Norfolk Archaeological Services Committee meeting of 13th September 1983. This report has only recently been released to public view in the Norfolk Record Office now that the 30-year embargo has expired. It does illustrate the lack of care for our cultural heritage in the countryside which the Department of the Environment were exhibiting at the time. In the text a comparison was made with Pudding Norton, recognised as the best-preserved deserted village in the county.

(a) Letton (in Cranworth parish) was a particularly extensive earthwork site relatively well preserved in parkland. It was probably as complete as Pudding Norton. The Archaeological Unit recommended scheduling in April 1977. After a site visit by an inspector, the Department decided to proceed with scheduling in September 1977, and a letter was sent to the farmer giving notice of the decision. We understand that the farmer asked for a site meeting before the site was scheduled. No meeting was arranged, and the site was eventually levelled and ploughed in 1978. In 1979 a very eroded and worthless fragment of a sunken roadway was scheduled long after it was too late.

(b) Godwick (in Tittleshall parish) is a good earthwork site but with many later features. Of the church only the much altered tower survives, and part of that collapsed in May 1981. After this happened the Unit wrote to the Department on 3rd June 1981 to tell them that the farmer, Mr J. Garner of Godwick Hall, wanted advice and help with restoration of the tower. Site visits and meetings then took place in the same year to agree on the best method of safeguarding the remaining parts of the tower, and to work out a Management Agreement for the whole site and to improve display and public access. Ever since then the farmer has been waiting for a decision from the Department. Over two years later he has made no progress, despite several promptings from us and letters from him.

(c) <u>Roudham,</u> near Thetford, was the only intact site left in the Breckland area. It was scheduled in 1970. On 18th May 1981 the Unit notified the Department that two areas, including some of the best earthworks, had been ploughed, but no action was taken for 18 months until eventually the Ancient Monuments Warden visited the site, but that was only after much pressure from us. Three areas of the scheduled site are actually being cultivated, and so far no action has been taken to stop this destruction. It now seems that no attempt will be made to bring a prosecution, even though the Department has been informed that there are two people willing to describe on oath what condition the site was in before cultivation took place.

The Chief Executive of the County Council then wrote to the Minister, Neil Macfarlane, about these particular cases. The feeble explanation about inaction over Roudham came back as follows: 'The events coincided with change in the areas of responsibility of some inspectors at the time of increasing pressure on all aspects of our work.' (*EDP* 14th September 1984).

In the 1980s there were two mechanisms by which sites could be protected from damaging farming operations. One was scheduling, and we have seen how very difficult it was to encourage English Heritage to respond to the need to schedule sites even where they were of obvious national importance. The other was for us to organise voluntary management agreements with farmers and landowners and to provide tax-free grants under Section 17 of the 1979 Ancient Monuments Act, usually for five years. This was the purpose of the Norfolk Monument Management Project which we began in 1990. In 1991 Countryside Stewardship Schemes were introduced by the Countryside Commission to pay farmers to protect farmland of environmental significance, but to begin with that had relatively little impact on archaeology conservation (Wade Martins, S. 2015, 144).

The real breakthrough came when I reached an understanding with English Heritage that they would fund the Norfolk Monuments Management Project which would cover *all* monuments of schedulable quality and not just those already scheduled (**p. 198-203)**. For English Heritage this was a new scheme, and the decision to include all sites which met their scheduling criteria was crucial to the project's success. English Heritage offered initially £10,000 a year for three years to fund these management agreements. I invited representatives from the Farming and Rural Conservation Agency, the Countryside Stewardship Officer, English Heritage, the Farming and Wildlife Advisory Group, the National Farmers Union (NFU) and the Country Landowners Association to join a committee which I chaired twice a year. We employed a part-time project officer, Helen Paterson who had been an English Heritage Field Monument Warden, in a pilot scheme to visit every known earthwork of schedulable quality in the county to discuss management options with farmers, land owners and their agents. The running costs were jointly funded by the County Council's Department of Planning and Transportation and the Field Archaeology Division of the Norfolk Museums Service (Paterson and Wade-Martins 1999). A project leaflet was produced for farmers with several air photographs of very visual sites with the message:

> TIMES HAVE CHANGED
> Some archaeological sites, such as Bronze Age burial mounds and medieval moated sites still survive as earthworks, even in a county like Norfolk which has been intensively cultivated since the last war. Many more have been lost through levelling and ploughing over the same period. Most of us can remember old meadows containing 'humps and bumps' which disappeared during the expansion of arable farming in the 1940s, 50s and 60s. This destruction was encouraged with government subsidies at a time when farmers were being urged to produce more food.
> Times **have** changed. We have now entered a period of food surpluses, of government conservation grants and Set Aside. Farmers are being increasingly encouraged to conserve the best of what remains .... The purpose of the Project is to encourage the farming and management of the field monuments in ways which conserve them for future generations to enjoy. We have so few good sites left in Norfolk now, that we owe it to our successors to protect the best of what previous farming generations have handed down to us.

The leaflet explained that the new project had the support of the Ministry of Agriculture, the county branches of the National Farmers Union and the Country Landowners Association to encourage the better management of the surviving archaeological heritage.

It was later agreed with English Heritage that Helen could take the place of their own Field Monument Warden who would not need to visit Norfolk monuments in the future.

The north-west part of the county was chosen as the pilot area, where 82 sites were identified for visits, and of these 22 had been scheduled. By October 1992 four management agreements had been concluded, and a further 13 were being considered for similar agreements.

By July 1997 Helen had visited 365 sites county-wide of which 307 were judged to be significant. The other 58 were considered too fragmentary or had disappeared since they were last recorded. The range of monuments to be covered included deserted villages, fishponds, castles, burial mounds, priories, ruined churches and moats. The Section 17 grants could cover the full capital costs of stock fencing, scrub clearance, tree felling and rabbit control plus ongoing maintenance. The grants were tax-free. Whenever the Farming and Wildlife Advisory Group organised a farm walk Helen was always invited along to talk about the archaeology, even if the walk was on a farm where earthworks were not present. Increasingly farmers began to realise that archaeology was an essential part of the conservation movement. This led to invitations for Helen to give talks at meetings of the local branches of the NFU and Young Farmers Clubs, and she wrote about her work for the local press (*EDP* 17th March 1995).

The outcomes of the visits to the 307 significant sites by 1997 were as follows:

- 23   Section 17 agreements signed
- 2   Section 17 agreements in preparation
- c.10   entered Countryside Stewardship or Environmentally Sensitive Area Schemes
- 104   management statements signed
- 50   management statements awaiting signature
- c.40   owners already managing sites voluntarily preferring not to sign statements
- 6   showed no interest in discussing better management*
- 72   further visits in hand

*This included one farmer who owned a scheduled site

This was overall a very encouraging response. When the project officer called on farmers of unscheduled monuments they were often surprised to learn that they had something of archaeological interest, and their responses were usually very positive, Goodwill and good communication were the key to the success of the project, helped considerably by Helen's warm personality. Unfunded management statements were often signed to record voluntary understandings, and when we had completed an earthworks survey of a site, that plan was attached to the management agreement or management statement. This helped to build up goodwill and better understanding. When we had taken an air photograph as well, that was included in the information pack to the farmer. Raising awareness was the key to the whole undertaking. During the 1990s the integrated approach of our air photography programme, the earthworks survey (below) and the NMMP combined with the new acquisition policy of the Norfolk Archaeological Trust (**p. 271-272**) ensured that archaeology was gradually recognised within the farming community as an essential part of good conservation.

The project was promoted through the NFU and the Country Landowners Association whose representatives were on the project committee, and we usually combined a committee meeting with a site visit to discuss practical issues. The model worked well, and the project is still going strong. The Committee itself has been wound up recently by the County Council, but a similar-sounding advisory group is currently being formed. The roles of the two project officers, Helen Paterson who was part-time from 1990 to 2006, and David Robertson since 2006, are described in their article in *Norfolk Archaeology* which celebrates the achievements of the project over its first 20 years (Robertson and Paterson 2010). Over 600 earthwork sites had been visited and 187 Section 17 Agreements had been signed covering 87 sites at a cost of £177,000 in grant aid. The project also gave advice to Natural England on the archaeology of more than 400 Higher Level Stewardship schemes. The success of this approach was gradually recognised by English Heritage which grant-aided 20 or more similar county projects elsewhere under their Historic Environment Countryside Advisory Services Scheme. Some counties have since, sadly, closed their monument conservation projects, although the Norfolk one, thank goodness, has continued to prosper.

The County Earthworks Survey, 1994-2000

Of all our projects, the one which gave me the greatest satisfaction was the county earthworks survey. It felt as though we were doing something which was absolutely right, and it has contributed considerably to our understanding of the county's archaeology. Some conservation specialists and advisers now tell me that the volume we produced, *Earthworks of Norfolk* in East Anglian Archaeology 104 (Cushion and Davison 2003), has become their bible for advising on good management of the county's earthwork archaeology, and that is immensely satisfying.

The *Earthworks of Norfolk* volume with 141 survey plans and supporting aerial photographs, was published in 2003 and represented the results of a six-year project which started in 1994. Full credit must go to the two authors. Brian Cushion produced the elegant site surveys, mainly at 1:1,000. He had just retired after 29 years as a surveyor in the Ordnance Survey and was familiar with working on his own with minimal equipment before the days of satellite positioning technology. His method was to start with a 1:2,500 base map enlarged to 1:1,000 and to plot features on to that using the Graphical Survey technique, all done by eye and with an optical square. That was his only instrument other than tapes and ranging poles. It was a very simple method which did not require a second person (*EDP* 16th November 1996). Helen Paterson, while working on the Monuments Management Project (**p. 198-203**), helped to identify some of the sites which needed surveying, while Alan Davison carried out the documentary background research for each site and wrote the informative background texts. The authors assembled a virtually complete corpus of all significant earthworks in grassland which we could identify at the time (*Figure 15.1*), although inevitably we missed a few. We had hoped that the project would be followed by another involving a systematic search of all the woodland, but with my departure from the Museums Service in 1999, that was not to be. However, Gerry Barnes and Tom Williamson have more recently carried out important work surveying 50 sample woods in the county recording the earthworks of moated sites in three of them plus many other historic features (Barnes and Williamson 2015, 34-37 and 160-251).

The volume illustrated and described 141 sites representing the full range of earthwork evidence from Romano-British to post-medieval settlements, moated manors, monasteries, castles, fishponds, water meadows, ridge and furrow, parks and gardens and even oyster beds. Brian and Alan worked for long periods on the project with great dedication. My problem was that English Heritage absolutely refused time and again to contribute to survey costs. So, I had to raid all sorts of pockets in our budget to cover them. I suspected that the English Heritage fear was that we would once again come up with a well-considered set of recommendations for scheduling more sites on top of the original barrow survey, which they could not handle. Full credit must go to my successor as County Field Archaeologist, Brian Ayers, who succeeded in obtaining English Heritage funding for the publication, so English Heritage had their logo on the cover after all! In my Editorial I said that only some 40% of monuments described in the volume then had legal protection, and 'It is to be hoped that English Heritage will follow the conservation process to its logical conclusion and consider scheduling most of the monuments illustrated here'. There was no response from English Heritage, but the information in that volume has often been used for conservation purposes within the Environmental Stewardship schemes funded by Defra.

For such an arable county it was surprising how much we found, mainly by searching air photographs. Even well-known sites, like Castle Acre Priory, had earthworks which proved to be much more intact and informative than we had expected. We called the report *Earthworks of Norfolk* rather than **The** *Earthworks of Norfolk* because some had already been covered elsewhere (the barrow survey in Lawson, Martin, Priddy and Taylor 1981 and Lawson 1986, the Iron Age forts in Davies, Gregory, Lawson, Rickett and Rogerson 1992, four out of five of the linear earthworks in Wade-Martins 1974a and moats which are often adequately recorded on Ordnance Survey maps and were also discussed in Dollin 1986).

CHAPTER 15: COUNTY-BASED CONSERVATION PROJECTS   205

15.1. An historic aerial photograph taken in 1933-8 by the old Norfolk and Norwich Aero Club of the fine motte and bailey castle at Horsford. The original negatives of this picture, along with the many other interesting aerial photos taken by the Club before the war, were all destroyed in their clubhouse by one of the first bombs to be dropped on Norwich at the start of the Second World War. This is one of a small group of Norman earthwork castles in the county consisting of a mound, or 'motte', on which a timber keep once stood surrounded by a deep ditch. Attached to that is a heavily defended oval bailey which contained the castle outbuildings. Access to the keep was through the baily and up over a bridge onto the motte. There was quite a fuss after the interior of the bailey was ploughed in 1986 and it was afterwards returned to grass. Although internal details were reduced during this activity, there was no prosecution because English Heritage judged that it was not possible to prove damage. The castle featured on the cover of the Norfolk Earthworks Survey EAA volume published in 2003 (TG2015/M/NNAC).

It is very difficult to single out particular earthworks to mention here, but I would highlight four:
- Denton Castle, a small but perfectly formed, motte and bailey castle in a small wood in the corner of a meadow called Darrow Wood now owned by the National Trust.
- Wormegay Castle, a larger motte and bailey castle with a wide low motte and superbly preserved bailey with an entrance opening directly onto the end of the village street.
- Castle Acre Priory precinct meadow with a surrounding wall surviving to full height in a few places. The meadow, which is full of humps and bumps, surrounds the well-known English Heritage Guardianship monument, but the earthworks in the field outside the English Heritage railings had received little recognition before the survey (*Figure 25.10*).
- Anmer deserted village, where extensive earthworks cover the parkland near the church.

It appears that about 35 out of 141 earthwork complexes, including deserted and shrunken villages, monasteries, moats and fishponds have been scheduled, or their scheduling has been revised, since the project started. But, a follow-up review to clarify these figures would be beneficial.

Chapter 16:
National Conservation Initiatives

The English Heritage Monuments Protection Programme (MPP), 1986-2001

Work started on this major national scheduling programme at English Heritage in 1986. But, unlike Michael Heseltine's re-listing exercise for historic buildings, it was not launched, as far as we were aware, with a ministerial statement, and it was never clear to me if this had the Minister's backing with additional funds or if it was purely an internal English Heritage initiative. Certainly its resources were limited. At the start a very analytical and rigid approach was taken to:

1. Review and evaluate existing information in all the county SMRs on sites of archaeological and historical interest so that those of national importance could be identified.
2. Recommend to the Secretary of State those monuments which should then be considered for scheduling. This included reviews of existing schedule descriptions.

To do that they decided to (a) define monument classes at national level, (b) then locally to evaluate the relative importance of individual examples within each monument class and (c) then make a preliminary selection of those believed to be of the highest quality within each class. The plan was for MPP fieldworkers to visit those sites which had been identified as of high quality within each class and to determine the best immediate course of action in each case. By April 1992 our Assistant Records Officer, Myk Flitcroft, funded by English Heritage, had over a period of only 16 weeks completed desk-based site assessments of 128 monument classes from the 28,000 records in the SMR. Helen Bamford, a prehistorian, had been appointed by English Heritage to commence site visits in the region, but she was one of only 18 fieldworkers to cover all 46 counties. In the spring of 1993 English Heritage were saying that field visits would soon begin and they intended to work through the task at a rate of 90 new schedulings a year in Norfolk. But by October 1993, 18 months after their fieldworker was appointed, no new sites had been scheduled in the county nor had any old schedulings been revised. It was not looking good.

In the spring of 1994 English Heritage explained that the lack of progress in Norfolk was due to the fact that we had one of the largest SMRs with 30,000 separate entries. It had taken them a long time to go through the data.

Nevertheless, they now had their East Anglian fieldworker working full time on Norfolk, and their target was 691 sites to be scheduled by the year 2003. However, the Department of National Heritage (DNH), to which their scheduling proposals had to be submitted, required much more extensive documentation than had been needed for the re-listing of historic buildings. An example was West Acre Priory where the proposal took ten days to write covering 30 pages! Anyway, English Heritage agreed to submit quarterly lists of the proposals they had sent to DNH. By June 1994 the lists showed that four new sites had been scheduled, including Wormegay Priory and West Acre Priory and 40 proposals had been submitted to DNH. These included some where the old schedulings had been revised. English Heritage appeared now to be meeting its national targets. By March 1996 71 new Norfolk schedulings had been completed, mainly for barrows, moats and their own Guardianship monuments. Although that was welcome, this figure had, in our view, been artificially boosted by multiple barrow cemeteries, such as a group of 28 on Salthouse Heath, which looked like a quick fix to get the numbers up. Nevertheless, the Programme seemed to be gaining momentum, although the emphasis on their own Guardianship monuments was puzzling when surely they were the safest and least urgent of them all. In late 1996 we invited Helen Bamford to write an article about her work in an 'Our Hidden Heritage' series we were producing for the local press (*EDP* 21st December 1996).

From 1980 to 2015 there were 233 new or revised schedulings, falling well short of the English Heritage 1994 predictions. We never saw the drive to protect unscheduled earthworks or vulnerable sites under cultivation on a scale we had earnestly hoped for. And, significantly, I don't recall that there was ever an opportunity to sit down regularly with the English Heritage designation team to discuss their programme or the possibilities for collaborative working as we frequently did with the project officers working for the Countryside Commission, MAFF, Defra and Natural England. With them we regularly met as colleagues and had review meetings on how they were developing their Countryside Stewardship and Environmentally Sensitive Area (ESA) schemes and they were always willing to discuss their work and their priorities with us. Not so English Heritage, which was very frustrating.

In 2000 English Heritage published a booklet, *MPP 2000: A Review of the Monuments Protection Programme, 1986-2000* (Schofield 2000), which summarised what had been achieved over the previous 15 years. Their work had been primarily to create a very elaborate system of Monument Class Descriptions while continuing to evaluate the resource data in the County Sites and Monuments Records, but 'at a strategic level'. Their continuing priority was this evaluation which would be achieved 'over the next few years'. A short piece of the concluding section of the report is worth quoting in full because it says so much about the philosophy of MPP:

> In addition, however, we need to constantly review what we mean by 'the archaeological resource' and 'the heritage' embracing where appropriate such things as the cultural diversity and social inclusion agenda into our evaluation and characterisation work.

The report is peppered with words and phrases like 'evaluate', 're-appraise', 'constantly review' and 'new strategy directions', and one has no clear sense of direction, purpose or commitment in the document. But it is nevertheless important to accept that there was some real progress with 5,000 newly-scheduled monuments created under MPP throughout England during the life of the project.

The report states that West Yorkshire had the greatest increase of 229%, from 96 to 316. In Suffolk there was a 36% increase with 66 new schedulings, There was no percentage available for our own county, but Norfolk and Lincolnshire with some of the largest proportions of arable farmland, where the need for conservation was most urgent, were in the lowest category with under 25%. There was an apparent reluctance to designate sites in arable land where continued ploughing would be a significant issue. Although the report gave the impression that MPP was very much in progress, it just died in 2001 without a formal announcement and with the job only half done. Where, we asked, was MPP? Nobody seemed to know, and it is possible that government and NFU pressure to limit regulation may have had a hand in the decision. Sadly, the archaeological community hardly made the closure of this potentially important initiative an issue for debate. It had died with hardly a whimper from the profession 'there being some consensus that management via the planning system was generally more appropriate' (Bryant and Wills 2016, 6). But in areas where the main damage was from cultivation that essentially urban approach to conservation simply would not work.

The English Heritage Monuments at Risk Survey (MARS), 1994-1996

Survey results

Meanwhile, there was the 'MARS' project, initiated by Geoff Wainwright, who was a most effective Chief Archaeologist at English Heritage from 1989 to 1999. This national survey was published in 1998 with the commendable aim of providing sound data on which future conservation policies would be based (Darvill and Fulton 1998). It was a substantial piece of work full of coloured maps and diagrams, running to over 300 pages plus the back-up archive data. The survey lasted from July 1994 to November 1996 during which a representative sample of 14,591 monuments (scheduled and unscheduled) were randomly selected and examined. Of these 16% had been completely destroyed prior to 1995, and about half of these losses were known to have occurred since 1945. Cultivation was the single biggest cause, accounting for 10% of wholesale monument destruction and 30% of piecemeal damage. The report concluded that:

> All across England archaeological monuments are in a sorry state. There is certainly no scope here for archaeological bodies or other agencies to relax their efforts to improve the conservation of monuments, indeed there is an urgent need to do much more (Darvill and Fulton 1998, 243).

Action to prevent damage

It was recognised that measures were needed to prevent more monuments being taken into cultivation and to remove those being ploughed from cultivation altogether. This required 'the extension of existing mechanisms to control changes in land use'. The survey found that scheduled monuments had suffered a lower than average rate of destruction, so one would have expected the MARS report to recommend that greater efforts be made to speed up the scheduling process. But that was not one of the key conclusions. The report just recommended that:

> The Monuments Protection Programme is continued to systematically review England's Schedule of monuments as the cornerstone of national conservation policy (Darvill and Fulton 1998, 242).

There was a big difference between simply 'reviewing the Schedule' and organising a crash catch-up programme, which the report clearly indicated was necessary, although that was not spelled out. When the survey had accumulated such a weight of evidence demonstrating the need for a lot more scheduling, one can't help thinking that someone had a hand in watering down the key recommendation. That would surely have been the moment to make a strong case to ministers to fund an accelerated scheduling programme in the areas not fully covered, just as Michael Heseltine did years earlier with listing buildings. Instead, as we have seen, MPP seems to have just disappeared unfinished four years later. But one can't imagine that the wildlife lobby would have accepted this so easily if it had been a habitats' review which was being closed down.

Natural England's Environmental Stewardship schemes

The third initiative under which sites could be protected was the new *Environmentally Sensitive Area (ESA)* schemes introduced following the 1986 Agriculture Act. These started in the Broads in 1986, following the uproar over the ploughing up of the Halvergate Marshes, and the *Countryside Stewardship* schemes ran alongside ESAs from 1991, all funded by the Ministry of Agriculture Fisheries and Food (MAFF).

Unlike with scheduled monuments, there were generous payments available under these schemes. But, in 1992 when I gave my presidential address to the newly-formed Norfolk Archaeological and Historical Research Group I still had to point out then that these ESA schemes showed little provision for conserving the historic landscape. For instance, the Breckland ESA, started in 1988, had a management prescription which provided payment to farmers who left uncropped 'wildlife strips' around arable field margins, but there was no equivalent prescription for leaving fallow the site of a Roman villa or a Saxon cemetery being damaged by ploughing and sub-soiling. The Countryside Commission's *Countryside Premium Scheme,* then available for Set-Aside land in the region, provided payments for the establishment of fallow for ground-nesting birds, for the creation of grazing areas for brent geese and new grassland for wildlife benefit on top of Set-Aside payments, but there were no management options under these measures to benefit the archaeology. The wildlife agencies had been much more successful than English Heritage in pressing for change within the new conservation schemes being introduced to the farming community by MAFF. This was partly because there was European legislation on the conservation of the *natural* environment dating back to 1993 with which the government had to show compliance or risk fines. There was no comparable European protection for the *cultural* heritage which was left to national governments. Nevertheless, there would soon be some real change.

Breckland Archaeological Survey, 1994-96

A Breckland survey, originally suggested by the Suffolk Archaeological Unit and financed by English Heritage, was run jointly by the Norfolk and Suffolk Archaeological Units from 1994 to 1996 and demonstrated the archaeological wealth of the Brecks, with many new sites recorded as a part of the survey. One of the principal aims of the survey was to make specific recommendations to MAFF, the Forestry Commission and Ministry of Defence, both of which manage large parts of the Brecks, for improved historic landscape conservation. The project officer, Kate Sussams, located 90 new earthworks, including round barrows, rabbit warren banks and flint mines, and emphasised the specialist nature of past land use on these dry sandy soils. The survey also highlighted the archaeological significance of the rabbit warrens (Sussams 1996).

Kate's report recommended that MAFF's ESA project officer should receive regular updates on the area's archaeology so that the information could be relayed via their ESA Agreement maps to landowners and farmers joining the scheme. There were four tiers of land management grant-aided under the scheme. Where there were earthworks on existing heathland (Tier 1) these earthworks should be managed to protect the archaeology, and where there were sites identified as artefact scatters on arable land (Tier 2) reversion from arable to grassland should be encouraged (Sussams 1996, 141-142).

It was also recommended that Forest Enterprise should receive updates on new archaeological information as it was entered into the SMRs (Sussams 1996, 143-150). Some earthworks could well lie unrecognised deep within the forests and might be subject to potentially damaging forest clearance operations. So, it was recommended that all forest compartments should be surveyed in advance of felling, with priority given to those still with first-rotation crops. The importance of these 'Rapid Identification Surveys' quickly became apparent by 1999 when Forest Enterprise funded a survey of 921 hectares of forest which produced 16 previously unrecorded possible burial mounds, an area of Neolithic flint mining and numerous probable post-medieval boundary banks (Paterson and Wade-Martins 1999, 147). These results were actually much better than Kate had predicted (Sussams 1996, 144).

It was at this point that MAFF accepted the importance of building provision specifically for archaeology into their Breckland ESA scheme, and I was asked to write the following piece for the Breckland ESA Spring 1998 Newsletter:

A New Prescription for Preserving Archaeological Sites in Breckland: a significant step forward

Archaeologists in Norfolk and Suffolk are delighted with a new option just announced for the Breckland ESA. Breckland is one of the richest areas for archaeology in the region, and at last payments are available specifically to encourage farmers to take important sites out of arable when they are at risk of damage by ploughing or sub-soiling. Conserving our archaeological heritage has now been placed on a par with wildlife habitats. This is a tremendous step forward.

Archaeological sites in the arable areas of Breckland are usually recorded in two ways, either as scatters of surface artefacts (pottery, metal object or flints) or crop-marks visible from the air. All the information is stored in the County Sites and Monuments Records at Gressenhall and Bury St Edmunds. Archaeologists at these two centres are eager to work with the ESA Project Officer to identify those sites where payments for arable reversion would be justified.

Not every scatter of prehistoric flints will qualify for the generous payment of £500 per ha. However, where there is evidence that important sites are being disturbed by cultivation or where significant crop-mark patterns have been identified on Breckland cereals, then payments can be made under the ESA Scheme.

The new prescription can be applied in two ways:

(a) archaeologists, through the ESA Project Officer, can 'target' sites where there is strong need for conservation measures, or
(b) farmers, again through the ESA Project Officer, can seek advice on which fields qualify on their land.
We will all have to feel our way forward carefully to establish how the option would be applied in practice, but Breckland is rich in archaeology and there are clearly many sites which would be eligible. Let us hope that there is a significant take-up to justify the Minister's decision.

This 1998 announcement was a real breakthrough and brought archaeology level with wildlife in the Ministry of Agriculture's ESA schemes for the first time with very generous payments to go with it. This provided a firm foundation for including archaeology in future agri-environment conservation schemes.

Meanwhile the Countryside Commission had brought in their *Countryside Stewardship Schemes* as a pilot project in 1991, and five years later these schemes were transferred to MAFF to be administered by their Farming and Rural Conservation Agency. The big difference between the two was that Stewardship was not confined to designated areas like ESAs, although it was discretionary. Stewardship offered much more generous payments for 'income foregone' than English Heritage was able to offer under their Section 17 management agreements, which were purely for capital works. So Helen Paterson for the Norfolk Monuments Management Project was able to encourage farmers to use the Stewardship route to obtain higher grants for the management of Ancient Monuments.

Countryside Stewardship for the first time provided generous grants for good archaeological conservation management on farmland under ten-year voluntary agreements, and I was able to make full use of these new grants for the Norfolk Archaeological Trust which had just acquired more land at Caistor St Edmund Roman town (**p. 274**). The Countryside Commission emphasised that the historic landscapes they wanted to preserve should be of cultural interest and they would give preference to proposals which included provision for people to enjoy and appreciate these landscapes through public access and educational visits. This fitted the Trust's plans perfectly since we intended to open the whole of the Roman town then in Trust ownership to the public and to provide a car park, a guidebook and a series of interpretation panels, which subsequently won several national awards. So, once the site was accepted into the Scheme, I was able to claim back for the Trust annual payments of £70/ha a year for maintaining existing grassland in good order and £225/ha for converting arable to grass. Much of the land we had bought at Caistor was arable, so these payments were a real blessing. For capital works we claimed £1.20 per metre for sheep fencing and £125 for each gate we installed. Caistor was actually the first large Stewardship scheme in the region, and when we opened the Roman town to the public on 10th June 1993, it was Sir John Johnson, as chairman of the Countryside Commission, who performed the ceremony (*Figure 22.2*).

Protection under the European Common Agricultural Policy from 2005

Perhaps the most significant change in farm subsidies and farm regulations came in 2005 with the introduction of new measures under the European Common Agricultural Policy (the CAP). Then a system for making *area* payments under a new Single Farm Payment Scheme replaced a multiplicity of crop and livestock subsidies. Any serious breach of the regulations governing conservation of the environment could then lead to a loss or a reduction of these area payments under 'Cross Compliance' regulations.

Protection of uncultivated land from 2006

An elaborate two-stage procedure for the protection of uncultivated land came into force in October 2006 under The Environmental Impact Assessment (Agriculture) (England) (No.2) Regulations. This is a formal procedure for controlling improvements to 'uncultivated land' which has not been cultivated or received increased levels of fertiliser or soil improvers or has not been drained in the last 15 years. But if a farmer can prove with witness statements that any of these activities *have* taken place in the last 15 years, then the regulations do not apply. They also only apply to areas of over two hectares, and most archaeological sites are under that, and, strangely, the presence of a scheduled or unscheduled monument is not, in itself, relevant at this initial stage.

Where the area is *over* two hectares and the work is likely to impact significantly on the natural or historic environment, then Natural England will usually, under their screening process, consult Historic England and the County Archaeologist and other relevant bodies. If there is a scheduled monument involved, Historic England will always be consulted. Natural England then has 35 days to decide if the proposed works could have a significant impact on the natural or historic environment.

If Natural England concludes that it does, then the farmer has to submit a formal application for consent which will need to include an Environmental Statement. This Statement will have to cover aspects of the environment likely to be affected, including biodiversity, historic features and landscape. Where a Scheduled Ancient Monument is present, then Natural England will consult Historic England and the County Archaeologist again. Members of the public are also consulted through an advert in a local newspaper. If a farmer starts work on the project without waiting for the consent, then Natural England can issue a stop notice.

Anyone who breaches these regulations risks prosecution and is liable to summary conviction and to a fine not exceeding £5,000. But with the rising price of farmland, that is hardly a significant sum. The farmer can be required to reinstate the grassland but *only* if the national total area of grassland has been shown to have declined. Nobody has been fined so far, and it is unlikely now that anybody will be because since 2015 all grassland recorded as 'temporary' for more than five consecutive years is now classified as 'permanent' by the Rural Payments Agency thus artificially boosting the national area of permanent grass. And, of course, once ploughed the damage has been done to the archaeology anyway.

So, under these cumbersome regulations there may be some limited conservation benefits, particularly at landscape level, but there is a very real danger that unscheduled earthworks under two hectares, such as round barrows, will easily slip through the net. It is really only a landscape protection measure to safeguard floristic diversity. All this could, of course, change when we leave the EU, but these measures are all we have for the protection of undesignated archaeology in grassland at the moment. Archaeology conservation can only, in reality, be enhanced when the importance of a site is flagged up by scheduling. So we come back again to the need for a system of legal designation to provide specifically for archaeological protection.

Chapter 17:
Some Rescue Excavations, 1972-92

Selecting some key excavations by the Archaeological Unit which have made the greatest difference to our understanding of the county's archaeology over 25 years or so will inevitably be based on the satisfaction they gave me personally as well as how much they have told us about the archaeology of the wider region. There were large high-profile excavations which were generally recognised as significant at the time, like the Spong Hill cemetery and the Castle Mall shopping centre in the castle bailey in Norwich, but there were much smaller ones which did not reach the headlines of the local press in the same way but which were no less significant. In the following pages I have chosen some favourite projects, with sincere apologies to those project officers whose work has not been included. The Castle Mall development is one of those not included here because it was all so big and complex that it is not easy to describe briefly. Similarly, the story of Seahenge, a Bronze Age timber circle found on the beach at Holme-next-the-Sea, which erupted following the publication of a photograph in *The Independent* in December 1998 is not included because it has already had heavy coverage elsewhere (Champion 2000; Pryor 2001b; Brennand and Taylor 2003; Watson 2005; *EDP* 14th January 1999).

The press when it covered stories put their own gloss on these events, and the relative significance of a site was not always fully understood by them. Press headlines are not by themselves a guide to a project's success, and it is still a popular belief that archaeologists dig 'to find things', a perception frequently re-enforced by museums which usually only display the finds as though it is only the finds that matter. Press photographs of excavators holding up objects to camera – a pot, a coin or even a skull often missed the point. While individual objects occasionally made a real contribution to our understanding of a site, it was the *totality* of the story - the artefacts, the post-holes, the walls, the ditches, the bones and the preserved seeds - when all pulled together - which painted the picture of life, or death, for the episode we were hoping to understand.

Spong Hill Anglo-Saxon cemetery, North Elmham, 1972-81 and 1984

The complete excavation and publication of the Anglo-Saxon cremation cemetery on Spong Hill in North Elmham was an enormous undertaking. The excavation ran from 1972 until 1981, and it is still the largest Anglo-Saxon cremation cemetery to be excavated in Britain. It must represent one of the great achievements of East Anglian Archaeology over the last 50 years.

Each season lasted for about three months, and for the first three years a team from the University of Warsaw, lead Dr Jerzy Gassowski, also took part, although that arrangement proved difficult to sustain for practical reasons. The excavation was run by Bob Carr and myself in 1972-73 (*EDP* 21st September 1972) and thereafter by Catherine Hills, then a research student at the University of London, who wrote her PhD on the burials excavated up until 1975 (Hills 1977). She was then appointed a lecturer in Anglo-Saxon archaeology at the University of Cambridge and remained there until her recent retirement. Catherine continued with the excavation and saw the post-excavation work through to completion.

Barbara Green in the Castle Museum in Norwich and I initiated the project with a trial excavation back in 1968 because part of the hill was threatened by a gravel concession, but that, thankfully, lapsed. This small trench demonstrated that while many of the cremation urns still survived, the damage to them by constant cultivation was severe. The case for the total excavation of the cemetery was made to the Department of the Environment by the Scole Committee, and the whole project through to publication was generously funded by the Department and then English Heritage with some additional support from the Norfolk Research Committee (*EDP* 14th October 1976). As we worked year after year on the site the field around us continued to be cultivated, often quite deeply for sugar beet and potatoes, so the task of clearing the whole cemetery was critical and urgent until it was finished. After we had finished, the excavated area was sub-soiled by the farmer.

Excavation completed

By the end of the 1981 season we had removed 2,323 cremations (*Figures 17.1 and 17.2*) and excavated 57 inhumations. Once lifted, the cremation urns were carefully emptied in shallow layers with cross sections of all the fills drawn and recorded. As the soil was sieved the smallest fragments of cremated bone and the grave-goods, many of which had been badly damaged in the cremation pyres, were all retained. This was the first time this had been done, and the results fully justified the extra effort involved. We had heard that on some other excavations of Saxon cemeteries the urns had been left to be emptied later, but the soil in the fill then dried out and set rock hard and the fill then proved impossible to remove. So, emptying the urns straight away was clearly essential.

In 1984 Andrew Rogerson went back to Spong to excavate a sample of the Anglo-Saxon settlement to the west with its post-holes and sunken featured buildings, but we did not have the resources then to excavate the whole settlement and its full extent remains unclear. But with a change of owner the field has been put down to grass and is now grazed by sheep, so the urgency to excavate the rest of the settlement has passed. Underlying the Anglo-Saxon cemetery there

17.1. Examples of some of the 2,323 Anglo-Saxon cremation urns excavated on Spong Hill, North Elmham over ten summers from 1972 to 1981. Some had their tops sliced off by the plough, and others had collapsed under the pressure of soil and tractor tyres from above, but all were in danger of being destroyed by constant cultivation and probable subsoiling (1012/1010).

17.2. An unusually large group of Spong Hill urns set in a pit just below plough depth (Photo by Catherine Hills).

was a landscape of Roman ditched enclosures, but we saw little sign of a Roman settlement. There was also a Bronze Age round barrow partially surviving to the north within the same field, so it was archaeologically a rich area, now thankfully protected by the grazing sheep under a Higher Level Stewardship scheme.

Potential disaster averted

While the study of all the finds was still at an early stage we had a shock in 1985 when the then site owner announced he was going to sell the whole collection, by auction if necessary, if we could not raise the money to buy it all from him. This shock came out of the blue, caused by my own naivety, and it put the whole project in real jeopardy. I had accepted casual verbal assurances (a normal procedure up until the 1970s) that the finds could all go to the Norfolk Museums Service but there was nothing in writing to confirm that understanding. The bombshell arrived after we had been excavating the site for ten years at considerable public expense and the conservation of the plough-damaged urns and the conservation and study of the other finds was all still in progress. The hero of the day was Francis Cheetham, Director of the Norfolk Museums Service, who raised the £120,000 from the National Heritage Memorial Fund needed to secure the whole collection in 1988 and to save it from dispersal (NCM 1994.192). The bitter irony of the whole business was that the nation had in the end to pay for it twice over, once to save it from the plough and then again after the collection was conserved to save it from dispersal. The obvious lesson from this episode was that it is essential to agree arrangements in writing with site owners *before* any excavation begins. Most amateur metal detectorists do that automatically now, and it is very important that they do.

Cemetery publication

We decided to publish catalogues of the cremations as the excavation progressed, rather than leave it all to the end. To wait until the excavation was finished would inevitably have created a formidable backlog, probably too large for anybody to manage. So, comprehensive cremation catalogues were published in a series of four volumes of East Anglian Archaeology (Hills 1977, Hills and Penn 1981, Hills, Penn and Rickett 1987 and 1994). Each represented around 600 burials, with the urns illustrated at 1:3 scale in order to show the often elaborate decoration, and all recognisable grave-goods were published at 1:1. The catalogue of the 57 inhumations appeared separately as Hills, Penn and Rickett 1984. There were further volumes devoted to the cremated bones by Jackie McKinley (1994), the prehistoric evidence by Frances Healy (1988) and the Iron Age, Roman and Anglo-Saxon settlements by Robert Rickett (1995). Early attempts at a computer-based analysis of the cremation burials were unsuccessful because of the great complexity of the data-set with potentially hundreds of descriptive attributes per burial. This work had to be delayed until there were computers available which were powerful enough to analyse the data, and then the massive final volume by Catherine and Sam Lucy could be published as a Cambridge MacDonald Institute research monograph in 2013 (Hills and Lucy 2013). The database can also be found online (www.repository.cam.ac.uk/handle/1810/274).

The key conclusion from all the analysis was that most of the cremations were buried in the fifth century, starting in the first quarter of the century, and that the final phase which coincided with the relatively small number of inhumations, had died out by the middle of the sixth century. Spong seems to represent the earliest phase of Germanic settlement in England. Most of the early cremations were contemporary with the continental cemeteries like Issendorf and Schmalstede in

17.3 An excavation plan of the Spong Hill cemetery showing the distribution of the earliest phase of cremations, dating to the first quarter of the fifth century, mostly located within a Roman ditched enclosure. Also depicted in light shading are the Anglo-Saxon inhumation burials, post-hole buildings and other structures.

17.4. One of the Anglo-Saxon post-hole buildings on Spong Hill under excavation.

Schleswig-Holstein. The styles of decoration on the pots and the use of miniature grave-goods and cruciform brooches link the early phase of settlement to this 'Anglian' region. The stamped pottery decoration and equal arm brooches in the middle and later phases relate more to the 'Saxon' Elbe-Weser area, suggesting that the population was of mixed Germanic cultural origins. There was very little evidence for the cultural attributes of the native British population who just seem to 'vanish' in the fifth century. They were either quickly assimilated into the new culture or they do not identify themselves easily to archaeologists by their burials. In a wider context Spong is part of an early wave (c. AD410-450) of Germanic Anglian settlement found in Norfolk

17.5. The seated figure of Spong Man in the Anglo-Saxon gallery at Norwich Castle Museum.

and Lincolnshire on both sides of the Wash. The earliest urns were not randomly located but centred on one corner of a Roman ditched enclosure (*Figure 17.3*). Nearby were a number of Anglo-Saxon post-hole buildings (*Figure 17.4*) showing that were was a settlement close by.

About three quarters of the pots were decorated, far more than in contemporary settlement sites, suggesting that much of the decoration had a strong funerary purpose. There was a correlation between the size, shape and decoration of the pots and the individuals buried in them. Small pots contained children: men were in large, narrow-necked highly decorated ones. Some pots were decorated using the same stamps and buried in clusters suggesting family groups. There were an unexpected number of cremated animals, including many complete horses, some in separate undecorated pots close to a decorated one probably for an associated human.

For Catherine this final volume is the culmination of what must have seemed like a lifetime's work. Kenneth Penn, Robert Rickett, Jackie McKinley, Frances Healy and Sam Lucy were also key players, and Ken and Robert, in particular, devoted a lot of their energies ensuring that there was a high quality excavation archive. A popular summary of the project by Catherine can be found in *British Archaeology* 140 (Hills 2015).

Spong Man

No mention of Spong Hill is complete without a mention of Spong Man, found in 1979 in one of a series of pits probably indicating later disturbance of the cemetery. This unique urn lid represents a human figure sitting on a wooden chair with hands resting to either side of his neck. He has been much discussed (Hills 2014), but in the end we need to admit we know little about him. He remains a mystery and takes pride of place sitting on a rotating pedestal in the Anglo-Saxon gallery in the Castle Museum (*Figure 17.5*).

Anglo-Saxon cemeteries at Bergh Apton and Morningthorpe, 1973-75

Bergh Apton, 1973

The new Norfolk Archaeological Unit had only been running a few days in April 1973 when we had our first emergency as news reached us that Anglo-Saxon grave-goods had been picked off a gravel screening machine at a quarry at Bergh Apton. Atlas Aggregates, and their area manager Peter Charlton, were immensely helpful and moved their machines onto a different working face so that the remaining graves could be excavated. Although not really his period, Chris Green took on this excavation with the help of Barbara Green, Keeper of Archaeology at the Castle Museum, and we recovered the remaining 63 inhumations. An important decision made early on was not to fully excavate grave-goods *in situ* but to bring them into the museum in lumps of soil and excavate them indoors. This procedure ensured better retrieval and recording of the more delicate objects. Because graves were being looted on the site at night, each grave had to be fully excavated by the end of the working day ('Pillaging of graves hits digs' *EDP* 20th June 1988). Consequently the excavation had to be run at some speed.

The bones were very poorly preserved in the gravel soils, but as one might expect, the men had spears, knives and shields and the women brooches, beads and other jewellery. There were magnificent gilded square-headed brooches from Grave 7 and 64 and a very florid gilded cruciform brooch from Grave 18 (*Figure 17.6*). Perhaps the most interesting object was a much-decayed wooden lyre from Grave 22, similar to the one from Sutton Hoo. The wood in the lyre only survived as a dark organic stain except when close to the metal fittings of the lyre. The cemetery was published just as a catalogue of graves by Barbara and Andrew in an EAA volume in order to make the results quickly available to researchers (Green and Rogerson 1978).

Morningthorpe, 1974-75

Then, in October 1974, Atlas Aggregates produced a second Anglo-Saxon cemetery with some 365 inhumations and 9 cremations still intact at their quarry at Morningthorpe which was excavated mostly by Andrew Rogerson over two seasons. The first season was rather hurried because it was anticipated that Atlas Aggregates would not be able to hold off their work on the quarry face for long. However, they very helpfully agreed to suspend further quarrying until funding could be found from the DoE for a second season. Excavation then resumed in April 1975 for eight weeks until clearance of the cemetery was complete. The team of four was supplemented by very enthusiastic members of the Norfolk Archaeological Rescue Group (NARG) who provided invaluable assistance. The bones were in an equally poor state to those at Bergh Apton due to the acid gravel soils. A second lyre was found, in Grave 97. There were five ring-ditches or penannular ditches of various shapes and sizes around graves, and there had been a crop-mark of a further ring-ditch in the area already destroyed by the quarry. Ring-ditches around graves had also been found at Spong Hill. This showed that not all ring-ditches need be prehistoric. As at Bergh Apton, the cleaning of grave-goods on site was kept to a minimum and the objects were quickly transferred to the Castle Museum. This ensured that the recovery of textile remains from the corrosion surfaces of metal objects in particular was much more successful. Again the cemetery was published primarily as a catalogue in EAA (Green, Rogerson and White 1987), funded largely by Atlas Aggregates (*DAFT* 8th April 1988).

The full discussion of Bergh Apton and Morningthorpe was run together with the 57 inhumations from Spong Hill (Hills 1977; Hills, Penn and Rickett 1984) and a Suffolk cemetery excavated by Stanley West at Westgarth Gardens in Bury St Edmunds in 1972 (West 1988). The four cemeteries together had produced about 500 inhumations and this provided a really worthwhile set of data for analysis.

17.6. A fine gilded cruciform brooch from Grave 18 of the Bergh Apton Anglo-Saxon cemetery excavated in 1973 (1011/25).

Discussion of both cemeteries

The heavily academic discussion volume on the four cemeteries appeared as an EAA volume by Kenneth Penn and Birte Brugmann in 2007. Except for Bergh Apton, there were cremations as well as inhumations on each site. A key issue was the relationship between the cremations and the inhumations when both rituals were clearly in use at the same time. Were the inhumations, sometimes surrounded by the ring-ditches, evidence for a rising elite in the sixth century; if not, what was the difference? While other researchers suggest this was the case, Penn and Brugmann seem to sit on the fence in their report. They did, however, identify significant changes over time. Female burials with dress accessories and male burials with weapons became more common towards the end of the fifth century. Around the middle of the sixth century wrist clasps and girdle-hangers were no longer buried, or at least not worn by women. By then great gilded square-headed brooches on women and larger weapons, particularly longer spearheads, on men had become the status symbols of the privileged few, leading to the emergence of a stronger social differentiation in the seventh century.

Sixteenth-century pottery kiln wasters from Fulmodeston, 1974

In June 1974 there was a knock on the door at our house at North Elmham, and there was a builder holding an armful of almost complete sixteenth-century pots he had picked out of a drain trench he had been digging for a new septic tank being installed for a cottage in the village of Fulmodeston, near Fakenham. He had struck a layer of almost solid earthenware pottery of considerable interest.

Because the Norfolk Archaeological Unit had been informed straight away it was possible to observe the trench before it was backfilled, and it was obvious that a high proportion of the pots were complete. But many were cracked or distorted, and they were clearly rejects from a kiln. The range of shapes was remarkable, and it looked like an important and unique collection which ought to be recovered. So, in the following September the Unit organised an excavation over three weekends with the help of members of NARG.

Once the area was excavated archaeologically we could see that the pottery formed a dump layer in a wide pit or ditch and that the pottery had all been deposited at one time. The pots were made of red earthenware, and the shapes of the jugs were so similar to medieval jugs that the group could hardly be much later than the early sixteenth century. The septic tank was working by then, but the gentle smell of sewerage did not distract from the fun of digging out one complete pot after another! We dug a second trench in an area not disturbed by the drains, and we struck lucky again. In that trench there was a different pit with a later group with many saggar fragments. Saggars are fairly crude pots with holes cut in the sides intended only to be used as kiln furniture; saggars limit the supply of oxygen so that pots put inside them come out black or grey, rather than the usual red. The saggars had only been used for firing tankards, of which there were many broken examples, and neither saggars nor tankards had been found in the earlier group.

The sheer quantity and variety of pots from the site was astonishing. We organised a weekly pot washing evening for volunteers at Gressenhall, and it took months to wash all the sherds. Nothing quite like this had been found before in the region. Some of the broken pots could be glued back together which was satisfying. From the earlier group (*Figure 17.7*) (from left to right) came large and small storage jars with and without handles, jugs, colanders, measures, bottles, costrels (water bottles with loops on the neck), stewpots, tall milk churns, pipkins (jars with feet and handles), chafing dishes (plate warmers for charcoal or hot water),

17.7. A selection from the earlier group of sixteenth-century pottery kiln wasters excavated from a domestic sewer outfall at Fulmodeston in 1974 (BVN3).

pancheons (large bowls), a warming pot or pomander (a shallow pot with handle and triangular holes), fire covers (to close down open fires at night), dripping pans and even sprinkler pots (watering pots - not illustrated).

From the later group (*Figure 17.8*) (from left to right) came pipkins, costrels, jugs, sprinkler pots, jars of all sizes with side handles or bucket handles, a ring-shaped flower vase decorated with floral stamps, chafing dishes, lids, possibly a drinking horn, colanders, dripping pans and even a circular chicken feeder as well as the saggars and tankards.

17.8. Some of the sixteenth-century pottery kiln wasters from the later group found at Fulmodeston (BVN14).

We searched for the kiln but could find no trace of it, so we were no closer to an understanding of why the pottery had been dumped where it was. We were unable to date the two groups with any certainty. Saggars were in use in Yorkshire in the fifteenth century to make Cistercian Ware, and while both groups probably date from the sixteenth century the time gap between them remains unclear.

The whole collection was given by Mr P. Riseborough of Little Snoring, the site owner, to the Norfolk Museums Service (NCM 974.735), and it forms a really very useful and attractive reference collection for the study of sixteenth-century pottery manufacturing in the region. The collection was published with 29 pages of drawings illustrating all the pot types prepared with great care by Sue White as EAA 19 (Wade-Martins 1983).

Norwich, Anglia TV site on the former Cattle Market, 1979

The excavation of part of the old Cattle Market behind the Agricultural Hall was organised by Brian Ayers in advance of the construction of a new office block for Anglia Television. For an excavation in a great urban centre like Norwich, the story which unfolded as the excavation progressed was remarkably simple. The Agricultural Hall Plain, as the area in this part of the old Cattle Market was called, lay within the north-east castle bailey, so we had expected castle outbuildings, but there were none. This bailey appears to have been no more than a meadow – an open space possibly for holding livestock for the castle in the Middle Ages - but underneath the castle levels the story was much more interesting. A part of the Late Saxon town had been cleared to build the castle, and because the north-east bailey had seen little activity after it was constructed, the underlying Late Saxon levels were remarkably undisturbed. There was the complete plan of a small pre-Conquest timber church surrounded by its own graveyard containing about 130 burials. The timber church had been rebuilt twice. The first two phases had been set into post-holes, with the second phase having been burnt down probably around AD 1000. The third phase was of post-in-trench construction with a rectangular nave 8 x 5 m and a small square-ended chancel 3 m square. To find the complete plan of a pre-Conquest wooden urban church was a pleasant surprise. It may have been one of the 40 or so Norwich churches mentioned in Domesday Book. A late tenth-century brooch was recovered from the nave floor, a useful dating indicator.

The skeletons in the churchyard represented a rare and relatively undisturbed Late Saxon urban group showing evidence for heavy manual work with few living beyond the age of 45. They were buried without coffins, sometimes with the heads supported on small pillows of flints. Several of the children suffered from rickets, a disease caused by Vitamin D deficiency, often resulting from an inadequate diet and lack of access to sunlight. It was an impoverished population (*Figure 17.9*). One burial was of special interest; it was almost certainly a woman of black African origin, and that raises questions about Late Saxon population movements and the slave trade. It was notable that one other Late Saxon black African burial had already been found in East Anglia, in the cathedral cemetery at North Elmham (**p. 57**). Indeed, the two groups, one urban and one rural of about the same date, provided useful comparative information. The site was published as EAA volume 28 (Ayers 1985) and in one of a series of the popular booklets on our Norwich excavations, *Digging Under the Doorstep* (Ayers with Lawson 1983, 11-17).

17.9. A part of the Anglia TV excavation within the north-east bailey of Norwich Castle showing some of the burials outside the timber church and to the left the foundation trench for the third phase of the church all under the castle earthworks (BFP2).

Norwich, St Martin-at-Palace Plain, 1981

After the Anglia TV site, Brian's next major project was to excavate part of the early waterfront in Norwich in advance of the construction of a new probation centre and magistrates' courts just to the east of Whitefriars' Bridge. Because the new court house was to be put on piles to take the weight of the building, the County Architect did not attempt to specify how deep we could go, thus making it possible to explore some of the Late Saxon waterlogged levels which would be damaged by the piles. We were allocated £15,000 by the DoE for the excavation which was hardly enough, but it was possible in those days to take on unemployed youngsters under a YOP Scheme (Youth Opportunities Programme) run by the Manpower Services Commission, and this helped. The area we could excavate was still less than ideal, but it enabled us to explore some of the early waterlogged deposits which were full of organic material, including wattle fences to retain the foreshore, a large piece of woollen cloth, leaves and thousands of articulated fish bones, mostly herring but with a wide range of other species. This was the heyday for trade on this part of the river, but as ships became larger by the late eleventh century commercial activity moved downstream to deeper waters off King Street.

The big surprise of the excavation was the uncovering of a large (17 x 9m) twelfth-century Norman house built endways on to the river in flint-coursed rubble with dressed Barnack limestone corners, surviving in excess of 2m in height with three windows and two doorways. The building also contained some Caen stone from Normandy. Both doorways had drawbar slots within the thickness of the walls to secure the doors, and an impressive feature was a cesspit tower in the north-east corner with a large arch open towards the river (Figure 17.10). The house was built at some time between 1140 and 1170, and it was a tremendous discovery, but by exposing this building we had over-reached our resources. Luckily, an additional £3,000 came from both the City Council and the County Council for the excavation to be completed. Everyone was so struck by the building that there was an immediate wish by the city and the county to preserve this Norman house under the new courts. Frank Tucker, the County Architect, was more than willing to modify his foundations so that the building could be retained, and the extra funding was quickly found as follows:

17.10. *The twelfth-century Norman house found within the St Martin-at-Palace Plain excavations in Norwich in 1981 with the cathedral behind (BWB6).*

> *City Council £3,000 for the repair and consolidation of the Norman stonework, City Planning Committee £25,000, Norfolk County Council £23,600, National Heritage Memorial Fund £20,000, DoE £6,500 and Norfolk and Norwich Archaeological Society £100. There may have been other grants for which I have no record.* **Total £78,200+.**

That compared with a total of only £21,000 plus the YOP team which was all we had managed to raise for all excavation costs. The irony was not missed on us, and it did show that civil engineers and their consultants, the architects and the contractors could all command, and expect to receive, much higher fees than archaeologists. Our profession still had some way to go before it was recognised as a mainstream activity. It was nevertheless a thoroughly creditable effort by all those concerned, particularly by Frank Tucker and by Francis Cheetham, the Director of the Norfolk Museums Service who obtained the funding from the National Heritage Memorial Fund. The site architect, Bob Goodyear, designed the clever new access to the Norman house which can still be seen by appointment under the magistrates' courts. The site was published as EAA volume 37 (Ayers 1988) and in *Digging under the Doorstep* (Ayers with Lawson 1983, 22-30).

To some extent the survival and preservation of this house made up for the loss in 1977 of the late twelfth-century house in Queen Street, King's Lynn, although there the front wall had actually survived almost to its full height (*Figure 12.3*).

Norwich, Fishergate, 1985

A few years later we had a chance to dig a trench, up to 4 m deep, on the north side of the river west of Whitefriars' Bridge within the area enclosed by the tenth-century town defences. The importance of this small excavation was the discovery of the largest quantity of Middle Saxon pottery, both locally-made and imported, found up to that time in any excavation in Norwich, together with a coin of *c*. AD 725 and two eighth-century brooches. These finds were in the earliest layers above the original valley marsh, radiocarbon dated to AD 800. They strongly suggested that there was an eighth-century trading settlement on the north bank, known possibly as *Northwic* or *Norwic* at which there was a mint by the 930s (Ayers 1994a, 22-25). The growth of this putative new *Norwic* coincides with the decline of the coin evidence from the Dunston Field area just outside the Roman town at Caistor St Edmund in the eighth century (**p. 283-289**). The excavation was published as EAA volume 68 (Ayers 1994b) and in *Digging Deeper* (Ayers 1987, 7-10). In 2005 there was also an excavation at 40 Fishergate by NAU Archaeology which produced similar results (sadly still unpublished). The early growth and development of Norwich, including these Fishergate discoveries, is discussed in a recent paper by Brian Ayers (Ayers 2011, 70-76). The date for the gradual transfer of trading activity from Caistor to the new Norwich now fits reasonably well, but more research is needed. This raises the interesting question of where was *Southwic*; was it Norwich south of the river or was it actually Anglo-Saxon Caistor?

Thetford, Fison Way, 1980-82

This site, which was initially referred to as 'Boudica's Palace', was by far the most extensive excavation we conducted, thanks to the major contribution made by the Manpower Service Commission who provided a digging team of YOPs, who were recruited locally to help with site work. The DoE provided the funding for the topsoil removal. But the success of the project depended much on the leadership skills and an extra-ordinary capacity for hard work of Tony Gregory who ran the project for two years while also performing his many other county-wide duties for the Norfolk Archaeological Unit. The report by Tony was published as EAA 53 after he had died, having just moved to Yorkshire (Gregory 1991a). Andrew Rogerson's Appreciation of Tony in the front of that volume was heartfelt and well deserved. Martin Millett in his review of the volume in *The Archaeological Journal* wrote 'This report is thus clearly the work of an archaeologist of the highest calibre'.... (which) .... 'will remain as one of several major memorials to him' (Millet 1992).

The crop-marks of the enclosure were first noticed in 1980 from the air by Bob Carr of the Suffolk Archaeological Unit while circling over Thetford waiting clearance from air traffic control at RAF Honington. This discovery took on particular significance because it was very close to a spot where several thousand Late Roman coins, pottery and building materials had been found (largely unrecorded by archaeologists) the previous year on the construction site for the Travenol factory. It was also at this time that the spectacular hoard of Late Roman gold and silver jewellery was discovered (Johns and Potter 1983). The field containing the crop-marks was also due for factory development, and so the excavation of the enclosure became an urgent matter.

Immediately after harvest in 1980 the whole area was subject to a detailed metal detector survey by local detectorists supervised by Tony Gregory who later used the survey and the subsequent use of detectors on the excavation as a model of how detectorists and archaeologists could work closely together (Gregory and Rogerson 1984). This revealed a thin scatter of several Early Roman brooches and coins and one Iron Age coin suggesting that the enclosure was earlier than all the nearby Late Roman finds had suggested (**p. 111**). Large-scale excavation began in January 1981, and the intention from the start was to ensure we had a comprehensive overview at an early stage of the whole enclosure complex. So, nearly 5 hectares had to be stripped and cleaned by hand-hoeing and then recorded before any excavation in depth could begin; that was a strategy which required great discipline. It could not have been easy to hold together a team of previously unemployed and untrained young people scraping and cleaning the dry sandy sub-soil month after month without there being a workforce mutiny, but Tony managed it (*Figure 17.11*). It was necessary to record the surface immediately

CHAPTER 17: SOME RESCUE EXCAVATIONS, 1972-92   233

17.11. At Fison Way. Thetford, Tony Gregory managed a team of unemployed youngsters who worked month after month cleaning and planning over nearly five hectares of sand in order to record the complex patterns of Iron Age intercutting features before there was any excavation in depth (5853/851).

after cleaning as sand windblows were prevalent. Only after the cleaning was complete and the overall plan of the features cut into the sand and gravel had been fully recorded on the surface could they be very selectively excavated. The final results were so extra-ordinary that in the end Breckland District Council refused a planning application for another factory, which was then dismissed on appeal, and the land was designated as an Area of Archaeological Importance in the Local Plan and it has remained an open space ever since, now, at last, protected by English Heritage as an Ancient Monument. It was eventually scheduled by English Heritage because such a small proportion of the features had actually been excavated; there was still enough available for further research in the future, but it took them *20 years* to decide.

For the layman, the excavation report is complex and difficult to understand. There is no simple convincing interpretation, and there is no straightforward concluding chapter which makes sense of it all, suggesting that Tony was not entirely sure what he had found. We may never be sure, although others have tried (Bradley 2005, 184-188, 203; Millett 1992). Tony's report has provided scholars with all the information available to attempt re-interpretation following his death, and no doubt many more will try in years to come. It is clear, however, that the phases of construction corresponded to the Late Iron Age/Early Roman overlap. It is equally clear that the post-holes and ditches represent an immense effort to build this place which was probably not used for long before it was pulled down. It was an extra-ordinary site without obvious parallel. The unique layout and prominent location of the site probably indicates a place of strong regional importance.

The main phase started as a single large square-shaped enclosure surrounded by a pair of ditches with an impressive gated entrance to the east. In the centre of the enclosure there was a single massively constructed round timber building facing towards the entrance. Then in the later phase, perhaps dating from the AD 40s to mid 60s, the enclosure was enlarged to form a rectangle aligned west-to-east, 220m x 175m, with an even more impressive entrance to the east. The enclosure then contained five large round buildings facing the entrance (*Figure 17.12*). New buildings were erected to either side of the original one to form a row at the back and there were two more in front of the outer pair. The original building was the largest, and it may have had an upper storey. Between the inner and outer surrounding ditches there were eight shallow gullies containing continuous rows of posts or possibly planted trees or bushes. It may be argued that these had the

17.12 The Fison Way, Thetford, Phase III Building II after post-holes and gullies had been excavated (5853/915).

effect of separating the inner space from the rest of the world, suggesting strong ritual and religious beliefs. In *Celtic Fire and Roman Rule* (Robinson and Gregory 1987, 46) Tony described the eight gullies as containing 'a complex entanglement of enormous timber fences. If the posts were 6ft tall then the total length of timber used was an astonishing 70 miles'. However, in the final report the interpretation picture by Sue White shows the gullies filled with rows of bushes, and it is clear that nobody was quite sure what had been found *(Figure 17.13)*. There can be no doubt, however, that it was an extra-ordinarily important Late Iron Age tribal centre. But the almost complete lack of domestic debris argues more that it was a ritual place than a royal palace. Its proximity to the Late Roman temple under the Travenol factory with its coin offerings and the great Thetford Treasure found nearby (**p. 108**) also argues for it being a religious centre of some kind.

It would be good one day if the site could be taken on by a conservation trust so that information panels could be provided in an attempt to explain this extra-ordinary place, although site management within an industrial area of Thetford may well have its problems.

17.13 Sue White's reconstruction of Phase III at the Fison Way site showing the Iron Age enclosure surrounded with planted rows of bushes. The purpose of this extra-ordinary structure will probably always remain a mystery (KBL28).

Norwich Southern Bypass, 1989-92

The funding dilemma

When the Unit started we knew that a major road scheme involving a new bypass all around the south side of Norwich was being designed. This would cut through one of the most archaeologically sensitive parts of the county, close to both the Roman regional capital at Caistor St Edmund and the well-known prehistoric timber henge monument at Arminghall. So, it was encouraging that we were able to work with the road engineers in County Hall and publish our 28-page report, *The Archaeological Implications of the Norwich Southern By-pass*, on the same day that the road corridor was announced on 13th November 1974. It was the first time that archaeologists had been given the opportunity to work with road designers in the county before a route was made public. The key point we wanted to make was that we needed to be in at an early stage and co-operate with everyone involved. There was no point in objecting to the road because there was clearly a need for one there, and we wanted to be seen as an essential part of the road planning exercise. Where there was a clear case for excavation, we urged that land should be purchased early to ensure that there was enough time for excavation before the earth-moving contractors started work. We argued that with sufficient forward planning and cooperation there would be no reason why the excavations should cause any delay to the road scheme at all (*EDP* 14th November 1974 and 21st November 1974). We identified 152 archaeological sites and historic buildings in the corridor which could be threatened by the road. The mistake I made was to allow our report a very provocative cover, with the word CONDEMNED! stamped across an air photo of the Caistor ring-ditches (*Figure 17.14*). This upset some County Councillors, and the road engineers felt that we had let them down. I agreed, and all I could do was apologise and let time be the healer.

After the protected route was announced we focused on those sites which seemed certain to be destroyed and produced a short-list for the DoE of those where excavation would need to be funded; they included two scheduled monuments (a crop-mark complex in Caistor and two ring-ditches in Bixley) and a Palaeolithic site at Kirby Bedon near the Whitlingham sewage works. We then waited for the delayed publication of the Draft Line Order due out by 1984. The whole process seemed to take a very long time (*EDP* 4th October 1986).

But, as the time for the excavation drew closer we found ourselves in the middle of a tussle between English Heritage, which was urging us always to seek funding for rescue excavations from developers, and the Department of Transport (DoT), in this case the developer, which was responsible for trunk roads. The English Heritage policy by then was that they would only fund rescue excavations where the threat lay outside planning controls, and these excavations would certainly be the result of planning decisions.

By 1989 it was our own County Council's policy to build archaeological costs into our own road schemes, such as the A149 Dersingham – Ingoldisthorpe – Snettisham bypass in 1988/89, and we took the view that the DoT should do the same (*EDP* 30th January 1989, 23rd April 1990, 30th May 1990 and 12th July 1990). But the DoT officials were behaving like dinosaurs. Their policy, which was vigorously opposed by English Heritage, was that government funding for rescue archaeology was all channelled through English Heritage and therefore English Heritage should pay. English Heritage had received an additional annual sum of £100,000 for *all* archaeology on trunk road schemes in England from the DoT, but we had estimated that the Norwich Southern Bypass excavations alone would cost about £114,000. We wrote to Paul Channon, the Secretary of State for Transport, and the reply came back dated 6th June 1989 that:

17.14. The Norfolk Archaeological Unit's 1974 report on the archaeological implications of the construction of the Norwich Southern Bypass. To stamp 'CONDEMNED!' across the picture of the ring ditches was politically a big mistake, although they were indeed destroyed during roadworks, but after excavation.

> No further and separate 'funding' can be made available and it is for English Heritage to decide on the priority for using the funds.

The DoT policy seemed to apply to all Crown developments, and we were also having an issue with the Lord Chancellor's Department over the new County Courts to be built in the historic core and on the medieval waterfront of King's Lynn. It was government policy to encourage developers to fund rescue work *except* where it was itself the developer! Meanwhile there was a London conference for developers and archaeologists attended by Virginia Bottomley, a Minister in the Department of the Environment, and she urged developers and archaeologists to work together to resolve possible conflicts between the two sides. Ministers were clearly not following their own advice.

The issue was not just confined to the Norwich Southern Bypass, for there were other trunk road schemes in the county where archaeology would be affected. There was the Dickleburgh bypass due to start by the end of 1990 (*EDP* 23rd April 1990, 30th May and 13th July 1990) and after that the Scole bypass, both with important Roman sites which would be destroyed. The beginnings of a breakthrough came when Chris Patten was Secretary of State for the Environment. In response to letters from several Norfolk MPs on the matter, he wrote in early 1991 that he had asked his officials to consider with other departments and the Treasury the implications of each department being responsible for funding archaeological works when they were the developer. He was 'concerned to explore fully the possibilities for changing current policies' which was excellent news, but too late for our current road schemes.

In the end the Norwich Southern Bypass excavation went ahead in 1989 funded by English Heritage. There was no excavation on the Dickleburgh bypass where both a Roman settlement and a previously unknown Anglo-Saxon cemetery were destroyed without record. English Heritage had, quite rightly, given priority to the Norwich Southern Bypass. Meanwhile, the Scole Bypass was delayed because a decision had been taken to re-design the route as a dual carriageway, and this gave us a breathing space. The new County Courts were built by the Lord Chancellor's Department in King's Lynn without an excavation on the medieval waterfront. But, the developers of Castle Mall in Norwich which would destroy the whole castle bailey had agreed to pay most of the archaeological costs amounting to some £700,000. With this sort of example the government would have to fall into line sooner or later.

By August 1991 the DoT had agreed to fund archaeological *evaluation surveys* in advance of trunk road schemes and we heard that they had actually paid £300,000 for the excavations on the new Winchester bypass. In July 1992 John MacGregor, Secretary of State for Transport, wrote a very encouraging letter to us saying that they would review their archaeology grants to English Heritage annually and 'There have been no recent cases where a lack of funding has prevented work on trunk road schemes.' They agreed to fund an evaluation survey of the A11 Wymondham bypass, so it seemed that it would only be a matter of time before Crown developer funding became the norm. We had moved the government a long way in three years. By the time the excavations took place in advance of the Wymondham bypass in 1992-93 (Ashwin 1996) and the Scole bypass in 1993-94 (Ashwin and Tester 2014) they were fully funded by the Highways Agency.

This had been a battle which we had to fight, and with the support of Norfolk MPs I think we played a significant role in ensuring that government policy was changed completely on this important issue.

The excavations

The Norwich Southern Bypass project consisted of a major series of excavations primarily at two locations, and also some watching briefs, directed by Trevor Ashwin (1963-2016) during the period 1989 to 1992. The whole excavation was then published in 2000 in two excellent volumes of EAA (Ashwin and Bates 2000; Penn 2000). Excavation was concentrated on the sites already known from aerial photography and all were Scheduled Ancient Monuments. Work started at Bixley in November 1989, but the 'extreme shortage of time' (to quote from the report) meant that excavation had to be very selective and there could only be minimal sampling of the actual ring-ditches. We had been trying to argue for almost exactly 15 years, since November 1974 in fact, that we needed adequate time and resources to do the excavation properly. But in the end the money that English Heritage could make available from their budget for trunk road projects was not sufficient for comfort, and tough decisions about excavation priorities had to be taken. Nowadays, no excavation project of this kind would take place without a thorough evaluation by trial trenching and field survey first, with the results of the evaluation being used to determine the eventual budget for excavation.

Bixley

The remains of three Late Neolithic/Bronze Age round barrows were recorded on a hill slope overlooking the Arminghall Henge, and we found that they had all suffered from very severe plough damage. One of them (site 6099) had been rebuilt at least twice and was represented by three concentric ring-ditches. In the centre was a dense intercutting group of inhumed and cremated burials, some with Collared Urns. The same mix of burial rites was found in another (site 9585 ring-ditch 7), while the smallest ring-ditch (site 9585 ring-ditch 1002) had just one exceptionally large Collared Urn cremation.

Harford Farm

We then had to move quickly on to the Harford Farm site in February 1990 after the NAU finally gained access to the area under a Department of Transport Compulsory Purchase Order. Before that order was issued Unit staff were not allowed even to set foot upon the area to be excavated – hardly an ideal prelude to a major project of this nature. And by then there was only funding for 12 weeks to excavate this large and complex site. After initial metal detecting, the topsoil was removed with a box scraper from the whole two hectare-area which was cleaned and planned before any excavation could begin (as at Thetford Fison Way). This created a basic record of the sand and gravel surface to determine where sample excavation would be most efficiently directed.

Five ring-ditches were excavated on the hill crest which had fine views over Caistor Roman town to the south and over the outskirts of Norwich to the north (*Figure 17.15*). A sixth ring lay outside the line of the road works and so was left undisturbed. They were of considerable size, so it was expected that some represented large settlement enclosures of the later Bronze Age of a kind represented at the North Ring in Mucking in southern Essex (Bond 1988). However, when excavated they turned out to be grand and complex burial monuments of the later Neolithic and Early Bronze Age, although no trace of mounds remained (*Figure 17.16*). One of the two largest examples was interpreted as a 'hengiform barrow', probably featuring a central ring of posts rather than a mound. Most of the graves identified were inhumations, and some had tree-trunk or plank coffins. Overlying all of that was an Iron Age settlement with post-built round houses and pits which had grown up in the spaces between the mounds and ditches of the barrows during the first millennium BC. Unusual small square ditched enclosures were probably Late Iron Age square barrows. One of these was surrounded by a post-in-trench wall or fence creating a plan similar to a Romano-Celtic temple or shrine. It is also possible, with the paucity of dating evidence, that these square enclosures represent Anglo-Saxon shrines demonstrating the longevity of the site as a sacred place (Pestell 2012, 74).

17.15. Aerial photograph of the Harford Farm excavations in progress in 1990 showing the four large Neolithic/Bronze Age rings recorded previously as crop-marks. Less visible are the traces of an Iron Age settlement and small square enclosures, which could have been Iron Age or even Early Anglo-Saxon, and the Anglo-Saxon cemetery beyond. This hilltop had clearly been a sacred place for a long time (TF2204/ADY/GFQ7).

17.16. One of the large Harford Farm rings under excavation (Photo Trevor Ashwin).

Perhaps the most surprising discovery was a cemetery with a total of 46 Anglo-Saxon graves lying west-to-east close to the Harford Farm buildings dating to the late seventh and early eighth centuries AD. Four of the graves were lavishly furnished with jewellery, including exceptional pieces of gold and silver. The star piece was an early seventh-century composite disc brooch from Grave 11 with gold sheet on the face, decorated with gold filigree inset with garnets and with bosses inset with coloured glass. The face of the brooch was damaged and repaired (*Figure 17.17*), and scratched on the back was animal decoration and a runic inscription translated as LUDA REPAIRED (THIS) BROOCH (Penn 2000, 45-49). The character of the grave-goods and the manner of burial put the cemetery in the 'late' or 'Final Phase' when the Anglo-Saxon population were gradually converting to Christian beliefs and rituals. Grave 18 also had near the head a pair of *sceattas* dating to the last two decades of the seventh century, with on the reverse a dove sat atop a cross representing the Christian soul, and these may have been laid on the eyes of the deceased (Hoggett 2010a, 109-111).

When the first graves were discovered it was clear at once that this was a cemetery find of national significance. To their credit, English Heritage responded quickly by granting additional funding towards both the excavation and the conservation of the gravegoods, which allowed us to finish the cemetery

17.17. The early seventh-century composite disc brooch with gold filigree inset with garnets and coloured glass from a grave at Harford Farm (7.3 cm wide) (9794/194).

during an additional six weeks. The objects are now star exhibits in the Anglo-Saxon gallery in the Castle Museum. This cemetery provides further evidence that Caistor Roman town and settlement in the surrounding area did not just all die with the Romans. It remained an important centre of trade and influence well into the eighth century. This conclusion fits in well with the recent research on the Norfolk Archaeological Trust's recently purchased Dunston Field on the west bank of the River Tas at Caistor where there is a scatter of seventh and eighth-century coins and an excavated eighth-century sunken featured building (p. 285-289). The Harford Farm hilltop had since the Late Neolithic been in use as a funerary centre, although the locations of the settlements for the people using this burial ground over much of this very long period remain elusive.

Barton Bendish parish survey, 1980-90

There were three separate successful projects in the parish of Barton Bendish in West Norfolk. One was the excavation in 1980 and 1981 by Andrew Rogerson of the site of All Saints' church demolished in 1789, the first rural church in Norfolk to be completely excavated (Rogerson and Ashley 1987). Another was the excavation of a part of the village by David Pritchard in 1987-88 (Pritchard 1997). The third was a fieldwalking survey of the whole parish from 1983 to 1990 by Andrew and the study of the parish documents by Alan Davison. This survey was devised as a study to put the excavated church of All Saints' into its Saxon and medieval context (Rogerson with Davison 1997). There was no better person to do this fieldwalking than Andrew because whenever he walked into a ploughed field he was always the first to pick up something of interest. If there was anything there to be found, he would find it. His uncanny ability to spot small grubby bits of soil-coloured pottery on the soil surface is extra-ordinary.

Parish fieldwalking

The survey of all the arable fields in this chalkland parish took 139 days, or part days, by Andrew working alone. Every effort was made only to walk the fields when the soil surfaces were well weathered. Freshly ploughed land was of little use, and days when the sun was at a low angle were to be avoided. The fields were walked in lines, and the different levels of searching were carefully recorded. The end result was an impressive series of distribution maps for Neolithic, Bronze Age, Iron Age, Romano-British, Early, Middle and Late Saxon and medieval flint and pottery finds. But it was only from the Iron Age onwards that the fieldwalking produced meaningful evidence for the distributions of settlement. The pottery finds were marked on period maps with red spots which coalesced into blobs at high concentrations. These maps are the most sensitive and meaningful fieldwalking distribution records covering the whole time span from Iron Age to medieval I have seen (*Figure 17.18*). To quote from Andrew's conclusions:

> At the very least this survey has gone some way beyond the random distribution of chance finds and visible monuments which form the mainstay of rural archaeology (Rogerson with Davison 1997, 41).

That was an under-statement.

The settlement sequence

For the Iron Age there were about 15 concentrations of pottery scattered over the parish with an average size of 0.3 hectares, representing a range from small isolated farms to larger hamlets. A thin scatter of Iron Age pottery between the settlements represented domestic refuse distributed with farmyard manure, suggesting that most of the parish was already under arable, as it is today. In the Roman period the pattern of well-scattered hamlets remained, with one having evidence for iron smelting. Again, manuring was widespread.

In contrast, the Early Saxon population was almost invisible. For the Middle Saxon period, the evidence was stronger with 133 sherds mostly clustered near St Mary's church at the west end of the village, suggesting that this was the origin of the modern nucleated settlement. From the late ninth century the arrival of Thetford Ware made it much easier to define the focus of activity which expanded from near St Mary's church eastwards to take up most of the area occupied by the modern village. By the eleventh century there were five manors as well as all three churches. An outlying southern settlement, called Eastmore, strung out along the edge of low-lying ground and probably used as common pasture, did not begin before *c.* 1100. Similar expansion onto commons has been seen in several

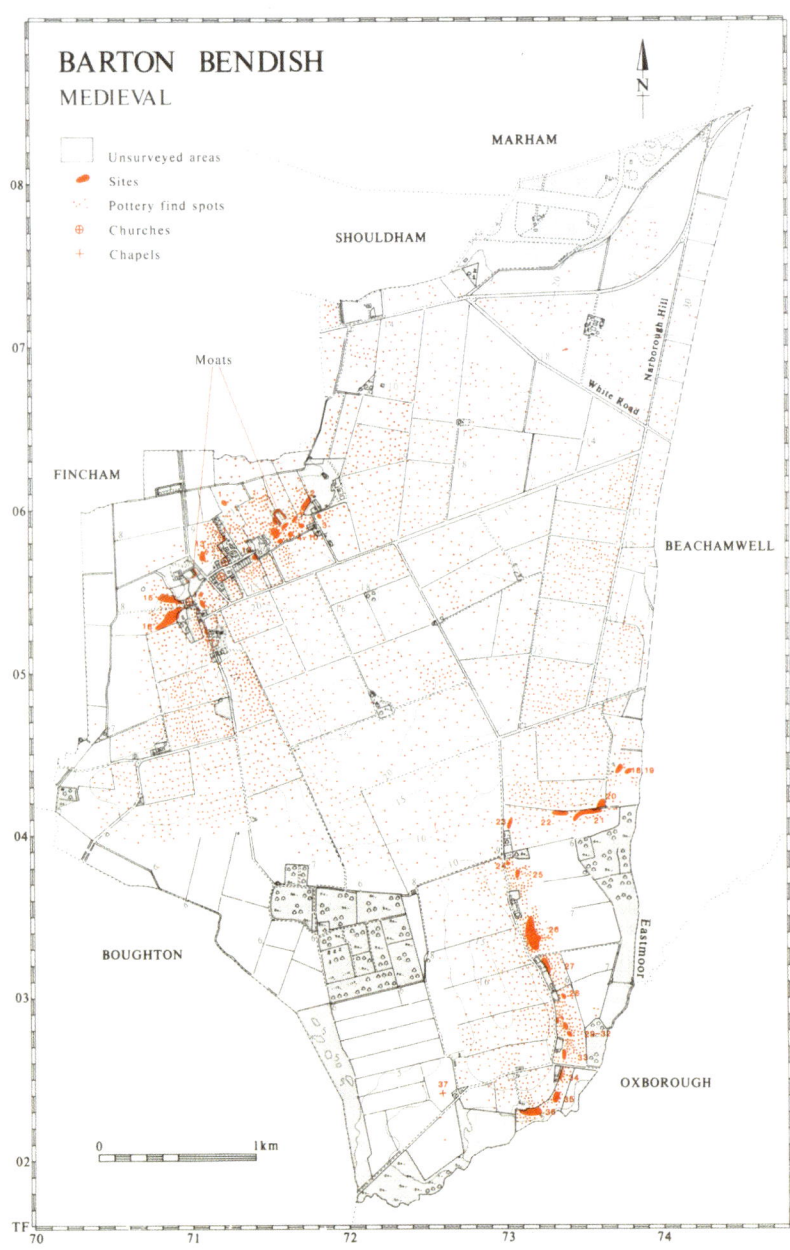

17.18. Barton Bendish parish survey: a distribution of medieval sites and finds.

other Norfolk villages **(p. 33-39)**. The twelfth century was the time when Eastmore expanded, but it then suffered severe decline in the fourteenth century. So, overall, these pottery scatters, recovered in a thoroughly disciplined and ordered manner, documented the fluctuations of settlement from the Iron Age to the post-medieval periods.

This integrated approach involving parish survey, village and church excavation is surely the best way to understand rural settlement.

Chapter 18:
Clearing the Publication Backlog from the Past, 1977-97

When the Unit started in 1973 we set ourselves the task of clearing the backlog of unpublished reports of excavations left unfinished by our predecessors. Writing up other peoples' excavations when their records often did not conform to the standards of a later time was never going to be easy, but by 1997 the job was done. These reports are listed below by period in alphabetical order followed by the publication reference:

Prehistoric

Bridgham Bronze Age barrow excavated by Clarke in 1953 (Lawson 1986),
Cockley Cley Bronze Age barrows excavated by Roberts in 1963 (Lawson 1986),
Eaton Heath Bronze Age barrows excavated by Tidder in 1969 and 1970 (Healy 1986),
Old Hunstanton Bronze Age barrow excavated by Gilding in 1968 (Lawson 1986),
Thetford Castle Iron Age fort and medieval castle excavated by Clarke in 1962 (Davies, Gregory, Lawson, Rickett and Rogerson 1992),
Thornham Iron Age ditched enclosure excavated by Butler in 1952 and by Clarke in 1955, 1956 and 1960 (Gregory 1986a; Gregory 1986f),
Trowse Bronze Age round barrow and burials excavated by Clarke in 1958 and 1959 and by Wade in 1967 (Healy 1982),
Warham Burrows Iron Age ditched enclosure excavated by Clarke in 1959 (Gregory 1986c),
Warham Iron Age Camp excavated by Clarke in 1959 (Gregory 1986d),
Weasenham Lyngs Bronze Age round barrows and enclosure excavated by Petersen in 1972 (Petersen and Healy 1986),
Wighton Iron Age ditched enclosure excavated by Clarke in 1957 and 1958 (Gregory 1986e).

Roman

Ashill Roman enclosure excavated by Barton in 1874 and by Clarke in 1961 (Gregory 1977),
Burgh Castle Roman fort excavated by Green between 1958 and 1961 (Johnson 1983),
Caister-on-Sea Roman fort and Anglo-Saxon burials excavated by Green in 1951 to 1955, by Ellison from 1961 to 1963, by Higgins in 1966 to 1968, by McEwen in 1979 and by Musty in 1972 (Darling and Gurney 1993),

Caistor Roman temple excavated by Clarke and Larwood in 1950, Knocker and Hughes in 1950, Baggs in 1956 and Mottram in 1957 (Gurney 1986),
Denver Roman salt-producing site excavated by Green in 1960 (Gurney 1986),
Feltwell Roman villa and bath-house excavated by Greenfield in 1962 and 1964 (Gurney 1986b),
Hockwold Leylands Farm Roman settlement excavated by Green in 1957 (Gurney 1986).

Anglo-Saxon

Thetford Anglo-Saxon town excavated by Knocker in 1948 to 1957 and 1959 (Rogerson and Dallas 1984),
Thetford Anglo-Saxon town excavated by Davison in 1964 to 1970 (Dallas 1993),
Illington Anglo-Saxon cemetery excavated by Knocker in 1949 (Davison, Green and Milligan 1993).

Medieval

Castle Rising Castle excavations by Beric Morley from 1970 to 1976 (Morley and Gurney 1997).

This was a large accumulation of some 28 excavations, and it took us 20 years to clear, but we could not just ignore the problem. Many of the older excavations had been funded by the Ministry of Works when it was their policy to pay archaeologists to excavate but not to write their reports afterwards. Yet, writing can easily take as long as the excavation itself, if not a lot longer. It was hardly surprising that all this unfinished work had accumulated, and it is difficult now to understand the mindset of those archaeologists who ran a system in the Ministry of Works whereby it was acceptable to pay professionals to dig but not to publish. The excavators could have refused to participate in this unreasonable practice, but they all continued digging, leaving the next generation to clear up their unfinished work. We eventually broke the practice over the North Elmham report in 1971 (**p. 59-60**), and thereafter government grants for post-excavation work were generally available.

The Caistor Roman town excavations of the 1930s

The high-profile excavations conducted from 1929 to 1931 and 1933 to 1935 at Caistor St Edmund Roman town by Professor Donald Atkinson for the Norfolk and Norwich Archaeological Society remained largely unpublished, except for a short summary by Christopher Hawkes (Hawkes 1949). When the British Association for the Advancement of Science held its meeting in Norwich in 1961 Atkinson was invited to give a lecture on his Caistor excavations in the hope he would thereby be encouraged to finish the report. But it made no difference, and I remember there was a moment in his lecture when he showed a slide of an unfinished section drawing, probably through the northern town bank, and said rather dismissively that he had not had time to finish it yet – and that after 30 years. Atkinson died two years later in 1963. Then Sheppard Frere commendably did what he could from Atkinson's inadequate records in his article on the forum and baths in *Britannia* in 1971 (Frere 1971).

Is history now repeating itself?

If I could go back in time I would dearly like to ask some of those early excavators why they did this to us. Why did they do so much excavating knowing that they would never complete the task and just leave the job to others? Excavating is an academic exercise, and to walk away and to leave it unfinished can surely bring little academic satisfaction to the excavator. Presumably, they thought that somehow or other they would find the time. We will return to this problem at the end, because over the last 25 years some contractors are now creating a much larger problem (**p. 339-342**).

Chapter 19:
Re-structuring Field Archaeology in Norfolk, 1991

Before the introduction of PPG 16 in 1990 (**p. 159-161**) the old Norfolk Archaeological Unit had run most of the rescue excavations in Norfolk because there was no other suitably qualified organisation available. Now, suddenly, with developers being expected to buy in archaeological services, a market place had been created for archaeological contracting work, and there could no longer be a monopoly. When we saw this coming, plans were made to restructure the old NAU into two quite separate organisations within a Field Archaeology Division under the general management of the County Field Archaeologist. There would then be a heritage management section and a contracting section with each section head being given responsibility for managing their own affairs. That was the only way to ensure that there was a credible 'Chinese Wall' between them. Then my own post as County Field Archaeologist could remain largely 'planning neutral' for as long as we retained a commercial contracting arm. My own role was to develop historic landscape conservation initiatives, like the county earthworks survey, a monument conservation advisory service for landowners and farmers and to work in support of the Norfolk Archaeological Trust and other agencies on historic landscape conservation and interpretation.

A very detailed report on the current structure and the proposed changes was presented to the Norfolk Archaeological Services Committee and approved in September 1990, and this new structure was introduced in April 1991. It was agreed that developers and others wishing to consult the Sites and Monuments Record for commercial purposes would now be charged. The world was indeed changing (*EDP* 23rd July 1991).

Norfolk Landscape Archaeology (NLA)

Under a new Principal Landscape Archaeologist NLA was to act as a curator of the county's archaeology by maintaining the Sites and Monuments Record, running air photography, advising and supporting amateur activity (including metal detecting) and giving advice to planning authorities. David Gurney was appointed to the post. Advice included issuing Briefs for archaeological work in response to enquiries from developers or in response to their planning applications. The planning authorities could now require a developer to carry out an archaeological evaluation of a development site *before* considering the planning application. The planning authority could then make an informed decision about the future of the site with advice from NLA based on the results of the evaluation work. This would normally involve some trial trenching. NLA would approve Specifications from the developer's own archaeologist both for the initial evaluation and for any further excavation which might be required. The quality of the archaeological work then had to be monitored to ensure that corners were not cut after the contracts had, in many cases, been won by competitive tendering.

Leaflets were prepared for developers setting out what the new procedures would be (*EDP* 5th May 1992). During 1991 all the archaeological contracting work was carried by the Norfolk Archaeological Unit, but the monopoly could not last long. The developer could, of course, employ any suitably qualified contractor from anywhere in the European Union! The main problem with archaeological contractors from outside the county was that they were not familiar with local artefacts, particularly the pottery, and their identifications could be, and sometimes were, seriously wrong. That could affect the dating of the deposits they were excavating. At times tactful guidance would be necessary.

Archaeological contractors

There were 11,246 planning applications in Norfolk during 1990/91, and in the period April 1991 to March 1992 NLA was consulted on exactly 1,000, nearly double the number of consultations in the previous year. In response to these consultations 86 Briefs were issued by NLA of which 48 were for evaluations, 19 were for full-scale excavations, 16 were for watching briefs, two were for building recording and one was for a survey. In 18 of these cases developers appointed archaeological contractors from outside the county. Competitive tendering was becoming commonplace involving both the Cambridge Archaeological Unit and the Fenland Archaeological Trust but without so far any decline in standards.

Sites and Monuments Record

By late 1992 the old six-inch SMR Record Maps had been replaced by re-drawn versions on the new 1:10,000 series. Copies of these were sent annually to the District planning authorities to keep them up to date with site locations for consultation purposes. More information was going into the SMR from metal detecting than from any other source, and we regularly quoted the figure of 20,000 as the number of objects being recorded per year at the Castle Museum and at Gressenhall. With the SMR fully updated and computerised, David Gurney could claim that it would now be possible to answer a question from a member of the public like 'Which sites in West Norfolk over one hectare in area have produced Roman finds (not including pottery) where A. Smith fieldwalked between 1978 and 1980?' !!

Archaeology and planning

There was an interesting case over a planning application for gravel workings at Mundham in 1993 where evaluation trenches produced a very high level of archaeological interest; the trial trenches had revealed more than 40 features cut into the sub-soil, including a Bronze Age pit, an Iron Age ditch, three Iron Age pits and two Anglo-Saxon sunken featured buildings with associated features. NLA recommended that full developer-funded excavation of the whole quarry site was required in line with PPG 16 as well as the Confederation of British Industry's own Code of Conduct for Mineral Operators and the County Council's own Structure Plan policy E17 (2). But after lengthy debate the County Council's Planning Sub-Committee resolved to require only a 40% excavation in order to limit the archaeological costs of the gravel company. This was the first time that financial reality clashed head-on with planning policy, and it was ironic that it should have been the County Council itself, and not the District Councils, which was the first to break its own guidelines, but it was relatively rare for planning committees to compromise in this way.

In 1993/94 NLA had been consulted on 1,357 planning applications and had issued 56 Briefs for either evaluations or excavations. Although the consultation process was very demanding, this was the key mechanism for ensuring that archaeology was fully integrated into planning procedures in the county.

By 1994/95 the annual number of planning consultations to NLA had risen to 1,547, although the number of Briefs for archaeological work had actually dropped a little to 47.

The new Norfolk Archaeological Unit

The Unit, in its new form, acted as a commercial contractor providing a consultancy and contracting service for developers run as a self-financing arms-length business unit. The new NAU could theoretically also operate outside Norfolk, although it seldom did in the early years. Brian Ayers was appointed as the Principal Field Archaeologist to run the Unit. Contracting work was bound to bring in more funding, and by October 1991 the NAU was already employing some 30 people. In the spring of 1992 Brian reported to the Norfolk Archaeological Services Advisory Committee that his teams had excavated ten acres of the Roman town at Billingford in Breckland, a salt-production site at Middleton, Middle Saxon deposits at West Walton and Walpole St Andrew for the Fenland Management Project (**p. 185-188**), an eleventh-century settlement area at Pott Row, an area of Iron Age occupation at Bittering and two sites in Norwich. These excavations were in addition to various site evaluations, surveys and watching briefs. And so it went on. Developer funding was now bringing in more than double the grants the NAU was receiving through

English Heritage. By the end of 1992 Brian could report that he was still winning most competitive tendering competitions. An interesting indication that the NAU was becoming integrated into the local business community was Brian's election in 1992 as chairman of the Norwich branch of the Construction Industries' Forum.

In October 1995 Brian was able to report that his unit had in the last six months carried out two desk-based site assessments, seven site evaluations, twelve watching briefs, five excavations and five site surveys. The staff were also engaged in writing up eight projects for publication.

Over 1994/95 the ratio of income was:
Private individuals 9%,
Local authorities 22%,
English Heritage 29%
Developers 40%.

This was all part of an extra-ordinary national upturn in the level of archaeology never seen before.

But, invisible below the surface there was already a problem developing which I did not at that stage fully appreciate. In response to the temptation to take on yet more contracts, insufficient resources were being put into writing project reports. The beginnings of a new backlog of unpublished excavations had started to accumulate only just after we had worked so hard to clear the old one going back to the 1940s (**p. 247-249**). That backlog then grew as the years went by.

A Five-year Development Plan for archaeology in the Museums Service

In July 1996, 23 years after we started the original Unit, we carried out a complete review of the non-contracting side of archaeological services in order to assist with the development of a new Five-year Plan for archaeology within all aspects the Museums Service. For each area of activity there was an indication of priorities for the next five years. This 35-page report was a detailed account of what we had achieved so far, and it is a useful point of reference. A summary of that review is in **Appendix 2**.

1996-99

Our identification work continued to grow, and by March 1997 there were six metal detecting clubs in the County, all of which needed regular staff visits. The previous year, 1996, had been spectacular for air photography, which was good, but it added to the growing and worrying backlog of prints to be located and filed. So, priority would just *have* to be given to the backlog in the future, however good crop conditions for further discoveries might be. The problem was rather like an excavation backlog; it just somehow had to be kept under control. There was also a view that there was no point in taking more aerial photographs if the resulting data was not being processed and used. The priority was to have the collection catalogued.

In 1996/97 the number of planning consultations rose even higher to 2,219, and 112 Briefs were issued for developer-funded archaeological works and this was only six years since PPG 16 came into force. In response to this ever-rising workload we appointed a Development Control Assistant with a very helpful 50% incentive funding for three years from English Heritage, and the rest came as grants from the Districts to help with the consultations they were generating. By 1997/98 consultations had risen to 2,649 and Briefs to 148. The mechanism for archaeology playing a central role in the planning process was now well embedded.

Curatorial standards

In April 1998 we introduced a new Curatorial Code of Practice governing the functions of Norfolk Landscape Archaeology for the 'preservation, recording, interpretation and presentation of the field archaeology, historic landscapes and built heritage'. This enshrined the standards we expected our field curators to maintain, and it was symbolically a stepping stone for Norfolk on the road to achieving total professionalism in the functions of a still young field archaeology service. In particular it was essential to ensure that contracting archaeology, usually subject to competitive tendering, followed best practice. This involved NLA issuing clear Briefs, rigorously examining Specifications and enforcing strict adherence to the highest possible professional standards.

County standards for field archaeology

In 1998 we also produced a draft of our own *County Standards for Field Archaeology in Norfolk* which was tested on excavations, particularly on the Norwich Millennium Library site, and was also subject to consultations during 1998 before being approved by NASAC just as I left in 1999. This substantial document, written by David Gurney, was based on the well-established excavation techniques and recording procedures developed by both NLA and the NAU since 1973. It was a gold-standard manual which all contractors working in the county would be expected to follow, and there was one Appendix on 'Guidelines for the organisation of excavation and field survey archives for deposition with the Norfolk Museums Service' and another on the 'Service Collecting Policy for Archaeology'. So it was very clear how excavation archives were to be assembled and what finds were, and were not, to be retained for permanent museum storage.

The County Council's own contracting unit goes into the red

But not everything was working well. An enormous deficit was exposed in the NAU's finances a year after I had left the Norfolk Museums Service. To create a business unit in 1991 still fully integrated within local government was not ideal, and the Council's own accounting procedures, which were the only procedures then available, later appeared to have been producing misleading information for several years, although the full story has not been made public. The figures generated by the County Treasurer's Department which I saw up until I left the Museums Service in 1999 always indicated that the Unit was generating a surplus. I had understood that half of this was to be put into a reserve fund for the Unit while half was being clawed back by the County Council. However, what was actually happening, according to press reports in 2000, was that, while on paper the Unit was making a profit, it was actually accumulating a substantial deficit because some invoices were not being issued, although they were showing up as credits in the computerised balance sheets. The story broke in the press in June 2000, with a debt of £454,000 being quoted initially. This rose to £545,000 when the Leader of the County Council was saying '…. the surprise to everyone was that it happened at all, given that the Council had accountants who were involved in managing the Unit.' (*EDP* 21st June 2000). A District Auditor's report was presented to County Council cabinet on 10th October 2000. This showed that the debt was actually £650,000. The report found no evidence of fraud or corruption or grounds for questioning the integrity of NAU staff, but 'perhaps just naivety' (*EDP* 19th September 2000 and 6th October 2000). The Director of Cultural Services said in answer to questions from County Councillors that 'people had been monitoring the wrong figures and drawing the wrong conclusions in the past.' However, it was announced that the Unit still had contracts worth £1 million and it would be given the opportunity to trade its way out of the deficit and would not be wound up (*EDP* 11th October and 18th November 2000). A new overseeing board had been established with a business plan aimed to put the unit back into profit within ten years.

By September 2001 the Head of Museums was able to say that the £1 million order book had showed 'how well the unit was regarded and how competitive it was becoming' (*EDP* 20th September 2001). In 2006 the unit was then transferred into a seperate company, Norfolk Property Services owned by Norfolk County Council and run fully along business lines. The unit was re-branded 'NPS Archaeology'. It did appear that the Unit was successfully trading its way back to health and was a successful business, but at what *archaeological* cost? That cost now appears to have been a serious failure to keep up with its excavation reports for publication and that there was apparently a policy of moving staff onto new contracts before completing their previous ones in order to generate more income from developers. All we knew for certain was that the reports were not appearing. So, in financial terms the Unit may have been doing well, but for archaeology the consequences were really quite serious. There was not sufficient financial data publicly accessible to assess why reports remained unfinished and there was no monitoring by archaeologists outside the Unit to assess the problem. This is an unhappy note on which to end the story of the Norfolk Archaeological Unit, but it does raise the far wider question of how to hold to account archaeological contractors who are not meeting their professional obligations (**p. 342**).

Chapter 20:
Time to Move On

Back in 1998, on the face of it, all was going well, but a new Head of the Norfolk Museums Service was appointed after the previous one appeared to leave in rather a hurry without waiting for a replacement to be appointed. At the Museums Committee meeting on 5th January 1999 the new Head received approval for an entirely new management structure for the service which involved replacing the old management team, on which I had served from the start, and it was time to go. At the next NASAC meeting she announced that all the existing posts in the management team had been 'deleted' and I and the others had accepted enhanced early retirement packages. I left at the end of March in great distress and in need of a long holiday. The last year or two had not been easy, with tensions in the old management team, which came to a head over a messy and unsuccessful attempt by the Rural Life Museum, which occupied the rest of the Gressenhall workhouse complex, to take over our wing. There had been no proper discussions about finding us alternative accommodation and when senior managers start scrapping like this in any organisation drastic changes are usually needed. If I had been the Chief Executive of the County Council I would have made a clean sweep too. The Museums Service as a whole would be better for it.

All change

It was hard to leave with such little acknowledgement of what we had achieved over the last 26 years, but such a situation was almost inevitable when there was nobody left in the County Council's senior officer hierarchy who was in any way familiar with the details. But that is always a problem in a large corporate institution with a fairly rapid turnover in senior posts. However, the elected members with longer memories at the March 1999 meeting of NASAC asked that their good wishes be recorded, and I left in time to lamb our flock of 40 or so Manx Loghtan sheep we had kept at North Elmham since 1979 (Wade-Martins 1990). I was asked if I wanted a leaving party in the Castle Museum, but I would have to pay for it myself. I refused, and months later when I was feeling stronger colleagues and friends held a tea party on the lawn at Gressenhall at which I was presented with a painting of Burgh Castle by Sue White and a fine replica of a medieval Grimston Ware face jug, both of which I do treasure.

In the meantime, the Norfolk Archaeological Trust had asked me if I would join them as their first Director, so after a long summer holiday I started in what was for me a dream job, developing the Trust as a significant force for conservation in the county. As one door had closed another had opened wide.

Meanwhile in 1999, Brian Ayers, who had been running the NAU, was appointed Archaeology and Environment Manager for the Museums Service in my place. It was a different job title, but with an almost identical job description. Then, in September 2008 he left to run the Butrint project in Albania and David Gurney took over. The three of us all had a very similar experience while sitting on the museums management team: field archaeology never did fit well into a museum environment because the two disciplines are actually poles apart; in the team meetings there was little about field archaeology the other members felt they ever needed to discuss with us and there was little we could contribute about the running of museums. So, it was good to hear that David had persuaded the County Council to transfer Field Archaeology on 1st April 2010 to the County Planning Department as part of a merger with their Buildings and Landscapes Team to form the new 'Historic Environment Service' (HES). Then, on 22nd November 2002 the Council accepted David's recommendation that the SMR should be re-named the Historic Environment Record (HER). This decision was much more than just a name change; it was part of a national movement to recognise that the old SMRs had outlived their original role and had actually become a record of the *whole* historic environment. They were no longer just about sites and monuments.

NASAC, the Norfolk Archaeological Services Advisory Committee, had its last meeting on 9th March 2012 when they recommended to the Joint Museums Committee that the reporting arrangements for the Historic Environment Service be changed. That was the last link with museums, and since then the HES has been run in a planning environment, but still based in the Gressenhall workhouse.

Chapter 21:
The Norfolk Archaeological Trust: a property-owning conservation trust

While this book has shown that in many ways ecologists are significantly ahead of archaeologists when it comes to conservation, there is one local conservation initiative where archaeologists are not so far behind. The Norfolk Archaeological Trust, which has proved to be an effective county-based conservation body for archaeology is still not well known. Its membership is under 100, yet it now owns some of the most prestigious sites in the county. The years which I spent supporting the Trust in acquiring many of these properties were wonderfully rewarding. I was at first their Archaeology Adviser and then from 1999 their first Director. This gave me an opportunity to demonstrate what could be achieved at local level in monument conservation. There is now really no reason why every county should not have a similar conservation trust devoted to the protection, and wherever possible the ownership, of a selection of the really significant sites and monuments in their area.

The programme to acquire these properties for the Trust was run from 1991 alongside two other projects organised by the Museums Service: the Norfolk Monuments Management Project (from 1990), which was devised to give conservation advice to farmers (**p. 198-203),** and the Norfolk earthworks survey (from 1994) which prepared detailed plans of all significant earthworks known at the time in grassland at a scale of 1:1,000. These were published as *Earthworks of Norfolk* in East Anglian Archaeology 104 (Cushion and Davison 2003) (**p. 203-206**). So, a farmer could be given advice on how to look after his monument often with a detailed site plan to identify its significant features. This three-part approach of acquisition, recording and advice is especially useful where there is pressure on the cultural heritage from intensive arable farming.

The early years of the Trust, from 1923

A leading figure in the early conservation movement was a Norwich solicitor, Basil Cozens-Hardy (1885-1976; obituary in Cresswell 1976), who was convinced that there was a need for a local conservation trust committed to the ownership and care of monuments and buildings (*Figure 21.1*). He saw that role as quite separate from the academic activities of the Norfolk and Norwich Archaeological Society which organised lectures and excursions and published an annual journal (**p. 69-70**). In those early years the Trust's conservation work was focused mainly on historic buildings probably because at the time they were most easily recognised as being of archaeological importance. He may well have been inspired by the activities of the Ministry of Works which had already started to take into Guardianship abbeys and castles to put them into good repair and open them to the public. The first of these in Norfolk was Castle Acre Priory, put into the Ministry's Guardianship by Lord Leicester in 1929. By the outbreak of war in England there were 147 such properties under government control (Thurley 2013, 99-161).

This was a time when the conservation movement on all fronts was making real progress. The National Trust had bought one of the last areas of un-drained Fenland at Wicken Fen in Cambridgeshire in 1899, then Blakeney Point in 1912 and Scolt Head in 1923 (Waterson 1994, 39-55).

Archaeological sites are given some legal protection

21.1. A portrait of Basil Cozens-Hardy, taken while he was Sheriff of Norwich in 1935. He was the founding Secretary of the Norfolk Archaeological Trust from 1923 and General Secretary of the Norfolk and Norwich Archaeological Society from 1928 until 1947.

Basil Cozens-Hardy had joined the Norfolk and Norwich Archaeological Society in 1919 and became their Excursion Secretary three years later and then their General Secretary from 1928. He was also Secretary of the Excavations Committee for Caistor Roman town which ran excavations there from 1929 to 1935 directed by Donald Atkinson (*Figure 22.9*). While Basil was Excursions Secretary he became familiar with historic buildings and archaeological sites all over the county and recognised that there was a need to provide them with some legal protection. As the local correspondent for the Ancient Monuments Board he compiled a comprehensive list of 188 monuments which had been scheduled or he would be recommending for scheduling under the 1913 Ancient Monuments Act. He wrote in the introduction to that list, which he put into *Norfolk Archaeology* in 1928, that 'It may be of interest to remark that with the possible exception of Wiltshire, Norfolk is head of the list in respect of the number of ancient monuments scheduled' (Cozens-Hardy 1926). The list included the Neolithic flint mines at Grimes Graves near Brandon (scheduled 1924), the interior of the Roman town at Caistor St Edmund (scheduled 1925) and the Roman Saxon Shore fort at Burgh Castle (scheduled 1929). It is not clear, however, how many of Basil's 188 sites were scheduled at that time. Certainly, they could not all have been. While the 1913 Act gave some protection, Basil believed that some better mechanism was still needed. This was where a local property-owning conservation trust could have a role. After all, the best possible way to protect a site is to own it.

Scheduling under the 1913 Act gave sites some legal status for the first time, and under the 1931 Act owners were required to give three months' notice of their intention to disturb or destroy a monument. The list of scheduled sites grew, although the details are almost impossible to find in the archives of Historic England. The County Council's Development Plan of 1951 shows that by then 155 had been scheduled and a further 64 were being considered (Ayton 2012, 25). Additional monuments included the site of the Roman Saxon Shore fort at Brancaster, which had been demolished in the eighteenth century.

A conservation trust for archaeology

Basil was a remarkable and energetic man. He had lost a leg while a pilot in the First World War, but that did not stop him riding a bicycle around Norwich. In the inter-war years he played cricket for Norfolk with the help of a runner, and like many of the early supporters of local charities he was a non-conformist. He was on the committees of many city charities as well as the Board of Norwich Union. He was made Deputy Lord Lieutenant in 1935, when he was also Sheriff of Norwich. The first meeting of the Norfolk Archaeological Trust was held in the Norfolk and Norwich Library in March 1923. A governing Council was appointed, which included well-known local antiquarians of their day like Beloe, Bolingbroke, Bradfer-Lawrence and Duleep Singh and county families like Colman and Gurney. One of the Council members was W.G. Clarke, author of *In Breckland Wilds* and the father of Rainbird Clarke who later became Curator of Norwich Castle Museum and energetic Secretary of the Norfolk Research Committee (**p. 8-9**). Basil was made Secretary from the start.

The aims of the Trust were set out in their 1923 Memorandum of Articles:

> *To promote and foster the discovery, excavation, preservation, recording and study of sites and objects of archaeological and historical importance within the County of Norfolk for public benefit.*

Under these terms the Trust could acquire, manage, excavate and 'lay bare' sites and historic buildings and issue appeals and procure funds in furtherance of its objectives. This was all a truly inspired and far-sighted concept. Their early years represented a great experiment in conservation at a time when grants were not available. While they tried to raise money through public appeals, acquisitions were often heavily subsidised by the trustees themselves using their own assets as security or by lending the money for the purpose (Wade Martins, S. 2015, 80-88).

A conservation trust for wildlife

Basil Cozens-Hardy's visionary efforts did not stop with an Archaeological Trust. He used the same model to help Sydney Long, a Norwich doctor, to establish the Norfolk Naturalists' Trust (later re-named the Norfolk Wildlife Trust) in 1926. This was after Sydney Long had persuaded a group of friends to acquire for £5,160 a block of 407 acres of the Cley Marshes, a wetland of international importance for bird conservation. He had invited them to a lunch at the George Hotel in Cley on 14th March to raise the possibility of the group collectively buying the marshes and to set up a county wildlife conservation trust. This was all agreed, and on 30th November 1926 the donors gave the marshes to the new Norfolk Naturalists' Trust at its first meeting to 'keep the property in perpetuity as a Bird Breeding Sanctuary' (Fowler 1976, 13-16; Wade Martins, S. 2015, 90-91; minute book held by the Wildlife Trust). Basil devised both trusts as companies 'limited by guarantee', and their early Council meetings were held in the chambers of Cozens-Hardy and Jewson in Norwich.

From that original donation the Norfolk Wildlife Trust has gone from strength to strength and now owns or manages around 50 reserves and has about 35,000 members. The Archaeological Trust had its early setbacks, as we shall see, and so it has grown more slowly. Nevertheless, both trusts have made great strides in recent years, and there is now a memorandum of understanding between them to work closely together when their interests overlap.

Archaeological Trust's first properties

Augustine Steward's House, Norwich, 1924

The first building the Trust acquired was Augustine Steward's House in 1924, a fine sixteenth-century timber-framed building in Tombland, Norwich, opposite the Erpingham Gate into the Cathedral Close. It had been built by Augustine Steward who was lord mayor of Norwich in 1534, 1546 and 1556, and it was in a poor state. A second building to the rear was bought the following year and the two were renovated and let. A carved stone tablet commemorating the fact that the Trust had saved the building in 1924 is still set into the south wall facing Tombland Alley. But 20 years later a fire partly destroyed the roof and further repairs were needed

Chapter 21: The Norfolk Archaeological Trust: a property-owning conservation trust

21.2. Augustine Steward's House in Tombland, Norwich, purchased in 1924.

in 1947. By 1960 the Trust's Council decided 'that in the opinion of the meeting the repair and presentation of Augustine Steward's House was beyond the financial capacity of the Trust and for this reason it should be sold'. The financial realities of owning and maintaining an historic building were already becoming apparent, and it was sold to the City Corporation. It has since been well maintained by the City Council and is now a notable landmark, saved from almost certain demolition (*Figure 21.2*).

Sprowston Mill

In 1926 it was recognised that timber-framed post-mills were fast disappearing, so it was resolved to acquire one. There was an opportunity to receive the eighteenth-century post mill at Sprowston as a gift provided that the Trust put it in good repair and leased it back to the owner. There were many delays, but matters progressed until 24th March 1933, the day before the mill was due to be handed over, when it was totally destroyed in a fire caused by sparks from the burning of adjoining brushwood. This must have been a great shock, and the trustees did not look for another windmill.

21.3. Pykerell's House, St Mary's Plain, Norwich, purchased in 1928.

Pykerell's House, Norwich, 1928

In 1928 Basil proposed that the Trust should buy and save from slum clearance a de-licensed pub known as the Rosemary Tavern in Norwich. This late fifteenth-century thatched hall-house on St Mary's Plain had been occupied by the mayor of Norwich, Thomas Pykerell, in the sixteenth century, and it had a fine oriel window and a queen post roof with elaborately carved spandrels over the open hall. The Trust bought it and carried out extensive repairs, and all went well until the war when the roof suffered severe bomb damage and needed further repairs. The house was re-thatched in 1948 and again in 2010, and this attractive house is now the only building left in Trust ownership (*Figure 21.3*).

St Peter Hungate church museum, Norwich, 1931

In 1931 the Trust took on the sub-lease of the redundant St Peter Hungate church in Norwich to convert it into an ecclesiastical museum. The church was put into good repair and opened to the public in 1933, and it was expected that the maintenance costs would be recovered from admission charges. But that was not to be. Trustees must have over-estimated the likely popularity of a church museum, and by 1936 the lease had been terminated. Nevertheless, the City Corporation retained the new church museum until it was eventually handed over to the Norfolk Museums Service, under its Director, Francis Cheetham who was building a County Museums Service as a part of local government re-organisation of 1974.

Greenland Fishery, King's Lynn, 1932

In 1932 the Trust bought an early seventeenth-century timber-framed and jettied merchant's house called the Greenland Fishery in King's Lynn from the King's Lynn solicitor and antiquarian Edward Beloe. It had been opened as a museum by Beloe in 1912 housing local antiquities, maps and manuscripts and was run under a volunteer curator (The Society of Antiquaries on-line newsletter, issue 349, 20-21). But more bad luck followed when this was also severely bomb-damaged in the war, and in 1945 Basil reported to Council that the building 'could never be used again'. But the building was subsequently repaired and let in 1951, while the

21.4. Greenland Fishery, King's Lynn, purchased in 1932.

Trust's share of the museum's collections was sold to the King's Lynn Corporation. Printed copies of the catalogue of the museum's collections can be found in some reference libraries. The costs of maintenance remained an on-going problem, and an attempt was made in 1996 to sell the building to the King's Lynn Preservation Trust. They declined to buy, and so it was given to them for £1 the next year (*Figure 21.4*).

Binham Priory, 1933

There was one Trust acquisition which was not a building in use but an archaeological site, and elements of this project proved to be a useful model for the Trust's revival years later. Back in October 1932 it was resolved to purchase part of the meadow on the south side of Binham Priory church where upstanding pieces of masonry and earthworks represented the site of the demolished priory cloisters and the east end of the priory church (*Figure 21.5*). The aim was to raise the funds for the purchase through a public appeal and then pass the site straight into the Guardianship of the Ministry of Works. It would be similar to the Ministry's acceptance of Castle Acre Priory from Lord Leicester three years earlier. Then it would be up to the Ministry, and not the Trust, to spend money on clearance and consolidation of the exposed ruins. The Trust would not have any responsibility for long-term maintenance. An appeal to cover the purchase was a success, presumably because the church with its famous west window was such an iconic landmark. The purchase and transfer into Guardianship all took place speedily during October 1933, and clearance began the following summer. By the outbreak of war all sides of the cloisters and the east end of the church had been exposed and consolidated by the Ministry.

21.5. The ruined area of Binham Priory before purchase in 1933 cleared by the Ministry of Works from 1934 to 1938.

The driving force behind it all was Henry Neville of Tasburgh Hall, recently retired from the Indian Civil Service, who, as far as we know, had no archaeological training. But at the time 'clearance' of ruins by the Ministry was not treated as an archaeological exercise and it was usual not to record layers or later structures which were usually removed. The aim at the time was simply to put the monument back into its 'original' form

(Thurley 2013, 146-47). If Neville did keep any records they did not survive his sudden death soon after the outbreak of war. The Ministry's files of the period in the National Archives contain detailed records of the costs of clearance and consolidation year by year, but there is no information about what was found by the workmen.

The Ministry were usually only interested in taking on the core buildings of a monastery, showing little interest in the rest of the precinct; sometimes even the gatehouse was left untouched. So, at Binham visitors had to drive through the derelict ivy-covered ruins of the gatehouse to reach the beautifully manicured lawns and consolidated stonework surrounded by boundary railings. But that was not unusual at the time (Thurley 2013, 145).

The monument is still in the care of English Heritage, while the Trust has ownership of a monument which has given pleasure to people for 70 years (*Figure 21.6*). This was achieved at no cost to the Trust, with the funds for the original purchase all coming from a public appeal. The only control the Trust has exercised since has been over the ownership of finds which have been given to the Norfolk Museums Service. The carved stone, and there is a lot of it, is kept in an English Heritage store.

21.6. A similar view of the cloisters of Binham Priory as they are today following the clearance of the 1930s.

The end of a remarkable experiment

There were other buildings which the Trust acquired and saved, like the Bishop Bonner's Cottages in Dereham (*Figure 21.7*), the Tudor Cottage in Field Dalling and the Great Hall in Oak Street in Norwich, but they were all eventually sold because of the prohibitive cost of keeping them in good order in relation to the income which could be derived from letting old properties. The records suggest that when the Trust was set up this problem had not been anticipated. Over the years the trustees had to deal with two accidental fires and three cases of bomb damage. Faced with these problems, the costs of routine repairs and a declining and elderly membership, they were close to closure by the 1980s (Wade-Martins 2014). It is nevertheless important to realise that despite their small numbers their achievements were impressive. Several historic buildings had been saved from demolition at a time when slum clearance was widespread. Measures to protecting historic buildings were not introduced until the Town and Country Planning Act of 1944 (Thurley 2013, 200-01). The trustees were a dedicated group and their achievements deserve to be more widely recognised.

21.7. Bishop Bonner's Cottages in Church Street, Dereham, purchased in 1939 and sold to Dereham Town Council in 1981. It has been leased to the Dereham and District Antiquarian Society since 1954 as the town's museum.

The Trust takes a new direction

The moment the Norfolk Archaeological Trust set itself on a new course can be accurately identified in the minutes of a Council meeting held on 21st July 1982 when the secretary, Jon Skelton who was an astute senior solicitor at Cozens-Hardy and Jewson, pointed out that the Trust had sold a number of its properties in recent years 'and it was important to take stock of the Trust's future to ensure that the Trust fulfils its objectives to the best of its ability'. In other words, he was asking the Trust how it was going to use its funds from the sale of properties to remain an effective conservation charity when there was clearly no appetite left for owning more historic buildings.

I had previously been looking unsuccessfully for a purchaser for the site of the Roman coastal fort which was under cultivation at Brancaster and had been on the market (Pearson 2002, 11-15). The trustees immediately recognised that there was an opportunity here to look out for other appropriate archaeological sites in need of care which might become available. Brancaster did come up for sale again, and this time it was bought in 1984 by the National Trust which also acquired at my suggestion in 1990 a fine little motte and bailey earthwork castle at Darrow Wood in Denton in South Norfolk (Cushion and Davison 2003, 168-9). But after Denton, an attempt to persuade them to take on New Buckenham Castle when that was up for sale did not succeed; two archaeological sites seemed enough for them at the time. So, the scene was set for a more local solution, just as Sydney Long had found for the Cley Marshes in 1926. Council then readily accepted the defended centre of the Roman town at Caistor St Edmund when it was offered as a bequest in 1984, and from that moment the Norfolk Archaeological Trust was ready for a real revival.

The 1991 re-structuring of the Norfolk Archaeological Unit, covered in a previous chapter (**p. 251-257**), gave me the time to stand back from routine administration to devote more energy to monument conservation. In particular this made it possible to support the Archaeological Trust in its efforts to acquire sites in obvious need of care and protection (Wade-Martins 1996 and 2008). The use of a charitable trust, limited by guarantee, could attract generous grants for both acquisition and repair, thereby allowing us to take control of sites suffering damage in various ways and then open them to the public with fresh new interpretation schemes. This could give the public access to a wider range of archaeological sites than English Heritage and the National Trust could provide. A similar approach was being used by my County Planning colleagues who were supporting the Norfolk Historic Buildings Trust and the Norfolk Windmills Trust. The main difference was that the County Planning Department had the resources to make grants to these trusts, while the Museums Service only *received* grants. So, for the Archaeological Trust we therefore had to obtain grants entirely from elsewhere, in particular English Heritage, the Heritage Lottery Fund, various local charities and district councils when sites fell within a council's remit. Then, as we started to accumulate properties we could begin to generate sufficient income from them to cover repair and management costs. It all seemed too good to be true, but it worked.

Most of this income from the properties has come from agricultural subsidies and support derived from the European Common Agricultural Policy. If the British government does not continue this support when Britain leaves the European Union, trusts which derive a significant part of their income from conservation farming could well have a problem. However, I remain an optimist and believe that the well-embedded farming and wildlife conservation lobbies will not let that happen.

Chapter 22:
Caistor St Edmund Roman Town

The Roman town at Caistor, or *Venta Icenorum* as it was called, is one of only three Roman regional capitals not built over in the Middle Ages, the others being Silchester in Hampshire and Wroxeter in Shropshire. Lying about five miles south of Norwich, the site was undisturbed except by cultivation, and the late Roman defences are clear on all four sides. The Trust's involvement with Caistor all began in 1984 when it received the centre of the town as a generous bequest from the late Mrs Edith Hawkins (*Figure 22.1*). The rest of the estate had been sold off by auction

22.1. Aerial photograph from the west of the region's Roman capital at Caistor St Edmund taken by Mike Page in 2013. This must by now be the best-known archaeological site in the region. It lies just outside Norwich and is mostly owned by the Norfolk Archaeological Trust. The town centre has been open to the public since 1993, and it is possible to walk around the town walls and in dry weather to see the parch marks of the streets within the walls. The streets were laid out at various times early in the life of the town, but the walls with a deep ditch in front were constructed later, in the third century, cutting through the street system. There were also extensive Roman suburbs in the background, and these run up the hill to the east outside the area of Trust ownership.

in the 1960s, and the bequest unfortunately did not include the town ditch, the Roman suburbs or the amphitheatre. So, as opportunities arose we acquired additional land in 1991 and a larger area in 1992. By the time the site was opened to the public in 1993 the Trust had possession of a 48-hectare block between the River Tas and the Norwich to Stoke Holy Cross Road, including about a quarter of the suburbs and the amphitheatre. These acquisitions had involved a series of very tough negotiations, but the outcome made the whole process worthwhile.

Countryside Stewardship Scheme

Just as the Trust was acquiring Caistor, the Countryside Commission launched an excellent new conservation-led 'Countryside Stewardship Scheme' in 1991. This provided for the first time the grants so necessary to encourage farmers to convert arable land into grass where there would be real conservation benefit. The Scheme provided generous annual payments to cover the difference between the income from arable and from less profitable grass farming, so the timing for us could not have been better. The Scheme also assisted with the capital costs of grass seeding, new fencing, gates and even water troughs. There were also regular payments for public access measures. Under these new Stewardship Schemes the farmer could sign up to a ten-year commitment to sow a mixture of old-fashioned and less productive grasses and not to use herbicides, insecticides, fertiliser or lime during the agreement period. That was a commitment which would not have suited all farmers, but it was perfect for us.

An immensely complicated funding package of about £250,000 from English Heritage, the Countryside Commission, the County Council, the District Council, the Norfolk Museums Service, Anglian Water, Shell UK and the Archaeological Trust covered land acquisition, consolidation of the Roman town walls, grassland creation, a series of interpretation panels, a car park and sets of steps up the Roman defences.

The field inside the defences which was the subject of the original bequest was already under grass following an earlier DoE Preservation Order. After purchase the surrounding fields were all lightly ploughed and also sown with grass. But prior to the seed germinating the bare soil was fieldwalked and surveyed with metal detectors by NARG (the Norfolk Archaeological Rescue Group). Of great interest was an area of Middle Saxon pottery on the north side outside the defences, indicating some occupation of the area after the Roman period. Since that discovery, it became standard practice to arrange for these surveys to be carried out after ploughing whenever newly-acquired land on other sites was sown with grass.

Site opening

Finally, on a wonderful sunny day in June 1993 all 48 hectares were declared open by Sir John Johnson, the Chairman of the Countryside Commission (*Figure 22.2*). He was persuaded to perform the ceremony because at the time Caistor was the largest area of farmland in East Anglia to be entered into a Countryside Stewardship Scheme. There was a free car park and open access to all the land. The interpretation panels, devised by Sue White, the illustrator in the Norfolk Archaeological Unit, were installed in time for the opening and they were very well received (*Figure 22.3*). The interpretation scheme subsequently won five awards. John Davies, a Roman period specialist and now Chief Curator in the Norfolk Museums Service, wrote the guidebook which was published in 2001. Sue, under John's guidance, did a superb watercolour reconstruction showing the town as it might have looked after the walls were constructed in the late third century, and that was used both in the

22.2. *The ceremony on 10th June 1993 when Sir John Johnson, chairman of the Countryside Commission (on the right) formally opened Caistor to the public. Since then the site has never been closed except during a foot and mouth outbreak.*

22.3. One of a series of award-winning information panels designed by Sue White which were installed for the site opening in June 1993. This one included the forum, temples and a pottery kiln.

guidebook and on the panels. In addition, an information pack for teachers to encourage school visits was designed by Katrina Silliprandi in the Education Department of the Museum Service. Sue also designed a leaflet printed onto waterproof paper to be sold through an 'Infopoint' vending machine in the car park, but sadly the machine was smashed up by someone with a sledge hammer to extract just a few £1 coins. These machines then cost £1,000 each, and after the second one was ruined in the same way we gave up the idea of providing leaflets on site. In 2015 the old panels were replaced with new ones which incorporated the results of recent excavations and gave the site a fresh look. But the old panels had done well, lasting over 20 years.

What we did *not* manage to do was to encourage the Castle Museum to revise their Roman displays to provide a real signpost to the site and to tell visitors at the museum where Caistor was, how to go there and what they would find if they did. But there were plenty of Roman objects from Caistor on display. New displays in 2016 have provided a better context for the finds.

Caistor has given a wonderful opportunity for people to enjoy the countryside within five minutes by car from Norwich. The interpretation panels were located on two walks, one around the town walls and the other along the River Tas, and they featured both the archaeology and the ecology. Of particular interest were areas of chalk-loving wild flowers on the town banks formed on soils derived from the mortar in the Roman stonework. All the grass is grazed on a seasonal basis by sheep provided by a local stockman, David Moore, and that arrangement has worked extremely well over the years, although visitors' dogs remain a real problem. Several times sheep have been chased into the river and drowned, and however much we have asked people to keep their dogs on leads, many do not do so.

22.4. There have been several attempts to consolidate and protect the town walls since the site was purchased by the Norfolk Archaeological Trust. This one on the north wall in 2013 was funded by Natural England under one of their Higher Level Stewardship schemes.

In April 1995 routine site management was transferred to South Norfolk Council which had been particularly supportive. Thereafter, the costs of site wardening, regular repairs and litter collection were all covered by the Council, whilst the Trust could benefit from the grazing rent and the annual payments under the Stewardship scheme. The walls were repaired with 100% grants from Natural England (Figure 22.4), and there were a series of annual Family Fun Days run by South Norfolk Council for children to learn about the Romans (Figure 22.5).

There was much debate over the years about whether or not there should be a visitors' centre and where it should be. South Norfolk Council organised a widespread public consultation in 2003, and in the end it was decided not to build one at all primarily because it was feared that the income would not cover running costs. Neither South Norfolk nor the Trust was willing to subsidise the running of the centre when there was a real fear it would prove to be a financial white elephant.

22.5. Family Fund Days at Caistor have been regular annual events organised by South Norfolk Council. In 2013 two Roman soldiers and Queen Boudica talked to children about life in the Roman army and about the Boudican revolt, with the Roman town walls as a backcloth to the event.

Caistor Roman Town Project

The site made the headlines in the local press for four years from 2009 while Will Bowden, an Associate Professor of Archaeology at the University of Nottingham, excavated for three weeks each August. Several thousand people visited Caistor each summer, no doubt encouraged by the efficient way Will organised visitor reception with displays in a large marquee and with volunteers on hand to answer visitors' questions.

In all, 30 hectares were subject to a magnetometer survey yielding the most remarkable results (*Figures 22.6 to 22.8*) (Bescoby, Bowden and Chroston 2009). Will's trenches were then carefully located to answer specific questions about the Roman town and its development arising from the survey. In the first season he dug two in the field to the south near the amphitheatre. Both trenches contained Roman burials including a first/second-century cremation in an urn and at least

22.6. Dave Bescoby in June 2006 just after he had started work on the magnetometer survey of the town for the Caistor Roman Town Project. Already the outline of a Roman crossroads near the town centre was showing up remarkably well from his survey data.

four inhumations orientated east-west, two dating to the fourth or early fifth centuries. In 2010 one trench within the defences was cut through the street which ran diagonally to the north-east corner revealing a complicated sequence representing bursts of urban renewal and decline. This

22.7. Over the next ten years Dave Bescoby has built up this impressive map of most of Caistor from his geophysical survey data which reveal so much more than can be seen from aerial photographs alone (Caistor Roman Town Project).

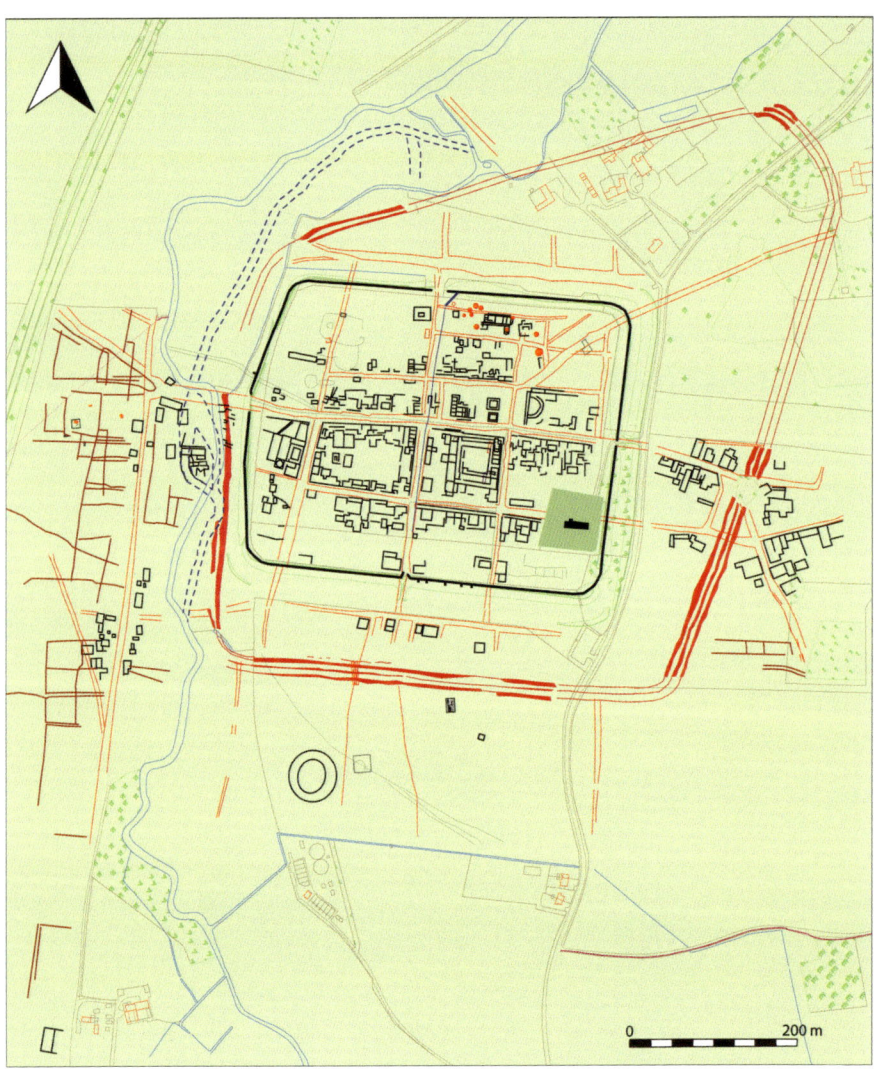

22.8. An interpretation map of the geophysical survey data showing masonry buildings (in black), streets and field systems (the latter probably not all of Roman date). The postulated course of the river in the Roman period is shown in dotted outline while possible pottery kilns in the northern part of the town are shown as red dots. The plan includes the extensive second-century triple-ditch circuit with its distinctive kite-shape outline. The oval shape of the amphitheatre lies to the south. (This contains OS data, © Crown copyright, and data copyright of the English Heritage National Mapping Programme licensed to Norfolk County Council).

suggested that Caistor was not a heavily built-up urban centre throughout its life as one might have expected. As Will in his interim report, distributed to members of the Trust and the Roman Town Project for that year, put it:

> *The lifespan of the town as a recognisable urban centre seems to have been quite short and much of it was never densely occupied. It was .... a place in which the Iceni fashioned a townscape that reflected local needs and values .... an ostensibly 'Roman' town of streets and public buildings was in fact a creation of its local inhabitants rather than simply a reflection of the requirement and values of a distant imperial power.*

As he said in his lectures, Norfolk people, then as now, always 'do different'!

In 2011 three trenches were dug into the forum (*Figure 22.10*). At the bottom of the sequence there was strong evidence for a first-century timber-framed building decorated with painted wall plaster, which was destroyed by fire. This had not been recognised in old excavations carried out in the 1930s. Then a new stone forum was built, but that was abandoned by the mid third century. After quite a gap there was a revival in the early fourth century when Caistor seems to have taken on a new strategic importance within the region. It is interesting to see how much excavation standards have changed since those conducted by Donald Atkinson in the 1930s (*Figure 22.9*).

In the final season a long trench was cut through the early town defences on the south side showing that they had been filled in during the second century AD. Also, one of the possible Anglo-Saxon sunken featured buildings seen on aerial photographs of Dunston Field (see **p. 283-289** below) was excavated with splendid results.

Overall Will's conclusions were that the well-known grid of streets, so often photographed from the air, may not have been laid out until several decades after the Boudican revolt and then not all at one time. The urban infrastructure therefore cannot be associated any longer with the pacification of Iceni, but with a gradual urban development during the second century (Bowden 2013a). He found that an early wooden forum was destroyed by a catastrophic fire, to be replaced by a monumental stone rebuild, two temples and a bathhouse in the latter half of the second century. This new high-status forum was abandoned in the third century, and then there was a revival in the late third or early fourth centuries associated with the creation of another new forum and the construction of the town walls (Bowden 2013b).

There were sporadic sherds of Early Saxon pottery in the uppermost levels of the trenches opened within the defences. There was also a post-hole structure associated with Early Saxon pottery in the trench cut through the early defences to the south. This all indicates some later activity, but twentieth-century ploughing

22.9. The first excavations at Caistor by Donald Atkinson in the 1930s were not good even by the standards of their day and were never fully published. Much of it was just wall following.

could well have removed much of the settlement evidence associated with the two Early Anglo-Saxon cemeteries on the hills around. Certainly, no sign of Early Saxon sunken featured buildings have been seen so far on the east side of the river. Will's technique was to select relatively small areas and excavate them in depth to understand the stratigraphic sequence of the town's development. Another option, which may or may not work in the future, is to open up wider areas to examine just the surfaces of the Roman rubble to see if there is any trace, however slight, of post-Roman structures as Phil Barker did on the basilica at Wroxeter Roman town from 1966 (Barker *et al.* 1997). Also, we still have the perplexing question of why massive earth banks were piled against the *outside* of the walls, almost reverting to earthwork defences at the end of the life of the town. Certainly the post-Roman period will deserve special attention whenever there is further excavation at Caistor.

We must now await Will's final report to assess the full significance of his discoveries, although meanwhile he has produced a popular summary of his research in *Current Archaeology* (Bowden 2012).

22.10. The contrast between Atkinson's work (Figure 22.9) and the recently completed excavations by Will Bowden are striking. Here in 2011 a trench in the forum exposed the white flint foundations of what Atkinson described as his Forum 2 cutting through a red layer of burnt soil and roof tiles from an earlier timber phase destroyed by fire. A wall of Atkinson's Forum 1 is visible behind the excavator.

Dunston Field, 2011

Ever since the 1993 opening, I had been looking across the River Tas to the 22-hectare field on the west side. This area between the river and the railway line was known to be a regular haunt for nighthawks. It had also been detected in the 1980s by genuine detector enthusiasts under the guidance of the late Tony Gregory (**p. 104-113**). The results had stunned archaeologists by the quality and richness of the finds produced, both legally and illegally. These included a series of 5,700 Roman coins, mainly of late Roman date, some Early Saxon metalwork and an outstanding series of seventh- to eighth-century *sceattas*. There was also a gold *tremissis* minted in Dorestadt in the Netherlands about 650 AD and a penny of Beonna, king of the East Angles in the 750s. This unparalleled collection of Middle Saxon coinage was the clearest possible evidence that the western side of the river continued to prosper as a trading centre into the eighth century until it moved to Norwich. This field contained the line of the main Roman road running up from Colchester (the Pye Road), many crop-marks representing an east-to-west street running towards the west gate of the town, Roman ditched enclosures and trackways and also sub-rectangular pits which looked remarkably like Anglo-Saxon sunken featured buildings (SFBs), as had been excavated at West Stow Anglo-Saxon village in Suffolk. It was a wonderful palimpsest, rich in archaeology. This crop-mark data had all been plotted out by the English-Heritage-funded National Mapping Programme team working at Gressenhall. Acquisition of the field had the potential to make the whole area into a low-key archaeology park with a river running through the middle, as well as an important conservation project.

It was known for several years that when the elderly lady who lived in Bottom End Farm died her land would be sold because her assets would need to be divided between several children. The area had been listed for the Trust Council as a worthwhile acquisition back in 2005, but when the moment came in October 2010 the question was: how were we to raise the anticipated price of £400,000 in a hurry? The land was due to be sold by private treaty in November, and there were several neighbouring farmers who might be interested in buying it. The preparation of grant applications to the Heritage Lottery Fund (HLF) had to go through two stages which usually took many months, and we just did not have that long.

I tried the National Heritage Memorial Fund (NHMF) first, but they deflected us to the Heritage Lottery Fund. A bid prepared in a hurry to the HLF, avoiding the usual two-stage process failed, as I knew it would, and then we were allowed to submit a bid to the NHMF for 82% of the total of the purchase price and professional fees in time for their Christmas deadline. This bid was presented as a bid of last resort, as indeed it was. Meanwhile, discussions with English Heritage produced an offer of £40,000 and South Norfolk Council agreed to contribute an emergency £20,000. The Trust Council offered to put in up to £20,000 if required. I was able then to relay those three decisions to the NHMF just in time for their committee meeting on 15th February 2011.

There was one problem, which highlights again the current English Heritage (EH) reluctance to schedule more sites unless they are known to be under real threat. Dunston Field was not scheduled despite the strong crop-mark and metal-detector evidence, both of which had been recognised for more than 20 years. All attempts by the Trust to encourage English Heritage to schedule *all* the land around Caistor containing the Roman suburbs had failed, with EH giving the usual reason that the matter was not urgent. However, the NHMF, quite rightly, took the view that they could not recognise the field as a monument of national significance *unless* it was scheduled. To their credit, EH responded by ensuring that the field was designated as a Scheduled Ancient Monument faster than I have ever seen them move before. Our bid to the Fund was also supported by a number of academics who appreciated the full archaeological significance of the field and wrote directly to the NHMF. I was on holiday in our croft house on the Isle of Eigg in Scotland when their decision came through, and that was a magnificent moment!

It is believed that this was the first time the NHMF had grant-aided the purchase of an archaeological site because their funds normally go to help the nation acquire great works of art. That, in itself, is an interesting issue. The purchase was completed on 12th August after some unseemly haggling with the vendors' solicitor over the ownership of the finds from the field. In the end, all agreed that the Archaeological Trust would indeed own the finds and that the vendors would only receive money from the finds in the future if the Trust was to sell them, which the NHMF would not agree to anyway, so the deal was settled.

This sequence of events raises three issues of national importance:
- The case does highlight again that there is a real need for Historic England, as it is called now, to get on with scheduling archaeological sites known to be of national significance.
- There is currently no suitable lottery funding process available to obtain grants to assist with the acquisition of important heritage items or properties when they come on the market at short notice. The application process to obtain grants from the HLF is slow and complex and usually involves two stages, but there is often not that time available unless vendors are prepared to wait. A separate additional short-cut procedure for 'heritage emergency acquisitions' would be a logical improvement of the present system.
- Acquisition is often the best way to protect a site from being damaged by cultivation and nighthawking. For this, there needs to be some sort of established procedure for national funding without having to go backwards and forwards between the NHMF and the HLF.

In Will Bowden's final season of excavations in 2011 he dug one of the sub-rectangular pits visible on the air photographs which we suspected were Anglo-Saxon sunken-featured buildings, and indeed this one was exactly where we hoped it would be (*Figure 22.11*). It was located by clever use of the geophysics (Bescoby and Bowden 2013). A *sceatta* dating from AD700-710 came out of the topsoil just above the pit and at the bottom was another *sceatta* minted about AD710-750 imported from the continent. Over the winter of 2011/12 we organised a very intensive metal-detector survey of the whole field before it was grassed over with a local very competent detectorist, Mark Turner (*Figure 22.12*), who plotted every find using GPS. Volunteers for the Caistor Roman Town Project did

22.11. As a result of Dave Bescoby's magnetometer survey it was possible to pinpoint exactly in Dunston Field the location of an eighth-century sunken featured building which was excavated in 2012.

22.12. Mark Turner at work on Dunston Field in 2013 searching for Roman and Anglo-Saxon coins. The coins were all recorded by him using GPS so that they could be plotted exactly against the background of the magnetometer survey.

a similar survey plotting their finds in 40 metre squares. These two surveys produced large numbers of Roman coins and a further 20 *sceattas*. The *sceattas* were clustered around a Roman crossroads just to the west of the river crossing opposite the west gate into the Roman town, suggesting that a bridge at this point continued in use for at least 250 years after the end of the Roman period (*Figure 22.13*). These discoveries, added to the *sceattas* recorded by Tony Gregory in the 1980s, brings the total to 44, the second largest collection from the county, making it a phenomenally important record of post-Roman activity. The Caistor Roman Town volunteers also collected pottery off the field and the resulting distribution plans of both the Roman and Middle Saxon pottery sherds should add to the picture built up from the metal-detector surveys.

CHAPTER 22: CAISTOR ST EDMUND ROMAN TOWN 287

22.13. *The results of the magnetometer survey of Dunston Field overlaid with the plots of the Roman and Anglo-Saxon coins found by Mark Turner. We believed that this was the first time that the two techniques had been used together to produce an integrated record of magnetic anomalies and surface metal finds.*

22.14. A major expansion of Trust ownership at Caistor Roman town came in 2011 when the 22-hectare Dunston Field to the west of the River Tas was purchased with a grant from the National Heritage Memorial Fund with additional support from English Heritage and South Norfolk Council. The field was then sown with a grass and wild flower mix to enhance the wildlife and also to protect the archaeology from further ploughing.

It is likely that some of the people who lived on Dunston Field at this time were buried in the Anglo-Saxon cemetery we had excavated at Harford Farm to the north in advance of the construction of the Norwich Southern Bypass (**p. 236-242**).

What is particularly interesting is that post-Roman coins have not been found on the opposite bank of the river *inside* the defences. So, it was Dunston Field which became the focus for trade in the eighth century before the focus all moved to Norwich. At least we now know where Norwich came from!

In the winter of 2011/12 three quarters of Dunston Field was also surveyed with a magnetometer by Dave Bescoby confirming the plan of the Roman suburbs, which included strong signs of industrial activity and a probable Roman water mill near the river. The geophysics and Mark Turner's detector finds were both

22.15. In 2013 with a grant from Norfolk County Council a fine new bridge was built across the River Tas to link Dunston Field to the centre of the Roman town.

located with great accuracy by GPS, and was one of the first occasions that the two techniques, combined with some limited excavation, had been used together. There has been a similar recent study of the site of Anglo-Saxon royal palace at Rendlesham in Suffolk.

In October 2012 Dunston Field was sown with a seed mix of old-fashioned grasses and wild flowers with 100% funding for the seed provided under our third ten-year Natural England Stewardship Scheme for Caistor (*Figure 22.14*). In July 2013 we built a new footbridge spanning the Tas with a grant from Norfolk County Council's Community Construction Fund (*Figure 22.15*) and installed a new seat on the high ground which gave superb views across the Tas valley. That completed the Dunston Field initiative. The only other view across a Trust property which is as good as this is from the viewing platform at Burgh Castle overlooking the River Waveney and the Halvergate Marshes (*Figure 22.9*).

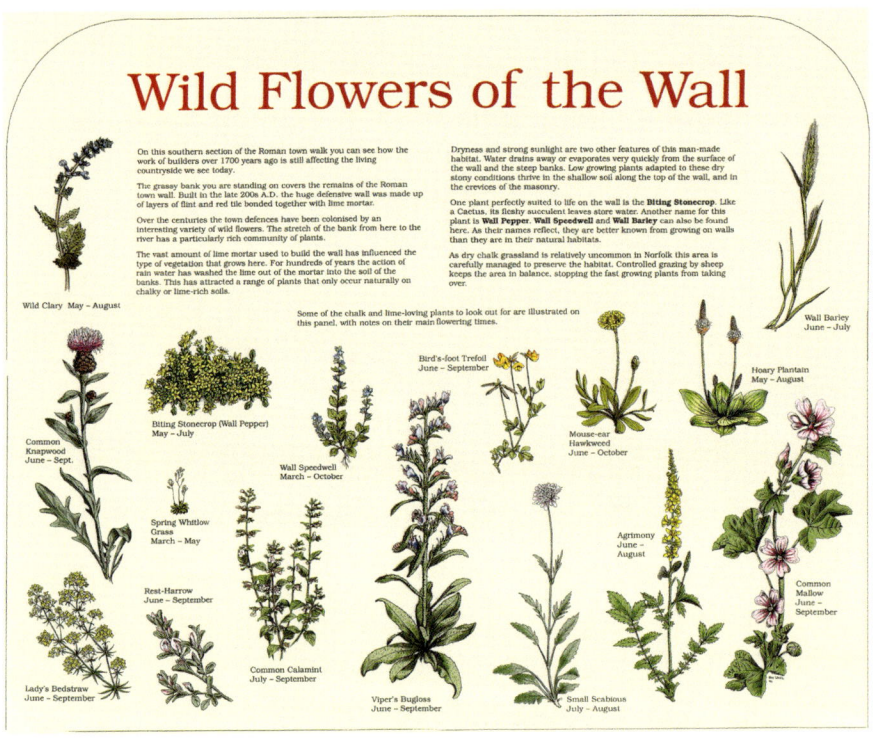

22.16. An information panel on the Roman town's southern defences located to help visitors identify the chalk-loving wild flowers which flourished on the mortar derived from the town walls.

Chapter 23:
Burgh Castle 'Saxon Shore' Roman Fort

Site purchase

'Colourful' was the best way to describe John Green, who was the owner of the Saxon Shore Roman fort at Burgh Castle (Pearson 2002, 17-19). John and I first arranged to meet at the church gates on 15th June 1993 and he drove up in a golden Rolls Royce. I *just had* to comment on his car, and his response in a good Norfolk accent was 'I've got two of these, and I keep the dog in the other one'. I don't think he did have two, but that remark made quite an impression. The meeting was the beginning of a long friendship, very tense at times because he was a tough negotiator, but I was determined to buy the spectacularly impressive Roman fort he owned, and there was a clear need for a change of ownership. He seemed willing to sell, but not at any price. He had grown up in the village and ran a business which he had inherited from his father. He was a demolition contractor and had a fleet of lorries for delivering aggregates from his own gravel quarries; these lorries and his mechanical excavators, all emblazoned with E.E. GREEN & SON, were a familiar sight in the Great Yarmouth area. By the time I first met John he had only one leg, which in itself set him apart from most people.

John frequently fell out with authority and enjoyed the publicity, especially if he could inconvenience Great Yarmouth Borough Council as well. He once took pleasure in tipping a load of pig manure on the steps of the town hall in Great Yarmouth and there was another occasion when he ambushed a Borough Council's refuse collection lorry by parking one of his mechanical excavators at the entrance to a narrow lane so the lorry could not get out. Needless to say, he rang the press, and a picture appeared in the local paper of him next to the captured lorry. John had been prosecuted by Norfolk County Council for damage to a scheduled monument by filling in a pit at Burgh Castle within the scheduled area close to the Roman fort and then scraping in soil off the surrounding field to cover it over. Later he was quite convinced that when the Norwich Central Library went up in flames in 1994 that was divine retribution on the County Council for prosecuting him for the scheduled monument offence which he felt was unfair. When he had to attend the Crown Court hearing he took with him a brick which had been made at the old Burgh Castle brickworks with 'Burgh Castle' stamped in the hollow side. When court security asked him why he was carrying a brick, he said it was to throw at the judge. Needless to say the brick was confiscated, although it was returned afterwards. One of my treasured possessions is that brick that he signed 'J.E. Green

1995' which he gave me after I finally bought the Roman fort and surrounding land from him. Sadly, he died in 2008 and is buried in the parish cemetery adjacent to Burgh Castle churchyard. I felt privileged to be invited to attend the burial with a small family group after the funeral service. His flamboyant gravestone in black marble must break all the rules about what one is allowed to erect in a churchyard, with pictures of his favourite dog on one side and a golden mechanical excavator on the other.

This sets the scene for the protracted negotiations I had with John which involved about 20 meetings over two years before we finally shook hands on a deal in June 1995. There is a picture of the two of us, just after that handshake, published in the Trust's Spring 2008 Newsletter, and it is fairly obvious that I was absolutely exhausted.

The case for acquisition was clear. The Roman fort walls were in English Heritage Guardianship and were safe and in good condition. The fort interior was down to grass and also safe, but the land around the fort, in which there was very strong air photo and metal-detector evidence for an extra-mural settlement, was being quite deeply cultivated, sometimes to bury offal from poultry processing or was being used by John for car boot sales, horse racing events or firework displays. It was all quite legal, but John enjoyed pushing boundaries, and it was causing general distress in the village. The area used for the car boot sales directly in front of the fort was surrounded by a barbed wire fence, and to stop people entering without paying he put tractor grease on the posts! As a result of all these activities John had actually made it relatively easy for me to raise the funds for the purchase because there was a strong community wish to see him gone. There was also development pressure in the vicinity, with caravan parks very close by, and a building company had an option on constructing a housing estate within the eastern part of the property if they could obtain planning permission. Much of the area of extra-mural settlement at the Brancaster Roman fort on the north coast had been lost to housing in the 1970s (**p. 150**), and I was determined that it would not happen at Burgh Castle. Also, John regularly held metal-detector rallies on the unscheduled areas of land outside the fort for which he charged £20 per head a day.

The 36 hectares of land we bought included the fort and its walls, the land around it to east and to north, a large field further east stretching as far as Butt Lane and the freshwater reed beds down to the River Waveney to the west (*Figure 23.1*). The reed beds were a SSSI (a Site of Special Scientific Interest) and a part of the Breydon Water Special Protection Area under the EU Wild Birds Directive. The price John wanted was £200,000 which was considered high at the time. The package of funding the Trust put together was made up of £80,000 from English Heritage and £40,000 each from the Countryside Commission, the Broads Authority

23.1. Aerial photograph by Mike Page from the south of Burgh Castle Roman fort beside the River Waveney, with the yellow reed beds and Breydon Water in the background. Breydon Water is all that is now left of the once great Roman inland estuary.

and Great Yarmouth Borough Council. There was also a small contribution from the Parish Council which did all it could to help. Some organisations found it easier to contribute their share than others. The County Council's committee which approved their grant was especially concerned about the high price until the outstanding significance of the well-preserved fort was fully explained. The officer presenting the request to committee turned to the members saying 'But how would you value the crown jewels?' We explained that the fort walls were probably preserved to their full height and it was one of the most impressive Roman monuments in Britain (*Figure 23.2*). It had also probably become an Anglo-Saxon monastery and was then converted into a motte and bailey castle. The shape of the Norman motte, or castle mound, was still visible in the south-west corner.

There was also a remarkable story to tell about how the marshes in the Roman period had been an open estuary where a Roman fleet was based at the fort. The marshes then silted up before they were drained with the characteristic windmills introduced in the eighteenth century. Then, as stronger pumps were installed in the 1960s and 1970s it was possible to lower water levels further and plough the marshes, thus wrecking an irreplaceable habitat (Wade Martins, S. 2015, 138-

23.2. Aerial photograph by Mike Page from the east of Burgh Castle showing the bastions, the east gateway and the River Waveney beyond.

144). This in turn led to the Halvergate Marshes Controversy and the birth of government conservation subsidies for farmers.

Despite the generous purchase price, John still imposed one condition: we must allow him to hold one more metal-detector rally. Although by then the land around the fort had all been scheduled in order to justify the English Heritage purchase grant, permission from English Heritage was given for the rally to ensure that the sale was not compromised at the last moment. That was a wise decision.

Site management plan

The funding package was assembled and John got his money. But there was a requirement attached to the grants from some of the funders that the Trust must prepare a management plan for the property. This must cover conservation policies for the land around the fort, improved public access, better site interpretation and the long-term protection of the setting of the monument. This was all quickly written and approved by September after consultations with over 20 interested organisations. The outcome was that a ten-year Countryside Stewardship Scheme was offered by the Countryside Commission and then landscape conservation could begin.

Chapter 23: Burgh Castle 'Saxon Shore' Roman Fort

23.3. The south-east bastion at Burgh Castle with the Halvergate Marshes in the distance.

The arable land outside the fort had all been under intensive cultivation, and the hedgerows were either heavily denuded or had been removed. The reed beds between the fort and the river had been shot over, and paths through the dryer areas of the reeds had been used regularly by duck shooters.

In 1996 we had the arable land shallow-ploughed and put down to old-fashioned grass varieties with Stewardship funding and the hedgerows were re-planted or their gaps filled. A wood was planted along the eastern perimeter of the property, outside the scheduled area, with funding this time from the Forestry Commission. The thinking was that this would provide a long-term visual barrier against any future development there might be to the east. The Trust decided to prohibit all further shooting, and to re-enforce that decision we dug a deep ditch, funded by Natural England, around the reed beds to keep people out. The reed beds were the only area where there would be no public access, and in the nesting season the reeds came alive with birdsong.

NAHRG (the Norfolk Archaeological and Historical Research Group), supported by an archaeological surveyor, organised fieldwalking and metal-detector surveys of the arable fields and all finds were carefully plotted with an electronic theodolite, before the days of GPS positioning. About 1,500 metal objects, mostly Roman coins, were retrieved even though John Green had already had his own detector rally. The data from these surveys is still held in the Historic Environment Record, but it has never been fully analysed because English Heritage would not fund it, and it was not easy for Natural England to fund archaeological research. For the same reason, it was not possible for Natural England to fund a geophysical survey, although the one the Time Team did for its TV programme at the Brancaster fort in August 2012 produced quite spectacular results (**p. 99**). To fund such a survey within the fort where the walls were in English Heritage Guardianship was seen quite logically to be the role of English Heritage.

A magnetometer survey completed in 2016 by Dave Bescoby with HLF funding for some of the fields outside the fort has yielded quite remarkable results (*Figure 23.10*). So, let's hope that the fort and all of the remaining extra-mural areas can soon be surveyed in this way.

The wildlife

Some benefits from our conservation work soon became apparent. After the shooting was stopped a pair of marsh harriers started to nest in the reed beds and have done so ever since. Other species of note included bearded tits and water rail as well as yellow wagtails, which in late summer and early autumn roost in the reeds. We soon found that there were as many visitors with binoculars as there were people interested in the archaeology, possibly more. In 2010 two pairs of marsh harriers nested in the reed beds and reared five young between them, which were all ring-tagged before they flew the nests. There was often a fine view of these magnificent birds from the new viewing platform. A genuine sighting of an osprey being chased off by the marsh harriers created quite a stir amongst the local birdwatchers. By 2011 Dr Paul Nokes, one of the local bird watchers had recorded 150+ bird species seen on the site regularly and

23.4. A local naturalist, John Burton, in 2010 who first found examples of bee orchids which sprang up in the meadows around the fort after the Archaeological Trust started to manage the land for the conservation of wild flowers and ground-nesting birds.

a further 100+ which visited from time to time. In 2012 one of the young marsh harriers tagged by Paul Nokes from that year was later recorded at the Tophill Low Nature Reserve in Yorkshire. It was not just the reed beds which attracted the birds, and there were six or seven pairs of skylarks nesting regularly in our new hay meadows.

As we removed the hay from the meadows each year, without applying fresh fertiliser, soil nutrients were gradually reduced, thus encouraging the establishment of a range of wild flowers. In 2010 we were rewarded with the discovery of a large colony of bee orchids outside the fort gate. By 2011 we had 25 recorded species of butterflies, no less than 16 species of dragonflies and three types of orchid. Records for 2011 by John Burton, another local naturalist, included the Pyramidal Orchid, the rare Green Hairstreak Butterfly and the Variable Damoiselle fly (*Figure 23.4*).

The trouble with car parks

In 2004 a bid to the Heritage Lottery Fund to build a car park, a covered interpretation area and toilets near the church with a long access road from Butt Lane failed because of the high cost of the access road. In 2006 we tried again, this time with a grant application to the Rural Enterprise Fund, but that failed for the same reason. Part of the problem was that nobody liked to pay for car parks,

23.5. A public consultation held in Burgh Castle village hall in November 2006 to explore different ideas for creating a car park for visitors which did not disrupt local traffic or intrude on the monument.

but one was essential here if we were ever to give adequate access to the site. In November 2006 the Parish Council called a public meeting to give us a chance to review options with members of the community (*Figure 23.5*). There was a lively debate, and there was full support for a different location close to Butt Lane which would not need such a long access road, but it would make a longer walk to the fort. Then a miracle happened. Natural England in 2008 offered an 80% Special Project grant to employ a landscape architect to design the car park off Butt Lane and a network of disabled access paths around the property so anyone in a wheel chair could actually go from the car park, around the fort and right down to the river. That was a major boost after a long period when there had only been space for about five cars near the church gates. A landscape architect, Sue Chisnell, then designed the scheme and we submitted a grant application for the full cost to Natural England. We were awarded the amazing sum of £408,000 to cover our 'Access for All' scheme, including all construction costs of the car park, the hardened pathways, a viewing platform overlooking the marshes and two covered areas for new interpretation panels. We announced this to Trust members in the 2008/9 Annual Report under the heading 'A new dawn for Burgh Castle' with a brilliant photo by John Russell of the sun rising through the east gate of the fort. The contractors were to be Giles Landscapes Ltd, and construction work started towards the end of 2008/09 (*Figure 23.6*). When it was finished the very attractive layout with the winding path up to the church was much admired (*Figure 23.7*).

23.6. The new car park under construction located so that it was completely invisible from the Roman fort.

23.7. The new landscaped footpath leading visitors from the car park towards the fort was laid out in March 2010.

Site interpretation

One of the reasons why the application for improved access was in the end successful may have been that Burgh Castle provided the best possible views of the Halvergate Marshes and it gave us the opportunity to tell the story of how this great area of wetland was saved from being converted into an arable wasteland like the Fens. This was a conservation story well worth telling.

After everything we had managed to do with the help of Natural England, we had sincerely hoped that English Heritage would fund the interpretation panels over the property including the introductory ones at the new car park, but they would not help except with those panels immediately around the fort. They wouldn't even work with us on devising a single integrated interpretation scheme for the whole property. They just did their own thing with their own (admittedly attractive) panels close to their Guardianship monument. Once again, Natural England came to the rescue and offered to fund all the rest of the interpretation including the archaeology. The contract for designing our panels went to Trevor and Imogen Ashwin after the first contractor withdrew. It was all a bit fraught, but

23.8. A pair of information panels under a pagoda near the car park. These were designed by Trevor and Imogen Ashwin to introduce visitors to the Roman fort and its wider landscape.

the panels were completed in 2012 (*Figure 23.8*). The site guidebook, *Outposts of the Roman Empire,* was ably written by David Gurney (2002).

Burgh Castle Parochial Church Council generously offered us a part of the unused north aisle of their church to erect an indoor interpretation scheme. But we were not able to take advantage of that offer because the church was structurally in a very poor condition and would need major repairs before we could think about displays in the church, which was a pity.

The need for site wardens

The site was extensive, and there was pressure from dog walkers who would *not* keep their dogs on leads in the wildflower meadows, although there were ground-nesting birds in the long grass. There were also complaints from visitors who found the dogs intimidating. In the summer teenage night-time drinking parties in the fort and regular attempts at over-night camping with camp fires were a problem too. And there was fly tipping in the car park (sometimes by the

23.9. The new viewing platform provided a fine view out across the reed beds, the River Waveney and beyond to the Halvergate Marshes.

truck load). We had problems here which we never experienced elsewhere. The wardening was largely funded with a package of grants from English Heritage, the Broads Authority, Great Yarmouth Borough Council and the Parish Council, but it was still a drain on our resources. Visitor pressure makes Burgh Castle not an easy site to manage, and many times we had to seek help from the police who were always supportive.

Special moments

Anyway, the job was done, and for me there will always be two 'Wow!' moments during any walk around the property. One is at the point where you leave Church Loke and first see the Roman fort standing to its full height facing you across the wildflower meadow. The other is when you reach the viewing platform and you look out over the reed beds to the great Berney Arms windmill, with a full set of sails, and beyond that to the Halvergate Marshes, now an RSPB bird reserve. Looking out over all of that, you can only feel at peace and enjoy it all (*Figure 23.9*).

23.10. A geophysical survey in 2016 by Dave Bescoby of two of the fields around the fort revealed a remarkable multi-period pattern of roads, boundary ditches and masonry buildings. The survey was undertaken as part of the Trust's 'Burgh Castle Fort: Life outside the fort walls' project funded by the Heritage Lottery Fund. Let's hope the Trust can continue this survey to include all the other fields in and around the fort to complete the picture.

Chapter 24:
Two Monasteries

Binham Priory

We have already covered how the area of the priory cloisters and the east end of the church at Binham were acquired by the Trust in 1933 and immediately handed over to the Ministry of Works, to be placed in Guardianship for clearance and consolidation (*Figure 24.1*). This was all finished just before the outbreak of war (**p. 268-269**). But little thought was given to the gatehouse and the rest of the monastic precinct, either because at the time the Trust could not afford to buy more land or because the Ministry of Works only wanted to take on the central area of the priory. In the sixteenth century when monasteries were being closed and demolished, gatehouses were often left standing, either complete or in ruins.

24.1. The striking early thirteenth-century west front of Binham Priory church with its early bar tracery, probably the earliest surviving in England. As a part of a project funded by the Heritage Lottery Fund the ruined north aisle was converted into a new entrance to the church with a kitchen and toilets, greatly increasing its potential as a tourist attraction.

24.2. The Trust purchased the derelict ivy-covered priory gatehouse in 2002 to carry out urgent repairs and to remove the nineteenth-century cattle shed built into its northern side.

We can see that at Castle Acre, Pentney, Little Walsingham, West Acre, St Benet's Abbey and others. At Binham the ruined gatehouse still stood derelict and covered in ivy and was on the English Heritage 'Buildings at Risk' register. Visitors had to drive through this to reach the priory church with its carefully maintained cloisters in the care of English Heritage. The contrast was most striking (*Figure 24.2*).

It was fortuitous that the Trust's decision to buy the gatehouse, the adjacent meadow and the precinct wall in 2002 coincided with a decision by the Parochial Church Council to improve facilities in the church to make it a more welcoming place. So, together we set up the Binham Priory Access and Conservation Project which the Heritage Lottery Fund liked and supported with a grant of £648,500, as did English Heritage which contributed a generous £55,000 towards the repairs to the gatehouse and the consolidation of the precinct wall (*Figure 24.3*). English Heritage also responded to the challenge to improve site interpretation by erecting excellent new panels in the cloisters and at the east end of the church. We then added our own panel for the gatehouse.

For their part of the project, the PCC rebuilt the ruinous north aisle with a new disabled access entrance, a kitchen and toilets. But, to create a level access through the new north door required archaeological excavations around the north-west corner of the church, conducted by Archaeology Project Services

24.3. Conservation work on the gatehouse under way with the church behind in 2007.

(APS) from Lincolnshire. APS found over 70 intercutting burials in this small area. Bones from three of the earliest graves were sent away for radio-carbon dating, and the results came back as AD 770-970, 1020-1170 and 1030-1220, which strongly suggested that some of the burials pre-dated the foundation of the priory in 1091. It is therefore not difficult to envisage a sequence where there was an earlier parish church where the nave was later built and that this earlier church remained in use until the east end of the priory church had been constructed. All the rest of the excavated bones were re-interred in the churchyard with due ceremony.

Wall bedstraw

Not long after we had announced the purchase of the gatehouse and precinct wall in the Trust's Spring 2003 Newsletter, one of our members, Gillian Beckett, co-author of the *Flora of Norfolk,* contacted us to say that growing on that wall was an extremely rare plant called wall bedstraw, or *Galium parisiense.* This wall was the only habitat for the species in the whole of north Norfolk, although it could be found in other locations in Breckland (Beckett and Bull 1999, 192). Without Gillian's warning we would certainly have removed the plant in the course of repairs not knowing it was there because it is so small and difficult to see.

Repairs to the gatehouse began in January 2007 and work to the precinct wall in the spring of 2008. The wall proved to be a mix of medieval work and many later alterations. The hardest sections to conserve were those where ivy roots had become so deeply embedded within the structure that it had pushed out the wall faces. So, in some places the facing had to be taken down and rebuilt. As a safety measure Gillian collected seeds of the wall bedstraw plants, some of which she sowed on the walls of the cloisters and the chapter house We also took her advice on which sections of the precinct wall should be left untouched in the hope that the plant would colonise from these reserves back onto the repaired sections. All was going well until 2009 when the vegetation on these reserves suddenly died soon after a contractor working for Norfolk County Council's Highways Department had sprayed weedkiller on the adjacent pavement. Luckily, some of the seed Gillian had collected was still available and could be used to re-establish the plant on the wall. So in places we cut holes in the new mortar and filled the holes with soil from the base of the wall and put in the seed. In 2010 the whole wall was declared a Roadside Nature Reserve, and marker signs were fixed at either end. Spraying near the wall is no longer permitted, and the latest reports suggest the plant is now doing well.

A report of the APS excavations and a study of the unpublished finds from the old Ministry of Works clearance of the 1930s was pulled together by Sue Anderson, of the archaeology consultancy Spoilheap Archaeology with funding from English Heritage. The combined report has appeared in *Norfolk Archaeology* in 2016 (Cope-Faulkner and Anderson 2015).

The final event was a thanksgiving service attended by the Bishop of Norwich of 17th May 2009 which brought the project to a close. The new church entrance, neatly inserted into the west end of the north aisle, with vaulting reconstructed in wood with a gilded central boss looked magnificent (*Figure 24.4*). There was a speech from a representative of the HLF and a fine sermon by the Bishop followed by refreshments which brought the project to a fitting conclusion.

24.4. *The new entrance to the church in the north aisle with the original medieval vaulting beautifully re-created in wood.*

St Benet's Abbey, Horning

In any conversation about St Benet's Abbey the word 'iconic' is soon used to describe this remarkable monument, located on a remote island called Cow Holm in the Broads' marshes beside the River Bure. It is a place which has a feeling of great isolation, with wide views all around. The remains of the church stand high on the centre of the island, and the site is surrounded by a D-shaped enclosure defined by a water-filled ditch (*Figures 24.5 and 24.6*). Along the inside edge of the ditch are the foundations of the precinct wall. The base of the wall can be seen in many places, but it only stands to its full height near to the famous fourteenth-century gatehouse. The gatehouse features frequently in nineteenth-century Norwich School paintings and drawings by artists such as John Sell Cotman, his older son Miles Edmund Cotman, John Berney Crome, John Thirtle, Henry Bright and James Stark. More recently, it was painted several times by that wonderful Norfolk artist Edward Seago. Their

24.5. *An aerial photograph of St Benet's Abbey from the west taken by Mike Page in 2013 to match exactly Sue White's reconstruction in the next picture (Figure 24.6). A D-shaped ditched enclosure surrounds the island with marsh on all sides except for the River Bure to the south. The entrance causeway runs up from the bottom left-hand corner to the ruined gatehouse with the eighteenth-century windmill built in front. From the gatehouse a strong desire-line marks the route visitors usually take to walk up to the remains of the abbey church on the highest part of the island. The impressive fishponds/water gardens lie to the left.*

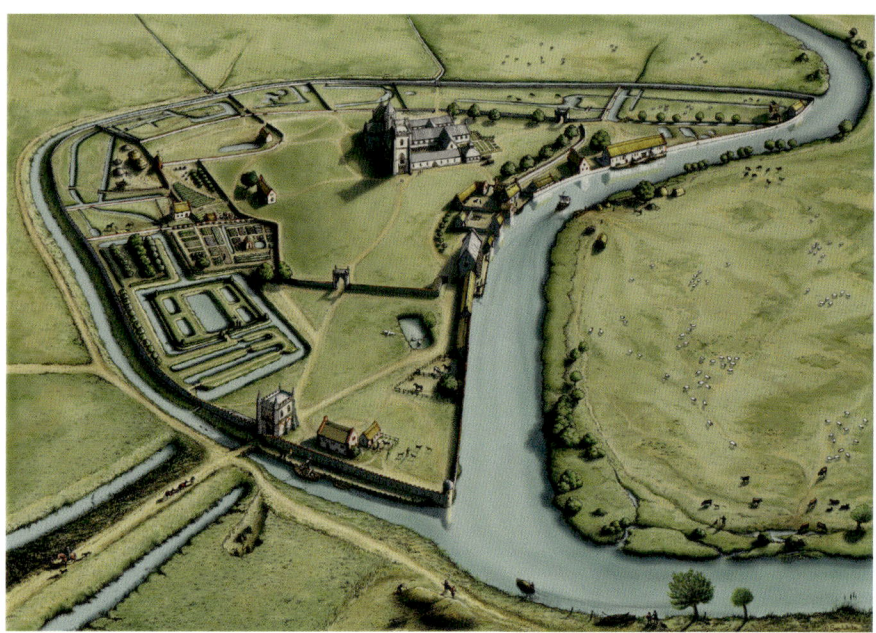

24.6. Reconstruction by Sue White, made for the 2008 guidebook, indicating how the monastery may have appeared in 1536 just before the Dissolution. This suggests that most of the buildings stood along the waterfront, a point confirmed by the 2014 geophysical survey which provided more detail than we knew at the time of this reconstruction (Figure 24.19).

works depict the gatehouse with a tall eighteenth-century wind-pump or windmill built onto its western side, thus covering the front arch. By the time the Norwich School artists came with their paint brushes, the upper floor of the gatehouse had been removed and a wooden platform built around the mill so that the sails could be turned manually with a long pole into wind (*Figure 24.7*). But there is also a pair of older ink drawings by the antiquarian John Kirkpatrick made sometime before 1722, showing the gatehouse before the windmill was built and with the upper floor still largely intact, although derelict (Norfolk Record Office Rye mss 17 Vol. 6, p.1) (*Figure 24.8*). The gatehouse and windmill have been painted, drawn and photographed so often that it is now one of the most recognisable historic landmarks in the region, and it never fails to evoke interest.

In the Middle Ages the abbey could be approached by land along a broad causeway from Horning to the north-west as well as by river. It is quite likely that the causeway was only usable during the summer, and no doubt before the marshes were drained in the eighteenth century Cow Holm was a true island in winter.

Site significance

St Benet's Abbey was the only Anglo-Saxon monastery in the county which continued in use throughout the Middle Ages. Further afield, there are comparable sites at Bury St Edmunds and Ely, but, unlike these, St Benet's remained undisturbed after the Dissolution because of its great isolation. While the monastic buildings were demolished, the place retained a fine set of earthworks, which have not been built over or dug into since. The whole place lies completely undisturbed. A very fine plan of the earthworks was made by the Royal Commission on Historical Monuments (RCHM) in 1994, and this showed the surface features, including the impressive fishponds in great detail (Cushion and Davison 2003, 148-151). That survey could not show, of course, what lies beneath. In this water-logged location, it is highly likely that the underlying archaeology contains well-preserved organic remains of Anglo-Saxon and medieval date of the greatest importance (Figure 24.19).

24.7. An early photograph of the windmill by Dr W.T. Bensley taken in 1856 when it was still in use as a drainage mill. The casing for the scoop wheel to lift water from the drains into the river is just visible to the right. The mill lost its sails in a storm in 1863 and they were not replaced.

The potential importance of St Benet's for the Anglo-Saxon period is enhanced by the fact that it stands at the tip of a peninsular projecting eastwards into the marshes cut off from the higher ground to the west by a very significant defensive linear earthwork running north from Horning church. The remains of this west-facing earthwork were discovered by F.W. Edwards and Edwin Rose in 1978 (Rose 1982). It is as yet undated, but probably derives from a time of great conflict in the fifth century when Roman government was collapsing and tribal groupings were defending their territories. A set of opposing earthworks in West Norfolk (the Launditch, Bichamditch and others) may well be contemporary (Wade-Martins 1974a, Reid and Wade-Martins 1980 and Wade-Martins forthcoming).

When Henry VIII appointed Bishop Rugge as Abbot of St Benet's in 1536 the king granted him all the abbey's properties in return for those of the Diocese, so this left the Bishop with the abbey estates, and the king never did close the monastery. The Bishop soon stripped the site, and the last monk left in 1545, although Rugge

24.8. *The manuscript drawing by the antiquarian John Kirkpatrick, made sometime before 1722, shows the gatehouse before the windmill was built and before the upper half of the gatehouse was removed so that the sails on the mill could turn.*

and his successors by perverse logic have retained the title of 'Abbot of St Benet's' ever since. So, this remote location beside the River Bure still holds a special place for the history of Christianity and for archaeology in the wider region.

When the surrounding marshes were drained in the eighteenth century the existing precinct ditch was used as a main drain and new dykes were dug to flow into it. A wind-pump to lift the water from the marshes into the river was first built at the *eastern* end of the precinct ditch, and this is shown in a map of 1702. There is no trace of this pump today, and in the mid eighteenth century it was replaced with the tall brick tower mill with a scoop wheel for lifting the water into the river at the *western* outflow into the Bure. The mill was used both as a wind-pump for marsh drainage and for milling.

A pub, called The Chequers Inn, stood mid-way along the riverbank until it was destroyed by fire in 1891. The name 'The Chequers' strongly suggests that it was faced, at least in part, with medieval chequer-board flushwork, or knapped flints and ashlar, similar to flintwork surviving in places on the outside of the north wall of the church. A description by G.C. Davies in his *Handbook to the Rivers and Broads of Norfolk and Suffolk* (1882) describes the interior as having 'arched doorways and strong walls .... whose cool recesses speak of ancient days' suggesting that there was medieval stonework inside the building. Two pencil and wash views of the interior of 1858 show the arched stone doorways, and a photograph of the building with flint walls and ashlar corners of about 1890 can be found in Bob Malster's book of old photographs of the Broads (Malster 2003, 32). It has been suggested that this may have been the abbot's lodgings, but there is no firm evidence for this.

Recent site history

By the time the Trust became involved with the site in 1998 there were several management problems at St Benet's. The site had been in divided ownership since the Church Commissioners sold off most of it in 1921 to a farmer, a Mr William Wright, retaining only the gatehouse and church. In 1946 Mr Wright sold the land to the Norwich Union but when their investment policy changed it was sold in 1992 to the Crown Estate. Two documents make it possible to tell the story from 1920; one is the old Ministry of Works file covering the period from 1920 to 1957, now held in the Public Record Office at Kew (WORKS 14/1735), and the other is the site file in the Historic Environment Record at Gressenhall.

The site was one of the first Norfolk monuments to be scheduled in 1915 when it was numbered 'Norfolk Ancient Monument No. 6'. It had been an early candidate for scheduling no doubt because it was already well known. The Church Commissioners clearly found continued ownership of the gatehouse a burden, and they had to pay for major repairs in 1921/22 and again in 1928 after 'trippers' (holiday makers) had made holes in the brickwork. A postcard picture showing the gatehouse surrounded by a formidably high corrugated iron fence, no doubt to keep the 'trippers' out, belongs to this time. While the work was in progress it was discovered that the top of the mill was in a bad state, so in 1929 the lead-covered roof was removed and the top of the brickwork was rebuilt. In 1954 further repairs were needed to the windmill after new holes were made in the brickwork. In 1980 there were more repairs to the windmill supervised by Norfolk County Council when the remaining internal timbers were removed.

So, it is hardly surprising that the church authorities tried three times between 1937 and 1954 to persuade the Ministry of Works to take the gatehouse into Guardianship, but without success. The responses suggest that the Ministry thought that a local organisation would be more appropriate to manage the monument, particularly if the rest of the site could be acquired. The Ministry were certainly influenced by the fact that the site was too isolated to attract many visitors. There the matter rested, with the reluctance of everyone to take on the monument, and the Church Commissioners must have regretted their 1921 decision to divide the ownership of the abbey.

Open-air service

The first open-air service was probably held on site in 1939, with the Bishop of Norwich as preacher. After the war the services were revived and have continued ever since except during Foot and Mouth outbreaks. The high point of the event is the arrival of the Bishop on a Broads' sailing wherry. The Bishop standing at the prow of the boat fully dressed in his golden cloak and mitre as the wherry silently glides up to the staithe is a powerful image which regularly features in the local press. A massive cross set in an above-ground concrete foundation was erected at the east end of the church in 1987 with oak brought from the Sandringham Estate, and this has since been the focal point of the annual service (*Figure 24.9*).

Trust purchase

With no one organisation in charge, it had been very difficult to develop an overall management policy for the property, despite the best efforts of a joint Committee of Management. The records of that committee do not survive, but it probably consisted of representatives of the Crown Estate, the Diocese, the tenant and an historic buildings adviser from Norfolk County Council. The committee had already been disbanded before the Trust started discussions with the Crown Estate. There was an obvious need to improve visitor facilities and provide better interpretation for people reaching the site down a long concrete farm track over the marshes. There was no car park and no on-site information. The foundations of the precinct wall were in places suffering from frost and cattle damage. But, worse than that,

24.9. The Bishop's annual open-air service at St Benet's, August 2009.

the constant wash from river cruisers was causing severe erosion of the riverbank, thus destroying the foundations of the medieval waterfront buildings which were falling into the water.

The land had been tenanted by the Ritchie family at Ludham Hall since the mid 1940s, and the site was in their farm ESA Scheme. Their cattle kept the grass down, visitors were permitted access, and it was all environmentally friendly and worked well. The problem was that the ESA Scheme was limited to the tenanted farmland and so could not provide for active conservation work on the gatehouse and windmill.

With two owners, the acquisition was not straightforward. The Trust first approached the Crown Estate through their managing agents in Cambridge in 1998, but there was not much enthusiasm for a deal, and discussions lapsed. Our second approach in early 2000 was more successful, and we had an indication that the Crown Estate would be willing to sell at the right price. By July 2000 a sale was agreed, although English Heritage and the Broads Authority both declined to assist because they had no funds available at the time. In the end we bought the land from the Crown Estate on 29th May 2002 for £55,000 with the help of grants of £20,000 from the Town Close Estate Charity and £7,500 from the Scarfe Charitable Trust. The balance came from the Trust's own funds. Then, nearly two years later, we bought the gatehouse on 13th January 2004 from the Diocesan Board of Finance for a nominal sum of £500, but the legal costs of the extended negotiations with the solicitors acting for the Diocese came to much more than the purchase price (*Figure 24.10*). The Diocese would not sell us the church because they were anxious to protect the Bishop's right to be called 'Abbot of St Benet's', but they agreed to a 199-year lease instead. So, that effectively gave us control of the whole place and made it possible for the Trust to devise a comprehensive management plan, and this was written and distributed to all interested parties by May 2004. There were so many people who felt that they had a stake in the place, and they all had to be consulted. Their representatives met on 14th July 2004 at the Broads Authority Field Base in Ludham and fully endorsed our proposals. So, we were able to proceed with the draft plan without amendments, although we didn't need to wait for the outcome of even these consultations before starting to restore the riverbank. The urgent need to prevent further erosion of the river's edge was obvious for all to see (*Figure 24.11*).

24.10. The gatehouse and windmill in 2007 after the Trust bought the structure from the Diocese in 2004.

24.11. After the Trust bought the abbey precinct from the Crown Estate in 2002 our first task was to rebuild the riverbank to stop the severe erosion of the medieval foundations exposed by the constant wash from the large numbers of river cruisers which go past the site during the tourist season.

Repairs to the riverbank

St Benet's is on an island and as the ground here is higher, riverbank protection was technically not necessary as a flood defence, but the Environment Agency agreed to stretch a point to fund this vital work, with some support from English Heritage. An engineering solution was devised by Broadland Environmental Services Ltd, and Nuttalls were the main contractors. In 2004 a wall of galvanised steel wire gabions (wire cages filled with stones) was constructed, and the space between the gabions and the old riverbank was filled with imported clay capped with river dredging (*Figures 24.12 and 24.13*). The scheme had the full approval of English Heritage on condition that a membrane of geo-textile matting was laid between the old riverbank and the imported fill to create a permanent separation between the archaeology and the new material. It would also be necessary to avoid using heavy machinery which would churn up the site, so most of the work was carried out from barges on the river. Later, to prevent cattle damage to the new riverbank it was fenced off, which was a pity visually, but that was the only way to stabilise the riverbank for the long term.

24.12. A new riverbank built of wire cages filled with stones, or gabions, created a protective wall to safeguard the medieval foundations.

Flooding of the low-lying area close to the gatehouse

The other engineering problem was an extensive area of wet ground between the gatehouse and the river which flooded in winter with water lapping up to the gatehouse walls. Local tradition suggested that the flooding here was gradually becoming worse, so the foundations of the gatehouse and windmill were probably being weakened. The only answer here was to fill the area with Broads Authority river dredgings. These dredgings shrink a lot when they dry out, so two layers were necessary to fill up the area, but in the end that worked well.

Guidebook

The original guidebook written by Joan Snelling in 1971 and revised by W.F. Edwards in 1983 had gone out of print, so the Trust invited Tim Pestell, who had just completed a thesis on the early establishment of monasteries in the region (Pestell 2004), to write a new one (Pestell 2007b). That was published in 2007 to be distributed through bookshops and local tourist outlets (*Figure 24.14*).

24.13. *Fishermen enjoying the restored riverbank in July 2009.*

Lottery funding

So, with the engineering works all finished we turned our attention to the next stage, but this would involve major repairs, some at quite a high level, both to the gatehouse and to the windmill, as well as the church and the precinct walls. The Trust's 2004 management plan became the basis of a bid to the Heritage Lottery Fund for the repairs and improvements to the visitor facilities. We submitted a Round One application to the HLF with the help of Anne Mason, who was very familiar with their application procedures, in time for their committee which met in September 2009. Their grant of £51,500 was approved despite heavy competition. This allowed us to appoint Anne Mason, supported by Hilary Brown as the project's accountant, to work up the Round Two bid. To test public reaction to our proposals we gathered together on 30th March 2010 all project partners and supporters at the abbey to explain our ideas and to invite discussion. There was a lively debate and we left the meeting knowing that everybody believed that

24.14. The launch of the new St Benet's guidebook by the Bishop of Norwich in a photo session in Norwich Cathedral, with Sue White who drew the reconstruction, Stephen Heywood, the architectural historian and Tim Pestell, the guidebook author in 2007.

our proposals were long overdue. There was concern, though, that we should take account of all aspects of the abbey, its history, its landscape and the wildlife as well as the archaeology. The point was well made that the dragonflies in the medieval fishponds deserved our attention just as much as the ponds themselves. The bid was submitted for the June 2011 committee meeting, and the call came through from the HLF regional office on 24th June to say we had been successful! That gave us £671,000 out of the £837,000 we needed, with the rest being offered as separate grants from a range of local bodies, particularly the Norfolk and Norwich Archaeological Society and the Geoffrey Watling and Town Close Estate Charities. There was also a very generous help in kind, valued at £58,000, from the Broads Authority at a time when they were faced with making severe cuts elsewhere in their budget.

Caroline Davison was appointed project manager, and the work was spread over the two years 2012-14. In summary the outcomes were:
- A new car park for 12 cars and cycle racks and a disabled access path to the gatehouse,

- Removal of the old wooden fence around the gatehouse and fresh landscaping and paths down to the new river moorings already provided by the Broads Authority,
- Full conservation of the gatehouse, windmill, abbey church and precinct wall, where it survived. This included using 3,500 hand-made bricks to replace those which had been severely eroded in the windmill over the previous 200 years, mainly on the inside of the mill (*Figures 24.15 to 24.17*),
- A new site interpretation scheme based on a website and a very limited number of panels, because the Broads Authority was concerned that more panels would be too intrusive,
- Detailed records of birds, butterflies (*Figure 24.18*), dragonflies and wild flowers were all assembled by enthusiastic volunteers, with the data fed into the county's Biological Record,
- The creation of a Friends organisation which took on routine maintenance, site wardening and organising guided tours in the summer,

24.15. The gatehouse and windmill under scaffolding for major repairs funded by the Heritage Lottery Fund.

24.16. The repairs involved cutting out and replacing thousands of hand-made bricks and re-pointing the stonework.

24.17. A visit by Norman Lamb, MP (on the left) with Caroline Davison, the project officer and Peter Griffiths, the Trust chairman in 2008.

24.18. A wonderful moment in June 2010 when a swallowtail butterfly landed on vegetation close to the author during a site meeting near the gatehouse! This part of the Broads is the area where the rare swallowtail is most often seen.

- With unspent funds, we were also able to re-furbish the site staithe where the Bishop of Norwich comes ashore for his annual service,
- and to build a scale model of the site which was put on display in the nearby Ludham church,
- and to carry out a magnetometer survey by Dave Bescoby, who had previously worked so successfully at Caistor (*Figure 24.19*). This covered the area between the church and the river revealing in remarkable detail the layout of medieval buildings along the river frontage not visible on the surface. That was the last activity I organised before leaving the Trust, and the results were very gratifying.

The final event on 9th May 2014 was the opening of an exhibition about St Benet's Abbey in the Norfolk Record Office featuring documents which covered the history of the abbey. The opening was performed by Sir Christopher Howes, a Council member of the Trust, who gave a masterly speech in which he recalled how as a small boy he had played on the site, and he said how much pleasure it had given him to know that 50 years later its future was secure.

24.19. *A magnetometer survey by Dave Bescoby of the area around the abbey church in 2014 revealed in astonishing detail the layout of streets and buildings not visible on the surface (Norfolk Archaeological Trust).*

Chapter 25:
Other Recent Acquisitions

Space does not permit detailed descriptions of the other properties we acquired over this period, but they need at least a mention.

Iron Age fort at Church Field, Tasburgh, 1994

This Tasburgh earthwork fort was purchased in 1994 to stop cultivation of the interior and its western defences. The northern earthwork bank is well preserved, and the outline of most of the rest of the perimeter is clear but not impressive. The parish church stands within the fort in its south-east corner, and the likely entrance is on the east side under the modern road near the church. The main field was owned by David and Silvia Addington of Tasburgh Hall next door. Silvia was the great Tasburgh fieldwalker and recorder of hedgerow species who wrote two important papers on the landscape history of this part of Norfolk (**p. 86-88**). Silvia had recorded the hedge along the north bank as being one of the most species-rich and therefore potentially one of the oldest in the parish.

The age of the fort remains uncertain because of the absence of datable finds from primary contexts. Silvia found almost nothing when she regularly fieldwalked the site while it was under cultivation. That is not unusual for such sites. Almost nothing was found at our South Creake hillfort which Alan Davison fieldwalked for us when we bought it in 2003, although it just *has to be* Iron Age (**p. 323-325**), and Rainbird Clarke found nothing to date Warham Camp in his 1959 excavations (**p. 9-11**). So, there is no reason at all why Tasburgh can't also be Iron Age, while others think it may be later (Rogerson and Lawson 1992). Our understanding of the site has just been greatly improved by a geophysical survey by Dave Bescoby of the interior, funded by the HLF, and a previously unrecognised entrance has been identified at the western end.

The field is grazed by David Moore's sheep, as at Caistor, and the Parish Council keeps an eye on the site for us. Our ownership created a public open space in the village which has been much appreciated by the locals. Bringing cultivation to an end, as well as creating a public space in the centre of the village, was really worthwhile, with both conservation and community benefits for Tasburgh.

Bloodgate Hill Iron Age hillfort, South Creake, 2003

Bloodgate Hill was another Iron Age hillfort. We rescued this from the constant ploughing of the whole site with a generous purchase grant from the Heritage Lottery Fund in 2003 (*Figure 25.1*). We then carried out some very limited excavation

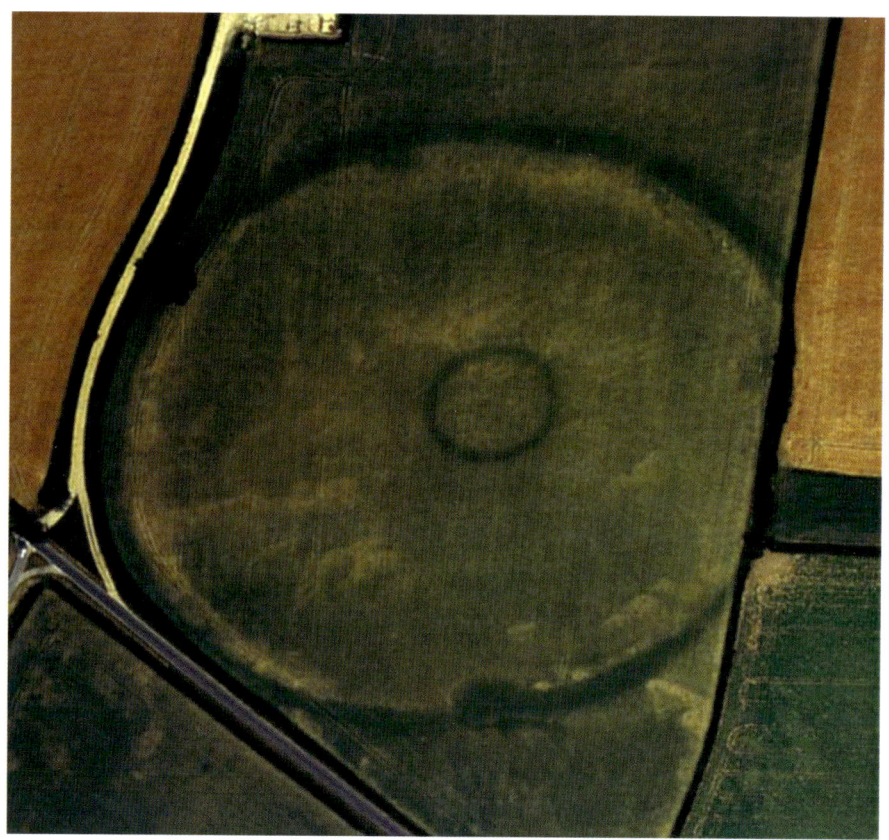

25.1. *An aerial photograph of the Iron Age hillfort at Bloodgate Hill, South Creake, which suffered from severe plough damage for many years before it was purchased by the Trust in 2003. (TF8435/ABE/SLIDE)*

to ascertain the date and the nature of the defences. A resistivity survey helped enormously in locating the site entrances and the internal layout of the fort (*Figures 25.2 to 25.4*) (Penn 2006). The site was given added interest by the discovery of an early seventeenth-century map of this part of South Creake parish with the layout of open fields both within and around the fort (Rogerson and Ashley 1997). This early ploughing did not include the defences which survived intact with the entrance still in use until 1827-28 when Rev. Bowman recorded in the parish marriage register that 'Bank of Burdyke encampment removed and set on land' as a part of agricultural improvements in the parish (Rickett 1992).

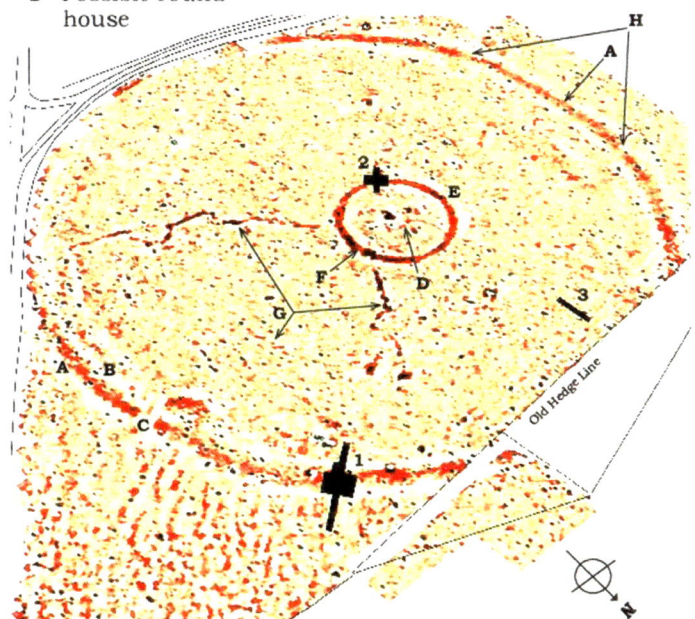

The 2003 geophysical survey and locations of excavated trenches

25.2. A resistivity survey of Bloodgate Hill at the time of purchase highlighted internal features including the inner circle, which was subsequently established by excavation to be contemporary with the fort.

Middleton Mount motte and bailey castle, 2006

The Mount is a fine motte and bailey castle near King's Lynn which we purchased in 2006 from Norfolk County Council when the Council was clearly struggling to look after the site. While the bailey had been flattened in the past, the small motte is most impressive and well worth protecting (*Figure 25.5*). Excavation in 1987 had been used to determine the extent of the bailey, which was left undisturbed as an open space when the castle was surrounded by a housing estate soon afterwards (Ashwin 2001).

25.3. Sue White's fine reconstruction of Bloodgate Hill used in one of the information panels erected in time for the 2005 site opening.

25.4. Sue White being photographed by an Eastern Daily Press photographer in June 2005 to publicise the installation of her interpretation panels at Bloodgate Hill.

25.5. Middleton Mount motte and bailey castle grazed very successfully by sheep in 2006.

Burnham Norton Carmelite Friary, 2010

In 2010 we took on a long lease of this super little friary site from the Holkham Estate for a peppercorn rent (Cushion and Davison 2003, 133). The problem here was similar to that at St Benet's Abbey with management divided, with the gatehouse and the west wall of the church under Norfolk County Council Guardianship, while the earthworks of the rest of the church and the cloisters remained nominally managed by the Holkham Estate (*Figure 25.6*). Here

25.6. The little gatehouse at Burnham Norton Carmelite Friary.

25.7. Aerial photograph by Mike Page of Burnham Norton Friary shortly after the Trust had taken on the lease and removed the fence enclosing the upstanding remains of the gatehouse and west wall of the church. Following scrub clearance, the rest of the church is now clearly visible as an earthwork.

again we were able to remove the fence separating the two and manage the whole precinct, with its surviving precinct walls, as a single monument (*Figure 25.7*). With English Heritage funding we were able to clear the earthworks which had become overgrown, and the precinct walls around the site are currently being consolidated with a grant from Natural England.

Fiddler's Hill round barrow, 2012

This Bronze Age round barrow is located at a crossroads on the Binham/Warham parish boundary, and was also owned by the County Council. Although it was laid out as a picnic area and planted with various local varieties of apple trees, it was becoming overgrown and inaccessible. We bought the site for £1 from the County Council in 2012, and with English Heritage funding we were able to have the place cleared and made accessible again (*Figure 25.8*).

25.8. Fiddler's Hill Bronze Age barrow after purchase and clearance of trees and undergrowth but leaving the County Council's planting of local varieties of apple trees around the barrow.

Castle Acre Priory meadows

The Trust and the Holkham Estate worked together in 2013 and 2014 on a project, funded by Natural England under an HLS scheme, to conserve the precinct wall around Castle Acre Priory meadow. While the upstanding remains of the main priory buildings were well cared for under English Heritage Guardianship (*Figure 25.9*), the rest of the precinct was rather neglected, and the precinct wall was buried deep in ivy and in urgent need of repair (*Figure 25.11*) The meadow containing the fine earthworks were those recorded by Brian Cushion as a part of the Norfolk earthworks survey (Cushion and Davison 2003, 136-137) (*Figure 25.10*). In 2014 the conservation of the walls had been completed (*Figure 25.12*), an information panel had been installed to explain the earthworks (*Figure 25.13*) and the lease for the Trust to manage the meadow had been drawn up by Holkham's solicitors all ready to be signed just before Lord Leicester's sudden death in 2014. At the time of writing the question of the precinct area being leased by the Estate to the Trust is unresolved.

This summary shows the range of archaeological properties acquired in recent years. There has been an unintended emphasis on Iron Age forts, Roman fortified sites and medieval monasteries because they became available. There is certainly a

25.9. Aerial photograph by Mike Page taken in 2012 of the upstanding remains of Castle Acre Priory, which have been in the Guardianship of English Heritage and its predecessors since 1929.

25.10. Aerial photograph taken by J.K. St Joseph of the rest of Castle Acre Priory precinct under a light covering of snow showing the priory earthworks outside the Guardianship area remarkably well (Cambridge University Collection of Aerial Photography AXA 65: copyright reserved).

CHAPTER 25: OTHER RECENT ACQUISITIONS   331

25.11. Work starts on the clearance of the ivy covering the Castle Acre precinct walls in 2013 funded by Natural England.

25.12. Conservation of the precinct walls all finished in 2014, with long lengths of the wall found to be almost complete.

25.13. An information panel, again funded by Natural England, using the photograph in Figure 25.10 with the precinct under snow, and others showing repairs to the wall in progress and the one short length of wall with the original flint capping intact.

strong case for taking on more Bronze Age round barrows if there is a conservation need, and the earthworks of a deserted village would provide real educational benefits. But, as we will discuss in the next chapter, opportunities for acquisition can appear when you least expect them.

Chapter 26:
The Future Role of the Norfolk Archaeological Trust and County-based Archaeology Conservation in Britain

The Norfolk Archaeological Trust has been successful over the last 30 years in building up a body of significant sites in its ownership and control where there has been an obvious need for care, good management and public access (*Figure 26.1*). While I have been critical in this book several times about the lacklustre role English Heritage has played in scheduling and protecting sites, their support for the Trust's conservation work at critical moments has been crucial, as indeed has the role of the Heritage Lottery Fund and the National Heritage Memorial Fund. The encouragement South Norfolk Council gave to our protection work at Caistor St Edmund Roman town in the early years was considerable. The help the Trust received from the Broads Authority, Great Yarmouth Borough Council, the County

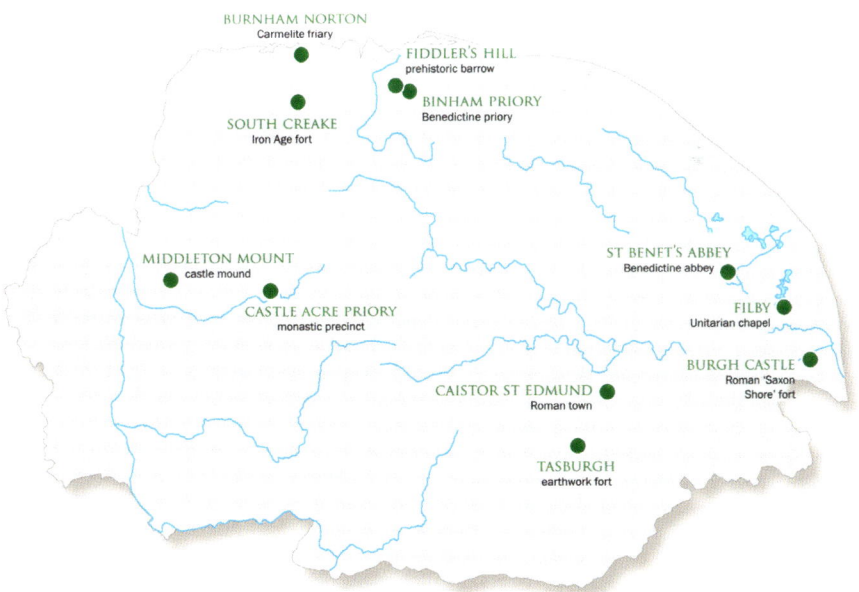

26.1. *Map of the county showing the sites acquired or leased by the Norfolk Archaeological Trust since 1991 (although the future management of the precinct at Castle Acre Priory has still to be determined at the time of writing).*

Council and English Heritage made the acquisition of Burgh Castle possible, and the outstanding generosity of Natural England over conservation management and public access at Burgh Castle was impressive. The Broads Authority also played a key role in supporting the public access works at St Benet's Abbey. Grants from such public bodies and from local charities are so important if conservation archaeology is to prosper.

My aim was to reach a point where the Trust would have enough critical mass to survive and grow as a force for site conservation and archaeological interpretation by the time I retired, and I believe the Trust had just about achieved that by August 2014 when it seemed right to go. There would still be real and obvious benefits in acquiring more land adjacent to some properties in order to make their conservation complete. The Trust also needs to seek out others where there is a clear case for providing better protection, particularly where ploughing and sub-soiling is causing serious harm. There would also be significant educational benefits in acquiring a wide range of monument types not currently accessible to the public. An obvious case would be the earthworks of a well-documented deserted medieval village with its streets, tofts, ruined church and moated manor. The acquisition of such a site where the evidence from archaeology, old maps, manorial records and other documents could be combined to explain landscape change would be a real bonus. And it would provide an ideal opportunity to demonstrate how evidence can be used to explain landscape change.

Ideally, a wide range of archaeological sites should be open in each region of Britain for the public to understand and appreciate. Close co-operation with the National Trust would have many benefits. And, let's face it, there is no reason why this can't be achieved if the will, determination and support is there. The public would appreciate seeing much more than just monasteries and castles which are usually all that archaeology can offer in many areas at the moment, however fascinating these sites can be (*Figure 26.2*).

The role of a county conservation trust for archaeology

Except for land adjacent to existing properties, it can be fruitless to compile an acquisition list of all suitable 'Trustworthy' properties because events don't usually work out like that. Trustworthy sites tend to come up when and where you least expect them, and when that happens it is important to dive in and never to miss the opportunity.

There is bound to be a debate sooner or later about the merits of buying a totally flat field where nothing at all is visible on the surface. One can envisage a situation where we know from aerial photographs or from rich metal-detector finds that underneath the surface there is a fine Roman villa or an Anglo-Saxon cemetery being hammered by cultivation or nighthawking. In these cases the removal of that site from the plough can have real conservation benefits. If conservation is our primary objective, then the Trust should not hesitate to act, as we did over Dunston Field at Caistor in 2011 (**p. 283-289)**. There will always be additional wildlife and public access benefits in almost any situation, and creating a new public open space can be a real bonus for any local community, as we saw at Tasburgh.

There then should be strict controls over excavation, which is always destructive. Usually there are other more endangered places to excavate. I always had deep misgivings about the very extensive excavations permitted at Sutton Hoo, the burial ground of the Anglo-Saxon kings of East Anglia near Woodbridge in Suffolk. Here a total of eight perfectly safe burial mounds were investigated, or re-examined, over an area of one hectare from 1983 (Carver 1992, 1998 and 2005). Every generation should have the opportunity to investigate its share of such a unique site. But the share taken by our own generation was too large, however well it was excavated, not leaving enough for the multitude of generations of archaeologists who, with more sophisticated techniques, will surely wish to follow. My views about the ethics of the excavation were well known before it all started and were recognised.

On the other hand, the excavations we ran on the Anglo-Saxon cemetery at Spong Hill, where it was not possible to prevent damaging cultivation on an entirely arable farm, was, I believe, fully justified, and we recovered much of the evidence only just in time (**p. 217-223**). We were not to know that years later the farm would be sold and that the new owner would put the whole field down to grass for his new flock of sheep. Judgements can only be made based on each situation as it is at the time.

At Caistor St Edmund Roman town Will Bowden had put forward a good academic case for excavation; his objectives were always precise and the areas to be disturbed carefully limited. The excavation on Trust properties, once they are in our safe hands, will always need very careful monitoring and should be strictly limited.

Low membership

The other issue for the Norfolk Trust, and for others if or when they are formed, will be low membership. While the Norfolk Wildlife Trust has a stable membership of about 35,000, the Archaeological Trust has under 100, with little sign so far of that number increasing. Yet, thousands of visitors enjoy free entry to our properties. The Trust Council has often debated the membership issue without reaching a firm conclusion. The low numbers have given some trustees a feeling of failure because the Trust has not persuaded the public to contribute to our work. Other trustees have taken the opposite view and said that a low membership makes it far easier to make difficult decisions.

Having started out with the firm intention of boosting membership to somewhere near the levels of the Norfolk Wildlife Trust, I came to the conclusion that this ambition was simply not achievable. Large numbers of people came to see the Caistor excavations, yet as far as I am aware not one visitor joined the Trust, neither did the supervisors or volunteers who actually took part in the excavations. Yet, without Trust ownership of the Roman town, I am 100% certain that no excavation would have been permitted.

When it comes to paying subscriptions the Trust just has to accept that, even though TV archaeology programmes like Time Team have attracted large audiences and considerable public interest, people will not feel they need to subscribe, particularly when access to our properties is free. But access is also free, except for car parking at RSPB reserves and at Wildlife Trust properties in the region, yet their memberships are large. There is a dilemma here, for which there is no logical answer. It is just a fact that people are much more attracted to fur and feathers than they are to bones and stones.

We also, of course, have four active county-wide archaeological societies: the Norfolk and Norwich Archaeological Society (NNAS), the Norfolk Archaeological and Historical Research Group (NAHRG) the Norfolk Industrial Archaeology Society (NIAS) and the Norfolk Historic Buildings Group (NHBG) which all provide lectures and excursions and member events. There is little point in competing by offering yet more of the same. It is best to focus on what a conservation trust can do best which is to act as a property-owning conservation charity. The low membership should certainly not act as a discouragement, and there is still so much more conservation work the Trust needs to do in all areas of intensive arable farming. But to win public understanding and support, education and site interpretation must remain central to our activities, particularly when it can be tied into museum displays. It is worth recalling how Sir Mortimer Wheeler quoted the eminent historian G.M. Trevelyan in 1956 in his *Archaeology from the Earth* (1956, 219) 'if historians neglect to educate the public, if they fail to interest it intelligently in the past, then all their historical learning is valueless except so far as it educates themselves'. So, the Trust needs to conserve and educate in equal measure.

The Norfolk Wildlife Trust was the first of its kind in the country, and there are now 46 others right across the British Isles. Perhaps the example of the Norfolk Archaeological Trust may still serve as a model to be repeated elsewhere one day soon.

Chapter 27:
A Time to Reflect

Where are we now?

It is worth reflecting how far we have progressed since the days when I first started as an enthusiastic volunteer in the Castle Museum and as an excavator with the Norfolk Research Committee in the 1950s. Field archaeology did not exist then as a profession. The mechanisms for protecting our cultural heritage were still very weak, and farming was just about producing more food after a long period of post-war austerity and rationing. Damage to the countryside was widespread and considerable. In the towns there was much demolition and rebuilding without excavation, particularly as a result of wartime bombing. In the countryside there had been real enthusiasm for amateur excavation, seen particularly with the digging of barrows before and after the war, when recording standards were low and little was ever published. And, as I nearly found to my cost, site safety standards on excavations were worse than poor. The need to dig carefully, record well and publish promptly had been well demonstrated by people like Sir Mortimer Wheeler, who worked at Maiden Castle between 1934 and 1937 and published in 1943 despite the war, but his example was seldom followed. The Ministry of Works had a hopeless system of paying archaeologists to carry out rescue excavations but then not to write up the results.

After the war the easy destruction of sites in the countryside was made possible by the rapid advances in mechanised earthmoving and in the development of diesel farm tractors. Urban renewal and farming had forged ahead of environmental awareness. In the 1970s there was no right of access and few resources to excavate sites before destruction. While the Norfolk Archaeological Trust had made valiant conservation efforts in the 1920s and 1930s to save some important historic buildings from demolition, it had since gone into a slow decline largely because their building maintenance costs were exceeding their income.

But, there were already some signs of real change, like Rainbird Clarke's ground-breaking efforts to compile England's first County Sites and Monuments Record (although it wasn't called that then). There was J.K.S. St Joseph who after the war was making a remarkable record of the historic and natural landscapes of Britain from the air as curator of aerial photography at Cambridge. By 1976 he held a third of a million negatives (St Joseph 1976, 5). In the 1950s there were two inspiring books which enhanced awareness of the antiquity of the countryside: Maurice Beresford's *The Lost Villages of England* (1954) and W.G. Hoskins' *The Making of the English Landscape* (1955). On the wildlife side, it was Rachel Carson's *Silent*

Spring (1962) which shook the ecologists into action. Following the birth of RESCUE in 1971 we started to see real change, but this placed great emphasis on rescue excavation and far less on conservation. Today that imbalance remains. There are still very few conservation archaeologists, but there are thousands of rescue excavators funded by developers. In 1990 before PPG 16 there were about 2,000 archaeologists in Britain, but that number rose to a little under 7,000 by 2007. In 1990 there were just over 400 excavations each year, but following PPG 16 that number had increased to over 1,400 by 2008 (Darvill 2016, 13). On the other hand, Norfolk is rare in having a county conservation trust dedicated to the protection and display of important archaeological sites, and the county's Monument Management Project is still prospering while many others have folded.

It is now essential to have a fully computerised Historic Environment Record (the old SMR) which continues to grow as a truly remarkable record of the county's cultural heritage. This will soon include all the supporting data, the grey literature reports, old Polaroid photographs and drawings of finds. There is also, of course, the large and comprehensive air photographs library. So, '…. researchers are fortunate that Norfolk possesses one of the richest archaeological records anywhere in England. The range and quantity of evidence available is largely the result of a proud research tradition ….' (Wright 2015, 169). Developers and their agents now accept without question that they must comply with the requirements of archaeology if they are to obtain planning consent. The publication series, East Anglian Archaeology, remains the main vehicle for publishing excavations and fieldwork in the region. Our record in encouraging the reporting of metal detector finds has reaped huge rewards in terms of our increased understanding of the region's archaeology, and the national Portable Antiquities Scheme (the PAS) has been very much modelled on the Norfolk approach. And, while there *were* black clouds on the horizon with Norfolk County Council proposing to cut all its funding for county staff in the PAS, the unprecedented public response encouraged councillors to drop that idea completely. Less good news is that the post of County Field Archaeologist has been deleted in a management re-structuring as from December 2016. This leaves us without a specialist archaeology manager ultimately responsible for the quality of most fieldwork in the county.

The Norfolk and Norwich Archaeological Society (NNAS), The Norfolk Archaeological and Historical Research Group (NAHRG), The Norfolk Industrial Archaeology Society (NIAS), the Norfolk Historic Buildings Group (NHBG) and the various metal detector clubs are all successful. So, professional and amateur archaeology can still flourish together.

Although this book is primarily about the history of field archaeology mainly in Norfolk since the 1950s as seen through the eyes of one participant, there is no harm in reflecting on some of the issues which are of national concern now and which may well be more so in the future. They may be painful and difficult to debate, but we need as a profession to find ways through them for the future.

And now a new, and potentially larger, publication backlog

While there are now strong procedures within the national planning system for ensuring that sites are excavated and recorded before they are destroyed by development, these powers do not ensure that excavation reports as grey literature are completed on time and that the more significant rescue excavations are adequately published as research reports. That raises the key question of what is the point of an excavation if the results are not afterwards made widely available to increase our understanding of the past? This is perhaps the most intractable problem facing British rescue archaeology today, and it is swept under the carpet all too often because there is no easy solution.

The usual procedure when there is a planning application on a site which may be of archaeological interest is for the planning authority to issue a Brief setting out what recording work will be required. Norfolk County Council's Historic Environment Service provides developers with between three and four hundred of these Briefs a year for surveys, site evaluations and larger excavations. An evaluation excavation can be used to identify the presence or absence of archaeological deposits and their condition. Further excavation or a watching brief (now called archaeological monitoring) may then be required. It is actually rare for an evaluation to uncover evidence which is so important that the development is recommended for refusal. There have been only half a dozen cases in the last ten years, and it is usually possible to re-design the scheme to overcome the problem.

Once fieldwork has been completed, the contractor is expected to produce an Updated Project Design (UPD) and a site assessment which includes a quantification of the site archive and an assessment of whatever post-excavation work is necessary. This assessment will include contributions from the specialists who have been involved. The UPD will contain a commitment to produce a report, an archiving strategy commensurate with the results and an indication of the time required for each task, but not a timetable with dates for completion. This documentation must comply with *Regional Standards* which arose out of *County Standards* (**p. 255**) and *Standards and Guidance* produced by the Chartered Institute for Archaeologists. In reality, the post-excavation work does not often merit more than a grey literature site report to be deposited in the HER and for the archive, including the finds, to go into museum stores. The intention in due course is to make all grey literature reports available on line through the HER, and if an excavation does produce very significant results, a research report for submission to a recognised archaeological journal will also be necessary.

The new backlog grows

One of the key tasks we set ourselves when we formed the original Norfolk Archaeological Unit in 1973 was to sort out the excavations not written up by our predecessors. It took us 22 years to clear up that inheritance of 28 unpublished research reports (**p. 247-248**). But now a significant proportion of current archaeological contractors, ranging from small consultancies to substantial companies, are slipping behind with their own report-writing commitments. A new rather alarming backlog spirals ever upwards.

In March 2016 the Norfolk's Historic Environment Service, when faced with the prospect of a Freedom of Information enquiry, revealed to the writer that there were a total of 369 grey literature reports, going back to 1994 which had not been submitted by 30 different contractors, with one contractor having 184 and another having 68 such reports overdue. This is serious. There are no figures available for how many research reports were outstanding, although there are a few excellent ones which have been published mainly in East Anglian Archaeology and *Norfolk Archaeology*. The temptation is for contractors just to put off post-excavation analysis, bank the post-excavation funds from the client, and move on to the next developer's project to generate more income. This is not deliberate dishonesty; it is the easy option. In March 2017 I asked the Historic Environment Service again for the latest figures for the total numbers of reports outstanding, but this time my request was declined on the grounds that the information was 'too sensitive'. Rumour has it that there are many hundreds outstanding.

This backlog does raise serious questions about how effective current mechanisms are for ensuring that grey literature reports are completed and deposited in the HER and research reports are published in one form or another when they can be justified. Once the consultant or contractor has notified the planning authority that the funding for the preparation and production of the reports proposed in their UPDs has been secured, the power of the planning condition lapses. So, there is no system to require further compliance, so surely a major review of the whole process is now overdue.

Examples of the failure to complete projects began to appear in the later years of the County Council's old Norfolk Archaeological Unit, since absorbed into Norfolk Property Services (NPS) but fully owned by the County Council. We have been waiting a long time for the NAU, and then NPS Archaeology, to produce research reports on some of the most significant excavations conducted in the county over the last 20 or so years. An abbreviated version of a list covering just some of their outstanding publications highlights the problem:

- The church of St Margaret *in Combusto*, Magdalene Street, Norwich, 1987 (only the graveyard burials have been published so far in EAA 129),
- 14 Calvert Street, Norwich, revealed the Late Saxon town defences, 1998,

- The site of the new Norwich Millennium Library within the Norman Borough, 1998-99,
- Bacton to Great Yarmouth pipeline with many important prehistoric and Roman settlements recorded, 1999,
- Norwich Castle mound and Shirehall redeveloped as part of a museum improvement scheme, 1999-2001,
- Norwich Cathedral Close in advance of an extension to visitor facilities, 2001-03,
- Shropham Neolithic, Bronze Age and Iron Age settlements, 2002,
- Harford Park and Ride Neolithic and Bronze Age settlement, 2003,
- Whissonsett Church Close Middle and Late Saxon settlement and cemetery, 2005,
- Middle Saxon occupation deposits close to the river at 40 Fishergate, Norwich, 2005.

The most high-profile example of the problem is the site of the fine Millennium Library in Norwich with its extensive underground car park. The excavation of the Norman Borough by the NAU ran from November 1998 to May 1999 with considerable local press publicity (*EDP* 24th October 1998; 17th November 1998; 4th December 1998; 19th January 1999; 23rd February 1999 and 22nd April 1999). The whole development was a £60 million project, 50% funded by the Millennium Commission, run by the Norfolk and Norwich Millennium Company Ltd in which there was a heavy County Council commitment. The funds available for the excavation must surely have been sufficient to cover both the post-excavation work and the research report. There is a similar situation over the NAU's work in the Norwich Castle mound undertaken between 1999 and 2001 as a part of the improvements to the museum and the adjacent Shirehall. Here again the County Council was the developer. This scheme included cutting a lift shaft deep into the Norman castle mound, which is a nationally important monument.

NPS Archaeology, which has been carrying out 60% of the archaeology contracting work in Norfolk, conceded to the writer in February 2016 that 19 of their research reports on significant excavations undertaken between 1987 and 2005 were overdue, and there are bound to be others conducted since 2005. NPS supplied a spreadsheet setting out a timetable for clearing some of the old backlog with submission dates for four reports in 2016 and four in 2017. That was encouraging, but by November 2016 rumours that NPS was trying to sell its archaeology contracting business left one anxious. I wrote to the NPS Group Director asking about progress but received a rather defensive response. Then on 14th December 2016 the staff were told that NPS were to close down their archaeology contracting work and make staff redundant by the spring (*EDP* 16th December 2016 'Anger as archaeology unit could be shut').

There is now the highly significant question of what has happened to the funds for the post-excavation and publication work offered or given to the NAU and then to NPS over the last 20 or more years. Money must have been offered, project by project, by developers for the post-excavation work so that the developers could have their commitments to the archaeological work signed off by the Historic Environment Service. So, when any archaeological contractor claims that they do not have the funds to produce a research report on any important rescue excavation one is bound to ask what has happened to the money. If it is no longer available then archaeology managers have either miscalculated their archiving and report-writing costs or the money was spent elsewhere. Either way, it is difficult to see the situation as representing anything other than a serious management failure. Requests in writing to NPS to explain what had happened to their post-excavation and publication funds produced no answers. The company would not say and we do not know. It is, of course, fully owned by Norfolk County Council.

This is a heartbreaking end to a bold vision. There is no other way to look at it. Right up to the end the senior managers within NPS would provide no explanation on how this could have happened (*EDP* 3rd April 2017).

The situation is not all bad. In 2009 NAU Archaeology published the massive two-volume account of the excavations of the whole of Norwich Castle bailey funded by English Heritage (Shepherd Popescu 2009) and there have been volumes on a small medieval cemetery at Ormesby St Margaret (Wallis with Anderson 2009), a Roman settlement at Billingford (Wallis 2011) and a substantial work with the Suffolk Archaeological Service on the Roman town at Scole (Ashwin and Tester 2014). There have also been some short reports in *Norfolk Archaeology*. But increasingly it has been contractors from outside the region (Northampton Archaeology, Oxford Archaeology, Network Archaeology and others) which have been setting the pace and making a real difference with their own EAA volumes.

As this book reaches proof stage (July 2017) there is encouraging news that the Norfolk Historic Environment Service (NHES) at Gressenhall has taken this matter in hand and is devising a series of volumes to cover the key outstanding NAU/NPS excavations. Much will depend on funding, but it is a step in the right direction. There is also an expectation that the NHES will in the future find ways to restrict the opportunities for archaeological contractors who fail to deliver high quality work on time from taking on more contracts in the county. At least some good will then have come out of the collapse of NPS Archaeology.

The county backlog is, of course, part of a wider national problem with origins already evident with the barrow diggers active in the inter-war years and the urban excavations of the 1970s. It is an age-old dilemma for which the profession still has to find a solution, and finding a solution will not be easy. It should not be for the previous generation of archaeologists to tell, or even to suggest, to the present one how to solve a problem which we could not solve ourselves, but it seems likely that the enforcement of professional standards through the Chartered Institute for Archaeologists may be the only option. A deterrent for failure to complete projects is certainly needed. This is one area where I really do have fears for the future of the profession. An acceptable way forward should be found if that is possible.

The long-term storage of excavation archives

The second issue is the long-term lack of storage space in museums for excavation and fieldwork archives. One has the impression that many museums throughout England do not have the resources to provide sufficient storage and they are also reluctant to accept the need to be much more selective about what is retained and what, out of necessity, needs to be thrown away. This is clearly a matter for national debate (Shepherd 2015, 143-45).

Each stage of the post-excavation process from the preparation of the archive through to publication is based on agreed professional standards. These were first set out locally in the *County Standards for Field Archaeology in Norfolk* drafted in 1998 and widely distributed in 1999. They were actually field tested during the Norwich Millennium Library excavation as a part of a professional consultation process (**p. 341**).

County Standards was replaced in 2003 by *Standards for Field Archaeology in the East of England* (Gurney 2003, 21). This also makes it clear that contractors are expected to deposit project archives in a form which meets the standards of the organisation receiving the material, in our case the Norfolk Museums Service. The contractor is also required to comply with guidance from the Chartered Institute for Archaeologists. If the owner of a site wishes to retain any of the artefacts he has a legal right to do so, but then the developer's contractor is expected to include in the archive a full record of the retained items.

In 2010 the Norfolk Museums Service issued their own guidelines on *Requirements for Deposition of Fieldwork and Excavation Archives with Norfolk Museums and Archaeology Service* containing very detailed advice on the boxes to be used, how they are to be labelled and how the documents and photographs are to be prepared for storage. There is further guidance available on what finds are to be retained and what can be discarded. Over the years there have been significant instances where researchers have gone back to an archive as techniques have improved and extracted information which was not recovered by the original excavators or by their specialists. So, it is important that fieldwork archives are assembled in good order and are accessible with the artefacts for further research in a safe place.

Storage facilities should include the long-term preservation in museums of the digital archives which now form a major part of the written records so that they can be studied alongside the finds. There is national guidance for this, although Record Offices always advise that paper copies are still the most secure way to preserve the written word. The Briefs issued in Norfolk to excavation contractors require them to use film-based black and white photography, which should survive better if kept in acid-free sleeves, while digital colour photography will be vulnerable.

Finding the space

As we have seen, excavation archives consist of both the finds and the records. The Norfolk Museums Service used to issue an accession number to excavators at the start of each project so that the finds and the records could all carry that number. However, in 2013 the Museum's Archaeology Department temporarily suspended accepting any more archives and stopped issuing further accession numbers because its stores were full. There were by then almost 350 outstanding numbers issued to contractors for which the material could not be accepted. Contractors in the county were filling their stores and their garages with un-numbered archives as an interim measure waiting for the Museums Service to come up with a long-term solution. By the end of 2015 the backlog had probably reached close to 500 project archives for which no space could be found. The good news is that early in 2016 extra space for a further 10 years was found, although it would involve a charging system for future excavations at a flat rate of £395 for the first six boxes and £100 per box thereafter. This is the commercial world in which rescue archaeology now operates. In addition, copies of all digital data from excavations will be stored on Norfolk County Council servers and will be safeguarded by the Council's routine back-up procedures. This is all a real leap forward for which the Service should be congratulated.

What this issue has highlighted is that museum storage generally has long been under-resourced, and that museums nationally were ill-prepared for the burst of excavation activity following the introduction of developer funding under PPG 16 in 1990 (**p. 159-161).** The need to store more and more finds from excavations might sooner or later encourage museum directors to be very selective about what material they can accept for permanent preservation in addition to the written, photographic and digital archive. Each region, or each county, will have to find its own storage solutions, but, clearly, this issue will be the subject of much agonised debate in the years to come.

It really goes without saying that there will also be a need for sufficient study space to spread out and work on the finds and the records so that these archives can become a real research resource for the future.

Protecting the field evidence in an arable landscape

The background

The third issue is the slow pace at which deserving field monuments and wetland archaeology has been given protection in the region by English Heritage and then Historic England over the last 40 years. There are several factors at work here. The system of European funding since 1993 provides a lot more resources for wildlife protection than it does for safeguarding the cultural heritage. The European requirements to protect wildlife do not extend to archaeology. In addition, the English legal background encourages Historic England to put much more emphasis on listing historic buildings than it does on scheduling archaeological sites. There has also probably been subtle pressure from the farming community and from successive governments not to increase the regulatory burden on farming. English Heritage/Historic England have had severe budget cuts since 2010, but the slow pace of extending protection for archaeology goes back long before that.

The result of all of this is that there has been great reluctance since the 1970s to schedule more sites in arable areas, and there are many very important sites in the East Anglian landscape still without legal protection. There is, of course, no developer funding to pay for the rescue excavation of sites being damaged by cultivation, so the sort of excavation we carried out on Spong Hill to save that great Anglo-Saxon cremation cemetery from being wrecked by the plough is unlikely to be repeated. This whole issue is so important that it is worth summarising from previous chapters some of the key points to show what little progress has been made in a region where the land is mostly under intensive cultivation.

In Historic England's *Heritage at Risk* Register published online in October 2015 there is a striking statement that arable cultivation is the greatest cause of damage to scheduled sites, affecting 39% of those on the Register. In the East of England the proportion is 73%. Analysis of entries shows that prehistoric barrows are one of the most 'at risk' types of archaeological site. That, of course, is nothing new, and much of the damage goes back to the development of more powerful diesel tractors and crawlers in the 1950s which were able to pull deep-digger ploughs and sub-soilers (*Frontispiece*).

The statistics just quoted highlight the damage caused to scheduled sites under cultivation, so one can only guess how much greater this damage must surely be to the mass of *un*scheduled sites. Plough damage to barrows is an issue we have been raising constantly since we started our barrow survey in 1973 (**p. 193-196**). In that, we compared our measurements with those recorded on the same mounds during a previous survey by the Norfolk Research Committee in the 1930s (**p. 193**). We calculated that for barrows under plough the average rate of destruction was two centimetres a year, or one metre in 50 years. Initially the Department of the

Environment's response was to schedule a few more barrows, which was good. But that did not stop the cultivation of the barrows already under the plough.

In 1982 we sent an annotated list of all scheduled barrows to the Department of the Environment indicating which ones urgently needed attention, and there was absolutely no response. So, in 1983 we carried out a fresh review of barrow survival and prepared a list of *all* barrows over half a metre high in need of protection and we marked up the list according to a scale of priorities from 'High' to 'Low'. This was then sent by Norfolk County Council's Chief Executive to English Heritage in May 1984. We were told in reply that there was little English Heritage could do until it started its 'proposed re-scheduling exercise'. In due course, we heard that this initiative was to be called the 'Monuments Protection Programme' (the MPP), but it was much delayed and it appears that no more barrows were scheduled until 1995.

Then, there was the 1994-96 English Heritage Monuments at Risk Survey (the famous 'MARS' project), an ambitious national survey with the commendable aim of providing sound data on which future conservation policies could be based (**p. 209-210**). Results showed that cultivation was the single biggest cause of loss, and it was recognised that there was a need to do more to improve monument conservation. The survey showed that monuments which were scheduled had suffered a lower than average rate of destruction, but the report did not then advocate a more active programme of site scheduling or a review of Class Consent Orders which surely should have been the outcome. The recommendations in the MARS report were a great disappointment, although they did lead later to the English Heritage 'Heritage at Risk' initiative which has played an important role in more recent years in encouraging farmers to apply for Natural England's agri-environment funds to bring more monuments *already* scheduled into benign management, but not to increase the number of scheduled sites.

Without that designation, farmers, landowners and land managers have no clear indication of the relative importance of sites under their control. There are many instances where recommendations for new schedulings have not been acted upon, ostensibly because the matter is not urgent or because the limits of a site are not very clear. After a while you just give up trying.

The fact that it took 20 years to persuade EH to schedule even the Late Iron Age ritual site at Fison Way, Thetford, which was under great pressure from industrial development (**p. 232-235**), is just one example of the problem. The outstandingly important Roman town at Great Walsingham with its temple and many associated votive offerings in the ploughsoil, other masonry structures and an apparent sub-Roman earthwork fortification still has no protection (**p. 115-198**). This refusal (and it has been a refusal) by English Heritage to schedule more sites in arable farmland unless they are in immediate danger is difficult to justify. We are nowhere near a situation where we need to say that 'The designations we have cannot be extended indefinitely to cover boarder and broader categories or larger and larger areas. To do so risks destroying the effectiveness of the whole designation system... (Fairclough 1999, 38)'.

Current Historic England policy

It is quite clear that the intention in the 1979 Ancient Monuments and Archaeological Areas Act was to give legal protection to archaeological sites accepted to be of national importance. There is no mention in the Act that this only applies to sites under threat. But, in 2011 English Heritage produced their *National Heritage Protection Plan* in which they committed only to provide that protection for sites 'where the threat is most urgent or where future threat may be most appropriately forestalled.' (English Heritage 2011, 80). That appears to be contradicted by the *Historic England Action Plan 2015-2018* which says that 'Designating heritage assets is at the very heart of Historic England's duties'. So where are we now?

It is Historic England's current policy to exercise judgement on the basis of (a) threat, (b) evident significance, and (c) research priority. People in Historic England who work on designation say that we are living through a period of deep suspicion of regulation and with successive governments determined to boost economic growth. Historic England prefers to see scheduling as part of a package of approaches in which it is just one element along with working with local authorities to protect non-scheduled sites. The point seems to be missed that local authorities have no control whatsoever over plough damage. There is also the issue of nighthawking on unscheduled sites known to be rich in artefacts where the loss of items from the soil can be considerable. If nighthawks are caught by police at night on a *scheduled* site the prospects of a successful conviction are much stronger. For *un*scheduled sites defence lawyers can convincingly make the case that if a field is not legally protected as being of national importance, then the removal of artefacts can hardly be regarded as a serious crime. We saw examples of this on the Roman temple field at Great Walsingham (**p. 116-117**). This is a serious matter not to be overlooked. The area around the British Museum's excavations of the hoards of Iron Age torcs at Snettisham is also still unprotected.

Ancient Monuments versus historic buildings

Historic England says that its budget has been cut by 50% since 2010 and their designation team is now the smallest part of their organisation in term of staff numbers and budget. While this may or may not be true, they always seem keen to list good examples of historic buildings, even quite modern ones, whether they are at risk or not. It is not unreasonable to suggest that they should put a larger proportion of their limited budget back into scheduling archaeological monuments and really make progress, particularly in arable areas where vulnerable sites are often most at risk. Then, archaeology designation could really be seen to be 'at the very heart of Historic England's duties'.

The legal problem here is that Section 1 of the Planning (Listed Buildings and Conservation Areas) Act of 1990 imposes a *duty* on the Secretary of State to compile or approve a list, or lists, of buildings of special architectural or historic interest as a guide to the planning authorities when carrying out their planning functions. However, under the 1979 Ancient Monuments Act the Secretary of State has the *discretion* to include monuments of national importance in the schedule. It was surely never intended in the 1979 drafting that archaeological monuments should receive less care than historic buildings. The difference has to be an historical accident due to the time between the two Bills. Surely both aspects of our cultural heritage equally deserve, and need, proper safeguarding.

Archaeology and wildlife

The disparity also between cultural heritage and wildlife conservation has been reflected in the European Commission's view on how the natural environment and cultural heritage should be treated. Nature is part of a common European inheritance and was thus enshrined in a legally binding Directive. When the Maastricht Treaty was drafted by the Council of Europe in 1991 and came into force in 1993, the protection of the cultural heritage was left to member states. The result was that wildlife sites were to be protected by European regulations while cultural heritage was left to national legislation. If there was competition between the two for European resources, then wildlife won. Hence, there has been a massive difference in the support available to Defra for wildlife conservation within farmland management issues, while cultural heritage is a very poor relative left to the Department of Culture, Media and Sport (DCMS), and it has been given a much lower resource base by government. Following the British referendum held on 23rd June 2016 when the decision was taken to leave the EU, this could all change. During the Brexit negotiations it will be vital to put pressure on the government to ensure that the conservation of the cultural heritage in the future has the same status as wildlife protection. For this we will need to look to Historic England.

English wetlands

The reluctance of English Heritage/Historic England to take a strong lead in archaeology conservation is equally apparent in wetland archaeology where English Heritage has not been a partner in the Wet Fens for the Future Project while all the other the leading national bodies, such as Natural England, the Environment Agency, the National Trust and the wildlife trusts, certainly are. English Heritage spent a very considerable sum on the highly successful Fenland Survey to gather all the data in preparation for just this sort of archaeological management of the Fens (**p. 180-185**), but then did nothing with it in their Fenland Management

Project **(p. 185-188)**, although the Wetland Vision Project was partly funded by English Heritage in partnership with Natural England and the RSPB. This sets out a 50-year vision for England's freshwater wetlands showing where new wetlands could be created and current wetlands restored. Let's hope that some of that vision can be converted into reality before the evidence has all gone.

Historic England says openly that the recent heavy reductions in their budget has meant that much of their strategic capacity has been lost. They say that it is very difficult to encourage wildlife organisations to take the historic environment seriously given the level of resources they now have available. The English Heritage 2004 Wetland Strategy did talk about developing conservation strategies for the most vulnerable wetland monuments. Time will show if these strategies can be converted into any real conservation, but there is little sign of that so far. In Exmoor National Park there has been an excellent example of archaeologists and ecologists working closely on the Exmoor Mires Project (Bray 2015). This is exactly what is needed in the Fens.

The success of Environmental Stewardship schemes

The good news is that since 2006 over 1,000 sites in England previously scheduled have been taken out of cultivation nationally through Higher Level Stewardship and related schemes run by Natural England. So, there is surely every reason to continue scheduling important sites and monuments endangered by cultivation in anticipation that they also can be rescued under similar Stewardship schemes in due course.

In the end, the root cause of Historic England's reluctance over the last 40 years to persist with a vigorous scheduling programme lies in the very nature of archaeology, where the pre-occupation and sheer weight of archaeological activity is in discovery, excavation and research. If every county had an active conservation trust for archaeology alongside their wildlife trust, we could be achieving so much more. But unlike ecology, the main focus is not on conservation. That is surely why the Norfolk Archaeological Trust has under 100 members while the Norfolk Wildlife Trust has 35,000. There are no signs that this will change, and the consequences will be seen in how much will be left for archaeologists working in arable areas to pass on to future generations. This is not said with bitterness; it is just a fact.

The achievements have been considerable

The last 50 years have been an exciting time to be an archaeologist, watching how the profession of field archaeology has developed from almost nothing when RESCUE was born at the large public meeting in the Senate House in London in

1971 (**p. 141-143**). All credit should go to Philip Barker, Martin Biddle and the many others who organised that event which started a real revolution in British archaeology. Before then we struggled, and that meeting was the turning point. The need for rescue recording is now fully embedded in the planning process, and we no longer need to beg a developer to allow access to record the archaeology before it is destroyed. The formation of the Chartered Institute for Archaeologists in December 2014 was another real step on the road to full integration into the hierarchy of the professions. The February 2016 decision of Norfolk County Council's Policy and Resources Committee to reject the proposed budget cuts to the Historic Environment Service after a public outcry and instead to increase Council Tax shows that local people really do care about their local heritage. But the post of County Archaeologist has since been quietly deleted by the County Council without any public consultation as from 31st December 2016. Responsibilities will now be divided between different parts of the Planning Department, and there will be no one person able to provide a strategic lead for field archaeology in the county. This is a part of a national trend, but without a strong overall leader who is a specialist in the subject the Historic Environment Service may have difficulty in the long term retaining its drive and any sense of direction.

On the conservation side, it remains a fact that while the need for research and rescue recording is widely accepted within the profession, pro-active protection of the archaeological heritage is still in its infancy. Nevertheless, the Norfolk Archaeological Trust may be showing a way ahead with a range of sites now conserved and open to the public. As a relatively new profession we have made a wonderful start, but in this area in particular there is still a long way to go.

Appendix 1:
Alan Davison's publications

1972: 'Some Aspects of the Agrarian History of Hargham and Snetterton as recorded in the Buxton MSS', *Norfolk Archaeology* 35, 335-355.
1980: 'West Harling: a village and its disappearance', *Norfolk Archaeology* 37, 295-306.
1982: 'Petygards and the Medieval Hamlet of Cotes', *East Anglian Archaeology* 14, 102-107.
1982: (with B. Cushion, G.Fenner, R. Goldsmith, J. Knight, N.Virgoe, K. Wade, P. Wade-Martins) *Some Deserted Village Sites in Norfolk*, East Anglian Archaeology 14, 40-101.
1983a: 'The Distribution of Medieval Settlement in West Harling', *Norfolk Archaeology* 38, 329-336.
1983b: 'The Documentary evidence', in A. Lawson *The Archaeology of Witton*, East Anglian Archaeology 18, 83-85.
1985: 'Keburn', *Medieval Villages Research Group* 33, 10.
1987: 'Little Hockham.' *Norfolk Archaeology* 40, 84-93.
1988 (with Brian Cushion and others): *Six Deserted Villages in Norfolk*, East Anglian Archaeology 44.
1988 (with E.Rose) 'St Catherine's Thorpe – The Birth and Death of a Myth.', *Norfolk Archaeology* 40, 179-181.
1990: 'Norton', *Medieval Settlements Research Group* 5, 27.
1990 (with Alayne Fenner): *The Evolution of Settlement in Three Parishes in South-East Norfolk*, East Anglian Archaeology 49.
1991: 'Holverston', *Medieval Settlements Research Group* 6, 30.
1991a: 'Great Hockham – A Village which has moved?', *Norfolk Archaeology* 41, 145-161.
1991b: (with Brian Cushion): 'Earthworks at Harling Thorpe', *Norfolk Archaeology* 41, 207-211.
1993: 'The Documentary Evidence' in C. Dallas 1993, *Excavations in Thetford by B.K. Davison between 1964 and 1970.* East Anglian Archaeology 62, 194-217.
1993a (with Barbara Green and Bill Milligan): *Illington: The Study of a Breckland Parish and its Anglo-Saxon Cemetery*, East Anglian Archaeology 63.
1994: 'The Field Archaeology of Bodney and the STANTA Extension', *Norfolk Archaeology* 42, 57-79.
1995: 'The Field Archaeology of the Mannington and Wolterton Estates', *Norfolk Archaeology* 42, 160-184.

1996: *Deserted Villages in Norfolk.* Poppyland.
1996: 'The Manors of West Walton', *Norfolk Archaeology* 42, 339-343.
1997 (with Brian Cushion): 'A Group of Earthworks in the Tat Valley', *Norfolk Archaeology* 42, 492-505.
1997a (with Mark Leah and Margaret Matthews): 'A Survey of the Earthworks at Hills and Holes Plantation, Marham, Norfolk', *Norfolk Archaeology* 42, 506-510.
1999: (with Brian Cushion) 'The Archaeology of the Hargham Estate', *Norfolk Archaeology* 43, 257-274.
2001: 'Great Hockham in 1599: a revision', *Norfolk Archaeology* 43, 667-669.
2003: 'The Archaeology of the Parish of West Acre. Part 1: Field Survey Evidence.' *Norfolk Archaeology* 44, 202-221.
2003 (with Brian Cushion): *Earthworks of Norfolk*, East Anglian Archaeology *104*.
2004 (with Brian Cushion): 'The Archaeology of the Parish of West Acre. Part 2: The Documentary Background', *Norfolk Archaeology* 44, 456-481.
2005 (with Brian Cushion): 'An Archaeological Survey of the Stanford Training Area, 2000-2.', *Norfolk Archaeology* 44, 602-616.
2005a (with Trevor Ashwin - eds) *An Historical Atlas of Norfolk.* Phillimore.
2005b 'Medieval Settlement Desertion' and 'The Decline in Population' in Ashwin and Davison (eds), *An Historical Atlas of Norfolk,* 88-89 and 90-91. Phillimore.
2006: 'A Fieldwalking Survey of the Morley Research Centre', *The Annual* 15, 17-22.
2007 (with an introduction by A. Rogerson): 'Investigations at Godwick and Beeston St Andrew.', *Norfolk Archaeology* 45, 141-154.

Appendix 2:
Summary of progress set out in the 1996 Five-year Development Plan for Archaeology in the Norfolk Museums Service

Recording services

- The SMR at the end of 1995 had reached 31,706 records, and it was one of the three largest in England. During the year 736 completely new records had been added and 1,800 old records enhanced with further information
- A pilot study for a separate Urban Archaeological Database for Norwich had just been completed.
- Around 14% of the SMR records related to churches and secular historic buildings.
- Most wreck sites around the coast had been plotted – 192 in all – but with no supporting data.
- Following the Norwich library fire, a complete security copy of the paper secondary files had just been created and was housed in a separate secure store.
- There had been fieldwalking surveys of some limited parts of the county. So we had detailed knowledge of parishes like Barton Bendish, Fransham, Hales and Loddon as well as the Mannington estate, the Wolterton estate, the Morley Farm Research Centre and those areas covered by the Fenland Project, while other parts were still largely blank.
- The county air photographs library was by far the largest in England with more than 78,000 prints. About 40,000 of these we had taken ourselves recording numerous discoveries of national importance. The negatives were all housed in a secure store separate from the prints.
- In a four-month period there had been 94 telephone enquiries, 7 postal enquires and 41 visitors for air photography, mainly as a result of press interest in the project. This was causing serious delays in routine cataloguing, and an unacceptable backlog of 3,500 new photos had been allowed to accumulate. Public access would now have to be limited and there could be no further flying unless the crop conditions were exceptional until it had been cleared.

Development control

- The number of planning consultations had risen steadily over the last five years as follows:
    1991-92   1,200
    1992-93   1,203
    1993-94   1,357
    1994-95   1,547
    1995-96   1,841

    In 1995-96 the 1,841 consultation (av. 35/week) resulted in 71 Briefs being issued for archaeological works under planning consents which would need subsequent monitoring.
- While the concept of developer-funded excavations under PPG 16 had readily been accepted by planning officers, our equivalent advice for historic buildings under PGG 15 was being accepted only slowly. Conservation officers in District Council planning departments were reluctant to recognise the need for archaeological recording of standing buildings.

Monument conservation and interpretation in the countryside

- For the Norfolk Monuments Management Project approximately 130 sites had been visited so far and 22 grants for improved management had been paid to farmers.
- The county earthworks survey had started in 1994 with a part-time consultant surveyor whose brief it was to make 1:1,000 plans of every schedulable earthwork in the county, except for barrows. By then 53 sites had been surveyed, including 14 scheduled monuments, and we estimated that there were a further 80 to do. We were aiming for publication in 2000. We were unable to persuade English Heritage to help with funding, even though the surveys could greatly facilitate their Monument Protection Programme.
- We had offered every possible assistance to the English Heritage Monument Protection Programme which had been running since 1992, and 71 sites had been scheduled so far. While we had suggested that we could modify the programme of our Earthworks Survey to support their work that offer had not been taken up.
- The Norfolk Archaeological Trust (NAT) had been founded in 1923. Its new role was to acquire field monuments in need of care and protection where public access could also be offered. The Trust now owned 120 acres at Caistor Roman town, 15 acres at the Tasburgh hillfort and 90 acres in and around Burgh Castle Roman fort, all of which it acquired with our support.

- I also acted as regional advisor for archaeology to the National Trust, and the NLA provided advice to the Forestry Commission and to farmers preparing applications for Countryside Stewardship schemes.

Presenting monuments to the public

- NLA had worked with the Norfolk Archaeological Trust to produce 12 interpretation schemes and exhibitions, including:
    On-site panels and leaflets at Park Farm Snettisham.
    Exhibition on 'The Thetford Story' in St Peter's church, Thetford.
    Text and design for panels for Thetford Priory.
    On-site panel for Middleton Mount
    On-site interpretation and presentation scheme at Caistor St Edmund Roman town which won several national awards

Identification service

- Staff at the Castle Museum and Gressenhall were often working long and unsocial hours to keep up with the flood of material, usually estimated at some 20,000 objects a year. This data contributed *more than a third* of the new records added to the SMR.
- In a sample of 136 planning Briefs issued since 1991 for non-urban projects there were 70 instances (51%) where information from the finds identification service was a significant factor in the assessment of a planning application.
- It was recognised that the absence of a member of the core staff at the Castle Museum or at Gressenhall with an expertise in prehistory was a serious weakness.

Outreach

- Traditionally the approach to educational outreach included:
    Lectures to local groups and societies,
    Organised site visits and public viewing of excavations,
    Liaison with metal detector groups and individuals
    Artefact identification,
    Temporary displays at the Norfolk Show and Castle Mall excavations,
    Publications like *Norfolk from the Air*, the *Norfolk Atlas* and *Digging Deeper*,
    Promotion of best practice amongst amateurs in fieldwork and while assisting on excavations.

Appendix 3:
List of those archaeologists who attended the February 1970 Barford meeting which represented the start of the RESCUE movement

P.V. Addyman
John Alexander
Paul Ashbee
Professor R.J.C. Atkinson
Philip Barker
K.J. Barton
Don Benson
Martin Biddle
H.C. Bowen
Professor Barry Cunliffe
John G. Evans
Peter Fasham
Peter Fowler
Professor W.F. Grimes
Douglas Hague
Tom Hassall
Brian Hobley
J.G. Hurst
Henry Hurst
Dr J.K.S. St Joseph
Chris Musson
Brian Philp
John Rhodes
Philip Rahtz
Trevor Rowley
A.D. Saunders
Professor Charles Thomas
Dr G.J. Wainwright
Dr G. Webster
D.R. Wilson

Bibliography

Adams, W.M., 1986. *Nature's Place: Conservation sites and countryside change.* Allen & Unwin.
Addington, S., 1978. 'The Hedgerows of Tasburgh' *Norfolk Archaeology* 37, 70-83.
Addington, S., 1982. 'Landscape and Settlements in South Norfolk' *Norfolk Archaeology* 38, 97-139.
Addyman, P., 2008. 'Before the Portable Antiquities Scheme' in S. Thomas and P.G. Stone (eds) *Metal Detecting and Archaeology,* 51-62. The Boydell Press,
Ager, B., Ashley, S. and Rogerson, A., 1993. 'Two Norfolk Finds of Imported Continental Brooches' *Norfolk Archaeology* 41, 510-512.
Allison, K., 1957. 'The Lost Villages of Norfolk' *Norfolk Archaeology* 31, 116-162.
Ashley, S., 2002. *Medieval Armorial Horse Furniture in Norfolk*, East Anglian Archaeology 101.
Ashley, S., 2015. 'Anglo-Norman Elite Objects from Castle and Countryside' in J.A. Davies, A. Riley, J-M. Levesque and C. Lapiche (eds) *Castles and the Anglo-Norman World.* Oxford.
Ashley S. and Marsden, A. (eds), 2014. *Landscapes and Artefacts: Studies in East Anglian Archaeology presented to Andrew Rogerson.* Archaeopress Archaeology.
Ashley, S. and Penn, K., 2012. 'Contained the bones of horses': an early Anglo-Saxon cemetery at Sporle with Palgrave', *Norfolk Archaeology* 46, 281-319.
Ashley, S., Penn, K. and Rogerson, A., 2011. 'Rhineland Lava in Norfolk churches' *Church Archaeology* 13, 27-33.
Ashton, N. and Pettitt, P. (eds), 1998. *Stone Age Archaeology.* Oxbow Monograph 2012.
Ashwin, T., 1996. 'Excavations of an Iron Age Site at Park Farm, Silfield, Wymondham, Norfolk', *Norfolk Archaeology* 42, 241-82.
Ashwin, T., 2001. 'Middleton Mount excavations in and around the eastern bailey of Middleton Castle by Andrew Rogerson, 1987' *Norfolk Archaeology* 43, 645-656.
Ashwin, T. and Bates, S., 2000. *Excavations on the Norwich Southern Bypass, 1989-91 Part I: Excavations at Bixley, Caistor St Edmund, Trowse, Cringleford and Little Melton*, East Anglian Archaeology 91.
Ashwin, T. and Flitcroft, M., 1999. 'The Launditch and its Setting: Excavations at the Launditch, Beeston with Bittering and Iron Age features and finds in the vicinity' *Norfolk Archaeology* 43, 217-256.
Ashwin, T. and Davison, A. (eds), 2005. *An Historical Atlas of Norfolk* (3rd edition) Phillimore.
Ashwin, T. and Tester A., 2014. *A Romano-British Settlement in the Waveney Valley: Excavations at Scole, 1993-4*, East Anglian Archaeology 152.
Atkin, M.W., 1983a. 'The chalk tunnels of Norwich' *Norfolk Archaeology* 38, 313-320.

Atkin, M.W., 1983b. 'The Anglo-Saxon urban landscape in East Anglia', *Landscape History* 7, 27-40.

Atkin, M., 1991. 'Medieval Clay-Walled Buildings in Norwich' *Norfolk Archaeology* 41, 171-185.

Atkin, M., 1993. 'The Norwich Survey 1971-1985: a retrospective view' in J. Gardiner (ed), *Flatlands and Wetlands*, East Anglian Archaeology 50, 127-143.

Atkin, M. W., and Carter, A. with Baxter M., Donaldson, P. and Roberts, J.P., 1976. 'Excavations in Norwich – 1975/6. The Norwich Survey – Fifth Interim Report' *Norfolk Archaeology* 36, 191-201.

Atkin, M.W. and Carter, A., 1977. 'Excavations in Norwich – 1976/7. The Norwich Survey – Sixth Interim Report' *Norfolk Archaeology* 36, 287-304.

Atkin, M., Carter, A. and Evans, D.H., 1985. *Excavations in Norwich 1971-1978 Part II*, East Anglian Archaeology 26. Norwich.

Atkin, M., Donaldson, P., Roberts, J.P. and Sutermeister, H. with Carter, A., 1982. *Excavations in Norwich 1971-1978, Part I*, East Anglian Archaeology 15.

Atkin, M. and Evans, D.H., 2002. *Excavations in Norwich 1971-1978 Part III*, East Anglian Archaeology 100.

Atkin, M. and Margeson, S., 1985. *Life on a Medieval Street: Excavations on Alms Lane, Norwich 1976*.

Atkin, M.W. and Sutermeister, H., 1978. 'Excavations in Norwich – 1977/8. The Norwich Survey – Seventh Interim Report' *Norfolk Archaeology* 37, 19-55.

Atkin, M., 1993. *Norwich History and Guide*. Alan Sutton Publishing.

Atkinson, R.J.C., 1953. *Field Archaeology, Methuen*.

Ayers, B., 1985. *Excavations within the North-East Bailey of Norwich Castle, 1979*, East Anglian Archaeology 28.

Ayers, B., 1987. *Digging Deeper: Recent Archaeology in Norwich.* Norfolk Museums Service.

Ayers, B., 1988. *Excavations at St. Martin-at-Palace Plain, Norwich, 1981*, East Anglian Archaeology 37.

Ayers, B., 1993. 'The urbanisation of East Anglia: the Norwich perspective' in J. Gardiner (ed) *Flatlands and Wetlands*, East Anglian Archaeology 50, 117-126.

Ayers, B., 1994a. *English Heritage Book of Norwich*. Batsford/English Heritage.

Ayers, B., 1994b. *Excavations at Fishergate, Norwich, 1985*, East Anglian Archaeology 68.

Ayers, B., 2004. 'The Urban Landscape' in C.Rawcliffe and R. Wilson (eds), *Medieval Norwich*. Hambledon and London.

Ayers, B., 2011. 'The growth of an urban landscape: recent research in early medieval Norwich' *Early Medieval Europe* 19 (1), 62-90.

Ayers, B., 2015. 'The Development of an Urban Landscape: Recent Research in Mediaval Norwich' in T.A. Heslop and H. Lunnon (eds), *Norwich: Medieval and Early Modern Art, Architecture and Archaeology*, British Archaeological Association Conference Transactions 38, 1-22.

Ayers, B., Bown, J. and Reeve, J. 1992. *Digging Ditches: Archaeology and Development in Norwich.* Norfolk Archaeological Unit, Norfolk Museums Service.

Ayers, B. with Lawson, A., 1983. *Digging Under the Doorstep: Recent excavations in Norwich.* Norfolk Museums Service.

Ayton, J., 2012. 'The Mid-Twentieth Century Norfolk County Survey and Plan – Part1' *The Annual* 21. Norfolk Archaeological and Historical Research Group.

Bagnall Smith, J., 1999. 'Votive Objects and Objects of Votive Significance from Great Walsingham' *Britannia* 30, 21-56.

Barker, P., 1974. 'The Origins and Development of RESCUE' in P.A. Rahtz (ed.) *Rescue Archaeology.* Penguin Books.

Barker, P., White, R., Pretty, K., Bird, H. and Corbishley, M. 1997. *The Baths Basilica Wroxeter.* English Heritage Archaeological Report 8.

Barringer, C., 2006. 'Alan Davison – an Appreciation' *The Annual* 15, 3.

Barnes, G. and Williamson, T., 2006. *Hedgerow History: Ecology, History and Landscape Character.* WINDgather Press.

Barnes, G. and Williamson, T., 2015. *Rethinking Ancient Woodland.* University of Hertfordshire Studies in Regional and Local History Vol. 13.

Beckett, G and Bull, A., 1999. *A Flora of Norfolk.* Gillian Beckett.

Bellamy, P.S. and Trevarthen, M., 2011. 'Excavations by the *Time Team* on the 14th-century Dominican Friary in the grounds of Thetford Grammar School, 1998' *Norfolk Archaeology* 46, 181-189.

Benson, D., 1972. 'A Sites and Monuments Record for the Oxford Region' *Oxoniensia* 37, 226-237.

Benson, D., 2013. 'In the beginning: memories of the first ten years in the field department at Oxford City and County Museum' in M. Henig and C.Paine, *Preserving and Presenting the Past in Oxfordshire and Beyond: Essays in Memory of John Rhodes,* British Archaeological Reports (British Series) 586.

Beresford, M., 1954, *The Lost Villages of England.* Lutterworth.

Bescoby, D., Bowden, W. and Chroston, P.N., 2009. 'Magnetic Survey at *Venta Icenorum* Caistor St Edmund: Survey Strategies and Initial Results' *Archaeological Prospection* 16, 287-291.

Bescoby, D.J. and Bowden, W., 2013. 'The Detection and Mapping of Saxon Sunken-featured Buildings at Caistor St Edmund, Norfolk' *Archaeological Prospection.* Published Online.

Biddle, M., Hudson, D. and Heighway, C., 1973. *The Future of London's Past.* RESCUE.

Bland, R., 2008. 'The Development and Future of the *Treasure Act* and Portable Antiquities Scheme' in S.Thomas and P.G. Stone (eds) in S. Thomas and P.G. Stone *Metal Detecting and Archaeology.* The Boydell Press, 63-85.

Blinkhorn, P., 2012. *The Ipswich Ware Project,* Medieval Pottery Research Group Occasional Paper 7.

Blinkhorn, P., 2015. 'Archaeology and the media: from Wheeler to Time Team' in P.Everill and P. Irving (eds), *Rescue Archaeology Foundations for the Future*, 258-269. RESCUE The British Archaeological Trust.

Body, R., 1987. *Red or Green for Farmers (and the rest of us)*. Broad Leys Publishing.

Bond, D., 1988. *Excavations at the North Ring, Mucking, Essex: A Late Bronze Age Enclosure*, East Anglian Archaeology 43.

Bond, R., Penn, K. and Rogerson, A., 1990. *Norfolk Origins 4: The North Folk; Angles, Saxons and Danes.* Poppyland Publishing.

Bowden, W., 2012. 'The Iceni under Rome: excavating at Caistor St Edmund' *Current Archaeology* 270, September, 28-35.

Bowden, W., 2013a. 'The Urban Plan of *Venta Icernorum* and its Relationship with the Boudican Revolt' *Britannia.* Published Online.

Bowden, W., 2013b. 'Townscape and identity at Caistor-by-Norwich' in H. Eckardt, H. and S. Rippon (eds), *Living and Working in the Roman World: Essays in Honour of Michael Fulford on his 65th Birthday*, 49-62. Portsmouth, Rhode Island.

Bowers, J.K. and Cheshire, P. 1983. *Agriculture, the Countryside and Land Use: An Economic Critique.* Methuen.

Bradley, R., 2005. *Ritual and Domestic Life in Prehistoric Europe.* Routledge. Abingdon.

Bray, L.S., 2015. *The Past and the Peat: Archaeology and Peatland Restoration on Exmoor.* Exmoor National Park.

Brennand, M. and Taylor, M., 2003. 'The Survey and Excavation of a Bronze Age Timber Circle at Holme-next-the-Sea' *Proceedings of the Prehistoric Society* 69, 1-84.

Bryant, S. and Wills, J., 2016. 'Before, during and after: life pre-PPG 16, its impact after 1990, and the current struggle to retain its legacy' *The Archaeologist* 98, 4-8.

Burnham, B.C., 1995. 'Small towns: the British perspective' in A.E. Brown (ed), *Small Towns in Eastern England and Beyond.* 7-17. Oxbow Monograph 52.

Buteux, S., 1997. *Settlements at Skaill, Deerness, Orkney: Excavations by Peter Gelling of the Prehistoric, Pictish, Viking and Later Periods, 1963-1981,* British Archaeological Reports (British Series) 260. Archaeopress.

Butler, L. and Wade-Martins, P., 1989. *The Deserted Medieval Village of Thuxton, Norfolk*, East Anglian Archaeology 46.

Carson, R.L., 1962. *Silent Spring.* 1987 25th Anniversary Edition Houghton Mifflin Co. Boston.

Carter, A., 1972. 'Excavations in Norwich 1971 – an interim report' *Norfolk Archaeology* 35, 410-16.

Carter, A., 1978a. 'The Anglo-Saxon origins of Norwich: the problems and approaches' *Anglo-Saxon England* 7, 173-204.

Carter, A., 1978b. 'Sampling in a medieval town: the study of Norwich' *in 'Sampling in contemporary British Archaeology,* British Archaeological Reports (British Series) 50, 263-77.

Carter, A., 1980. *The Norwich Survey 1971-1980.* Centre of East Anglian Studies.
Carter, A. (ed.), 1982. *Excavations in Norwich 1971-1978.* East Anglian Archaeology 15.
Carter, A. and Roberts, J.P., 1973. 'Excavations in Norwich – 1972. The Norwich Survey – Second Interim Report' *Norfolk Archaeology* 35, 443-68.
Carter, A., Roberts, J.P. and Sutermeister, M.A., 1974. 'Excavations in Norwich – 1973. The Norwich Survey – Third Interim Report' *Norfolk Archaeology* 35, 39-71.
Carver, M., 1992 (ed). *The Age of Sutton Hoo.* The Boydell Press.
Carver, M., 1998. *Sutton Hoo: Burial Ground of Kings?* The British Museum.
Carver, M., 2005. *Sutton Hoo: a seventh-century princely burial ground and its context.* Report of the Research Committee of the Society of Antiquaries of London, No. 69.
Champion, M., 2000. *Seahenge: A Contemporary Chronicle.* Barnwell's Timescapes.
Chester-Kadwell, M., 2009. *Early Anglo-Saxon Communities in the Landscape of Norfolk,* British Archaeological Reports (British Series) 481.
City of Norwich Museums, 1966. *Bronze Age Metalwork in Norwich Castle Museum.*
Clark, J.G.D., 1953. 'The early Iron Age site at Micklemoor Hill, West Harling, Norfolk' *Proceedings of the Prehistoric Society* 19 (1), 1-40.
Clark, J.G.D., Godwin, H. and Clifford, M.H., 1935. 'Report on recent excavations at Peacock's Farm, Shippea Hill, Cambridgeshire' *Antiquaries Journal* 15, 284-319.
Clarke, H., and Carter, A., 1977. *Excavations in Kings Lynn 1963-1970,* Society for Medieval Archaeology Monograph Series, No.7.
Clarke, R.R., 1949. 'The Snettisham Treasure' *East Anglian Magazine* 8 (6), 282-290.
Clarke, R.R., 1952a. 'Roman Norfolk since Haverfield: A Survey of Discovery from 1901' *Norfolk Archaeology* 30, 140-155.
Clarke, R.R., 1952b. 'Notes on Recent Archaeological Discoveries in Norfolk (1943-8)' *Norfolk Archaeology* 30, 156-159.
Clarke, R.R., 1956. 'The Snettisham Treasure' in R.L.S. Bruce-Mitford (ed.), *Recent Archaeological Excavations in Britain,* 21-42. Routledge & Kegan Paul.
Clarke, R.R., 1960. *East Anglia.* Thames and Hudson.
Clarke, R.R. 1961. 'Archaeology' in *Norwich and its Region,* British Association for the Advancement of Science.
Clarke, W.G. 1925. *In Breckland Wilds.* W. Heffer & Sons.
Cleere, H., 1980a. 'Editorial: Stop Taking our Past' *CBA Newsletter and Calendar* IV/1 (March).
Cleere, H., 1980b. 'Editorial: STOP has started!' *CBA Newsletter and Calendar* IV/2 (April).
Cleere, H., 1980c. 'STOP: a progress report' *CBA Newsletter and Calendar* IV/3 (May).
Coles J.M. and Hall, D.M., 1983. 'The Fenland Project' *Antiquity* 58, 212-14.
Coles, J and Hall, D. 1998. *Changing Landscapes: The Ancient Fenland.* Wetland Archaeology Research Project.
Cope-Faulkner, P. and Anderson, S., 2015. 'Binham Priory: Recent Excavations and Artefact Studies' *Norfolk Archaeology* 47, 133-169.

Cozens-Hardy, B., 1926. 'Scheduling of the Norfolk Ancient Monuments' *Norfolk Archaeology* 22, 221-26.

Cresswell, I., 1976. 'Obituary: B. Cozens-Hardy Hon Life Fellow' *Norfolk Archaeology* 36, 283-4.

Crowson, A., 2004. *Hot rocks in the Norfolk Fens: the excavation of a burnt flint mound at Northwold, 1994-5*, East Anglian Archaeology Occasional Paper No. 16.

Crowson, A., Lane T., Penn, K. and Trimble D., 2005. *Anglo-Saxon Settlement on the Siltland if Eastern England*, Lincolnshire Archaeology and Heritage Reports Series No. 7.

Crowson, A., Lane, T. and Reeve, J., 2000. *Fenland Management Project Excavations 1991-1995*, Lincolnshire Archaeology and Heritage Reports Series No. 3.

Crowther, D.R., 1983. 'Swords to ploughshares: a nation-wide survey of archaeologists and treasure hunting clubs' *Archaeological Review from Cambridge* Vol 2:1, 9-20.

Culpin, C., 1938. *Farm Machinery.* Crosby Lockwood & Son.

Cumberpatch, C., 2015. 'In conclusion' in P. Everill and P. Irving (eds), *Rescue Archaeology Foundations for the Future*, 270-283. RESCUE The British Archaeological Trust 2015,

Cushion, B., Davison, A., Fenner, G., Goldsmith, R., Knight, J., Virgoe, N., Wade K and Wade-Martins, P., 1982. *Some Deserted Village Sites in Norfolk*, East Anglian Archaeology 14, 40-101.

Cushion, B and Davison, A., 1991. 'The Earthworks at Harling Thorpe' *Norfolk Archaeology* 41, 207-211.

Cushion, B. and Davison, A., 2003. *Earthworks of Norfolk*, East Anglian Archaeology 104.

Dallas, C., 1993. *Excavations in Thetford by B.K. Davison between 1964 and 1970*, East Anglian Archaeology 62.

Daniel, G., 1965. Obituary to Rainbird Clarke, *Norfolk Archaeology 33*, 240-241.

Darling, M.J. and Gurney D., 1993. *Caistor-on-Sea Excavations by Charles Green, 1951-55*, East Anglian Archaeology 60.

Darvill, T., 1987. *Ancient Monuments in the Countryside: an archaeological management review*, English Heritage Archaeological Reports no. 5.

Darvill, T. and Fulton, A.K., 1998. *MARS: The Monuments at Risk Survey of England, 1995, Main Report.* School of Conservation Sciences, Bournemouth University and English Heritage.

Darvill, T., 2016. 'What's been going on?' *The Archaeologist* 98, 12-13.

Davies, J.A., 1996. 'Where Eagles Dare: The Iron Age of Norfolk' *Proceedings of the Prehistoric Society* 62, 63-92.

Davies, J.A., 2008. *The Land of Boudica.* Oxbow Books.

Davies, J.A., Gregory, T., Lawson, A.J., Rickett, R. and Rogerson, A. 1992. *The Iron Age Forts of Norfolk*, East Anglian Archaeology 54.

Davison, A., 1980. 'West Harling: a Village and its Disappearance' *Norfolk Archaeology* 37, 295-306.
Davison, A., 1982. *Petygards and the Medieval Hamlet of Cotes*, East Anglian Archaeology 14, 102-107.
Davison, A., 1983a. 'The Distribution of Medieval Settlement in West Harling' *Norfolk Archaeology* 38, 329-336.
Davison, A., 1983b. 'The Documentary Evidence' in A. Lawson *The Archaeology of Witton, near North Walsham*, East Anglian Archaeology 18, 83-85.
Davison, A., 1988. *Six Deserted Villages in Norfolk*, East Anglian Archaeology 44.
Davison, A. with Fenner, A., 1990. *The Evolution of Settlement in Three Parishes in South-East Norfolk*, East Anglian Archaeology 49.
Davison, A., 1991. 'Great Hockham – A Village which has moved?' *Norfolk Archaeology* 41, 145-161.
Davison, A., Green, B. and Milligan, B. 1993. *Illington: The study of a Breckland Parish and its Anglo-Saxon Cemetery*, East Anglian Archaeology 63.
Davison, A., 1994. 'The Field Archaeology of Bodney and the STANTA Extension' *Norfolk Archaeology* 42, 57-79.
Davison, A., 1995. 'The Field Archaeology of the Mannington and Wolterton Estates' *Norfolk Archaeology* 42, 160-184.
Davison, A., 1996. *Deserted Villages in Norfolk*, Poppyland.
Davison, A., 2003. 'The Archaeology of the Parish of West Acre. Part 1: Field Survey Evidence' *Norfolk Archaeology* 44, 202-221.
Davison, A. and Cushion, B., 2004. 'The Archaeology of the Parish of West Acre. Part 2: The Documentary Background' *Norfolk Archaeology* 44, 456-481.
Davison, A., 2005. 'The Decline in Population, 1300-1450' in T. Ashwin and A. Davison (eds), *An Historical Atlas of Norfolk*, 90-91. Phillimore
Davison, A., 2007. 'Investigations at Godwick and Beeston St Andrew' *Norfolk Archaeology* 45, 141- 154.
Davison, A. with Cushion, B., 1999. 'The Archaeology of the Hargham Estate' *Norfolk Archaeology* 43, 257-274.
Davison, A., Cushion, B., Fenner, A., Fenner, G., Reid, A., Wade-Martins, P. And Yaxley D., 1988. *Six Deserted Villages in Norfolk*, East Anglian Archaeology 44.
Davison, A. with Fenner A., 1999. *The Evolution of Settlements in Three Parishes in South-East Norfolk*, East Anglian Archaeology 49.
Dollin, B.W., 1986. 'Moated sites in north-east Norfolk' *Norfolk Archaeology* 39, 262-277.
Drewett, P., 1976. *An Extensive Survey of Plough Damage to Known Archaeological Sites in West and East Sussex*, Institute of Archaeology, University of London.
Dunmore S., 1978. *221-222 Northgate Street, Great Yarmouth*, East Anglian Archaeology 8, 73-85.
Dymond, D., 1985. *The Norfolk Landscape*. Hodder and Stoughton.

Ede, J., Virgoe, N. and Williamson, T., 1994. *Halls of Zion.* Centre of East Anglian Studies.

Edwards, D., 1976. 'The Air Photography Collection of the Norfolk Archaeological Unit' *Norfolk,* East Anglian Archaeology 2, 251-269.

Edwards, D., 1977. 'The Air Photographs Collection of the Norfolk Archaeological Unit: Second Report' *Norfolk,* East Anglian Archaeology 5, 225-237.

Edwards, D. and Williamson, T., 2000. *Norfolk Country Houses from the Air.* Sutton Publishing.

Editorials in *Current Archaeology* 35 for November 1972 and in *Current Archaeology* 44 for May 1974.

English Heritage, 2011. *National Heritage Protection Plan.* English Heritage.

Evans, A.C., 1986. *The Sutton Hoo Ship Burial.* The British Museum Press.

Fairclough, G., 1999. 'Protecting the Cultural Landscape: National Designation and Local Character' in J. Grenville (ed.) Managing the Historic Rural Landscape, 27-39. Routledge

Felder, K., 2014. *Girdle-hangers in fifth- and sixth-century England: A key to Early Anglo-Saxon Identities.* University of Cambridge Dissertation.

Fisher, E.A., 1962. *The Greater Anglo-Saxon Churches.* Faber and Faber.

Fletcher J. and Switzur, R., 1973 'North Elmham: The Dating' *Current Archaeology* 36, 25-28.

Fletcher, J., 1992. 'Dendrochronology of the preserved timbers from Well II excavated in North Elmham Park' *Norfolk Archaeology* 38, 192.

Fowler, E., 1976. 'Some Norfolk naturalists: a historical survey' *Nature in Norfolk: a Heritage in Trust,* 9-17. Jarrolds.

French, C.A.I., 1994. *Excavations of the Deeping St Nicholas Barrow Complex, South Lincolnshire,* Lincolnshire Archaeology and Heritage Report Series No. 1. Heritage Trust of Lincolnshire.

Frere, S.S., 1971. 'The Forum and baths at Caistor by Norwich' *Britannia* 2, 1-26.

Gardiner, M., 2014. 'An Archaeological Approach to the Development of the Late Medieval Peasant House' *Vernacular Architecture* 45, 16-28.

Godwin, H., 1978. *Fenland: its ancient past and uncertain future.* Cambridge.

Green, B., 1986. 'Roy Rainbird Clarke, 1914-1963: An Appreciation' in *Excavations at Thornham, Warham, Wighton and Caistor, Norfolk,* East Anglian Archaeology 30, x-xi.

Green, B. and Gregory, T., 1977-8. 'An initiative in the use of metal detectors in Norfolk' *Museums Journal* 77, 161-2.

Green, B. and Rogerson, A., 1978. *The Anglo-Saxon Cemetery at Bergh Apton, Norfolk: Catalogue.* East Anglian Archaeology 7.

Green, B., Rogerson, A. and White S. G., 1987. *The Anglo-Saxon Cemetery at Morning Thorpe, Norfolk Volume 1: Catalogue, and Volume 2: Illustrated Grave-goods,* East

Anglian Archaeology 36.
Green, C., 1977. 'Excavations in the Roman Kiln Field at Brampton, 1973-4' *Norfolk*, East Anglian Archaeology 5, 31-95.
Gregory, T., 1977. 'The Enclosure at Ashill' *Norfolk*, East Anglian Archaeology 5, 31-95.
Gregory, T., 1983a. 'Archaeology and treasure hunting; a view from the other side' *Treasure Hunting* (April), 45-8.
Gregory, T. 1983b. 'The impact of metal detecting on archaeology and the public' in R. Bewley (ed.) 'Archaeology and the Public' *Archaeological Review from Cambridge* 2(1), 5-9.
Gregory, T., 1986a. *An Enclosure of the First Century AD at Thornham*, East Anglian Archaeology 30, 1-13.
Gregory, T., 1986b. 'The Iron Age and Romano-British Sites at Warham and Wighton' *Excavations at Thornham, Warham, Wighton and Caistor, Norfolk*, East Anglian Archaeology 30, 14-16.
Gregory, T., 1986c. 'Warham Burrows' *Excavations at Thornham, Warham, Wighton and Caistor, Norfolk*, East Anglian Archaeology 30, 17-21.
Gregory, T., 1986d. 'Warham Camp' *Excavations at Thornham, Warham, Wighton and Caistor, Norfolk*, East Anglian Archaeology 30, 22-26.
Gregory, T., 1986e. 'An Enclosure at Wighton' *Excavations at Thornham, Warham, Wighton and Caistor, Norfolk*, East Anglian Archaeology 30, 27-31.
Gregory, T., 1986f. 'Enclosures of 'Thornham' Type in Norfolk' *Excavations at Thornham, Warham, Wighton and Caistor, Norfolk*, East Anglian Archaeology 30, 32-35.
Gregory, T., 1991a. *Excavations in Thetford 1980-1982, Fison Way* (2 vols), East Anglian Archaeology 53.
Gregory, T., 1991b. 'Metal Detecting on a Scheduled Ancient Monument' *Norfolk Archaeology* 41, 186-196.
Gregory, T. 1992. 'Excavations at Thetford Castle, 1962' *The Iron Age Forts of Norfolk*, in J.A. Davies et al. 1992 East Anglian Archaeology 54, 3-17.
Gregory, T. and Rogerson, A., 1984. 'Metal-detecting in archaeological excavation' *Antiquity* 58, 179-84.
Grinsell, L.V., 1953. *The Ancient Burial Mounds of England* (2nd edition) Methuen.
Gurney, D., 1986. *Settlement, Religion and Industry; Three Romano-British Sites in Norfolk*, East Anglian Archaeology 31.
Gurney, D., 1986a. 'A Romano-Celtic Temple at Caistor St Edmund' *Excavations at Thornham, Warham, Wighton and Caistor St Edmund, Norfolk*, East Anglian Archaeology 30, 37-54.
Gurney, D., 1986b. *Settlement, Religion and Industry on the Fen-Edge; Three Romano-Brtitish Sites in Norfolk*, East Anglian Archaeology 31.

Gurney, D., 1995. 'Small towns and villages of Roman Norfolk. The evidence of surface and metal-detector finds' *Roman Small Towns in Eastern England and Beyond*, 53-67. Oxbow Monograph 52.

Gurney, D., 1997. 'Archaeological Finds in Norfolk 1996' *Norfolk Archaeology* 42, 539-46.

Gurney, D., 1998. *A Romano-British Cremation and Inhumation Cemetery at Bawburgh*, East Anglian Archaeology Occasional Papers 4, 9-19.

Gurney, D., 2002. *Outposts of the Roman Empire*. Norfolk Archaeological Trust.

Gurney, D., 2003. *Standards for Field Archaeology in the East of England*, East Anglian Archaeology Occasional Paper 14.

Hadley, D.M., 2010. 'Burying the Socially and Physically Distinctive in Later Anglo-Saxon England' *Burial in Later Anglo-Saxon England c. 650-1100 AD*. Oxbow Books.

Hall, D.N, 1987. *The Fenland Project: No. 2: Fenland Landscapes and Settlement between Peterborough and March*, East Anglian Archaeology 35.

Hall, D.N., 1992a. *The Fenland Project, No. 6: The South-western Cambridgeshire Fenlands*, East Anglian Archaeology 56.

Hall, D.N., 1992b. 'The Fenland Project' *Antiquity* 251, 436-38.

Hall, D., 1996. *The Fenland Project, No. 10: Cambridgeshire Survey, The Isle of Ely and Wisbech*, East Anglian Archaeology 79.

Hall, D. and Coles, J. 1994. *The Fenland Survey; an essay in landscape and persistence*. English Heritage Archaeological Report No. 1.

Harrod, H. 1864. 'On the site of the bishopric of Elmham' *Proceedings of the Suffolk Institute of Archaeology* 6, 7-13.

Hart, R., 1844. *The Antiquities of Norfolk: A Lecture*. Charles Muskett, Norwich.

Harvey, G., 1997. *The Killing of the Countryside*. Jonathan Cape.

Hayes, P.P. and Lane, T.W., 1992. *The Fenland Project No. 5: Lincolnshire Survey, The South-West Fens*, East Anglian Archaeology 55.

Hawkes, C.F.C., 1949. 'Caistor-by-Norwich, the Roman town of Venta Icenorum' *Archaeological Journal* 106, 62-65.

Healy, F., 1982. 'A Round Barrow at Trowse: Early Bronze Age Burials and Medieval Occupation' *Barrow Excavations in Norfolk, 1950-82*, East Anglian Archaeology 14.

Healy, F., 1986. 'The Excavations of Two Early Bronze Age Round Barrows on Eaton Heath, Norwich, 1969-1970' *Barrow Excavations in Norfolk, 1950-82*, East Anglian Archaeology 29, 50-58.

Healy, F., 1988. *The Anglo-Saxon Cemetery at Spong Hill, North Elmham, part VI: Occupation during the Seventh to Second Millennia BC*, East Anglian Archaeology 39.

Healy, F., 1996. *The Fenland Project, No. 11: The Wissey Embayment: Evidence for Pre-Iron Age Occupation Prior to the Fenland Project*, East Anglian Archaeology 78.

Heywood, S., 1982. 'The ruined church at North Elmham' *Journal of the British Archaeological Association* 135, 1-10.

Heywood, S., 2014. 'The Elmhams re-visited' in S. Ashley and M. Marsden (eds)

Landscape and Artefacts. Archaeopress Archaeology.

Hills, C. M, 1977. *The Anglo-Saxon Cemetery at Spong Hill, North Elmham Part I: Catalogue of Cremations Nos. 20-64 and 1000-1690*, East Anglian Archaeology 6.

Hills, C. M., 2015. 'Spong Hill and the origins of England' *British Archaeology* 140. Council for British Archaeology.

Hills, C., 2014. ' 'Spong Man' in context' in Ashley and Marsden (eds), *Landscapes and Artefacts: Studies in East Anglian Archaeology presented to Andrew Rogerson.* Archaeopress Archaeology, 79-88.

Hills, C. M., 2015. 'Spong Hill and the origins of England' *British Archaeology* 140, 20-27.

Hills, C. M. and Penn, K.J., 1981. *The Anglo-Saxon Cemetery at Spong Hill, North Elmham, Part II: Catalogue of Cremations 22, 41 and 1691-2285*, East Anglian Archaeology 11.

Hills, C.M., Penn, K.J and Rickett, R.J., 1984. *The Anglo-Saxon Cemetery at Spong Hill, North Elmham, Norfolk, Part III: Catalogue of Inhumations*, East Anglian Archaeology 21.

Hills,C.M., Penn, K.J. and Rickett, R.J., 1987. *The Anglo-Saxon Cemetery at Spong Hill, North Elmham, Part IV: Catalogue of Cremations*, East Anglian Archaeology 34.

Hills, C.M., Penn, K.J. and Rickett, R.J., 1994. *The Anglo-Saxon Cemetery at Spong Hill, North Elmham, Part V: Catalogue of Cremations*, East Anglian Archaeology 67.

Hills, C. M. and Lucy, S., 2013. *Spong Hill Part IX: chronology and synthesis.* McDonald Institute for Archaeological Research, University of Cambridge.

Hills, C. and Wade-Martins, P., 1976. 'The Anglo-Saxon Cemetery at The Paddocks, Swaffham' *Norfolk,* East Anglian Archaeology 2, 1-44.

Hinchliffe J. with Green, C.S., 1985. *The Excavations at Brancaster 1974 and 1977*, East Anglian Archaeology 23.

Hobbs, R., 2003. *Treasure; Finding our past.* The British Museum Press.

Hogg, A.H.A., 1938. 'Preliminary report on the excavation of a long barrow at West Rudham, Norfolk' *Proceedings of the Prehistoric Society* n.s. 4, 334-6.

Hogg, A.H.A., 1941. 'A long barrow at West Rudham, Norfolk. Final Report' *Norfolk Archaeology* 27, 315-32.

Hoggett, R., 2010a. *The Archaeology of the East Anglian Conversion.* Boydell Press.

Hoggett, R., 2010b. 'The Early Christian Landscape of East Anglia' in N.J. Higham and M.J. Ryan (eds) *The Landscape Archaeology of Anglo-Saxon England.* The Boydell Press, 193-210.

Hoskins, W.G., 1967. *Fieldwork in Local History.* Faber and Faber.

Hoskins, W.G., 1955. *The Making of the English Landscape.* Hodder and Stoughton.

Howlett, R., 1914. 'The Ancient See of Elmham' *Norfolk Archaeology* 18, 105-128.

Hurst, J.G., 1956. 'Deserted Medieval Villages and the Excavations at Wharram Percy, Yorkshire' in R.L.S. Bruce-Mitford (ed), *Recent Archaeological Excavations in Britain,* 251-273. Routledge and Kegan Paul.

Jackson, R.P.J. and Potter, T.W., 1996. *Excavations at Stonea, Cambridgeshire 1980-85.* British Museum Press.

Jennings, S., 1981. *Eighteen Centuries of Pottery from Norwich*, East Anglian Archaeology 13.

Johns, C. and Potter, C., 1983. *The Thetford Treasure*, British Museum Publications.

Johnson, S., 1983. *Burgh Castle: Excavations by Charles Green, 1958*-61, East Anglian Archaeology 20.

Johnson, W., 1982. 'The Application of hedgerow dating techniques in South Norfolk' *Norfolk Archaeology* 38, 182-191.

Jope, E.M., 1952. 'Excavations in the City of Norwich, 1948'. *Norfolk Archaeology* 30, 287-323.

Kelly, S., Rutledge, E. and Tillyard, M., 1983. *Men of Property* edited by Ursula Priestley. Norwich Survey.

Kershaw, J., 2013. *Viking Identities: Scandinavian Jewellery in England.* Oxford University Press.

Knowles, A.K., 1977. 'The Roman Settlement at Brampton, Norfolk: Interim Report' *Britannia* 8, 209-221.

Knowles, V., 1983. An appreciation to John Turner, NARG News 25, 19.

Ladbrooke, R., 1843. *Views of the churches of Norfolk.* 5 volumes. Norwich.

Lambert, J.M., Jennings, J.N., Smith, C.T., Green, C., and Hutchinson J.N., 1960. *The Making of the Broads: A reconsideration of their origin in the light of new evidence.* Royal Geographical Society Research Series No. 3.

Lane, T.W., 1993. *The Fenland Project, No. 8: Lincolnshire Survey, the Northern Fen-Edge*, East Anglian Archaeology 66.

Lane, T. and Coles J. (eds), 2002. *Through Wet and Dry: Essays in Honour of David Hall*, Lincolnshire Archaeology and Heritage Reports Series No. 5.

Lane, T. and Morris E.L. (eds), 2001. *A Millennium of Saltmaking: Prehistoric and Romano-British Salt Production in the Fenland*, Lincolnshire Archaeology and Heritage Reports Series No. 4.

Lane, T. and Trimble, D., 2010. *Fluid Landscapes and Human Adaption: Excavations on Prehistoric Sites on the Lincolnshire Fen Edge 1991-1994*, Lincolnshire Archaeology and Heritage Reports Series No. 9.

Larwood, G.P., 1952. 'A Medieval timber-framed well at Happisburgh' *Norfolk Archaeology* 30, 226-231.

Lawson, A., Martin, E., Priddy, D. with Taylor A., 1981. *The Barrows of East Anglia*, East Anglian Archaeology 12.

Lawson, A., 1976a. 'The Excavation of a Round Barrow at Harpley' *Norfolk*, East Anglian Archaeology 2, 45-63.

Lawson, A., 1976b. 'Excavations at Whey Curd Farm, Wighton' *Norfolk*, East Anglian Archaeology 2, 65-129.

Lawson, A., 1983. *The Archaeology of Witton, near North Walsham*, East Anglian Archaeology 18.

Lawson, A., 1986. *Barrow Excavations in Norfolk, 1950-82*, East Anglian Archaeology 29.

Lewis, M. (ed), 2013. *The Portable Antiquities Scheme Annual Report 2013.* The British Museum.

Longcroft, A., 2004. 'Archaeology and the Vernacular Threshold' *The Annual - the Bulletin of the Norfolk Archaeological and Historical Research Group* 13, 3-18.

Longcroft, A. and Wade Martins, S., (eds) 2013. 'Building an Education: An Historical and Architectural Study of Rural Schools and Schooling in Norfolk c.1800-1944' *Journal of the Norfolk Historic Buildings Group* 5.

Malim, T., 2005. *Stonea and the Roman Fens*. Tempus.

Malster, R., 2003. *The Norfolk and Suffolk Broads*. Phillimore.

Margary, I., 1967. *Roman Roads in Britain,* John Baker.

Margeson, S., 1993. *Norwich Households: The Medieval and Post-Medieval Finds from Norwich Survey Excavations 1971-1978*, East Anglian Archaeology 58.

Marsden, A., 2014. 'Satyrs, leopards, riders and ravens' in S. Ashley and A. Marsden (eds), *Landscapes and Artefacts,* 45-72. Archaeopress Archaeology.

Martin, E., 2012. 'Norfolk, Suffolk and Essex: Medieval Rural Settlement in 'Greater East Anglia'' in N. Christie and P. Stamper, *Medieval Rural Settlement Britain and Ireland, AD 800-1600*. Windgather Press, 225-248.

Martins, S., 1971. 'Aids to recording (8). A small fish processing community in Great Yarmouth: a training course in field techniques' *Industrial Archaeology* 8, 247-63.

McCann, J., 1987. 'Is Clay Lump a Traditional Building Material?' *Vernacular Architecture* 18, 1-16.

McCann, J., 1997. 'The Origin of Clay Lump in England' *Vernacular Architecture* 28, 57-67.

McK. Clough, T. and Wade-Martins, P., 1970. 'A Late Bronze Age Hoard from Foxburrow Farm, North Elmham, Norfolk, 1970' *Norfolk Archaeology* 35, 6-18.

McKinley, J.I., 1994. *The Anglo-Saxon Cemetery at Spong Hill, North Elmham, Part VIII: The Cremations*, East Anglian Archaeology 69.

Millett, M., 1992. Review of Excavations in Thetford, 1980-82, *Archaeological Journal* 149, 426-8.

Morley, B. And Gurney, D., 1997. *Castle Rising Castle, Norfolk*, East Anglian Archaeology 81.

Murawski, P., 2003. *Benet's Artefacts of England and the United Kingdom*. Greenlight Publishing.

Myres, J.N.L. and Green, B., 1973. *The Anglo-Saxon Cemeteries of Caistor-by-Norwich and Markshall, Norfolk,* Society of Antiquaries Research Report No. 30.

Newby, H., 1988. *The Countryside in Question*. Hutchinson.

Northover, P. And Bridgeford S.D., 2002. 'The Characterisation of a Bronze Age Weapon Hoard' *Materials Research Society Proceedings* 712.

Owen, D.M., 1984. 'The Making of Kings Lynn: A Documentary Survey' *The British Academy Records of Social and Economic History New Series* 9.

Parker, V., 1971. *The Making of Kings Lynn: Secular Buildings from the 11th to the 17th Century*. Phillimore.

Paterson, H. and Wade-Martins, P., 1999. 'Monument Conservation in Norfolk: The Monuments Management Project and other schemes' in J. Grenville (ed.) *Managing the Historic Rural Landscape,* 137-147. Routledge.

Pearson, A., 2002. *The Roman Shore Forts: Coastal Defences of Southern Britain.* Tempus.

Penn, K., 2000. *Excavations on the Norwich Southern Bypas, 1989-91 Part II: The Anglo-Saxon Cemetery at Harford Farm, Caistor St Edmund, Norfolk*, East Anglian Archaeology 92.

Penn, K., 2006. 'Excavations and Survey at the Iron Age Fort at Bloodgate Hill, South Creake, 2003' *Norfolk Archaeology* 45, 1-27.

Penn, K. And Brugmann, B., 2007. *Aspects of Anglo-Saxon Inhumation Burial: Morning Thorpe, Spong Hill, Bergh Apton and Westgarth Gardens*, East Anglian Archaeology 119.

Pestell, T., 2004. *Landscapes of Monastic Foundation.* The Boydell Press.

Pestell, T., 2007a. *Landscapes of Monastic Foundation.* The Boydell Press.

Pestell, T., 2007b. *St Benet's Abbey: A guide and history.* Norfolk Archaeological Trust.

Pestell, T., 2012. 'Paganism in Early Anglo-Saxon East Anglia' in T.A. Heslop, E. Mellings and M. Thofner (eds) *Art, Faith and Place in East Anglia,* 66-87.

Pestell, T., 2014. 'Bawsey – a 'productive' site in west Norfolk' in S. Ashley and A. Marsden (eds) *Landscapes and Artefacts: Studies in East Anglian Archaeology presented to Andrew Rogerson*, 139-165. Archaeopress Archaeology.

Petersen, F.F. and Healy, F., 1986. 'The Excavation of Two Round Barrows and a Ditched Enclosure on Weasenham Lyngs, 1972' *Barrow Excavations in Norfolk 1950-82*, East Anglian Archaeology 29, 70-103.

Pett, D.E.J., 2010. 'The Portable Antiquities Scheme's Database: its development for research since 1998' in S. Worrell, G. Egan. J. Naylor, K. Leahy, and M. Lewis (eds), *A Decade of Discovery: Proceedings of the Portable Antiquities Scheme Conference 2007*, British Archaeological Reports (British Series) 520.

Phillips, C.W., 1951. 'The Fenland Research Committee, its past achievements and future prospects' in W.F. Grimes (ed.) *Aspects of archaeology in Britain and beyond: Essays presented to O.G.S. Crawford*, 258-73.

Phillips, C.W. (ed), 1970. *The Fenland in Roman Times: studies of a major area of peasant colonisation*, Royal Geographical Society Research Series 5.

Phillips, C.W., 1987. *My Life in Archaeology.* Alan Sutton.

Pollard E., Hooper M.D. and Moore, N.W., 1974. *Hedges.* Collins.

Powell, A.B., 2009. 'Preserving the John Wymer Archive' *Norfolk Archaeology* 45, 539-541.

Powlesland, D., 2015. 'Crisis in the Countryside' in P. Everill P and P. Irving (eds) *Rescue Archaeology Foundations for the Future,* 107-120. RESCUE The British Archaeological Trust,

Priestley, U. and Fenner, A., 1985. *Shops and Shopkeepers in Norwich 1660-1730.* Centre of East Anglian Studies.

Pritchard, D., 1997. 'Excavations at Church Street, Barton Bendish' *Barton Bendish and Caldecote: Fieldwork in South-West Norfolk,* East Anglian Archaeology 80, 43-76.

Pryor, F., 1992. 'Flag Fen: Introduction' *Antiquity* 66, No.251, 438-57. Thames and Hudson.

Pryor, F., 2001a. *The Flag Fen Basin: Archaeology and environment of a Fenland landscape.* English Heritage.
Pryor, F., 2001b. *Seahenge: New discoveries in Prehistoric Britain.* Harper Collins.
Pryor, F., French, C., Crowther, D., Gurney, D., Simpson, G. and Taylor, M., 1985. *The Fenland Project, No. 1: Archaeology and Environment in the Lower Welland Valley*, East Anglian Archaeology 27, Volumes 1 & 2.
Reid, A. and Wade-Martins, P., 1980. 'A Re-consideration of the Panworth Ditch, Ashill' *Norfolk Archaeology 37*, 307-312.
Rahtz, P., 2001. *Living Archaeology.* Tempus.
Richmond, H. and Taylor, R., 1976. '28, 30 and 32 King Street, King's Lynn: An Interim Report' *Norfolk*, East Anglian Archaeology 2, 247-249.
Richmond, H., Taylor, R. and Wade-Martins, P., 1982. 'Nos. 28-34 Queen Street, Kings Lynn' *Norfolk,* East Anglian Archaeology 14, 108-124.
Rickett, R., 1992. 'The Other Forts of Norfolk' *The Iron Age Forts of Norfolk*, East Anglian Archaeology 54, 59-68.
Rickett, R., 1995. *The Anglo-Saxon Cemetery at Spong Hill, North Elmham, Part VII: The Iron Age, Roman and Early Saxon Settlement*, East Anglian Archaeology 73.
Rigold, S., 1962-3. 'The Anglian Cathedral of North Elmham, Norfolk' *Medieval Archaeology 6-7*, 67-108.
Roberts, J.P., Donaldson P., Esmonde Cleary, A.S. and Dunmore, S.L., 1975, 'Excavations in Norwich – 1974. The Norwich Survey – Fourth Interim Report' *Norfolk Archaeology 36*, 99-110.
Robertson, D. and Paterson, H., 2010. 'The Norfolk Monuments Management Project 1990-2010: Twenty Years Conserving the County's Rural Historic Environment' *Norfolk Archaeology 46*, 15-28.
Robinson, B., 1981. *Norfolk Origins 1: Hunters to First Farmers.* Acorn Editions.
Robinson, B. and Gregory, T., 1987. *Norfolk Origins 3: Celtic Fire and Roman Rule.* Poppyland Publishing.
Robinson, B. and Rose, E.J., 1983. *Norfolk Origins 2: Roads and Tracks.* Poppyland Publishing.
Rogerson, A., 1976. 'Excavations at Fuller's Hill, Great Yarmouth' *Norfolk*, East Anglian Archaeology 2, 131-245.
Rogerson, A., 1977. 'Excavations at Scole, 1973' *Norfolk,* East Anglian Archaeology 5, 97-224.
Rogerson, A., 1991. 'Tony Gregory, 1948-1991: An Appreciation' *Excavations in Thetford 1980-1982, Fison Way*, East Anglian Archaeology 53, xi-xii.
Rogerson, A., 1995. *Fransham: and Archaeological and Historical Study of a Parish on the Norfolk Boulder Clay,* unpublished Ph.D. thesis, University of East Anglia.
Rogerson, A., 2006. 'Obituary to James John Wymer' *Norfolk Archaeology* 45, 138-39.
Rogerson, A., 2007. Introduction to A. Davison 'Investigations at Godwick and Beeston St Andrew' *Norfolk Archaeology* 45, 141- 154.

Rogerson, A., 2017. ' 'a great icrease in reported, provenanced, archaeological finds' Norfolk before the Portable Antiquities Scheme' *Public Archaeology* on-line journal, 15.

Rogerson, A. and Ashley, S.J., 1987. *The parish churches of Barton Bendish: the excavation of All Saints' and the architecture of St Andrew's and St Mary's*, East Anglian Archaeology 32.

Rogerson, A. and Ashley, R., 1997. 'Bloodgate Hill, South Creake: a recently discovered early seventeenth-century map' *Norfolk Archaeology* 42, 535-37.

Rogerson, A. and Ashley, S., 2009. 'A selection of finds from Norfolk recorded in 2009 and earlier' *Norfolk Archaeology* 45, 556-570.

Rogerson, A. and Ashley, S., 2011. 'A selection of finds from Norfolk recorded in 2011 and earlier' *Norfolk Archaeology* 46, 248-262.

Rogerson, A. and Dallas, C., 1984. *Excavations in Thetford 1948-59 and 1973-80*, East Anglian Archaeology 22.

Rogerson, A. with Davison, A., 1997. 'An Archaeological and Historical Survey of the Parish of Barton Bendish, Norfolk' *Barton Bendish and Caldecote: Fieldwork in South-West Norfolk*, East Anglian Archaeology 80, 1-42.

Rogerson, A., Davison, A., Pritchard D. and Silvester, R., 1997. *Barton Bendish and Caldecote: fieldwork in south-west Norfolk*, East Anglian Archaeology 80.

Rogerson, A. and Lawson, A.J., 1992. *The Earthwork Enclosure at Tasburgh*, in J.A. Davies, T. Gregory, A.Lawson and A.Rogerson, East Anglian Archaeology 54, 31-58.

Rogerson, A. and Silvester, R.J., 1986. 'Middle Saxon Occupation at Hay Green, Terrington St Clement' *Norfolk Archaeology* 39, 320-22.

Rose, E., 1982. 'A Linear Earthwork at Horning' East Anglian Archaeology 14, 35-39.

Rotheram, I.D., 2013. *The Lost Fens: England's Greatest Ecological Disaster.* The History Press.

Royal Commission on Historical Monuments (RCHM), 1960. *A Matter of Time: An Archaeological Survey.* Her Majesty's Stationary Office.

Rye, W., 1909 (ed.) compiled by F. Leney. *Catalogue of antiquities found principally in East Anglia.* Norwich Castle Museum.

Sainty. J.E., Watson, A.Q. and Clarke R.R., 1938. 'The first Norfolk Long Barrow: Interim Report on excavations at West Rudham, 1937' *Norfolk Archaeology* 26, 315-329.

Saville, A., 1977. *Archaeological Sites in the Avon and Gloucestershire Cotswolds.* Committee for Rescue Archaeology of Avon, Gloucestershire and Somerset.

Schofield, J., 2000. *MPP 2000: A Review of the Monuments Protection Programme, 1986-2000.* English Heritage.

Scott, M., 1989. 'Scheduled but unprotected: ancient monuments at risk' *Rescue News* 49, 4.

SHARP, 2014. *Digging Sedgeford: A people's archaeology.* Poppyland Publishing.

Sheldon, H., Dennis, G. and Densem 2015. 'RESCUE: historical background and founding principles' in P. Everill and P. Irving (eds), *Rescue Archaeology Foundations for the Future*, xiii-xxiii. RESCUE The British Archaeological Trust,

Shepherd, J., 2015. 'Museums, archaeologists and archaeological archives' in P. Everill and P. Irving (eds), *Rescue Archaeology Foundations for the Future*, 132-146. RESCUE The British Archaeological Trust.

Shepherd Popescu, E. 2009. *Norwich Castle: Excavations and Historical Survey, 1987-98*, East Anglian Archaeology 132.

Shoard, M., 1980. *The Theft of the Countryside*. Temple Smith.

Silvester, R.J., 1988. *The Fenland Project No. 3: Marshland and the Nar Valley, Norfolk*, East Anglian Archaeology 45.

Silvester, R.J., 1991. *The Fenland Project No 4: The Wissey Embayment and the Fen Causeway, Norfolk*, East Anglian Archaeology 52.

Silvester, R.J., 1993. *The Addition of More-or-less Undifferentiated Dots to a Distribution Map? The Fenland Project in Retrospect*, East Anglian Archaeology 50, 24-39.

Simpson, W.G., Gurney, D.A., Neve, J. and Pryor F.M.M., 1993. *The Fenland Project No. 7: Excavations in Peterborough and the Lower Welland Valley 1960-69*, East Anglian Archaeology 61.

Sims, J. 2010. 'Oxwick – Looking for the Lost Chancel' *The Annual* 19, 32-46.

Smith, H., 2003. 'The Norwich Survey: Recollections of the Late Alan Carter' *The Annual* 12, 26-31.

Smith, R. and Carter, A. 1983. 'Function and Site: aspects of Norwich buildings before 1700' *Vernacular Architecture* 14, 5-18.

St Joseph, J.K.S. (ed), 1976. *The Uses of Air Photography*. John Baker.

Stamper, P., Stocker, D., Rees, S. and Richards, J.D., 2015. 'Lives Remembered: Lawrence Butler, F.S.A.' *SALON* 335 (2nd February).

Sussams, K., 1996. *The Breckland Archaeological Survey*. Suffolk County Council.

Swan, V. 1984. *The Pottery Kilns of Roman Britain*, Royal Commission on Historical Monuments Supplementary Series: 5.

Taylor, H.M. and Taylor J., 1965. *Anglo-Saxon Architecture* I. Cambridge University Press.

Taylor, T., 1999. 'Bawsey St James' *Time Team 99: The Site Reports*, 66-73. Channel 4 Television.

Taylor, T., 2013. 'Mapping Roman Brancaster' *British Archaeology* March/April 2013. Council for British Archaeology.

Tester, A., Anderson, S., Riddler, I. and Carr, R., 2014. *Staunch Meadow, Brandon, Suffolk: a high status Middle Saxon settlement on the fen edge*, East Anglian Archaeology 151.

Thomas, S., 2008. 'Introduction' in S. Thomas and P.G. Stone (eds), *Metal Detecting and Archaeology*. The Boydell Press.

Thomas, S. and Stone, P.G. (eds), 2008. *Metal Detecting and Archaeology*. The Boydell Press.

Thurley, S., 2013. *Men from the Ministry: How Britain saved its Heritage*. Yale University Press.

Wade, K., 1983. 'The 1973 Excavations' in A. Lawson, *The Archaeology of Witton*, East Anglian Archaeology 18, 53-68.

Wade-Martins, P., 1961. 'Preliminary Report on Excavations by Bloxham School Archaeological Society on a Romano-British Settlement (Map ref. SP/423360) NW of Bloxham Village' *Cake and Cockhorse: The Magazine of the Banbury Historical Society* Vol. 1, No. 8. 106-109.

Wade-Martins, P. and Wade, K., 1967. 'Some Deserted Villages in Norfolk: Notes for Visitors' *Norfolk Research Committee Bulletin* 17, 2-8.

Wade-Martins, P., 1968. 'North Elmham' *Current Archaeology* 6, 148-152.

Wade-Martins, P., 1969a. 'Excavations at North Elmham, 1967-8: An Interim Report' *Norfolk Archaeology* 34, 352-397.

Wade-Martins, P., 1969b. 'A Polychrome Jug from Welborne' in B. Green, G.C. Dunning and P. Wade-Martins 'Some Recent Finds of Imported Medieval Pottery' *Norfolk Archaeology* 34, 403-405.

Wade-Martins, P., 1970a. 'North Elmham' *Current Archaeology* 19, 226-231.

Wade-Martins, P., 1970b. 'Excavations at North Elmham, 1969: An Interim Report' *Norfolk Archaeology* 35, 25-78.

Wade-Martins, P., 1971a. The *Development of the Landscape and Human Settlement in West Norfolk from 350-1650 AD, with particular Reference to the Launditch Hundred*, unpublished Ph.D. thesis, the University of Leicester. (Copies are held at the University and at the Historic Environment office at Gressenhall. A third copy was given to the Norwich Local Studies Library, but it is assumed that copy was destroyed in the library fire in August 1994).

Wade-Martins, P., 1971b. 'Excavations at North Elmham 1970: An interim Note' *Norfolk Archaeology* 35, 263-268.

Wade-Martins, P., 1972. 'Excavations at North Elmham' *Norfolk Archaeology* 35, 416-428.

Wade-Martins, P., 1973. 'North Elmham' *Current Archaeology* 36, 22-24.

Wade-Martins, P., 1974a. 'The Linear Earthworks of West Norfolk' *Norfolk Archaeology* 36, 23-38.

Wade-Martins, P., 1974b. 'The Norfolk Archaeologial Unit' *Current Archaeology* 44. 281-284.

Wade-Martins, P., 1975. 'The Origins of Rural Settlement in East Anglia' in P.J. Fowler (ed.), *Recent Work in Rural Archaeology*, 137-157. Moonraker Press,.

Wade-Martins, P., 1977a. *The Demolition of 28-32 Queen Street, Kings Lynn*. A typescript report with photographs, dated 19th January 1977, widely distributed in

January 1977; copies are held in the Historic Environment Record.

Wade-Martins, P., 1977b. 'The Roman Road between Billingford and Toftrees' *Norfolk*, East Anglian Archaeology 5, 1-3.

Wade-Martins, P., 1978. 'Excavations of a Roman Road at Brisley' *Norfolk*, East Anglian Archaeology 8, 29-32.

Wade-Martins, P., 1980. *Fieldwork and Excavation on Villages Sites in Launditch Hundred, Norfolk*, East Anglian Archaeology 10.

Wade-Martins, P., 1980b. *Excavations in North Elmham Park 1967-1972*, East Anglian Archaeology 9.

Wade-Martins, P., 1983. *Two Post-Medieval Earthenware Pottery Groups from Fulmodeston*, East Anglian Archaeology 19.

Wade-Martins, P. (ed.) 1987. *Norfolk from the Air*. (1st edition) Norfolk Museums Service.

Wade-Martins, P., 1990. *The Manx Loghtan Story*. Geerings of Ashford.

Wade-Martins, P. (ed), 1993a. *An Historical Atlas of Norfolk*. (1st edition) Norfolk Museums Service.

Wade-Martins, P., 1993b. *Black Faces*. The Norfolk Museums Service in association with Geerings of Ashford.

Wade-Martins, P. (ed.), 1994. *An Historical Atlas of Norfolk*. (2nd edition). Norfolk Museums Service.

Wade-Martins, P. (ed) 1996. 'Monument conservation through land purchase' *Conservation Bulletin* 7, 8-11. English Heritage.

Wade-Martins, P. (ed.) 1997. *Norfolk from the Air* Vol. 1 (2nd edition). Norfolk Museums Service.

Wade-Martins, P. (ed.) 1999. *Norfolk from the Air* Vol. 2 (1st edition). Norfolk Museums Service.

Wade-Martins, P., 1992. 'Looking Back and Looking Forward' *The Annual* No. 1, 2-12.

Wade-Martins, P., 1999. 'Discovering our Past' in T. Heaton (ed.) *Norfolk Century*, 309-327. Eastern Daily Press.

Wade-Martins, P., 2008. 'Managing archaeological sites in Norfolk' *Conservation Land Management* 6, 14-18. Natural England.

Wade-Martins, P., 2014. 'An Experiment in Conservation: The Early Years of the Norfolk Archaeological Trust' in S. Ashley and A. Marsden (eds), *Landscapes and Artefacts: Studies in East Anglian Archaeology Presented to Andrew Rogerson*. Archaeopress Archaeology.

Wade-Martins, P., forthcoming. 'The Date of the West Norfolk Linear Earthworks – An Unresolved Debate' *Norfolk Archaeology*.

Wade Martins, S., 2015. *The Conservation Movement in Norfolk*. The Boydell Press.

Waller, M., 1994. *The Fenland Project, No. 9: Flandrian Environmental Change in Fenland*, East Anglian Archaeology 70.

Wallis, H., 2002. *Roman Routeways across the Fens: Excavations at Morton, Tilney St Lawrence, Nordelph and Downham West*, East Anglian Archaeology Occasional Papers 10.

Wallis, H., 2011. *Romano-British and Saxon Occupation at Billingford, Central Norfolk*, East Anglian Archaeology 135.

Wallis, H. with Anderson, S., 2009. *A Medieval Cemetery at Mill Lane, Ormesby St Margaret, Norfolk*, East Anglian Archaeology 130.

Waterson, M., 1994. *The National Trust: The First Hundred Years.* The National Trust BBC Books.

Watson, C., 2005. *Seahenge: An Archaeological Conundrum.* English Heritage.

Watts, D., 1988. 'The Thetford Treasure: A Re-appraisal' *The Antiquaries Journal* 68, 55-68.

West, S.E., 1988. *The Anglo-Saxon cemetery at Westgarth Gardens, Bury St Edmunds, Suffolk: Catalogue*, East Anglian Archaeology 38.

West, S.E., 2015. 'A life in archaeology' *Proceedings of the Suffolk Institute of Archaeology and History* 43, 428-438.

Wheeler, R.E.M., 1943. *Maiden Castle, Dorset.* Report of the Research Committee of the Society of Antiquaries of London, No. 12.

Wheeler, R.E.M., 1956. *Archaeology from the Earth.* Penguin Books.

Williamson, T., 1993. *The Origins of Norfolk.* Manchester University Press.

Williamson, T., 2014. 'The Franshams in Context: Isolated Churches and Common Edge Drift' in S. Ashley and A. Marsden (eds), *Landscapes and Artefacts: Studies in East Anglian Archaeology presented to Andrew Rogerson*, 167-179. Archaeopress Archaeology.

Wilson, P., 2015. 'Metal detectors: friends or foes' in P. Everill and P. Irving (eds), *Rescue Archaeology Foundations for the Future*, 259-172. RESCUE The British Archaeological Trust.

Woodward, B.B., 1864. 'The Old Minster, South Elmham' *Proceedings of the Suffolk Institute of Archaeology* 4, 1-7.

Wright, D. W., 2015. *'Middle Saxon' Settlement and Society.* Archaeopress Archaeology.

Yaxley, D., 1980. 'Documentary Evidence' in P. Wade-Martins, *Village Sites in Launditch Hundred, Norfolk*, East Anglian Archaeology 10, 96-99.

Index

Acle 73
Addington, Silvia 79, 86-88, 323
Advice to farmers 155
Advice to planning authorities 155
Aerial photographs library 167-169
Aerial photography 155, 167-180
Alderton, Anne 182
Alexander, John 142
All Party Parliamentary Group of MPs 126
Allison, Keith 70
Amateurs, role of 78-79, 337
Amery, Julian, 143
Amphitheatre, Caistor 278
Ancient Monuments and Archaeological Areas Act (1979) 158, 196, 348
Ancient Monuments Board 262
Anderson, Sue 306
Anglia TV site, Norwich 9, 153
Anglian Water 274
Anglo-Saxon diocese 41
Anglo-Saxon graves 241
Anglo-Saxon timber buildings 44, 47, 53-56
Anmer 206
Apling, Harry 64, 72
Appleton 74
'Archaeological blight' 160
Archaeological contractors 252
Archaeological Project Services (APS) 304-306
Archaeology and Planning 253
Archaeology and wildlife 348
Area Archaeological Advisory Committee 148

Area Museums Service for South-Eastern England 106, 107
Area of Archaeological Importance 233
Arminghall henge 236
Ashill 10, 247
Ashley, Hallam 8
Ashley, Steven 103, 124, 191
Ashwin, Trevor 85, 167, 239, 299
Association of County and District Councils 109
Association of County Archaeological Officers 109
Association of Local Government Archaeology Officers (ALGAO) 190
Aston, Mick 22
Atkin, Malcolm 20, 131, 132, 134, 135, 136, 139
Atkinson, Donald 248-249, 262, 281, 283
Atkinson, Richard 8
Atlas Aggregates 224
Augustine Steward's House, Norwich 264-265
Ayers, Brian 139, 153, 156, 204, 253, 260

Bacton to Great Yarmouth pipeline 341
Baggs, Tony 8
Bagnall Smith, Jean 124
Bamford, Helen 207, 208
Barford meeting (Warwickshire) 141, 144
Barker, Philip 17, 141, 142, 282, 349
Barnes, Jerry 87, 204
Barnes, Ruth 75

Barnett, G.W.T. 74
Barrow digging 69
Barrow survey 72, 193-196
Barton Bendish 32, 242-245
Bawburgh 88
Bawsey 99
Bearded tits 296
Beckett, Gillian 305
Bee orchids
Begley, Michael 71
Beloe, Edward 263
Bennett, Don 112
Bensley, W.T. 309
Benson, Don 165
Beonna 111, 283
Beresford, Maurice 25, 337
Bergh Apton 149, 224
Berney Arms windmill 301
Bescoby, Dave 123, 279, 286, 288, 302, 321, 323
Biddle, Martin 129, 130, 138, 142, 143, 145, 349
Bidewell, Bob 42
Billingford 83, 253, 342
Binham Priory 268-269, 303-306
Birmingham University 21-22
Bishop Bonner's Cottages, Dereham 270
Bishop Losinga 57
Bishop of Norwich 59, 69, 306, 312
Bishop Rugge 309
Bishops of East Anglia 41
Bittering 253
Bixley 236, 239
Black African burials 57, 229
Blakeney Point 262
Bloodgate Hill, South Creake 323
Bloomfield, Francis
Bloxham School, Oxfordshire 6-8
Body, Richard 199

Bolingbrooke, L.G. 263
Bottomley, Virginia 237
Boudica 278
Boudican revolt 281
'Boudica's Palace' 232
Bowden, Will 278, 283, 335
Bowen, H.C. 141
Bowman, Rev. 324
Bracken impressions 66
Bradfer-Lawrence, H.L. 263
Brampton 88-98, 149, 150, 198
Brancaster 149, 150, 175, 263, 271
Brandon (Suffolk) 46
Breckland 210-214
Breckland Archaeological Survey 211-212
Breckland Environemtally Sensitive Area 212
Brexit 348
Breydon Water 292
Bridewell Museum, Norwich 76
Bridgham 247
Bright, Henry 307
Brighton, John 151, 152
Brisley 58
British Association for the Advancement of Science 9
British Museum 101, 111, 182
Broadland Environmental Services 315
Broads Authority 292, 318, 319, 333, 334
Bronze Age hoard 64, 114, 118
Broome 172
Brown, Basil 61
Brown, Hilary 317
Brown, Steve 119-121
Brugmann, Birta 225-6
Bryant, Stewart 189
Bure, River 89, 307

Burgh Castle 8, 70, 113-114, 158, 263, 291, 334
Burgh Castle detector rally 113-114
Burials 56-58, 239, 228-229
Burnham Norton 327-328
Burnham, Barry 88
Burnt clay daub 48
Burton, John 296, 297
Burwood Hall 26
Buteux, Simon 22
Butler, Lawrence 18-19
Butler, R.M. 141
Butler-Stoney, Richard and Rosamund 26
Butterfant, Paul 112

Caister-on-Sea 8, 74, 105, 150, 158, 247
Caistor Roman town defences 281, 282
Caistor Roman town Early Saxon pottery 281
Caistor Roman town excavations of the 1930s 248-249, 262
Caistor Roman town interpretation map 280
Caistor Roman Town Project 278-289, 336
Caistor Roman town proposed visitor centre 277
Caistor Roman town site opening 275-276
Caistor Roman town street grid 281
Caistor Roman town wild flowers 288, 290
Caistor St Edmund 70, 74, 88, 112, 121, 158, 213. 231, 236, 240, 248, 263, 271, 273-283, 333, 335
Caithness, Lord 197
Caley's manor, Mileham 23
Calvert Street, Norwich 340
Cambridge Archaeological Unit 252

Capon, Barry 107
Car parks 275, 297-298, 318
Carr, Bob 146, 218, 232
Carson, Rachel 337-338
Carter, Alan 129, 131-139, 144, 189, 192
Carter, Frances 136
Cartwright, Tony 75
Castle Acre Priory 206, 262, 268, 304, 329-332
Castle bailey, Norwich 228, 342
Castle Mall, Norwich 79, 153, 238
Castle mound, Norwich 341
Castle Rising 248
Castles 204
Cathedral Close, Norwich 341
Cattle market, Norwich 228
Central Excavation Unit, Department of the Environment 150
Centre of East Anglian Studies (CEAS) 147
Chafing dishes 226-227
Charlton, Peter 224
Chartered Institute for Archaeologists 343, 350
Cheesman, Clive 125
Cheetham, Francis 106, 148, 151, 220. 231
Chequers Inn, St Benet's Abbey 124, 311
Chester-Kadwell, Mary 124
Chicken feeder 227
Chisnell, Sue 298
Church Commissioners 312
Church, cropmarks of 177
Clark, J.G.D. 73
Clarke, Helen 129
Clarke, Rainbird 1, 8, 10, 13, 15, 70, 72, 73, 74, 75, 165, 193, 247, 263, 323, 337
Clarke, W.G. 70, 263

Class Consent Orders 197
Clay lump 19-20
Cleere, Henry 109
Cley Marshes 264, 271
Cockley Cley 247
Code of Conduction for Mineral Operators 252
Colanders 226, 227
Coles, John 182
Collared urns 239
Collecting policy for archaeology 255
Colman, Timothy 167
Common Agricultural Policy (CAP) 1, 214, 272
Community engagement by the NAU 155-157
Composite disc brooch 241
Compulsory Purchase Order 239
Confederation of British Industry 253
Construction Industries' Forum 254
Costrels 226, 227
Cotman, John Sell 307
Cotman, Miles Edmund 307
Council for British Archaeology (CBA) 24, 102, 105, 109, 143, 144
Country Landowners Association (CLA) 201
Countryside Commission 200, 208, 210, 274, 275, 292, 295
Countryside Premium Scheme 211
Countryside Stewardship Scheme 299, 201, 208, 213, 274, 275, 294
County Courts site, King's Lynn 237
County Field Archaeologist, Norfolk post deleted 338, 350
County Standards for Field Archaeology in Norfolk (1998) 255, 343
County Structure Plan 159, 253
Couts, Ian 151
Cow Holm 308

Cozens-Hardy, Basil 72, 261-264
Crawford, O.G.S. 15, 165
Crome, John Berney 307
Cromer Museum 94
Crowfoot, Elizabeth 66
Crown Estate 312, 313, 315
Crowther, David 108
Cunliffe, Barry 142
Curatorial standards 255
Cushion, Brian 83-84, 85, 203, 329

Darrow Wood, Denton 271
Data retrieval in SMR 165-166
Davies, G.C. 311
Davies, John 113, 118, 275
Davison, Alan 32, 84-86, 167, 204, 323
Davison, Brian 150
Davison, Caroline 318, 320
Deeping St James 185
Denton 206, 271
Denver 248
Department of Culture, Media and Sport (DCMS) 101, 348
Department of Local History, University of Leicester 32
Department of the Environment (DoE) 59, 91, 131, 147, 148, 150, 151, 161, 189, 199
Department of the Environment, Farming and Rural Affairs (Defra) 206, 208, 348
Department of Transport (DoT) 236
Department of Urban Archaeology for the City of London 143
Dersingham – Ingoldisthorpe – Snettisham bypass 237
Deserted Village Research Group 18, 85
Deserted villages 70, 79, 178
Destruction in the countryside 15

Developer funding 153
Dickleburgh by pass 77, 238
Digging under the Doorstep 155-156
Diocesan Board of Finance 314
Distribution maps from fieldwalking 243
Dixon Hewitt, H. 72
Dollin, Bert and Barbara 79
Don, Robin 42, 42
Dowes Green 22, 23
Dowes Green 22, 23
Dragonflies 318
Drewett, Peter 199
Drinking horn 227
Dripping pans 227
Ducker, B.F.T. 75
Duleep Singh 263
Dunston Field, Caistor Roman town 122-123, 231, 242, 281, 283, 287, 288, 289, 335
Dunthorne, Steve 112
Dymond, David 149

Early Medieval Ware 53, 55
East Anglian Archaeology (EAA) 189-192, 338
East Norfolk Metal Detecting Society 105
Eastmore, Barton Bendish 243
Eaton Heath 247
Ede, Janet 79
Eden, Peter 132
Edingthorpe 73
Edwards, Derek 146, 167-180
Edwards, F.W. 309, 316
Elmham Festival 45
English Heritage (EH) 41, 91, 102, 113, 117, 132, 135, 180, 181, 194, 201, 207, 209, 236, 238, 241, 255, 269, 271, 274, 284, 292, 315, 328, 333, 342, 346, 348
English Heritage Wetland Strategy 349
Environment Agency 187, 315, 348
Environmental Sensitive Areas (ESAs) 208, 213, 313
Escritt, Janet 24
Evans, Dave 131, 134, 135, 136, 137
Everett, Susanna 13, 21, 24, 165
Excavation archives 160
'Excavatores Brantunae' 88-96
Exmoor Mires Project 349

Fakenham 77
Family Fun Days, Caistor St Edmund 277, 278
Farming and Rural Conservation Agency (FRCA) 201, 213
Farming and Wildlife Advisory Group (FWAG) 201, 202
Faxton (Northamptonshire) 20
Federation of Norfolk Historical and Archaeological Organisations 80, 167
Felder, Kathrin 124
Feltwell 248
Fenland Archaeological Trust 188, 252
Fenland Evaluation Project 184-185
Fenland Management Project 185-188, 253
Fenland Research Committee 71, 181
Fenland Survey 180-184
Fenner, Alayne 85, 133
Fenner, George 78, 92
Fens 180-188
Fiddler's Hill round barrow 328-329
Fieldwalking 31, 79, 84-88, 242-245
Fincham 118

Finds Liaison Officers (FLOs) 102, 113, 119
Fire covers 227
First computer 166
Fishergate, Norwich 231, 341
Fishponds 204, 318
Fison Way, Thetford 110, 111, 232-235, 239, 346
Five-year Development Plan for Archaeology in the Norfolk Museums Service (1996) 254-255, 353-355
Flag Fen (Peterborough) 188
Fletcher, John 51
Flint mines 211
Flint-cobbled yards 19, 25
Flitcroft, Myk 207
Forestry Commission 211-212
Foulsham 65
Fowler, Peter 32, 142
Fox, Dave 114-118
Foxburrow Farm, North Elmham 64, 65
Fransham 39, 125
Frazer-Allen, Eileen 3
Frere, Sheppard 249
Fulmodeston 78, 150, 226-228

Gallows Hill, Thetford 108
Garboldisham History Society 80
Gardiner, Julie 191
Gassowski, Jerzy 218
Gayton 120, 121
Gelling, Peter 22
Geoffrey Watling Charity 318
'Geonex' aerial survey 168
Geophysical surveys 278, 279. 285, 287, 296, 302, 321, 322, 325
Germanic Anglian settlement 222
Giles Landscapes 298

Girdle-hangers 225
Glazebrook, Jenny 190, 191
Global Positioning System (GPS) recording 112, 120, 122
Godwick 37, 199
Goodyear, Bob 231
Graveyard 228
Great Hall, Oak Street, Norwich 270
Great Ryburgh 57
Great Walsingham 115, 117, 118, 124, 149, 346
Great Yarmouth 29, 76. 150
Great Yarmouth Borough Council 291, 293, 333
Green (Sparey), Chris 146, 224
Green Charles 8, 13, 150
Green Hairstreak Butterfly 297
Green, Barbara 104, 157, 165, 218, 224
Green, John 113, 291-296
Greenfield, Ernest 13
Greenland Fishery, King's Lynn 267-268
Gregory, Tony 9, 75, 91, 92, 104-113, 116, 125, 155, 232-235, 283, 286
Grenstein 22-29, 30, 33, 56, 145, 252
Gressenhall 77. 148, 252
Greynston Green 22
Griffiths, Peter 320
Grimes Graves 263
Grinsell, Leslie 72, 73
Ground Penetrating Radar 99
Guardianship monuments 262, 268, 329
Guidelines for project archives 225
Gunton Park 77
Gurney, David 92, 93, 251, 252, 255, 260, 300

Hales 32, 85
Hales/Loddon survey 79, 85

Hall, David 181, 182
Halvergate Marshes 210, 289, 294, 299, 301
Happisburgh 74
Harford Farm 239-242, 288
Harford Park and Ride 341
Harpley 73, 149, 196
Harvey, Graham 198
Hassell Smith, Alfred or 'Hassell' 130, 136
Hawks, Christopher 248
Hay Green, Terrington St Clement 184, 185
Hayes, Peter 182
Healy, Frances 220, 222
Heckingham 32, 85
Hedges, John 189
Hen Domen (Montgomery) 17
Heritage at Risk Register 345
Heritage Lottery Fund (HLF) 98, 102, 271, 303, 304, 317, 319, 323, 329, 333
Herring bones 230
Heseltine, Michael 196
Heywood, Stephen 47
Higher Level Stewardship Schemes (HLS) 112, 203, 220, 329, 349
Highways Agency 238
Hills, Catherine 67, 218-224
Hindringham 115, 116
Historic Buildings and Monuments Commission 112
Historic England 117, 180, 214, 349
Historic England Action Plan 347
Historic Environment Record (HER) 88, 103, 260, 338
Historic Houses Association 109
Historical Atlas of Norfolk 155, 166-167
Hockwold 248
Hogg, A.H.A. 73

Hoggett, Rick 39
Holkham 23, 32, 83, 329
Holme-next-the-Sea 217
Home Office 109
Horning 309
Horsford Castle 158, 205
Hoskins, W.G. 8, 32, 87, 337
Houghton Hall 196
Howes, Christopher 321
Hoyle, Mark 191
Hurst, John 17, 18, 60, 145, 148

Illington 9, 74, 248
'Infopoint' vending machine 276
Inquests 111
Interpretation panels 276, 326, 332
Interrupted ditched enclosure 171
Ipswich (Suffolk) 138
Ipswich Ware 33, 52, 121
Isolated churches 31
Issendorf (Schleswig-Holstein) 221
Itteringham 177

Jennings, J.N. 75
Jennings, Sarah 134, 139
Jermy, Terry 126
Johnson, Goddard 69
Johnson, John, 275
Johnson, Wendy 87
Jope, Martin 73
Jordon, Paul 153
Judge, Philip 132, 136
Jugs 226

Kelly, Serena 133
Kershaw, Jane 124
King Street, King's Lynn
King's Lynn 29
King's Lynn Museum 165
King's Lynn Preservation Trust 129, 268

King's Lynn Survey 129, 150
Kirkpatrick, John 308, 310
Knocker, Guy 9, 13, 74, 150
Knowles, Keith and Vivienne 88

Lacons Brewery site, Great Yarmouth 150
Ladbrook, Robert 70
Lakenheath Fen
Lakenheath Fen 187
Lamb, Norman 320
Lambert, J.M. 75
Lane, Tom 182
Larwood, G. 73, 74
Launditch Hundred 31-39, 46
Lava querns 20
Lawson, Andrew 73, 81, 82, 85, 146, 193-194
Lenwarde 77
Letton 199
Lewton-Brain, Charles 8
Lincoln 138
Linear earthwork 309
Little Cressingham 158, 194
Little Walsingham 80, 304
Local Studies Library, Norwich 77
Loddon 32
London 138
Long barrow 170
Long, Sydney 271
Longcroft, Adam 20
Longcroft, Adam 80
Longham 33, 38
Lord Leicester 262, 268, 329
Lottery funding 285
Lowestoft Museum 94
Lucy, Sam 221
Ludham Hall 313
Lyres 224, 225

Maastricht Treaty 348
Macfarlane, Neil 200
Macgregor, John 238
MacGregor, Neil 103
Macreth, Don 130, 135, 139
Maiden Castle, Dorset 337
Malster, Bob 311
Malt, Dick 169
Mann, Commander F.R. 74
Manning, Derek and Mary 76
Manpower Services Commission (MSC) 229, 232
Margeson, Sue 108, 135, 137, 138, 139
Market Place, North Elmham 58, 59
Markshall 73
Marsden, Adrian 103
Marsh harriers 296
Martin, Edward 37
Martins, Ernest 3, 4
Mason, Anne 317
Maxey (Northamptonshire) 141
McCann, John 20
McClough, Tim 65
McKinley, Jackie 222
Measures 226
Medieval peasant houses 17-21
Mercury 115
Metal detecting 2, 101-127, 252, 338
Metal detecting code of conduct 101, 105, 106
Metal detecting on a Scheduled Monument 102, 294-295
Metal detector survey 108, 295-296
Micklemoor Hill, West Harling
Middle Saxon carpentry 51
Middle Saxon pottery 231, 274, 286
Middleton 253
Middleton Mount 325, 327
Mileham 24, 26, 33, 37

Milk churns 226
Millennium Library, Norwich 255, 341
Miller, Barbara 136
Millett, Martin 232
Milligan, Bill 108, 137
Ministry of Agriculture, Fisheries and Food (MAFF) 208, 210, 211, 213
Ministry of Defence 211
Ministry of Public Buildings and Works 43
Ministry of Works 18, 262, 303, 312, 337
Moated manors 204
Monasteries 204
Monument Protection Programme (MPP) 196, 198, 207-209
Monuments at Risk Survey (MARS) 209-210, 346
Moore, David 276, 323
Morningthorpe 78, 224-226
Morris, A.J. 73, 74
Mucking 240
Murawski, Paul 95
Murphy, Peter 150
Museum displays 157-158
Museums Association 105, 109
Mustkett, Charles 69
Myres, J.N.L. 74

NARG survey of chapels and meeting houses 79
National Archaeological Service 142, 143
National Farmers Union (NFU) 201, 202, 203
National Heritage Act (1984) 159
National Heritage Memorial Fund (NHMF) 220-231, 284, 333
National Heritage Protection Plan (2012) 347
National Land Utilisation survey 75

National Mapping Programme 180, 280, 284
National Monuments Record Aerial Photography Unit 166
National Trust 187, 262, 271, 348
Natural England 187, 208, 277, 298, 299, 329, 331, 334, 349
Nene Valley Research Committee 130
Network Archaeology 342
Neville, Henry 268
New Buckenham 80
New Buckenham Castle 271
New Mills, Norwich 77
Nicholson, Fred 64, 65, 152
Nighthawks 102, 113, 116, 121, 125, 283, 285, 335, 347
Nokes, Paul 296, 297
Norfolk and Norwich Archaeological Society (NNAS) 29, 69, 70, 80, 147, 189, 262, 318, 336, 338
Norfolk and Suffolk Metal Detecting Society 105
Norfolk Archaeological and Historical Research Group (NAHRG) 77-80, 114, 295, 336, 338
Norfolk Archaeological Rescue Group (NARG) 77-80, 105, 226
Norfolk Archaeological Services Advisory Committee (NASAC) 146, 152, 195, 199, 251, 253, 259, 260
Norfolk Archaeological Trust (NAT) 259, 261-336, 337
Norfolk Archaeological Trust membership 349
Norfolk Archaeological Trust Memorandum and Articles 263
Norfolk Archaeological Unit (NAU) 116, 145, 147, 252, 340

Norfolk Archaeological Unit archive 146
Norfolk Archaeology 70, 189
Norfolk Biological Record 319
Norfolk coroner 126
Norfolk County Council (NCC) 144, 271, 274, 289, 291, 312, 328, 333
Norfolk County Council Development Plan (1951) 263
Norfolk County Council Policy and Resources Committee 151, 152
Norfolk Earthworks Survey 85, 261, 329
Norfolk from the Air 169-170
Norfolk Historic Buildings Group 80, 336, 338
Norfolk Historic Buildings Trust 271
Norfolk Historic Environment Service (NHES) 260
Norfolk Historical Atlas 155, 169-179
Norfolk History Fair 80
Norfolk Industrial Archaeology Society (NIAS) 76-77, 336, 338
Norfolk Landscape Archaeology 251-252
Norfolk Monuments Management Project (NMMP) 197, 198-203, 261, 338
Norfolk Museums Service (NMS) 131, 151, 167, 220, 267
Norfolk Naturalists' Trust (NNT) 264
Norfolk Property Services (NPS) 340
Norfolk Record Office 107, 130, 133, 321
Norfolk Research Committee (NRC) 29, 70, 71-76, 88, 105, 144, 147, 168, 193, 337
Norfolk schools survey 80
'Norfolk System' of metal detector recording 104-113
Norfolk Wildlife Trust membership 335, 336, 349

Norfolk Windmills Trust 77, 271
Norman house 230
Norman house, Norwich 230
North Elmham cathedral 47
North Elmham Park 41-45, 145, 229
Northampton Archaeology 342
Norwich 47, 56
Norwich Anglian Metal Detector Club 122
Norwich building surveys 133-134
Norwich Castle Museum (NCM) 8-9, 42, 46, 64, 65, 69, 94 103, 107, 113, 115, 116, 119, 135, 136, 157, 165, 242, 252, 337
Norwich City Council 131
Norwich court rolls 133
Norwich enrolled deeds 133
Norwich excavations 152-153
Norwich School of painters 307
Norwich Southern Bypass 79, 236-242, 288
Norwich Survey 129-140, 152
Norwich Survey excavation reports 134-139
Norwich Survey structure 130-131
Norwich Survey vision 132
Norwich Union 311
Nuttalls 315

Old Hunstanton 247
Olivier, Adrian 136
Open-air service, St Benet's Abbey 312, 313
Orkney 22
Ormesby St Margaret 342
Osteoarthritis 57
'Our Hidden Heritage' series 208
Owen, Dorothy 129
Owles, John 81-82, 149, 193
Oxford Archaeology 342

Oxfordshire City and County Museum 165
Oxwick 79
Oyster beds 204

Paddocks, Swaffham 66, 67
Pancheons 227
Parker, Helen 129
Parker, Vanessa 129
Parks and gardens 204
Patchett, F. 74
Paterson, Helen 201-203
Patten, Chris 238
Peasant houses 19-21
Peddars Way 174
Penn, Kenneth 222, 225-226
Penrose, David, 144
Pentney 304
Pestell, Tim 103, 316
Pipkins, 226, 227
Planning (Listed Buildings and Conservation Areas) Act (1990) 348
Planning advice 252
Planning applications 252
Planning consultations 252, 253, 255
Planning Policy Guidance (PPG) 15, 161-163
Planning Policy Guidance (PPG) 16, 159-161, 338
Planning Policy Statement 163
Pommander 227
Pooley, Graham 79
Pope, John 78, 89, 92, 96
Popyland Publishing 80
Portable Antiquities Scheme (PAS) 102-104, 119, 127, 338
Portable Antiquities Scheme database 124
Post-holes 53, 54

Pott Row, Grimston 253
Pottergate, Norwich 138
Prehistoric Society of East Anglia 70
Preservation Orders 158, 161, 194, 274
Priestley, Ursula 133
Primary record cards 165
Pritchard, David 242
Protection of cultural heritage 348
Protection of uncultivated land under CAP 214-215
Pryor, Francis 188
Publication 59
Publication backlog 155, 340-343
Pudding Norton 199
Puddy, Eric 72
Pulham Market 148
Pykerell's House, Norwich 266
Pyramidal Orchid 297

Quebec Hall, Dereham 5, 6
Queen Street, King's Lynn, 161-163, 231

Rabbit warrens 211
Radio-carbon dating 305
Rahtz, Philip 22, 141
Record maps for SMR 165
Reedham 99
Reffley 74
Regional History Dining Group, UEA
Renfrew, Colin 126
Report writing 20-21, 59-60, 247-249
Requirements for Deposition of Fieldwork and Excavation Archives with Norfolk Museums and Archaeology Service (2010) 343
RESCUE 59, 109, 142-145, 148
RESCUE public meeting 142, 349
Review of barrow survival 346

Rickets 229
Rickett, Robert 220, 222
Ridge and furrow 204
Ring-ditches 169, 172, 225, 239-241
Riverbank at St Benet's Abbey 314, 315, 316
Roadside Nature Reserve 306
Roberts, Charles 169
Roberts, Jan 131,139
Robertson, David 203
Robinson, Bruce 112
Rogerson, Andrew 32, 39, 84, 85, 103, 111, 113, 118, 120, 124, 146, 218, 232, 242
Role of a county conservation trust for archaeology 334-335
Roman forts 173, 174, 175
Roman road 83-84
Roman tiles 47
Roman villa 176
Rose, Edwin 146, 166, 309
Rotherham, Ian 181
Roudham 200
Rougham 178
Roughton 171
Royal Air Force 1946 Air Survey 17, 168
Royal Commission on the Historical Monuments of England (RCHME) 131, 141, 168-169, 182, 309
Royal Society for the Protection of Birds (RSPB) 187, 336, 349
Rumbelow, P.E. 73
Rural Enterprise Fund 297
Rural Life Museum, Gressenhall 259
Rutledge, Elizabeth 133
Rye, Walter 69

Saggars 226, 227
Saintonge polychrome jug 63
Sainty, J.E. 72, 73

Salter, H.E., 133
Saunders, Andrew 60
Saville, Alan 199
Scarfe Charitable Trust 314
Sceattas 285, 286
Scheduled Ancient Monument 214
Scheduled Monument Consent 158
Schmalstede (Schleswig-Holstein) 221
Schwabe, P. 72, 74
Scole 144, 149
Scole bypass 238
Scole Committee 91, 93, 94, 106, 144-145, 149, 152, 155, 189, 218
Scolt Head 75
Sea Bank, Marshland 183
Sea Henge 217
Seago, Edward 307
Secondary files for SMR 166
Section 17 Management Agreements 213
Sharrock, Barrie 112
Shell UK 274
Shewring, Colin 162
Shoard, Marion 198-199
Shropham 341
Silchester (Hampshire) 273
Silliprandi, Katrina 276
Silvester, Bob 182-183
Site interpretation schemes 276, 299-300
Site wardens 301
Sites and Monuments Record (SMR) 15, 155, 160, 165, 212, 252, 337
Sixteenth-century pottery 226-228
Skelton, Jon 271
Smith, C.T. 75
Smith, Robert 132, 133, 134
Snelling, Joan 316
Snettisham 15, 74, 117

Society for Medieval Archaeology 129
Society for the Protection of Ancient Buildings 129
Society of Museum Archaeologists 109
South Creake 118, 323-325
South Elmham 41
South Norfolk Council 274, 284, 333
Specifications for archaeological contracts 252
Spong Hill 32, 41. 149. 150, 151, 152, 157, 217-224, 225, 335, 345
Spong Man 223
Sporle with Palgrave 69
Sprinkler pots 227
Sprowston Mill 265
Square ditched enclosures 240
Square-headed brooches 225
St Benet's Abbey 304, 307-322, 334
St Margaret's *in combusto*, Norwich 153, 340
St Martin-at-Palace Plain, Norwich 153, 229-231
St Peter Hungate, Norwich 266-267
St. Joseph, J.K. 23, 42, 70, 141, 330, 337
Standards for Field Archaeology in the East of England (2003) 339, 343
Standing Conference of Archaeological Unit Managers 109
Stark, James 307
Steensberg, Axel 17
Steers, J.A. 74
Stewpots 226
Stiffkey 114
Stonea Grange (Cambridgeshire) 181, 184
STOP campaign 109
Storage jars 226
Stow Bardolph 77
Suffolk Archaeological Service 342

Suffolk Archaeological Unit 147, 232
Suffolk Institute of Archaeology 147
Sunken featured buildings (SFBs) 281, 282, 286
Sussams, Kate 211-212
Sutermeister, Helen 133, 139
Sutton Hoo (Suffolk) 61, 101, 335
Swaffham 176
Swallowtail butterfly 321
Swan, E.L. 75
Swan, Vivien 88
Swanton Morley 173
Switsur, Roy 51

Talbot, Eric 129
Tankards 227
Tas, River 274, 276
Tasburgh 86-88, 323
Temple to Minerva, Stonea Grange 184
Textile impressions 66
Thatcher, I.J. 74
Thetford 10-13, 21, 41, 46, 74, 75, 76, 98, 117, 247, 248
Thetford Ware 33, 39, 52, 53, 55
Thirtle, John 307
Thomas, Charles 32, 142
Thoresby College, Kings Lynn 129
Thornham 13, 75, 247
Thorpe Station, Norwich 179
Thuxton 15-21, 29, 30, 56, 168
Tillyard, Margot 133
Timber church 228
Timber-lined wells 49-52
Time Team 98-99, 336
Times, The 59
Tindall, Adrian 189
Tittleshall 22
Toftrees 83
Tombland, Norwich 264

Town Close Estate Charity 314, 318
Town Close, Norwich 5
Townsley, Gerald 5
Travenol factory, Thetford 232
Treasure 103
Treasure Act 1996 101-102
Treasure Trove 111
Trephinations 66
Trevelyan, G.M. 336
Trowse 247
Tucker, Frank 230, 231
Tudor Cottage, Field Dalling 270
Turner, John 73, 82
Turner, Mark 121-123, 285, 286, 287, 288
Tuttington 170
Tyrell-Green, Rev. 72

United Kingdom Institute of Conservation 109
University of East Anglia (UEA) 131
Updated Project Design (UPD) 339

Variable Damoiselle fly 297
Village greens 31
Virgoe, Norma 78, 79
Virgoe, Roger 130, 139
Voodoo village 45

Wade, Keith 29, 146
Wade-Martins, Susanna 80
Wainwright, Geoff 159
Walker, Philip 186
Wall bedstraw 305
Wall consolidation 277, 329, 331
Waller, Martyn 182
Wallis, Ken 19, 20, 26
Walpole St Andrew 253
Walpole, Robin 105, 152
Walsingham Way 41, 43, 58

Wanborough (Surrey) 110
Warham 1, 9, 10, 11, 70, 75, 76, 247, 323
Water meadows 204
Water rail 296
Waterden 118
Watson, A.Q. 72, 73
Waveney, River 289
Weasenham 33, 34, 35, 36
Welborne 4, 63
Wells, Calvin 8, 46, 57, 66
Wessex Archaeology 146
West Acre 10, 86, 208, 304
West Lexham 32, 37
West Rudham 73
West Stow 284
West Walton 253
West, Stanley 144, 146, 151, 185, 189, 225
West, Susie 191
Wet Fens for the Future 186-187, 348
Wetland conservation 348-349
Wetland Vision Project 349
Wharram Percy (Yorkshire) 17, 24
Wheeler, Mortimer 61, 336, 337
Whetstones 29
Whissonsett 341
Whitaker, F.O. 74
White, Sue 78, 191, 235, 259, 275, 276, 307, 308, 326
Whitefriars' Bridge, Norwich 229, 231
Wicken Fen (Cambridgeshire) 262
Wighton 75, 116, 247
Wildfowl Trust 187
Wildlife conservation 348
Williamson, Tom 39, 87, 180, 204
'Willow' Walpole 24
Winchester (Hampshire) 130, 138, 145

Wireless Telegraphy Act (1949) 114
Wisbech 117
Witton 81-82, 149
Woodman, Frank 132, 134
Wormegay 119, 206, 208
Wright, William 311
Wrist clasps 225
Wroxeter (Shropshire) 17, 273, 282

Wymer, John 144, 194-196
Wymondham bypass 238

Yaxley, David 58
York 138
Young Farmer's Clubs 202
Youth Opportunities Programme (YOP) 229, 232